CAPTAIN AMERICA,
MASCULINITY, AND VIOLENCE

Television and Popular Culture
Robert J. Thompson, *Series Editor*

OTHER TITLES IN TELEVISION AND POPULAR CULTURE

*Black Male Frames: African Americans
in a Century of Hollywood Cinema, 1903–2003*
Roland Leander Williams Jr.

*Inside the TV Writer's Room: Practical
Advice for Succeeding in Television*
Lawrence Meyers, ed.

Interrogating The Shield
Nicholas Ray, ed.

Reading Joss Whedon
Rhonda V. Wilcox, Tanya R. Cochran,
Cynthea Masson, and David Lavery, eds.

Screwball Television: Critical Perspectives on Gilmore Girls
David Scott Diffrient and David Lavery, eds.

*"Something on My Own": Gertrude Berg
and American Broadcasting, 1929–1956*
Glenn D. Smith Jr.

TV on Strike: Why Hollywood Went to War over the Internet
Cynthia Littleton

*Watching T.V.: Six Decades of American
Television,* expanded second edition
Harry Castleman and Walter J. Podrazik

J. Richard Stevens

CAPTAIN AMERICA, MASCULINITY, AND VIOLENCE

THE EVOLUTION OF A NATIONAL ICON

SYRACUSE UNIVERSITY PRESS

First Edition 2015

15 16 17 18 19 20   6 5 4 3 2 1

∞ The paper used in this publication meets the minimum requirements
of the American National Standard for Information Sciences—Permanence
of Paper for Printed Library Materials, ANSI Z39.48-1992.

For a listing of books published and distributed by Syracuse University Press,
visit www.SyracuseUniversityPress.syr.edu.

ISBN: 978-0-8156-3395-2 (cloth)   978-0-8156-5320-2 (e-book)

Library of Congress Cataloging-in-Publication Data

Stevens, J. Richard, author.
  Captain America, masculinity, and violence : the evolution of a national icon /
J. Richard Stevens. — First edition.
      pages cm. — (Television and popular culture)
  Includes bibliographical references and index.
  ISBN 978-0-8156-3395-2 (cloth : alk. paper) — ISBN 978-0-8156-5320-2 (e-book)
1. America, Captain (Fictitious character)   2. Superheroes in literature.
3. Masculinity in literature.   4. Violence in literature.   5. Comic books, strips,
etc.—United States—History and criticism.   I. Title.
  PN6728.C35S77 2015
  741.5'973—dc23   2015005191

PUBLISHED WITH A GRANT FROM
FIGURE FOUNDATION
SOVEREIGNTY CROWN, ODYSSEY PEOPLE.

To Peter, the little fan who continues to instruct me

J. Richard Stevens is an associate professor in the Department of Media Studies at the University of Colorado, Boulder. His research delves into the intersection of ideological formation and media message dissemination. This work comprises studies on how cultural messages are formed and passed through popular culture, how technology infrastructure affects the delivery of media messages, how communication technology policy is developed, and how media and technology platforms are changing American public discourse.

Contents

PREFACE · *xi*

1. Introduction: *Sentinel of Liberty* · *1*

2. The Anti-Hitler Crusader (1940–1949) · *24*

3. Commie Smasher! (1953–1954) · *57*

4. The Man out of Time (1963–1969) · *75*

5. The Liberal Crusader (1969–1979) · *98*

6. The Hypercommercialized Leader (1979–1990) · *124*

7. The Superficial Icon (1990–2002) · *183*

8. Captain America's Responses to the War on Terror (2002–2007) · *210*

9. The Death and Rebirths of Captain America (2007–2014) · *256*

NOTES · *297*

BIBLIOGRAPHY · *341*

INDEX · *377*

Preface

For some reason, whenever an author writes a book analyzing an aspect of popular culture, he or she inevitably precedes the work in question with an introduction that offers the reader a form of apology.

I'm not sure if this apology is for the benefit of the author or the reader. There exist certain stigmas around the consumption of popular culture that marginalize its study within the confines of academic inquiry. And yet how members of our culture play can be every bit as informative as how we work or what we create.[1]

Popular culture has long existed as a core component of Western societies. In his justification for the study of popular culture, John Storey links the emergence of European nationalisms to the emergence of popular culture.[2] Popular culture texts do not simply reflect the events of history; they typically create conformity while simultaneously depoliticizing a society's working class. At its heart, the struggle over popular culture is a struggle over meaning, a renegotiation of the significance of events or of the power of ideology in the public world. Because the superheroic version of the American monomyth (comprehensively discussed in chapter 2) emerged within a mass-media context, scholars have a tremendous opportunity to dissect its origins. By definition, mass culture reduces more complex ideology into simplistic themes and patterns for easier consumption by the working class.[3]

I came to this particular inquiry in a gradual way. As a young man, I had read Marvel comic books (as well as the occasional DC Comics title), and perhaps the largest proportion of what I read was *Captain America*. I cannot recall precisely what originally brought me to seek out the exploits of the star-spangled avenger, but I remember even as a youth struggling to reconcile the Captain America of that contemporary age (the 1980s) with the Cap I found in back-issue copies I picked up from bargain bins and the long boxes in comic book stores. The Captain America of the 1980s experienced very different adventures from the Captain America of the 1960s and 1970s. "My" Cap dealt with much more individualized problems, whereas the back issues I read seemed to indicate a broader struggle against social problems, problems about which I was largely ignorant and less than enthused to read about between the covers of a comic book.

To my embarrassment, I remember looking at those past issues, published a few years before I was born, and thinking that because they engaged social issues such as race relations and sexism, they were somehow the antithesis of entertainment, within which my youthful mind considered education and advocacy inappropriate. But read them I did, and I confess those stories eventually did have some influence on my developing worldview. I did not, as a young man, think that racism was a contemporary problem. To my naïve mind, racism belonged in the history books under subtitles such as "American Slavery," "The American Civil War," and "The Emancipation Proclamation." I had a few African American friends, but I did not perceive any bias in myself or in my community against members of their race.

However, in the early 1970s Captain America had struggled rather explicitly with complex questions of race, with feminist critiques, and even with antiwar voices, so in the part of my mind that dreamed about other realities and possibilities, I acknowledged that, at least in the Marvel Universe, such problems existed.

It was not until I went to college and then on to graduate school to be trained in social science that I gained the intellectual tools necessary to think more critically about the world in which others live. Such is the plight of the white American male—or at least for some of us: it requires the ability to see beyond our own experiences, to consider the experiences of others, to understand how others see the world. Comic books and other forms of popular entertainment are vehicles for such considerations. Captain America did not open my eyes, but his struggles gave me a context in my fantasy world to consider alternative views of my world, a metaphor to cling to as I began to see American culture as a series of overlapping social structures.

While in college, I stopped reading comic books to engage in more intellectual pursuits. I occasionally became roughly aware of the changes wrought on the comic book medium in the 1990s, though I wouldn't understand any of those events as significant until years later. My reintroduction to Captain America and comic books came during the Christmas season of 2003, when I was shopping for a gift for a young nephew. This endeavor led me into the local toy store, inside which I was struck by the amount and variety of Marvel Comics merchandise.

As I was checking out, I was confronted by a set of small, framed posters featuring Marvel characters. The posters presented the best-known heroes in classic poses, with an inspirational inscription below each. The Captain America version caught my eye. Beneath the classic depiction of Captain America appeared the word *Patriotism*, which was followed by a roughly reworked quote from President John F. Kennedy's 1961 inaugural address: "Wish our country well or ill, but know this . . . we will pay any price, bear any burden, and meet any hardship . . . to assure the survival of our freedom."

The poster drew a smirk. In the context of the still-young US war on terror, those words seemed to have an almost ironic meaning. I bought it, and over the next few days the juxtaposition of the original context of Kennedy's words and the poster continued to bother me. And then I became curious: How *had* Captain America responded to the events of September 11, 2001? Was he the calm and neutral hero I remembered from the 1980s, the one who often sought a relatively nonviolent solution to conflicts? Or had he returned to the jingoistic superpatriot I had occasionally come across from earlier eras of his publication history?

I visited a comic book store and encountered the cover of the trade hardback collecting the first six issues of the fourth volume of *Captain America*. The cover portrayed a dramatic nationalist image of Captain America reminiscent of World War II propaganda posters. Assuming that the jingoistic poster on the cover represented a shift toward blind support of the American war on terror, I purchased the trade and prepared to watch my childhood hero betray the ideals I had come to associate with him. To my surprise, the storyline (written by John Ney Rieber) presented a sophisticated treatment of the relationship between overt nationalism, cultural imperialism, military might, and terrorism at a time when many such treatments were not available.

The Rieber storyline, one that involved Captain America confronting terrorism while simultaneously criticizing the US government for its role in fostering terrorism through its foreign policy, was eye-opening. I suddenly understood that this version of Captain America was radically different from the one that I had read about in my youth. And that, in turn, led me to wonder about other changes over time. More than ten years later this book is the result of that simple moment of curiosity.

Satisfying that curiosity would lead me down several different paths: thinking about patriotism and nationalism in American culture, looking at intersections of violence embedded in American mythology, conducting the kinds of counting and measurement activities consistent with social science, looking through the lenses of cultural theory, reading through fanzines of different eras, reading letter columns in the back of Captain America comic books, and finally bringing each of those instruments to bear on the questions of masculinity in American culture.

By learning more about Captain America and the writers and artists who created and continually re-created him as a cultural text, I began to see parallels with similar movements in other facets of American culture. Captain America, it turns out, has much to teach us about the ideals of American mythology—first and foremost, that such ideals are not nearly as static as seems to be generally presumed.

And so this book was intended to track the major moves in Captain America's evolution, to allow the text to make explicit what is too often implicit about American values (at least regarding how those values are expressed through a commercial commodity purposed with perpetually seeking consumer popularity).

This work has consumed a significant portion of my scholarly energy. I am forever indebted to so many people, probably most significantly the numerous friends who were subjected to late-night monologues as I sought to clarify my thinking by explaining why I was reading comic books at work. In particular, I need to thank Robert Jewett and John Shelton Lawrence. After coming across their series of books dealing with the American monomyth, which they convincingly argue is expressed in its purest forms through narratives involving superheroes, Western gunslingers, and 1980s action-movie figures, I contacted them with questions. Dr. Lawrence engaged with me in lengthy email discussions, nudging my thinking and even suggesting edits to my manuscript. Dr. Jewett met with me in a restaurant when he happened to be traveling through my area and critiqued an early draft of chapter 1. I disagree with each of them on certain points, which is what scholarship is all about, but their willingness to personally address my concerns proved invaluable.

And of course I must mention my research assistants' contributions over the years in editing my words and challenging my claims, most notably Christopher Bell and Shannon Sindorf. The staff at Syracuse University Press who handled and promoted my words deserve some special gratitude, in particular, Deborah Manion, Fred Wellner, Jennika Baines, and Mona Hamlin, along with freelance copyeditor Annie Barva. To that list, I should add the large number of friends and family who endured long discussions about this text over the years. In particular, Bryan Wade nudged me back into comics as a teenager. My youngest brother, Chuck, listened to me and contributed to long conversations that went through many a night. Carter Mullen often argued passionately with me about minutia in those ways brothers often do. Robert Foster pushed my intellectual boundaries around some of the related material in the first chapter. Friends such as Mark Huslig, Kelly and Christi Romeo, Jeff Stanglin, and Phillip Ratliff stoked the fires of my passions at various points. And Kimberly Donovan cheered me along over the final hurdles as I lurched toward completion. And of course my nephew Bradley Stevens, who helped inspire the original moment of curiosity.

But when it came time to dedicate the book, I had to dedicate it to my son. Peter, who is three years old as I write this preface, arrived at an interesting time. Comic books are often stereotypically considered the domain of children, but one of the surprises of my early parenting involved the stress associated with sorting through such texts and deciding which among them I felt comfortable bringing into my son's formative experiences. To my delight and horror, Peter was strongly attracted to Captain America, along with other heroes such as Spider-Man. I found that few pressures like grandiose concerns about influencing the early life of a child can drive a scholar to critically examine the implicit messages of popular entertainment.

CAPTAIN AMERICA,
MASCULINITY, AND VIOLENCE

1

Introduction

Sentinel of Liberty

On March 8, 2007, the *New York Times* ran as its featured book article a story on the assassination of Marvel Comics' Captain America.[1] The web version of the story appeared the evening before the printed edition and was briefly presented as the site's feature news story. Within minutes of the story's appearance, dozens of readers began to respond to it, including the following three examples:

> Capt. America dead? It is no wonder when Americans themselves think little of Americans.
>
> Capt. America might be dead, now, as also seems America—but, he should rise up, filled with hope, with pride, with the strength of the desire to live free as in 1776.
>
> Capt. America represents America in more ways than his ability to sell comic books. He fights with every man and woman in Iraq, against religious Islamic fascism. He fights with every New Yorker, looking to regain their lives in these last years since 9-11. He fights in the inner cities, in the farthest farm and in the most average suburb against those who would try to steal America's right to pray or not to pray, to say what they want to say—for the freedoms that make this country great.
>
> Get up, Capt. America. We need you now as much we needed you in 1941, when you fought for our fathers and grandfathers. Hitler is dead, but bin Laden lives on. Struggle to your feet, man. The fight is still worth fighting.

> I think this is the end. If you notice how it is becoming popular around the world to despise USA. this has been creeping into our own

population of passive Americans. I think that Marvel is throwing out this superhero because it is ashamed to be proud when everyone else is firing insults. We have forgotten the good which we stand up for. we are becmming wishy-washy europeanized country that can't stand up on it's own. we are afraid of saying we're great and ashamed of what we've done to help this world. THey killed Captain America in the Comic but our people of the USA are killing this great nation.

This is sick and unAmerican. What do the writers mean they new [*sic*] this was coming for a long time. In this world of conflict where America and democracy are fighting an existential battle against the forces of darkness, why would you have Captain America killed while trying to promote democratic ideals. Shame on these fools. Thousands of Americans were murdered on 9/11 and our soldiers die everyday fighting for liberty but these spoiled brats "kill Captain America." Disgusting. I would boycott Marvel Comics period.[2]

This type of rhetoric is hardly unusual for responses to the Captain America character. Nor was the commentary limited to fan dialogue. Original *Captain America Comics* writer Joe Simon told reporters he thought, "It's a hell of time for him to go. We really need him now."[3] Contemporary writer of *Captain America* Ed Brubaker commented, "What I found is that all the really hard-core Left-wing fans want Cap to be giving speeches on the street corner against the Bush Administration, and all the really Right-wing fans all want him to be over in the streets of Baghdad, punching out Saddam."[4]

Throughout the character's history, which contains messages varying from ultranationalist jingoism to a critique of the role of nationalism in the propagation of racism and terrorism, his narratives have provoked incredibly articulate responses. Since December 1940, Captain America has appeared in more than ten thousand stories in more than five thousand comic books, books, trade publications, and other media formats. To speak with a voice relevant to each era of American history, the character has undergone several transformations. Values, ideals, and even moral codes have adjusted at times to meet the needs of contemporary society.

Captain America is also an important text to consider because of the character's centrality to the Marvel Universe. Researchers Ricardo Alberich, Joe Miro-Julia, and Francesc Rosselló conducted an analysis that considered all of the characters of the Marvel Universe as members of a social network. Looking at the connections among characters within comic texts, they calculated that the average distance between two characters in the Marvel Universe network is 2.63. The researchers found that Captain America is the center of the network, with an average distance of 1.70 to other characters, making him the character most connected to all other characters.[5]

My own survey of the *Captain America* comic books found several distinct embodiments of the character, reflecting different conceptions of American culture. For example, despite beginning as a jingoistic prowar hero, Cap became a liberal crusader in the late 1960s, teaming up with the Falcon, the nation's first African American superhero to fight against corruption within the American establishment. In the 1980s, he reflected the Cold War morality and consumerism of the Reagan era. He became a superficial icon in the 1990s, a conflicted agent of the war on terror in 2002 (as well as a neoconservative zealot in Marvel's *Ultimates* line), a passionate advocate of wartime civil liberties in 2005 (culminating with his assassination in 2007), and finally a frustrated symbol of Obama administration optimism that struggled to define the role of government in regulating a new-world order.

Within Captain America's narratives, his actions, political stances, and speeches have frequently drawn attention and criticism from various sources outside the world of comic book publishing, particularly during times of social turmoil. In fact, the character has died several times (sometimes metaphorically and sometimes literally, though perhaps none of these deaths was as high profile and culturally significant as his assassination after Marvel's 2007 *Civil War* series), and he has been reborn each time to epitomize an updated sense of patriotism, American society, and power.

Through the years, Captain America's views have changed with the times, but it is a central component of his myth that his character has not changed (or that the change noted is an evolution of a new understanding of previously held ideals). This seeming paradox fits perfectly into the language of comics, where continuity is continually updated to fit the needs of the serialized present.

Fan Reception and the Struggle for Continuity

Of course, popular texts such as comic books also provide insight into their fan communities as well as into the population at large. In their recent book about the study of fandom, Jonathan Gray, Cornel Sandvoss, and C. Lee Harrington organize fandom studies into three stages: the initial studies emerging from Michel de Certeau's exploration of the use of popular mass media as a site of cultural resistance; the "fandom is beautiful" trend, which allowed fans to speak about and for themselves; and a third wave the authors describe as the study of the role of fandom in everyday life.[6]

In the third wave, fans are recognized not as resistors of the social order but as accessible exemplars of the maintainers of the social order in all its nuances. As the authors argue, "Here fandom is no longer only an object of study in and for itself. Instead, through the investigation of fandom as part of the fabric of our everyday lives, third wave work aims to capture fundamental insights into modern life. . . . Hence, studying fan audiences allows us to explore some of the key mechanisms through which we interact with the mediated world at the heart of our social, political, and cultural realities and identities."[7] The third wave of fandom studies will likely prove a boon to studies examining comic book fans, for such fans have consistently been framed in research literature in precisely this way. As the chapters in this book show, fan interactions (letters, articles, and consumer behavior) have been instrumental in influencing the Captain America texts. Like previous forms of popular culture, such as dime novels in Michael Denning's account,[8] comic books represent struggles both at the point of production and at the point of consumption. Even as readers consume popular culture, they act through their consumption and fan activity to resist and reform that culture. It because of the recognition of those dual points of struggle that this book seeks to account both for the structural accounting of a comic book text's generation (by analyzing the pertinent industry history) as well as the agency of those consuming it (by delving into the reactions of members of various fan cultures to the texts themselves).

Like many popular culture narratives, superhero comics contain and embody political texts. Heroes operating in a realistic universe must encounter and react to familiar conditions within their society. But politics shift over the life of a society, often more quickly than can be easily dealt with in the continuity of a comic book. Contemporary understandings of US history rely as much on mythological stories as on historical facts,[9] and myths are by definition stories that banish contradictions through rote simplification.[10] So comic creators are faced with a structural tension: heroes who change too quickly become unrecognizable to casual readers, and yet heroes must react to a changing world, or they will not resonate with devoted readers.

Jason Dittmer calls this tension the "tyranny of the serial."[11] Because heroes act as agents of the status quo, they tend to redefine themselves continually in terms of the society around them (in contrast, villains, Dittmer points out, are agents who work to impose their attitudes and beliefs on society) even as the status quo changes:

> Ultimately, national identity is not a static and timeless concept, as national mythmaking would have it, but instead a continually changing discourse that structures the nation's sense of collective self and its relationship with others. Because of this, serial narratives such as monthly comic books, the nightly news, and weekly television dramas can be seen not only as a venue in which national identity is constructed in regular chronological intervals, but also as an archive of discourses that can be studied longitudinally. If a serial narrative lasts long enough, it will certainly have to change in order to maintain a link to the society that is consuming it. However, serial narratives have a general inability to produce systematic social change and are therefore innately conservative.[12]

The tyranny of the serial makes long-standing superheroes magnificent representations of how values within a society develop and change as well as of how present citizens reconcile their values with those of an age long passed. In addition, to remain popular enough to stay in circulation, superheroes must represent social values (or sometimes embody a critique of contemporary values) that appeal to their audience.

As Terry Wandtke points out, the struggle to balance story advancement and a recognizable status quo within serialized superhero comic books creates a tension in how previous narratives are related to current story lines. When tensions arise, the present interpretation of a character is normally privileged over previous forms of and stories featuring that character, causing contemporary writers to reinterpret the significance of past events to reconcile previous forms with the attitudes and tones of contemporary comic continuity. The result is the "transhistorical presence" through which superheroes simultaneously signify cultural permanence even as their values change.[13]

Richard Reynolds describes three types of continuity within comic book discourse. Serial continuity dictates that events portrayed in a comic book cannot directly contradict the events in previous books. If a character is presented as an only child in a previous comic, he or she cannot encounter a sibling without significant explanation within the narrative to clarify why this contradiction is acceptable. Hierarchical continuity controls the relationships of power between the various characters within a comic universe. Neither heroes nor villains should exhibit new abilities or increased power from story to story without explanation. Finally, structural continuity governs the relationships between characters and stories in a given universe. What occurs in one text should not explicitly contradict a story in another text.[14]

Continuity is extremely important in serialized story forms because readers often drop into and out of awareness of the stories, and the authors and artists who work on a series frequently change during the life of a long comic narrative. Keeping up with how the events of a specific story fit into the broader narrative restricts the range of story elements for the sake of coherent stories. In addition, fans of comic narratives expect a certain consistency in the offered stories because detailed knowledge of the conventions of a comic's continuity creates a form of social capital for the consumers of a given story.[15] The result of these competing forces is a tension through which history is revised, blurred, and reconditioned to fit present understandings. Unlike many other comic publishers (and particularly in contrast to chief competitor DC Comics), Marvel pursues narrative continuity with an almost religious zeal. The disparities caused by differences in various eras of US history are reconciled by heavy use of retroactive continuity, "retcon," narratives. History is regularly updated and adjusted to make the past fit with the present.

Historians and historiographers have noted such adjustments as consistent with the manner in which Americans consider their own history. Because so many Americans arrived in their new country to escape their past conditions, history has long been a fluid concept for most of them, wherein the ability to reconstruct and reinvent origins serves as a central component of American mythology.[16]

In this sense, Captain America represents the ultimate American story: permanent enough to survive more than seventy years of continuity but with a history hazy enough to be constantly reinterpreted to meet the needs of the contemporary culture through which he walks from decade to decade. This phenomenon is common among long-standing comic book characters. Umberto Eco discusses in his classic book *The Role of the Reader* the root of this paradox when exploring the mythology surrounding Superman. Superman had indeed been fighting a "never-ending battle for Truth, Justice and the American Way" for forty years by the time Eco deconstructed his narratives. And yet Superman himself would not have possessed forty years of memories as a result of his adventures. Eco explains that comic book authors maintain a type of "oneiric climate—of which the reader is not aware at all—where what has happened before and what has happened after appear extremely hazy."[17]

This haziness in the Marvel Universe means that origin dates are adjustable despite the careful focus on continuity. The explosion of superhero activity in the 1960s can move forward in time as the characters do. It is generally assumed in Marvel Comics that only ten to twenty years have passed since the arrival of the Fantastic Four, the Avengers, and the X-Men. The introductory date can be assumed to be relevant to the era in which the characters reside. In Captain America's case, his World War II–era stories are treated as canonical accounts (although they are often augmented through flashbacks, and they all are compressed into a short span of a few years). In order to reintroduce Cap to the late twentieth century, Marvel writers used a plot device that has Cap frozen in a block of ice near the end of World War II and revived by the Avengers in *The Avengers* volume 1, number 4.[18] However, since his revival, it has been customary to frame Cap stories as if he had been revived for about ten years, no matter how much time actually passes in the real world. Reynolds discusses the root of this problem when he explains how Marvel's structural continuity allows Cap to remain perpetually young: "[S]ince 1964, time has continued to roll on. The time that has passed since 1964 has been telescoped into continuity, which is openly non-historical and doesn't move forward at any set pace. But the period of time when Captain America was out of continuity altogether was treated as historical—the time when no Captain America stories were being published, or at least none which are [*sic*] now considered canonical. Yet Steve Rogers/Captain America has now remained 'frozen' in his late twenties for far longer than he was literally frozen in the ice."[19]

This solution causes other problems for Captain America continuity because the character often reacts to dated cultural events and meets up with government officials as a matter of his duties as the nation's defender. For example, during the supposed ten years that Cap has existed since his revival, he has interacted with both Richard Nixon and Barack Obama (as well as with nearly every president in between). As a result of such paradoxes and to meet the needs of contemporary plot twists, Cap's history (and, by extension, America's) is frequently reinterpreted, reformed, and revised. References to particular events and historical moments are not erased per se, but they are often de-emphasized into a hazy recollection of when certain actions occurred and in what specific cultural context. Cap's character and personality are continually renegotiated to keep the character popular and relevant to contemporary American consumers. This seeming paradox of context (adaptability and apparent permanence) allow Captain America narratives to serve as time capsules of their age, particularly when it comes to the role of patriotism and nationalism in American culture, race relations, gender relations, the acceptability of violence in armed conflict, and the appropriate levels of respect awarded to governmental institutions and agencies.

Marvel *Civil War* series writer Mark Millar explained that he had a time capsule in mind when he wrote the series:

> You know, I WANT this book to be dated in 10–20 years. I want it to be dated in FIVE years. The thing about comics is that it's a pop medium and a mistake people make is dreaming of posterity. We're a disposable pulp medium in the sense that most readers don't keep or re-read our work, they just move on to the next pop thrill. A good comic book, to me, perfectly encapsulates the time period it was created in. *Dark Knight* and *Watchmen* are probably the two greatest comic books ever and are both absolutely rooted in Cold War and Reaganomics. A good comic is a 22-page time-capsule whether it's the Fantastic Four talking about the Beatles or Bush-era super-people worried about civil liberties.[20]

As Millar points out, because most readers of a given comic are reading contemporary stories with limited understandings of the past, writers operate within a haze that allows more freedom in storytelling. Contradictions are thus left to be noted by long-term collectors or explained away by the next writers should the continuity developments prove too inconvenient for future stories.

Human beings naturally refine their history by altering details during recollection. Psychologists call this reinterpretation process "destructive updating" because the original memories of an event are often lost as new interpretations of events are recalled.[21] Human memory is never an objective record of the past but rather reflects what Maurice Halbwachs calls "a reconstruction of the past achieved with data borrowed from the present."[22]

Captain America represents one of the greatest examples of how responsive comic book heroes must be to their audience. In the 1950s, Atlas Comics (historically considered the reconfiguration of Timely Comics and the predecessor of Marvel Comics) revived Cap to continue his defense of American values against the forces of communism. Although his adventures were entirely consistent with his actions and attitudes presented in the 1940s narratives, the *Commie Smasher!* book did not sell well and was canceled after only three issues. Years later Marvel sought to repair a breach in continuity by having the more liberal 1970s Captain

America battle the 1950s Captain America, who was retroactively recast as a separate person who had been driven to his "Commie Smasher" zeal by a defective compound. In this way, Marvel was able to explain how Cap had appeared in favor of the establishment during the early years of the Cold War but then opposed to it during the 1960s and 1970s without straining longtime readers' credulity over this glaring disparity.

To study comic books as cultural expressions is to run headlong into the relationship between fan culture and dominant culture. Henry Jenkins has written extensively on this topic, producing perhaps no finer exploration of fan culture than his 1992 treatise on the topic, *Textual Poachers*. Focusing primarily on television texts, Jenkins discusses how fans use favored texts to reconstruct and reconfigure cultural significance in their own lives.[23]

My own exploration of Captain America comic books does not present these negotiations except in extremely superficial ways. For instance, conservative social critics Michael Medved and Michael Lackner clearly approached the fourth volume of *Captain America* differently than the numerous critics and fan writers who took issue with their analysis of the character.[24] I briefly explore the differences in interpretation (as in the 1970s letter columns fight in chapter 4, the 2003 Medved controversy in chapter 8, and the subsequent debates surrounding the character's assassination), but my analysis focuses primarily on how the text itself has adapted to conform to the popular expectations necessary to sell comic books over the years.

Jenkins points out that television consumption is difficult to definitively categorize: "television is watched for many reasons and with different degrees of attentiveness as it is inserted into a range of viewing contexts."[25] It might be argued, at least philosophically, that comic book consumption can be subject to some minor variance in reader experience related to such variables (in particular, the discussion of the meaning of comic texts occupies a significant space in print and online materials). However, the static (if ephemeral) nature of comic book narratives does lend the medium to a heavier emphasis on textual analysis techniques.

It is also important to point out that fan culture is extremely important to modern comic narratives. As opposed to the limited ways in which

Jenkins identifies interactions between the producers and consumers of television shows, comic fans and creators have usually engaged in a much tighter dialogue that more dramatically affects the point of production. As readers will discover in chapter 5, the fans of *Captain America* comics in the 1970s actually influenced the direction of the book's narrative when the creators and editors at Marvel Comics interpreted the influx of fan letters as a referendum on the character's status quo. But it is this tighter relationship that makes the comic text such a source of potential value to historians. To speak with a relevant voice to each era of US history, the character has endured several transformations. Values, ideals, and even moral codes have adjusted at times to meet the contemporary society's needs, and these changes are reflected in the corresponding texts. However, the final chapter of this book also argues that the emerging primacy of the Marvel Studios movies may be changing this relationship.

Works of popular culture have a symbolic relationship to their socio-historical context, serving as both descriptions and explanations of the cultural systems that produced them.[26] Reynolds claims that superhero narratives give us insight into "certain ideological myths" about American society,[27] and, of course, the Captain America narrative seems particularly suited for encouraging a greater degree of articulation about these myths.

This book is an attempt to identify key changes in the Captain America narrative (focusing primarily on masculinity, as informed by the American monomyth, which in turn allows an exploration of attitudes concerning violence, patriotism, race relations, and gender roles), changes that provide insight into the makeup of the cultural environment to which the character has adjusted to remain relevant. Superhero narratives generally maintain the status quo,[28] and Captain America is no exception. According to his own continuity, the US government created Cap to battle the Nazi disruption of the pre–World War II American way of life.[29]

Thomas Andrae notes that although iconic heroes such as Superman—whom Gary Engle cites as deeply representative of American character[30]—tend to reinforce dominant ideology, they also offer social criticism.[31] Geoff Klock points out that superhero narratives, in particular those that have been running for more than six decades, are a wonderful source for understanding cultural transition because "reinterpretation becomes part of [their] survival code."[32] Andrew MacDonald and Virginia Macdonald argue that the 1960s and 1970s Captain America evolved into a character that "accurately caught the changing mood of the past thirty years."[33]

Salvatore Mondello asserts that Cap's contemporary, Spider-Man, offers a liberal perspective on social issues in his comics, even as the conservative climate in which he operates is reinforced.[34] Matthew McAllister shows that comic books are well suited to raising awareness of social issues and problems, such as the spread of AIDS.[35]

Captain America stories are often composed to demonstrate how competing American values (for instance, freedom of speech versus security) create conflict among the citizenry. According to his continuity, Captain America was frozen near the end of World War II, only to be awakened in 1963. His reaction to the culture of 1960s America and of later decades as he encounters them allows him to comment (mostly through silent thoughtful brooding) on the paradoxes of his contemporary surroundings. In this manner, Cap presents himself as a symbol of a culture in which he is an alien. As he reacts to the events unfolding around him, he allows his readers to have personal access to the shifting definitions of American culture.

Comic Narratives as Open Texts

Despite the historic dearth of comics scholarship, recent works have examined comic book narratives to describe social developments over time, such as Will Brooker's analysis of Batman comics and entertainment properties.[36] Others have examined many themes in a particular era—for example, Mike DuBose looks closely at *The Dark Knight Returns*, *The Watchmen*, and the 1980s *Captain America* comics to uncover heroic themes during the Reagan administration.[37] Finally, there have been several notable studies of representation, including the portrayals of women,[38] homosexuals,[39] and Arabs,[40] in comics.

In *The Role of the Reader*, Eco argues that Superman comic narratives are a closed text, unable to adapt to new circumstances or social understandings because the character's mythic dimensions embody timeless laws (in particular the empowerment needed to overcome industrial-era impotence), making his adventures predictable and formulaic.[41] Eco claims that because the character's serial adventures rely on a set of conventions established by the circumstances under which the character emerged, Superman should be considered an iconic text, consistently a single text throughout its existence. Eco published his analysis near the end of the height of this character's popularity,[42] the late 1970s, noting the paradox that Superman's creators faced when trying to interact with contemporary issues while holding to the timeless mythology.

My book argues that many of the narratives contained in Marvel Comics products should be approached as open texts in the same vein that Tony Bennett and Janet Woollacott argue that James Bond narratives are open. Critiquing Eco's analysis of Bond as a text possessing a mythic formula, Bennett and Woollacott effectively conclude that because Bond novels, movies, and derivative works cover thirty years of history, the backdrop and permutations of the character's exploits have made him a "sign of his times."[43] Such a positioning of Bond texts allows these authors to examine the ideology represented in different Bond texts and to draw conclusions about the immediate context in which those texts were produced.

The location and status of the texts are important in that an open-text narrative about cultural conflict will more readily draw on the social environment to feed its allegory, making the arguments within the text a time capsule of specific conflicts and specific eras in a society. Max Skidmore and Joey Skidmore describe comic books as a reflection of the political conditions in which they were produced.[44]

From its resurgence in popularity in the 1960s, Marvel Comics has produced open textual narratives that wrestle with the politics of representation.[45] The company's success has been linked to its efforts to create characters that "talk like real people and react like real people."[46] By linking its stories to events and locations in contemporary society, Marvel has sought to create characters that seem like "real, living, breathing people whose personal relationships would be of interest to the readers."[47]

Methods and Notes

Since the beginning, the writers, editors, and artists producing Captain America narratives have drawn on contemporary political situations of their day. The social commentary embedded within Captain America's adventures is seldom measured. Rather, the producers of Captain America often experiment with circumstances contemporary to their experience and create a need for narrative renegotiation as more facts or perspectives emerge over time.

Captain America narratives give us a snapshot of what it meant for Americans to live with the anger of watching the footage of Pearl Harbor at the local movie theater or with the fear resulting from witnessing the September 11, 2001, attacks on television. But these narratives also show us how we construct, deconstruct, and reconstruct the meanings of events and, as a result, how we build myth in our society.

Therefore, this book seeks to segregate different eras of Captain America stories for analysis to demonstrate how different eras of Americans conceptualize patriotism, the role of America in the world, and underlying concepts of American power.

In his analysis of the development of the superhero genre, Peter Coogan offers the following dates as boundary markers for different eras of comic book genre development:

1. The Golden Age of comic books. This era began with the first appearance of Superman in *Action Comics number 1* (June 1938) and ended with *Plastic Man* volume 1, number 64 (November 1956), which Coogan views as a symbolic end to the "simple" approach to comic heroes. This era contained the establishment of the superhero genre conventions.

2. The Silver Age of comic books. This era began with the appearance of the first modern Flash in *Showcase* volume 1, number 4 (October 1956), and concluded with *Teen Titans* volume 1, number 31 (January 1971). The superhero conventions reached an equilibrium in this era in which author and audience shared mutual understanding and expectation of the narratives. This age is well known for its stability and its episodic (if not formulaic) approach to comic narratives.

3. The Bronze Age of comic books. This era began with *Superman* volume 1, number 233 (January 1971), and ended with *The*

Legion of Superheroes number 259 (January 1980). This era was characterized by adjustments to the conventional superhero formula, resulting in the weakening or restructuring of certain heroes and the shuffling of hero team memberships. Though many of the conventions remained unchanged, the characters showed some growth and change in their development.

4. The Iron Age of comics. This era began with *DC Comics Presents* number 26 (October 1980) and concluded with *Justice League of America* volume 1, number 261 (April 1987). In this era, the form and its embellishments are accented until they become the "substance" or "content" of the work.

5. The Renaissance Age of comic books. This era began with *Justice League* number 1 (May 1987) and may not yet have concluded. In this era, the conventions of the superhero genre have been reestablished, and several new aesthetics have emerged.[48]

Coogan admits that these boundaries are a constant source of controversy within comic book fandom but believes that the eras he has defined reflect a general consensus. Other authors pick different boundary points and different labels. Mark Voger calls the "Renaissance Age" (or at least a portion of it) the "Dark Age" because of the excesses and grimness that permeate much of the genre in this period.[49] And it would appear that both authors allow for another age to exist following their final boundary, although neither provides a name for it.

When considering major developments of comic book history, scholars differ on organizing principles largely because of different approaches to the medium: textual analysts look for content trends; social scientists look to industry trends; critical theorists look for ideological shifts. Such diversity of approaches allows for competing ways to conceptualize the organization of comic book history. However, the frameworks listed earlier are useful in giving general guidelines (with certain modifications) for touring the mythic dimensions of Captain America across several generations of comic readers. Since 1941, there have been more than five thousand Captain America comic books (and counting because the character appears in twelve to eighteen stories each month) in which some version of Captain America has appeared (the uniform is worn by Steve Rogers, Bucky Barnes, William Naslund, Jeffrey Mace, William Burnside, Bob Russo, Scar Turpin, Roscoe, John Walker, Sam Wilson, Clint Barton, and Isaiah Bradley at various points). This book surveys the collected works, dividing the books into representative categories defined by dramatic changes in the character's personality or behavior. I identified and analyzed core traits using textual analysis to determine contextual clues about the presentation of culture. My survey of the books resulted in the following divisions, each featuring a Captain America character created to meet the needs of a different era:

1. Captain America: Anti-Hitler Crusader (269 comic stories appearing from 1940 to 1950)
2. Captain America: Commie Smasher! (16 comic book stories appearing from 1953 to 1954)
3. Captain America: Man out of Time (202 comic book stories appearing from 1963 to 1971)
4. Captain America: Liberal Crusader (322 comic book stories appearing from 1971 until the end of the Falcon's inclusion in the title in 1978)
5. Captain America: Individualist Consumer (582 comic book stories appearing from 1978 to 1990)
6. Captain America: Superficial Icon (906 comic book stories appearing from 1990 to 2002)
7. Captain America: Soldier in the War on Terror (548 comic book stories appearing from 2002 to the death of Steve Rogers in 2007)
8. Captain America: Postidealist Commando (approximately 1,450 comic book stories and counting, appearing from 2007 to the present)

I drew this list using a variety of sources, including the official indexes and websites published by Marvel and comic book information sites such as the Grand Comic Book Database, Comic Vine, the Comic Book DB, and the Marvel Database Project. The sample includes titles in which Captain America is a featured character (such as the various volumes of *The*

Avengers or the character's self-titled comic volumes) as well as titles in which he makes a guest appearance. I ignored strict reprints. For example, I omitted reprinted stories in comics such as *Marvel Super Action* and *Marvel Super-Heroes* from the sample (as I did all trade collections and hardback collections of previously printed materials unless they contain original story material), but I included Captain America's appearances in *Marvel Saga* because of the textual narration that accompanied the reprinted material from previous works.

Considering the Masculinity of Hypermasculine Superheroes

Each chapter addresses a particular era of publication (with some reference to other eras), including some of the cultural and historical context needed to draw attention to the relationships between text and culture. Of particular importance is the masculinity of Captain America as expressed in each era of his narrative. Masculinity as a concept has long been understudied because people tend to think of it as an obvious and constant concept, a "belief," reports Kenneth Mackinnon, "that men cannot fundamentally change, that there is a fixed masculinity."[50] But scholars have recently begin to argue that masculinity is better understood as "fluid, time-related and variable across cultures and eras as well as subject to change over the course of a person's life, and within any given society at any one time."[51] Or, as Mackinnon notes, "masculinity alters over time and amid changing circumstances. It cannot, by that understanding, be a monolith, but is protean—changing shape and emphasis—and also plural."[52] This understanding indicates that the longitudinal study of hypermasculinity over long-existing texts should show differences in how various eras present men and male behavior.

In a longitudinal context, masculinity should be understood as much for what it is not as for what it is. Though masculinity is broadly seen as being about "a man in power, a man *with* power, and a man of power,"[53] it is widely recognized that the given ideals of an era's views on masculinity are not gathered or explicitly performed by actual men but rather "formed from the people's common sense by, perhaps above all, television, film, advertising and sport as relayed to and received by huge audiences."[54]

In other words, masculinity is a social construct informed by the performance of exemplars,[55] most often through mediated representations or fantasy representations needed to embody particular frames of masculinity not generally found among men.[56] In this way, masculinity may be understood as a "condensing point of broader social discourses about the way in which we should live, about how to be a man—in short, about morality and masculinity,"[57] and the more idealized expressions drawn from media exist as a kind of hypermasculinity not generally practiced by men. In fact, it may very well be that the lack of faith in masculine power in society is what creates demand for representations of such power (such as violence) in media.[58] Thus, an expression of hypermasculinity "exposes, rather than allays, anxiety about masculinity."[59]

When considering the hypermasculine ideal presented by Captain America, several factors should be considered. How Captain America's male body is drawn is obviously an item of interest. Male body representations are objects of social practice,[60] and given Captain America's near-perpetual framing as the epitome of physical male perfection, how different artists have drawn his body says something about ideal views of physical male perfection during the time a given text appears. However, to simply conflate masculinity and the male form would miss other important socially constructed dimensions of masculinity,[61] and so more central to this book's analysis is how Captain America's masculinity is used to explore the intersections of components such as violence and morality. Given some scholars' framing of masculinity as a discourse informing men about the moral use of their power[62] and the "persistent cultural belief" in an "almost unbreakable relationship between men and violence,"[63] this work looks for masculinity as a function of the intersections of violence and morality (morality, in turn, being informed by patriotism and the ever-changing hero code to which Captain America subscribes).

In some ways, the evolution of Captain America puts the evolution of hypermasculinity on display as it shows how the American monomyth developed in different eras of US history. To better locate Captain America's emergence at a particular time in US history, chapter 2 includes a summary of the historical emergence of the American monomyth (the distilled conventions for all superheroes, action heroes, and Western-themed heroes), in particular the contributions of American theology to the creation of the peculiar American cultural mythology that breathed life into the superhero genre. It covers the Captain America narrative from the character's birth shortly before America entered World War II until this character's book was discontinued due to waning interest in it in postwar American culture. Other chapters devote space to tracking major developments in the comic book industry. Chapter 3 covers the brief reemergence of Captain America in the mid-1950s. Chapter 4 describes the birth of Marvel Comics and the resurrection of Captain America in the pages of *The Avengers*. Chapter 5 covers the character's involvement with the "relevant comics" movement. Chapter 6 follows the captain's exploits as the character embodied many of the consumerist trends of the 1980s. Chapter 7 follows Captain America through the superficial and hypercommercial era of comic books when art began to be valued over textual content and, at times, storytelling. Chapter 8 explores Captain America's response to the terrorist attacks of September 11, 2001, and the reemphasis on his character as a soldier struggling to find his role in the global war on terror. Chapter 8 also examines the character's involvement in the Marvel Comics Civil War event as Captain America became a symbol of the resistance to the surveillance state. Chapter 9 explores the environment left by Captain America's death and subsequent return to both comic books and film.

This research project was not an explicit attempt to reconcile mainstream Marvel continuity and largely ignores concerns about continuity except at times to chronicle how and why creators changed aspects of Captain America's backstory and characterization. This book is meant to examine Captain America's mythology, not to reconstruct his history. As a result, I did not attempt to segregate alternate universe storylines from stories that appeared in mainstream continuity. I offer two justifications for this more comprehensive inclusion: first, comic creators often experimented with characters in alternate titles such as Marvel's *What If?* in order to manipulate the mainstream character's attributes; and second, some of the alternate portrayals of Captain America were later incorporated into his mainstream continuity. An example of this incorporation can be found

in the feature story of *What If?* volume 1, number 4, in which two additional men are portrayed as taking up the identity of Captain America
after Steve Rogers's retroactively framed 1945 disappearance.[64]

After Cap's history was reconfigured to account for the 1950s incarnation, the story introducing these two men was canonized into the mainstream Marvel continuity. So although at the time the stories of the late
1940s and 1950s were written the comic creators involved clearly intended
the character be the same man who first put on the uniform, today's comic
creators presume that some 1940s (and 1950s) adventures were experienced by individuals other than Steve Rogers. The scope and analysis of
the work in this book do not hinge on such details, although they often
engage the reasons such hand-wringing was performed to bring Captain
America's history into conformity with contemporary concerns or values
(for example, the fact that Steve Englehart and Sal Buscema repurposed
the 1950s Captain America into a separate individual to battle with Steve
Rogers over the evils of Red baiting is certainly pertinent to discussions
about politics, patriotism, and masculinity). Nor does this survey attempt
to reconstruct continuity resulting from modern stories set in different
eras; for example, the critically acclaimed *Truth: Red, White, and Black*
series, which portrays the experiences of Isaiah Bradley in the 1930s and
1940s, is considered in the chapter dealing with all texts that appeared in
2003. The publication and release dates were the organizing principle for
selection, for regardless of the era portrayed in the comic book in question
the consumers of each particular era in US history were the target of the
text's creation and sale.

This book draws primarily from content analysis and textual analysis
techniques (counting examples of violent actions or comparing political
frames to contemporary texts, for instance), but it also consults sources in
news media and popular press items for context. I also pay close attention
to reader letter columns that have appeared in the back of most Marvel
Comics since the 1960s.

Finally, a few notes about some idiosyncrasies are important to help
those not familiar with certain aspects of the medium of comic books
understand how specific texts can be located. Throughout this book,
the dates reported for specific stories are the publication dates printed

on the covers or in copyright notices of the various books under scrutiny. However, I should point out that the dates listed are not the dates of release. Periodicals are often dated forward to allow newsstands and resellers to gauge when the publication may be removed from circulation and returned to the publisher or destroyed (or placed in the "back issues" bin of a comic book store). Comic books are normally dated two to three months ahead of their release date, although every company uses its own internal policies to govern this practice. So a comic dated "June 1996" probably was available to consumers in early April 1996. This discrepancy can make a significant difference in how *Captain America* comics are perceived. For example, *Captain America Comics* number 1 is cover-dated March 1941. This cover date often leads authors to claim that the historic punch to Adolf Hitler's jaw featured on the cover of the first issue appeared "more than six months before Pearl Harbor."[65] According to an advertisement inside the cover of *The Human Torch* number 3 (December 1940) that shows the cover drawing for *Captain America Comics* number 1, including the Hitler punch, the latter was scheduled for release "around December 20, [1940]."[66] According to *Marvel Mystery Comics* number 15 (itself cover-dated January 1941 but actually appearing at newsstands on November 27, 1940), the third issue of *The Human Torch* was released on December 10, 1940,[67] which means *Captain America Comics* number 1 was created at least twelve months before America declared war on the Axis powers. In recent years, both the publication date and the release date have been used to date comic books. In this book, dates reported are almost always the publication dates, not the release dates.

This distinction may seem trivial, but understanding the dating system changes the immediate context in which books were released. *Captain America Comics* number 13, dated April 1942, whose cover features Cap punching a bespectacled and fanged Japanese officer in the face, became available mere weeks after Pearl Harbor. Similarly, when Steve Englehart wrote into his "Secret Empire" story arc that the enemy conspiracy was headed up by President Nixon (*Captain America* volume 1, number 175, dated July 1974), he revealed that he was scrambling to comment on events he observed in the impeachment hearings occurring in May as the book was going to press. Similarly, the casual reader can lose sight of the timing of the portrayal of the September 11 terrorist attacks portrayed in *Captain America* volume 4, number 1 (dated June 2002), which appeared only a few months after the attacks.

Another note of interest concerns page numbering in comic books, which has adhered to different conventions at different points in the medium's history. In Golden Age Timely/Marvel comic books, pages were numbered by story. *Captain America Comics* number 1 contained five stories, and each story had a page 1. Marvel comics published in the 1960s also tended to number each page in each comic but skipped numbering for pages that contained advertisements. Marvel Comics in the 1970s sometimes counted page numbers across multiple stories that appeared in the same comic book, particularly when the stories were considered chapters of a larger story, as in early stories featured in *The Invaders*. Beginning in the late 1970s, Marvel comic books began to count advertisement pages as numbered pages in the comic. Around 1995, Marvel stopped putting page numbers in comic books, which is the convention in contemporary Marvel comic books. And, of course, publishers other than Marvel Comics have used a variety of page-numbering systems throughout the years.

Such differences in numbering conventions can make research projects such as mine rather daunting. If printed page numbers appear in a comic, I use those numbers to help readers locate specific pages. When page numbers are not given (as in post-1995 Marvel comic books), I manually counted pages, including advertisement pages, following the last page-numbering convention used by Marvel when it was still giving page numbers in its comic books. These numbers usually conform to informal indexes published on sites such as Grand Comics DB, but on occasion my manual page count differs from pagination in other sources because of alternative methodologies. And it should be noted that trade paperbacks that collect multiple issues of a comic in a bound edition almost always exclude advertisements.

Finally, although most books written in one of the major academic styles list only the writer when sourcing comic book stories, I list both the writer and the lead artist. This method of sourcing is necessary because of the emergence of the "Marvel Method" in the 1960s, in which writers and artists at Marvel collaborated more closely in the creation of stories than they did at other companies. Separating authorship of most post-1963 Marvel Comics would be a difficult proposition at best, so both writer and artist are listed. But many of the Timely/Atlas-era comic books showed no author credentials. As Timely artist Allen Bellman explained recently, "I was always made to feel that Timely didn't want you to sign your work while you were on staff. I also remember being told that they didn't want other publishers grabbing you."[68] In cases in which Golden Age creators could be identified from biographical works or industry interviews, I have restored author credits, but the creator credits for most Timely and Atlas-era comic books are difficult to verify.

Although changing conventions such as page-numbering systems can be frustrating for those who study long-running comic book narratives, such differences also serve as guideposts within an evolving medium. Captain America is nearly as old as the comic book medium itself, and to follow his history through the ages is to observe the history of comic books from its earliest age to the present. And just as Cap's narrative has evolved in response to the challenges in each era, so too has the comic book industry evolved in response to changing tastes, attitudes, and patterns of consumption in America culture.

2

The Anti-Hitler Crusader
(1940–1949)

"As the ruthless war-mongers of Europe focus their eyes on a peace-loving America . . . the youth of our country heed the call to arms for our defense . . . but great as the danger of foreign attack . . . is the threat of invasion from within . . . the dreaded fifth column."[1] These words, set against images of domestic sabotage by Nazi secret agents, open the first story presented in *Captain America Comics* volume 1, number 1. The initial story presents the origin of the character in the Oval Office with a meeting between President Franklin D. Roosevelt and his top military advisers. Decrying spies within the ranks of the armed forces, the officers are authorized by the president to accompany an FBI agent to look in on an experiment that might help with the fifth-column threat to America.

From here, the story incorporates narrative elements that would be ritualistically reproduced and reinterpreted more than a dozen times (whenever the character needed to be reestablished or the character's direction was changing): a rundown curio shop with a female agent wearing a mask to make herself look old, a hidden laboratory, a Jewish scientist with an experimental compound, and a young, scrawny man named Steve Rogers. Drinking a secret formula (later renditions would vary the treatment to include radiation as well as chemical injections), the young man who had been turned away from military service because of his frail condition suddenly grows physically larger. He becomes the perfect human specimen in strength, speed, agility, and intelligence, intended to be the first of a new corps of superagents. Another tenet of the mythology is realized when a secret Nazi agent draws his pistol and shoots the lead scientist dead before Rogers springs into action and kills him.

In the next page and a half, Rogers is transformed from the first of a corps of supersoldiers into a costumed symbol to combat spies and saboteurs; creates a secret identity as a common army private; and acquires his sidekick, Bucky Barnes. Thus emerges the heroic story that would frame this character's relevance (or irrelevance at times) for the next seventy-plus years.

There are several interesting differences between the first origin story and later drafts of the same events, but perhaps none is more telling than the results of the hero's confrontation with the Nazi agent. In later origin renditions, when Captain America leaps at the agent, he spooks the spy into killing himself. In the original version, Rogers lands two blows, and the agent stumbles into a bank of machinery that electrocutes him. As Rogers looks over the body, he proclaims, "Nothing left of him but charred ashes . . . a fate he well deserved!"[2]

Some later versions of this story portray Rogers attempting to warn the agent before his death, and no future origin stories have Rogers boast over the slain body (when Jack Kirby would draw a later version of the origin story, the character would boast about his new mission, but Rogers would never again boast about the Nazi agent's plight being "deserved"). This difference is hardly insignificant, for it sets the tone for Cap's approach to enemies of America. In the early years of Captain America narratives, Cap's foes wind up dead almost as often as they end up in the justice system, and a disproportionate number of them expire after Cap knocks them into dangerous circumstances. The perfect human specimen seems often to misjudge his own strength to the detriment of those who oppose him. Or perhaps he understands his strength all too well and merely plays at the innocence and righteousness that his promoters ascribe to him. In either interpretation, Cap would seem to capture profoundly the spirit of internal inconsistency that surrounds the behavior of the nation whose flag he wears on his body, a nation whose reputation as a benevolent superpower is being forged by the war he is designed to promote.

Although America would not enter World War II until after the Japanese bombing on December 7, 1941, Timely publisher Martin Goodman resolved as early as 1938 to use his company as an engine of anti-Nazi propaganda.[3] Even before Cap's first adventure, Nazi forces had already been portrayed as foes to a couple of the Timely heroes: the Sub-Mariner (Namor McKenzie), who grapples with a Nazi U-boat in Marvel *Mystery Comics* number 4, and the original Human Torch, who faces Axis enemies in the first issue of his self-titled comic. Goodman was reportedly looking to address world events in a way that those who were not educated in world affairs (such as children) could comprehend and become involved in the struggle against the rising Nazi influence in Europe.

The purpose of the Captain America comic was not merely to entertain or even to simply inform, for presented in each of Cap's early comics was an invitation to join the Sentinels of Liberty, a fan club that encouraged readers to actively engage in Cap's struggle. To join, readers had to submit a dime and sign a document that proclaimed, "I solemnly pledge to uphold the principles of the Sentinels of Liberty and assist Captain America in his war against spies in the U.S.A."[4] In return, members of the fan club received a membership card and a metal badge.

Each issue featured a new advertisement. *Captain America Comics* number 3 proclaimed that "[e]very Red-blooded young American boy and girl will be proud to be a member of this club!" The next issue encouraged readers to join the ranks because "[m]any thousands of Sentinels of Liberty are daily waging a war to the finish against spies and traitors to our country." By issue 5, the ads exerted classic appeals to peer identification: "Captain America wants YOU to join more than 10,000 red-blooded young Americans in a gallant crusade against the spies and traitors who attempt treason against our nation!! Be a Sentinel of Liberty!—And wear the badge that proves you are a loyal believer in Americanism.—OUR GOAL—100,000 members by July 4 and it looks like we'll make it!"[5] On the inside back cover of *Captain America Comics* number 7 appeared a full-page ad titled "Captain America Declares a 'State of Unlimited Junior National Emergency'!" This ad offered the delivery of a "special Charter of Membership" to any group of Sentinels with fifteen or more registered members. The ad created a rank structure to "authorize each club to elect its own Captain. The Captain may then send me a memorandum about the conduct of two of his Sentinels. If I approve of the report, I'll authorize the Captain to appoint the two Sentinels as Lieutenants under him."[6] Sentinel clubs were offered special certificates of merit based on deeds (apparently reporting on the suspicious activities of those around them was sufficient) as well as offers of promotion to general for captains whose clubs earned such recognition. Cap creator Joe Simon described what happened next:

> Bags of mail were dumped in the Timely waiting room daily. Sentinel of Liberty clubs were being formed by the hundreds to serve their country as instructed by Captain America. Young patriots accused others of treacherous and nefarious deeds. People with Teutonic-sounding names reported that they were being accused of suspicious radio transmissions and Fifth Column activities. One youngster told of strange noises such as groans and bed-shaking from his parents bedroom. Others vowed to kill Cap in cold blood. Little girls wanted to meet Bucky.[7]

Far from merely an anecdote of historical trivia, events such as the activity surrounding the Sentinels of Liberty clubs (and across the ocean in the much larger organization the Hitler Youth) provide interesting insight into the burgeoning youth culture of the early twentieth century as well as latent American attitudes concerning the relationship between the individual and society. The fact that young readers proved so willing to inform on their neighbors and parents demonstrates the influence of media propaganda during the 1940s and foreshadows the rise of McCarthyism in the 1950s. At least some young Americans appeared willing to put their ideals and passions ahead of their loyalties to family and the status quo.

But whatever the meaning of the fan club activity, it at the very least demonstrates that Captain America had resonated with the younger patriots Goodman was targeting. But who was this character that served to focus so much young attention on the global conflict?

The Anti-Hitler Captain America

Posing by day as an American soldier, by night Captain America dons a mask to conceal his identity in order to circumvent the law and restore justice with his fists. Although the genre of "superhero" would eventually be defined according to this formula, it was a relatively new construction when Captain America leaped onto the scene and, as some argue, a formula that poses significant implications for the development of postwar American ideology.

In his 1976 book *The Captain America Complex*, Robert Jewett used the character to illustrate how American religion and popular culture had begun to influence each other.[8] Tracing American history through the lenses of theological movements and moralistic zeal, Jewett argued that America's struggle against communism in general and against its entry into Vietnam specifically were the results of a mindset of righteous crusade against evil. Jewett updated his book in a second edition in 1984 to address the Reagan administration's foreign policy and to discuss the hope he held for the rechanneling of the "fight for right" zealousness into a more realistic approach.[9]

The "Captain America complex," as Jewett defined it, embodied a spirit of national zealousness that reduced struggles of foreign policy to caricatures of forces of good opposed to the forces of foreign evil, informed equally by American theology and popular culture. Arguing as a theologian, Jewett posited that the popular constructions had drowned out the "prophetic realist" theological position maintained by America during World War I and replaced it with the Captain America complex after World War II as the Cold War became a defining struggle of American culture.

In 2002, John Shelton Lawrence and Jewett approached this subject from a different angle in *The Myth of the American Superhero*.[10] Drawing on Joseph Campbell's archetype analysis of world mythology in *The Hero with a Thousand Faces*,[11] the authors adapted Campbell's "classical monomyth" to argue that superhero narratives (encapsulating Western and action-hero movie narratives as well as comic book superheroes) represented the emergence of a peculiar "American monomyth" not previously seen in other civilizations' cultural artifacts.

After the terrorist attacks of 2001 and the American people's nationalistic reactions leading up to the invasion of Iraq, Jewett and Lawrence applied their notion of the American monomyth to US foreign policy in *Captain America and the Crusade against Evil: The Dilemma of Zealous*

Nationalism. The American monomyth follows a predictable pattern, one that the authors argue was formed in a particular time and place:

> [H]elpless communities are redeemed by lone savior figures who are never integrated into their societies and never marry at the story's end. In effect, like the gods, they are permanent outsiders to the human community. . . . The tales of the American monomyth depicting threatened communities typically express frustration with the limitations of constitutional government and with its allied ideals of reconciliation and compromise. These stories show that, when confronted with genuine evil, democratic institutions and the due process of law always fail. In the face of such threat, democracy can only be saved by someone with courage and strength enough to transcend the legal order so that the source of evil can be destroyed. Hence the superhero, who couples transcendent moral perfection with an extraordinary capability for effective acts, spends much of his time in hiding, because he cannot be an identified voice in the corrupt democratic process. Even when present in public, the superheroes of the comics and movies wear a mask or uniform that hides their identity as citizens. The American monomyth thus embodies the vigilante tradition, in which redeemer figures who often wore the white robes of the Book of Revelation rid the community of its ostensible enemies.[12]

In particular, Jewett's primary criticism of the superhero version of the American monomyth is the undemocratic nature of masked vigilantism:

> There is a profoundly undemocratic quality to the superheroic version of the story, however. The democratic public is a mere spectator in the struggle for justice; constitutional government is always depicted as powerless to cope with evil; total powers must be granted to extralegal redeemer figures; in contrast to traditional stories of heroes with fatal flaws, these stories always end with triumph. The public is restored to a millennial paradise through the destruction of its enemies by superheroic powers exercised by self-appointed redeemers.[13]

It should be noted that the specific versions of the American monomyth that concern Jewett and Lawrence the most, the ones that create a "cultural matrix for action,"[14] first appeared in the superhero archetype Captain America. In other media, earlier elements of the American mono-myth had appeared since the founding of the country. For example, Jewett points to four stages of development that led to the superheroic mono-myth narrative: (1) the Native American captivity narratives published in colonial America, (2) the Leatherstocking novels of the early nineteenth century, (3) the Western cowboy narratives of the late nineteenth century, and (4) the superheroic tales of the twentieth century.[15]

In *Regeneration through Violence*, Richard Slotkin argues that US foreign policy in the post–Civil War period and during the Spanish-American War were wrapped in the Western-motif need to "rescue white captives" from the brutal savages in other cultures.[16] And certainly the introduction of characters such as Zorro in 1919, the Lone Ranger in 1933, and the "mystery men" archetype provided fertilizer for the specific points of ideology underpinning the development of a new national mythology. But the publication of *Captain America Comics* was noteworthy for two reasons: its immediate popularity—the first issue sold out within days, and the second issue approached the million-copy mark[17]—and the sociopo-litical orientation of the Captain America character.

As Bradford Wright explains in his book *Comic Book Nation*, the superheroes who predated Captain America (most notably Superman and Batman) began their narratives as pacifists and noninterventionists. It was not until after America entered World War II that these heroes adopted a patriotic stance, and even then they did not actually serve in the military or fight in the war.[18] Even the Shield, the patriotic precursor to Captain America, did not battle abroad, choosing instead to operate domestically to help the FBI protect America from the spies of fictional countries.[19]

According to comic book scholar Jules Feiffer, Captain America's cre-ators were the "two prime exponents" of the "golden age of violence."[20] Though Jewett selected the title *The Captain America Complex* because of Captain America's nationalistic uniform and mission, it would appear Captain America is a most fitting originator of the comic book version of the formula Jewett found objectionable.

This is not to suggest that Simon and Kirby created violent tendencies in the American character. Rather, through Captain America, they tapped into themes in the American unconsciousness not yet present in comic books. To understand how the authors connected with such an unlikely collection of appeals at least a year before fighting the Nazis was considered politically correct, a brief tour through the development of American mythology is in order.

Myth and the American Mind

In *Myths America Lives By*, theologian Richard Hughes explores the mythology of American history from a perspective parallel to Jewett's, with insights that frame the cultural context that gave birth to Captain America. Whereas Jewett framed his inquiry from a foreign-policy perspective, Hughes focuses instead on conceptions of American domestic issues, in particular historic attitudes of race relations and social justice.

Hughes describes six cultural myths in American history, beginning with the migration of the Puritans from England to the New World and culminating in the twentieth century as America became a world power. He argues that each myth is still present in Americans' minds (albeit at an unconscious level) and that it was the specific combination of these mythic frameworks that created the modern American society, tolerating racial inequality while simultaneously believing in the virtues of freedom and quality for all.

As Hughes demonstrates, the "Myth of the Chosen Nation" and the "Myth of Nature's Nation" became "a badge of cultural superiority, not an incentive to extend compassion to the poor and the oppressed. In due time, therefore, many came to believe God had chosen America for special privilege in the world, precisely because America was thought to be a Christian Nation."[21] In this way, the reformative message of the attempt to reconnect with religious authority in turn institutionalized American culture in moralistic terms among the general population. Many Americans began to think of themselves as inherently moral—that because they were among the chosen, they were naturally moral and were members of a Christian nation. The combination of these earlier American myths encouraged American colonists to see their own culture and communities as "Eden," leading them to frame conflicts with Native Americans and others as "invasions" and their own actions as righteous.[22]

Adding to this recipe of what would eventually be known as American exceptionalism was the fourth myth, the "Myth of the Millennial Nation," encapsulating the belief that America's presence in the world will make the world freer by its example.[23] When one considers the obvious connections between this theological development and the earlier mythic frameworks, it is not difficult to see how Americans arrived at the doctrine of Manifest Destiny (the development of which Hughes discusses at length).

Throwing in the influence of the growing cultural authority of capitalism, Hughes depicts the coalescence of the myths over time into the final myth, the "Myth of the Innocent Nation."[24] It is this myth that underpins the worldview in *Captain America* offered by creators Joe Simon and Jack Kirby as well as Jewett's Captain America complex. By intertwining the mental conceptions of the country and its citizenry embedded in these mythic frameworks, many Americans came to understand their culture as innocent of the cultural baggage and guilt other nations possessed. Although much of American history contains violent atrocities against native peoples and political enemies, Americans maintain this sense of innocence by not critically examining these events or by relegating those actions to individuals who somehow operate outside the cultural authority of American society. Although it was too early for the evangelical "born again" rhetoric to have gained popular acceptance, one can see the mythic roots in the culture of the 1940s and 1950s: Americans were a "start over" people, free from the very judgment they leveled against outsiders. As Hughes observes, "In effect, then, America had removed itself from the power of human history with all the ambiguity that history inevitably bears. In this way, America emerged, as it were, as an innocent child among the nations of the world, without spot or wrinkle, unmarred and unblemished by the finite dimensions of human history."[25]

Ironically, this innocence was forged largely during violent actions, displaying the growing paradox that surrounded the intersection of righteous violence and cultural judgment in the American mind. By participating in (and winning—a necessary component, as we will see) righteous wars, twentieth-century Americans redeemed their social virtues through violence. War correspondent Chris Hedges points to the moral certitude of a nation at war that held many of the same characteristics of a religious truth or, more directly, a "kind of fundamentalism."[26]

Just wars make a nation just. And in Americans' collective memory, no war was as just or as culturally purifying as World War II: "World War II," comments Hughes, "was especially important in this regard, for it allowed Americans to imagine that because they faced great evil, they themselves were altogether righteous in both intent and behavior and therefore innocent in the world."[27] The link between religious conviction and popular culture might seem a strange one to those approaching either topic without a deep understanding of both. Where the two cultural forces intersect is the construction of myth.

In fact, Christopher Knowles, author of *Our Gods Wear Spandex*, argues that although several scholars have demonstrated that popular culture can drive or reinforce particular religious understandings, the relationship also appears to go the other way. Superhero fandom can and does contain some of the trappings of a secularized civic religion. For example, when discussing superheroes, Knowles points out that

> [i]t is precisely the reverential treatment of these characters—the essentially religious portrayal of them—that resonates with the mass audience today. We have, in fact, witnessed the emergence of a strange kind of religion here. Indeed, superheroes now play for us the role once played by gods in ancient societies. Fans don't pray to Superman or Batman—or at least won't admit to doing so. But when you see fans dressed as their favorite heroes at comic conventions, you are seeing the same type of worship that once played out in the ancient pagan world, where celebrants dressed up as the objects of their worship and enacted their dramas in festivals and ceremonies.[28]

Knowles describes Captain America's emergence as the introduction of a new form of messiah character, the "science hero."[29] Borrowing mythic elements from religion and mythology, he points out that Cap represents the secularization of the messiah myth. Instead of being sent from an unearthly father, Rogers is transformed into a perfect human through a scientific rather than a supernatural gift by a Jewish scientist (in the 1940s scientists held their own mythic status as dealers of esoteric wisdom) who is subsequently murdered. Reborn perfect, with a murdered father, Rogers immediately pledges himself to defend America (the civic religion, incorporating the sacred Western values) against those committed to bringing down the US government (enemies who would often be characterized as "evil" because they oppose the secular American "good"). Jewett also posits that the emergence of the superheroic formula in the 1930s supplanted religion as a surrogate belief structure that underpins American mythology.[30]

Embedded within Captain America's identity and mission is the formula that most superheroes would in time follow. But also embedded in Captain America are the seeds of an ideology that allowed him to resonate with a culture challenged to redefine itself through global conflict. Jewett and Lawrence define the American monomyth as "[a]n archetypal plot pattern emerging in American popular culture in which a community threatened by evil is redeemed through superheroism."[31] The American monomyth is embodied in Captain America's origin story. In fact, Captain America may have served a role in institutionalizing the American monomyth by bridging the earlier Indian captivity narratives into a more concentrated mythological form that was in turn disseminated to an expanded audience of consumers.

Wartime Comic Books

Before America's entry into World War II, more than twenty-five patriotic superheroes had appeared in comics.[32] Captain America was not the first patriotic hero—that honor belongs to the Shield, who debuted in *Pep Comics* number 1, cover-dated January 1940—but he is the most enduring patriotic hero.[33] Patriotic heroes have not been among the most resilient comic book characters, largely because the circumstances that provide the relevance needed for their message to resonate are more ephemeral than the less-defined formula underpinning other iconic heroes.

Wartime comics as a genre sold exceptionally well not only because the conflict provided a seemingly inexhaustible supply of content but also because the books were shipped in large quantities to American troops stationed overseas. At the height of the war, 44 percent of men in training camps read comics regularly.[34] Publishers of that era knew they had two primary audiences: children at home and soldiers abroad, and the stories were crafted to reflect these readers' interests.

Captain America in particular benefited from this arrangement because of his patriotic elements, but his comic slumped in the late 1940s and was canceled when the postwar culture turned away from superhero comics. But before he was forced to adapt, Cap came to fruition in the environment for which he had been born: America's participation in World War II. The Golden Age of Captain America consists of 269 comic stories spread through 139 comic books (I have excluded two reprinted stories and six textual stories from this survey, although they are counted in Mike Nolan's "official" count of 277 Cap appearances in 140 comic books[35]). A brief tour of the character's initial narrative is important to establishing the context for analysis.

As noted, Captain America first appeared in his own title, which was a rare occurrence: Superman, Batman, Wonder Woman, the Sub-Mariner, the Human Torch—even the Shield, the first patriotic superhero—had first appeared in collected titles before being considered for a self-titled publication. At this point in the medium's development, comic books were typically sixty pages in length, each comprising three to four stories. This led most publishers to feature a variety of characters and storylines in a single book to increase the appeal of a particular book across a larger audience and improve its sales. Thus, early heroes usually shared space in individual books. But not Captain America. After the first issue sold out in a number of days, the second issue of *Captain America Comics* approached the million-copy mark,[36] and the title was instantly recognized to rival the established heavyweights such as Superman and Batman.[37] The character's popularity in his titled comic book (which initially contained three to four of his own stories in each comic) would lead to his appearance in other characters' books in an attempt to bolster their sales.

Though Adolf Hitler appeared on the cover of *Captain America Comics* number 1, the Nazi leader did not make an actual appearance in the comic book itself. However, he did appear in the comic's second issue (as well as on the cover), and he and then chief lieutenant Hermann Göring suffered the indignity of being kicked by Cap's sidekick, Bucky Barnes, and newspapers in the comic suggest the Nazis found their leader stuffed in a trashcan the following morning.[38]

Joe Simon, half of the creative team responsible for the introduction of Captain America, later revealed that those with Nazi sympathies were incensed by their fuehrer's treatment. In his book *The Comic Book Makers*, Simon describes the initial reaction over the debut issues: first came threatening letters, then the assembling of members of the German American Bund outside the McGraw Hill building resulted in police protection and assurances from Mayor Fiarello La Guardia that the comic's First Amendment rights would be protected.[39] But publisher Martin Goodman, anticipating that Hitler would be quickly defeated, ordered that future Cap books focus primarily on domestic concerns in order to keep the character relevant.[40]

No enemy faced Cap more consistently than the Red Skull, a Nazi assassin fond of using poisons and gimmicks to kill his prey. Introduced in Cap's first issue, the Skull would continually serve as Cap's primary enemy from 1940 until the present day. Like Batman's Robin and the Human Torch's Toro, the sidekick Bucky served to infuse the storylines with youthful passion and exuberance (and often as an excuse for a Captain America rescue mission), adding appeal for Timely's younger audience.

The second issue also introduced Captain America's spherical shield, a mainstay in successive Cap narratives. The change from the wedge-shaped shield featured in Cap's first issue reportedly came after threats of litigation from M.L.J. Publications, which argued the shape and coloring closely resembled the breastplate of the Shield, the company's competing character.[41] This issue also saw the comic book debut of Stan Lee (future face of Marvel Comics), who wrote a text story about Captain America.

Through the first few issues, Nazis and domestic criminals were the foes of Captain America and Bucky. But *Captain America Comics* number 5 (cover-dated August 1941) was notable for featuring "Orientals" as the villainous foils.[42] Modeled after a storied tradition of the "Oriental villain," the archetype (and stereotype) had faded from usage in comics a few years earlier in favor of the mad scientist.[43]

At first, the references were vague: which "Orientals" were menacing America were not specified. That, of course, changed with the bombing of Pearl Harbor, which was first addressed on the cover of *Captain America Comics*, volume 1, number 13 (cover-dated April 1942). Captain America and Bucky face a fanged Japanese officer, whom Cap is punching in the face, declaring, "You started it! Now—We'll finish it!" In the bottom left-hand corner appears a small circular seal appealing to the reader to "Remember Pearl Harbor!"

In the next month's issue, Cap faces his first Japanese opponents, a group of Japanese soldiers masquerading as Native Americans. Cap predictably kills the lead villain, who turns out to be an American sympathizer attempting to help overthrow America for the Japanese.[44] Cap's first authentic Japanese villain would present himself in *All Winners* number 5 (cover-dated July 1942). A Japanese scientist transforms himself into a vampire, but Cap kills him and sends a threatening letter to Japan afterward. The Japanese readers of the letter (dropped en masse from Allied planes) declare their intention to commit suicide immediately.[45] Cap and Bucky would also visit Pearl Harbor in *Captain America Comics* number 18.[46]

Cap also addressed the emerging atomic age in his conflicts with the Japanese. *Captain America Comics* number 51 (December 1945) featured a story titled "Mystery of the Atomic Boomerang," in which Cap and Bucky track down a new atomic explosive weapon developed by a Japanese scientist. Clearly cognizant of the tactical theory of the use of weapons of mass destruction, Cap observes, "Using the 'Atom-Water' you save thousands of soldiers and weapons for fighting us! At the same time you hope to raise the Japanese morale on the home front!"[47] Later, when Cap and Bucky return to the Allied command with a sample of the Japanese "atomic water," an officer tells them, "America is miles ahead of the Japs! You see, we've just perfected something called the ATOMIC BOMB! It will end the war immediately!" Cap responds, "And in the meantime, the Japs' 'atom-water' has been a boom—it's killed off thousands of their own men!"[48]

Though Simon and Kirby began the depicted violence against America's enemies, they were not part of the team that brought Cap into direct conflict with the Japanese. The contemporary comic book industry has often wrestled with the tension over whether the comic book is an art form or a commodity, but the scales were overwhelmingly tipped toward commodity early on.[49] After a compensation dispute, Simon and Kirby accepted an offer to jump ship and join rival DC Comics, leaving Timely owner Goodman scrambling to keep Captain America staffed after Simon and Kirby finished *Captain America Comics* number 10 (cover-dated January 1942). Before Simon and Kirby left Timely, they also created the initial issues of *All Select Comics*, a composite book featuring individual tales of Captain America, the Human Torch, the Sub-Mariner, and other Timely properties, as well as *Young Allies*, a book featuring a team composed of the primary heroes' sidekicks. After the exodus, Stan Lee became the editor of the comic book division and oversaw the Captain America comic (because of the lack of credits on early stories, it is difficult to ascertain which stories were written by Lee and which were written by others), while the artist duties were handled first by Al Avison and later by Syd Shores.[50]

Throughout the war years, Captain America and Bucky fought the Axis forces (and various agents of mixed allegiances) in virtually every theater of war imaginable. Wherever the story led Cap and Bucky, there Steve Rogers and Bucky Barnes would be stationed. In addition to regular missions into Berlin, Rogers and Barnes were stationed in Panama, India, Egypt, Washington, DC, the South Pacific, Baghdad, Great Britain, southern China, northern Africa, California, southern Italy, New York, Texas, New England, and even fictitious nations such as "Barbaria." Wherever Captain America visited, his prowess, bravery, and spirit proved greater than the foes he encountered.

As the war drew to a close, the readership began to lose interest in the exotic locales and foreign missions. Stan Lee, desperate to keep the superhero narrative relevant, took a page from competitor National/DC Comics and decided to experiment with superhero team narratives.[51] Until *All Winners* number 19, the "All Winners Squad" had battled together only on the comic book covers. But in issues 19 and 21 (because the title was renamed *All-Teen Comics* for issue 20, there was not an *All Winners* number 20), Captain America, Bucky, the Human Torch, Toro, the Sub-Mariner, the Whizzer, and Miss America joined forces in the comic text. But the excitement generated by the team-up was not enough to save the superhero war comics.

Lee tried to adapt Cap's narrative further. *Captain America Comics* number 59 (cover-dated October 1946) represented the first postwar Captain America narrative. With the war over, Steve Rogers settles into a teaching job,[52] and he and Bucky fight primarily domestic villains. The sales continued to sag at the newsstand, though, while Timely saw increasing sales success with animal comics and romance stories built around characters such as Millie the Model, Patsy Walker, and Nellie the Nurse.

Captain America Comics number 65 tried to blend the romance appeal into Cap's book when Captain America falls for a criminal who tempts him to retire from his heroic lifestyle. Bucky battles Cap but then helps him uncover the involvement of Cap's woman in the criminal conspiracy.[53] The very next issue (cover-dated April 1948) institutionalized the marriage of narrative genres. While facing a female villain named Lavender, Bucky is shot in the stomach and critically injured. Fearing the loss of comradeship in his mission, Cap recruits familiar female agent Betsy Ross[54] to become his new partner, Golden Girl. Cap reveals his secret identity to Ross (setting the stage for one of the more humorous moments in Golden Age comics when Ross realizes with an exclamation that the crime fighter "Bucky" is actually "Bucky Barnes!"), and after a rough beginning, Golden Girl takes down Lavender. Caught up in the jubilation of her first crime-fighting success, Golden Girl flings her arms around Cap, who initially balks but then kisses her.[55] Bucky would appear in one more Captain America story, *Marvel Comics* number 86 (presumably written before the publication of *Captain America Comics* number 66).[56] Golden Girl would be Cap's partner for the remainder of his Golden Age stories.

But even this change was not enough to increase sales. *Captain America Comics* number 68 signaled another turning point as Cap narrates only one story,[57] plays an inconsequential role in a second story,[58] and participates in a third story in which he and Golden Girl exhibit few superhero narrative attributes.[59] The next issue featured a story in which Cap (without Golden Girl) reenacts the tales of Gulliver[60] and another crime story with Cap again playing the narrator.[61] Issue 70 featured a science fiction story in which Cap's role was so generic that the story was later republished in a science fiction comic with Cap's role omitted.[62]

This trend continued for the remainder of the run of *Captain America Comics*. Captain America's role became increasingly irrelevant, until a title change to *Captain America's Weird Tales* in October 1949 signaled an attempt to embrace the rising monster story trend with a story about Cap battling the Red Skull in hell with Satan looking on.[63] This was to be Cap's last Golden Age appearance, for *Captain America's Weird Tales* number 75 (cover-dated February 1950), the final issue in the series, did not even feature the hero on the cover or in any of the stories.

Despite this litany of adaptation attempts, the costumed hero created specifically to sock Hitler in the jaw had trouble relating in meaningful ways to the more domestic concerns of a postwar America. As the writers at Timely struggled to keep the character relevant, they often sacrificed key formulaic components of Cap's early narratives. But, in the end, changes to American interest did what neither the Red Skull nor even Adolf Hitler had been able to do: kill Captain America. The Golden Age Cap did not survive to see the 1950s. The precise formula that made his stories so compelling in the 1940s made him irrelevant in peacetime. As Americans began to put their flags and patriotic banners back in the closet, Cap's ability to communicate to the popular audience diminished.

The distinct character born in the 1940s would never successfully command comic book readers' attention again. Even the revival efforts in the 1950s Cold War climate (discussed in the next chapter) failed to engender much interest. It would take significant changes to Cap's formula to make the character appeal to future audiences. The attitudes and ideology wrapped up in the 1940s anti-Hitler Captain America simply could not survive the changes in cultural climate.

The Anti-Hitler Captain America

Because Cap's narrative remained relatively consistent for nearly a decade and yet experienced a startling decrease in popularity, one can conclude that various attributes resonated closely with an audience in a particular time and place but did not resonate in a different time, making the 1940s Captain America narratives a time capsule of sorts for what appealed to the readers of comic books during the war years. Although Jewett (among others) has offered strong criticism of the character, the fact that the popular audience that once numbered in the millions began to dwindle when the war ended suggests that the explicit Captain America complex (at least as it related to the specific text from which the complex draws its name) is at worst temporary and at best more nuanced than it would seem critics generally believe.

Why did Captain America fall out of favor? Was it simply the downside of the hyper-relevance of a character built for a specific cultural context? How does a character whose patriotic fervor commands such attention lose that attention? Did American comic fans become less patriotic? Were the readers from the early and late narratives drawn from different interest groups? Or did how American consumers think about patriotism change?

Readers of 1940s comic books are difficult to examine and measure except in controlled circumstances (such as examining American servicemen in a foreign country). The breadth and depth of market research available to publishers today were largely absent during this period. Martin Goodman had no reason to believe *Captain America Comics* would be a success before the copies began flying off the news rack. But it did, making the text an item of interest for understanding what about the character was appealing in that place and time.

Readers and fans of Captain America from the 1960s or even the more contemporary stories would recognize some rather stark differences between the character they are most familiar with and his original expression. For example, one of the tenets of modern Captain America stories is the indestructible disc-shaped shield he carries. Modern storylines, such as the origin narrative presented in *Captain America* number 255 (cover-dated March 1981), determine that Cap received this shield from President Roosevelt shortly after he began his career. Since his early adventures, Cap's trusted shield has been a constant.

But this part of Cap's lore is clearly a later creation. In *Captain America Comics* number 50, Cap's shield is apparently severely damaged and must be repaired.[64] But even the ambiguity surrounding this event cannot account for the instance in which Cap's shield is sliced in two in USA *Comics* number 17 in 1945.[65] The purpose of raising this superficial example of incongruity is not to challenge the serial or the structural continuity of the 1940s Captain America comics. The reality is that with dozens of creators touching the character across perhaps a dozen 1940s books, incongruities were inevitable. The importance of such incongruities (even superficial ones such as the damage to Cap's shield despite its later claimed indestructible nature) is the recognition that different narrative elements often signal deeper indicators of the nature of the consumer environment for which the text was produced.

The Captain Americas of the 1960s, 1970s, and 1980s are mired in Cold War ideology. Cap is primarily a defender, rarely taking overtly offensive action. His impenetrable shield is a core element of this narrative ideology. Through great skill and intelligent tactics, he is often spared death or dismemberment at the hands of far more powerful adversaries. The defensive weapon of a Cold War Captain America must be presented as unyielding, for he (like the nation he represents) is constrained to defensive postures only.

The Captain America who fights Nazis in World War II, in contrast, is not ideologically or structurally bound in this way. The original Cap is not opposed to using guns or grenades, making the indestructibility of his shield less important than a Captain America who approaches opponents with a shield as his only weapon or defense.

These differences are what make examining Captain America in different eras interesting: his continual adjustment to appeal to contemporary tastes of patriotism and violence. A closer look at each of these broader categories provides insight into the popular appeal of these values for at least some Americans living during World War II.

Attitudes Concerning Violence and Patriotism in the 1940s

From his first story, the original Captain America displays a moral certitude that allows him to take life without guilt or reservation. After he receives the treatment that transforms his frail body into human perfection, his first action is to exact righteous violence upon his enemy. The Golden Age version of Captain America uses his superior prowess to end the threats against his country and its citizenry with righteous violence. In the 269 stories portraying the Golden Age Cap, he and his youthful sidekick kill or try to kill their opponents 119 times (and many of these attempts are against multiple foes).

It is perhaps prophetic that Cap knocks his Nazi adversary into a bank of equipment, for this is his most common means of stopping his enemies: in the Golden Age, Cap knocks no fewer than thirty-two of his opponents into electric currents or fires or into close proximity with dangerous substances or animals. Next to shooting his opponents with conventional guns (twenty-two times), his third preferred means of opponent disposal is to cast his foe from a great height, which he achieves eighteen times.

The Golden Age Cap and Bucky are also not above using grenades (twelve instances), setting or dropping explosives (eleven instances), or firing artillery (seven instances). Each of these events results in the death of at least one human being, and several (in particular the explosives and artillery) take the lives of many of their opponents simultaneously. Cap also manages to kill three people by striking them directly with his shield, and in an utterly disturbing display in *Captain America Comics* number 30 Cap actually uses a syringe to inject a downed Nazi soldier with a poisonous substance.[66]

Nor is this Cap above committing mass killing. In several instances, Cap kills dozens, hundreds, or even thousands of enemy soldiers, such as when he destroys a submarine full of Nazis in at least two instances.[67] As previously mentioned, he uses the Japanese "atom-water" to kill thousands of Japanese soldiers. But none of these acts compares to Cap's body count in *Captain America Comics* number 42, in which Cap disrupts a plot to transport a Japanese army to America in a subterranean ocean tunnel. He and Bucky trap the soldiers in their tunnel and detonate explosives, drowning approximately one million of them.[68]

Nor does Cap refuse to use fear and torture when it suits his purposes. When he encounters a Nazi spy in his first issue, he proves he is not above physical coercion to extract information:

CAPTAIN AMERICA: If you enjoy life at all . . . you'll start talking
  . . . fast!
NAZI AGENT: My kind never talks!
CAP (squeezing): Now isn't that just too bad! This calls for the tight-
  ening of the windpipe!
NAZI: No . . . NO! Ag-GH! I'll . . . I'll talk![69]

This act is not an isolated incident, either in occurrence or intention. Captain America would often torture his foes, such as in *All Select* number 4,
when he threatens a Nazi rather explicitly: "Come on, you—take me to
the hideout, or I'll put this knife in your heart!"[70]

Less violent but perhaps more troubling to those familiar with the
contemporary Captain America characters is how the 1940s Cap sometimes treats Americans with whom he disagrees politically. On several
occasions, Cap renders judgment upon someone who expresses what he
considers a "weak" perspective on foreign relations or on the war itself.

Perhaps the most explicit example occurs in the first story of *Captain
America Comics* number 15. Steve Rogers and Bucky Barnes are touring
New York City when they hear a member of the German American Bund
saying, "It is useless to resist the Axis Powers." Rogers pushes through the
crowd and punches the man in the face.[71] Later, after witnessing several
citizens' fear and dejection, Rogers and Barnes hear a group of sailors talking, saying they don't believe they have a chance against the Nazis. Rogers
responds, "Bucky, there are about four un-American sailors over there, so
let's start acting." Changing into their battle togs, they attack the sailors.
As Cap bowls over the bunch, he remarks, "This is what you deserve, traitors!"[72] In the context of the story, each of the citizens to receive a beating
is actually a secret German Bund agent who is actively trying to demoral-
ize Americans, but how Captain America can tell this is not apparent:
he appears simply to attack anyone who expresses fear or doubts at the
prospect of battling the Axis forces.

Again, the purpose in pointing out these examples is not to question
which of Cap's incarnations over the years is the definitive one (no version
of Captain America since his 1964 revival would so blatantly torture an
enemy or strike an unarmed man who merely disagrees with his politics)

but to recognize what narrative elements were acceptable at different times. If sales are any indication, the readers of wartime Captain America narratives were not concerned with seeing a hero representative of the spirit of the United States (and in many ways of its specific foreign policies) torturing a Nazi or Japanese enemy to get information or even assaulting American serviceman and civilians who express disagreement with the US war effort. This lack of concern at the time suggests a difference in such attitudes between readers in the 1940s and readers in other eras.

The patriotism exhibited by Captain America and his allies in the 1940s comics is tied directly to a peculiar matrix of violence and Western ideology. This chapter has framed the 1940s Captain America as the "anti-Hitler Cap," for, indeed, it is hard to argue against the fact that the character was created to oppose this real-life villain (according to his creators). But because Cap's very foundation was forged as the opposition of a man (Hitler) and the ideology that man represented (in Cap's initial origin story, Simon and Kirby stated his official mission as opposing the "vicious elements who seek to overthrow the U.S. government"), his own ideology remains unexamined. He represents the interests of the US government (at least as Simon and Kirby saw those interests), but beyond that his values and judgments seem little better (if not occasionally worse) than the enemies he seeks to destroy. Even on the rare occasions when Cap appears to give some thought to his ideology, the thoughts appear to revolve around the pragmatism of power politics and the jingoism of vaguely defined constructs.

Perhaps the best example of Cap's 1940s ideology is presented in a speech the hero makes to Bucky in *Captain America Comics* number 19: "Bucky, have you stopped to think what we are making America safe for? Have you realized what we are REALLY fighting for? Bucky, American countryside seems to me to be the most beautiful in the world! But today a terrible menace is closing in upon us from all sides! It is the menace of fascism, lad! The menace of hate and oppression, of tyranny and evil which is sweeping over the world! East and West, our nation is menaced as never before! Our people are facing the greatest danger they have ever known, and they must be made to realize it!"[73] From here, Captain America moves to implore Bucky (and his readers) to buy war bonds "not because we ask you to . . . but buy them as though your life depends on it . . . BECAUSE IT DOES!"[74] Even when he sets out to explain "what we are making America safe for," Cap defines his mission in terms of protecting his culture *against* outside threats (he never gets around to explaining what America is *for*). This lack of fundamental definition leads to some telling juxtapositions in Cap's adventures.

In the same comic in which Cap fails to explain the purpose of his mission, he demonstrates an amusing paradox. As he and Bucky invade Berlin, he knocks two Nazi soldiers off a rooftop. Both men fall to their death. The caption for the panel below the second fallen soldier reads, "And so, in the somber night, against a backdrop of an avenging R.A.F. Air raid, two gallant figures race onward on a mission of mercy and justice!"[75] Apparently, "mercy" and "justice" also entail Cap knocking yet another soldier into a burning fire.[76]

Such constructions of justice and mercy also create apparent paradoxes in portrayals of US foreign policy. In *Captain America Comics* number 50, Cap comes to the defense of Laura Porter, whose brother, John, has developed a "death rain" weapon that can wipe out an entire population. John Porter decides to take the secret of the weapon to his grave not because of the questionable morality of taking so many lives but because it may fall into enemy hands and be used against the United States.[77] Cap outmaneuvers the Japanese agents seeking the secret formula, and the formula is lost. Cap declares this loss "just as well. We'll never be in such dire straits that we'd have to use a thing like that against our enemies!"[78] No character in the story seems to perceive the ethical dimensions of killing an entire population at once. The weapon is an important objective only because of its possible use against the United States. The writers of the comic apparently did not question the morality of using weapons of mass destruction so long as "the enemy" was the target of such wanton destruction.

Cap's closing comment, that America would never need a weapon of mass destruction because it would never be in "such dire straits," is both telling and interesting, particularly in light of the fact that in the very next issue Cap and Bucky would learn about the existence of the atomic bomb. In that story, Cap lays out the justification for deploying the atomic bomb in a critique he offers of the Japanese use of an "atom-water" weapon: "Very clever, professor Rudo. Using the 'Atom-Water' you save thousands of soldiers and weapons for fighting us! At the same time you hope to raise the Japanese morale on the home front!"[79] The writers and readers of Captain America stories apparently had little trouble moving from considering weapons of mass destruction as unnecessary because America was winning the war to considering the "clever" use of weapons of mass destruction as a demoralizing tool.

As for America's enemies, their apparent motives are most often political ambition, the possibility of monetary gain, or an inherently evil nature. The original Red Skull (Marvel continuity later posited that multiple men had taken up the mantle of Red Skull) postulates one interesting illustration of this set of motives. In their first encounter, the Red Skull tells Cap, "Of course you realize the main item in overthrowing a government is money!"[80] The profits of war would also become a consistent motive among American traitors.

The result of Captain America's not having an explicitly expressed ideology and his opponents' possessing motives generally considered evil reinforces the "innocent nation" mythology Hughes describes. Because Cap (and symbolically America) stands poised to defend the vagaries of the American Dream (which Cap's writers never quite explicate) against those seeking to gain from its destruction, Cap is able to commit heinous actions against his enemies and maintain plausible justification for being considered "righteous." This righteous use of violence is entirely consistent with earlier expressions of the American monomyth.

Captain America, born into violence with the death of his proverbial father, is thus inoculated against the judgment leveled against other foes and nations. And thus is born Jewett's Captain America complex, under which US foreign policy cannot be compared to that of other nations because America's motives are assumed pure and innocent even when the tactics employed on both sides appear indistinguishable. As mentioned, Cap and Bucky's actions against their wartime opponents (and against the occasional traitorous businessman or mob gangster) heralded the beginning of the "golden age of violence."[81] Although Cap was not the first superhero, his body count loomed higher than other heroes', and he employed tactics with a more consistent brutality than his contemporaries, save perhaps those employed by Batman in his earliest adventures (another hero whose identity would evolve before becoming an American icon).

It would be a few decades before the Captain America his modern fans recognize would emerge: the idealist, the hero who refuses to use weapons or take lives under any circumstances. Captain America is an image that shifts over the years to fit the foreign-policy climate during which his tales are presented (or at least the contemporary understanding of those policies in the popular consciousness).

Attitudes Concerning Race and Gender in the 1940s

Of course, part of this difference can be directly attributed to differing attitudes about racial diversity, particularly in the case of Japanese opponents. In his survey of the renditions of wartime enemies in popular media, Robert MacDougall finds that although all enemies tended to be dehumanized, neither the Germans in World War II nor the Communists in the Cold War were demonized as blatantly as the Japanese in World War II.[82] MacDougall quotes historian Allan Nevins, who wrote in 1946, "[N]o foe has been so detested as were the Japanese."[83] William Savage describes the portrayals of America's enemies in wartime comics in specific terms: "rodentlike Japanese and bloated, sneering Germans. Japanese troops wore thick glasses and displayed prominent teeth, while German officers possessed monocles and dueling scars."[84]

Captain America narratives in the 1940s were no exception and perhaps exemplified the most regrettable negative racial stereotypes. In the very first Cap comic written after the attack on Pearl Harbor, *All Winners* number 5, the comic begins with a headline that reads, "Japs reported to be dropping disease germs on China! Thousands of Chinese Perish!"[85] This headline sets the tone for Cap and Bucky's attitude toward their first Japanese foe. As expected, Cap kills the first Japanese villain he faces (a vampire named "Togo," perhaps drawing an allusion to Imperial Japanese Army general Hideki Tojo) but then takes the extra measure of arranging for hundreds of copies of the following letter to be distributed throughout Japan by plane:

Dear saps:—

Your vampire, Togo, has been taken care of! This is just to let you know that 130,000,000 Americans are beginning to march towards Tokyo! We'll be seeing you soon! Our slogan for Japs: Keep 'em dying!

Captain America and Bucky.[86]

MacDougall points out that the most common caricature of Japanese individuals during World War II was the monkey or ape.[87] Captain America narratives did verbally refer to Japanese soldiers as "yellow monkeys"[88] but also commonly used the terms "dirty Jap"[89] or "dirty yellow Japs."[90] Some of the battle cries Cap and Bucky emit during their conflicts are even more racially objectifying, such as when Cap strikes two Japanese soldiers while bellowing, "Just like slicing yellow cheese!"[91] In most narratives, the character of the Japanese villains is portrayed as "treacherous," as when Cap is "downed by a treacherous blow from behind,"[92] despite the fact that he and Bucky themselves routinely attack their opponents from behind.

In terms of their physical appearance, the Japanese in these comics usually appear inhuman but tend to resemble vampires more than apes (in fact, Cap's first Japanese opponent is a vampire). Many of the narratives featuring Japanese soldiers and officers, including the very first such narrative, depict Japanese characters as demonic, possessing fangs and sometimes pointed ears.[93]

Perhaps the most disturbing treatment of those of Japanese descent is the portrayal of internment camps in *Captain America Comics* number 38, in which approximately one hundred Japanese Americans escape from a half-dozen California internment camps and begin to build bomber aircraft to launch a surprise attack from within US airspace. Predictably, Cap and Bucky are captured, escape, and foil the plans, but not before Cap mows down a group of Japanese enemies with an aircraft-mounted machine gun, destroys two planes full of Japanese aviators while they are still on the ground, and has his compatriots detonate explosives previously placed under a castle, killing dozens more.[94]

Compared to the Japanese antagonists, Cap's German foes fare somewhat better. Like all foreign characters, Germans appearing in Captain

America's early comics tend to speak in broken English, even when they talk among themselves. Also like the Japanese, Germans (in particular prominent Nazi officers, such as Adolf Hitler and his lieutenants) are portrayed as buffoons, making obvious errors in judgment, gloating, and revealing their master plans to captured American heroes shortly before those heroes inevitably escape and thwart those plans.

Physically, the Germans appear white and European, though they occasionally are portrayed with fangs.[95] More typically, Cap and Bucky equate German features with Nazism, even when those individuals are encountered on American soil. For example, when Cap and Bucky down a group of mysterious ghouls terrorizing a midwestern railroad, as Bucky unmasks an unconscious individual, he remarks that he "looks like a Nazi."[96] Or when investigating a mysterious figure terrorizing a New England town, Bucky exclaims, "Wow! What a Nazi-looking sourpuss!" the first time he glimpses the stranger's face.[97] Americans who appear to be of Japanese or German descent do not appear to get the benefit of the doubt in Captain America's wartime adventures. Each time Cap and Bucky encounter a character of Japanese or German ethnicity, the character turns out to be a villain. Not once does a Japanese American or German American character prove to be anything other than an Axis spy or soldier.

Of course, other racial stereotypes abound within these comic texts, in particular those of Native Americans and African Americans. Ethnic characters are consistently portrayed as ignorant and superstitious or at least misinformed about the character of mainstream America. Bradford Wright suggests this general approach to Native Americans was consistent with comic narratives of the 1940s: "A recurring theme found superheroes urging American Indians to abandon their traditional hostility towards the United States for the sake of the national war effort."[98]

In *USA Comics* number 16, Cap and Bucky investigate a series of killings that appear to be the work of Native Americans. Traveling to Canada (presumably so the creators can avoid directly portraying Native American reservation culture), Cap confronts the tribal chief and engages in the following exchange:

CAPTAIN AMERICA: I have read how the white man discovered a gold mine where your sacred totem stood!

CHIEF: We were driven from our land! Many white men have died and many more shall!

CAP: That's not true! The white man bought the land from your forefathers and gave them other, more fertile land![99]

This dialogue encapsulates Cap's belief structure concerning Native Americans: reading books leads one to realize that the complaints of injustice leveled by Native Americans are unfounded, for they have been treated more than fairly, and the various tribes were given a choice in their relocation. Any claim to the contrary is simply "not true."

Cap and Bucky are captured and placed atop a giant death trap in the form of a hundred-foot totem pole that is set ablaze. They manage to escape, and the totem collapses on the tribe, killing everyone. Even with the sight of their deaths, Cap offers little remorse:

BUCKY: Gosh! That's the end of the whole tribe!

CAP: It's best, lad! They were madmen—dedicated to murder![100]

In this regard, Cap goes further than his contemporary heroes at National/DC and other publishing houses. Where other heroes redeem Native Americans and recruit them to the war effort, Cap simply eliminates the threat of cultural critique. Like so many of his opponents, the Native Americans (forced to relocate to Canada) represent a threat to the status quo and so are better off dead. The fact that some in the tribe might be uninvolved with the previous murders does not seem to concern Cap, nor does the alleged presence of women and children (although not shown in the narrative) in the camp when Cap destroys it.

African American characters in Captain American comics are consistent with the terrible racial stereotypes Wright ascribes to comics of the 1940s: though largely invisible in comic stories, when black characters did appear, they normally "appeared as either brute savages or minstrel-show stereotypes with huge white eyes and white-rimmed lips, often speaking an imbecilic hybrid of pidgin English and exaggerated African-American slang. Above all, they were stupid."[101] *Captain America Comics* number 22 contains just such a stereotype in the character of Sam, an African American chauffeur. Although his involvement does not seem to advance the plot, Sam demonstrates an unreasonable fear of ghosts, deserts his post, and is more helpless than the white female character. Sam speaks in the hybrid language Wright describes: "Mah haid say wait for Mr. Barlow—but mah feet says—get on outta heah!"[102] These portrayals also appear in the only other presentation of African Americans in *Captain America Comics*, when servants in a white manor appear to be the only characters frightened of the monster menace or the prospect of ghosts.[103]

Perhaps the worst example of African American stereotypes can be found in the character of Whitewash Jones, member of the Young Allies. The Young Allies were a team of young boys brought together by Bucky and Toro, sidekick of the Human Torch. Joe Simon reportedly drew the idea from *The Boy Allies*, a novel about youths participating in World War I, and was attempting to extend the appeal of wartime support to the Sentinels of Liberty youth fan club by presenting youths fighting alongside the two superhero sidekicks.[104]

Introduced in *Young Allies* number 1, Whitewash stands apart from his partners. In their first mission, the Young Allies pose as American troops to trick a group of Nazi soldiers into surrendering. As the Nazis depart, the young men gloat, except for Whitewash, who hides until he is assured the coast is clear. When the youths become playful, Whitewash trips and breaks his rifle in two, crying out, "Owoo! Ah done stubbed mah toe—and busted mah rifle!"[105] The sound alerts the Nazis, who return to threaten the youths. Toro dispatches the Nazis, and the group finds Agent Zero, a secret agent, who gives the team an opportunity to introduce themselves.

The youths fit a mosaic of backgrounds: streetwise Irishman Percival Aloysius "Knuckles" O'Toole, white inventor Jefferson Worthington Sandervilt (whose parents are reportedly listed in *Who's Who*), and fatman Henry "Tubby" Tinkle. Whitewash Jones is the only boy without a proper name (unless his parents named him "Whitewash") and, in contrast to the merits of his teammates, is described as someone who can "make a harmonica talk" and "is also good on de watermelon!"[106]

In the second chapter of *Young Allies* number 1, the group enters a graveyard, allowing Whitewash to display his superstitious fear and be called ignorant by Sandervilt. His bumbling saves the Young Allies from the Red Skull but only because he misunderstands the function of a lever.[107] In the third chapter, Whitewash gets his teammates captured when he stupidly pretends to be a talking mouse.[108] In chapter 5, Whitewash assists the team by appearing on stage as "Growlo, the Ape-Man."[109]

During the twenty-issue run of the *Young Allies*, each youthful member has bumbling moments, and each gets a turn at saving the day. But the contrast between Whitewash and his white counterparts is stark: his bumbling appears more a result of ignorance than of inexperience, as in his compatriots' case, and he spends most of his storylines being captured by enemies so his white teammates can rescue him.

Other ethnic groups also became victims of negative stereotypes. In *All Winners* number 2, Cap and Bucky are stranded on a Malaysian island on which the Nazis exploit the natives' ignorance and superstition because the natives have "never seen a white man."[110] In *Captain America Comics* number 20, "The Fiend That Was the Fakir" (November 1942), Cap and Bucky are stationed in India and are captured by forces allied with the Japanese, until they are aided by an Indian soldier, who says, "I have been to state school. . . . I have read of you and your deeds! America is the hope of the world! Go free, brave sahib, and crush the evil Fakir who sells us to the little brown devils!"[111]

Nor is this Cap above racial profiling. When again stationed in India in *Captain America Comics* number 23, Cap and Bucky have the following exchange:

BUCKY: Look at that, Steve! It's a funny time to go for a row!
STEVE ROGERS: —They're a strange couple, too—A Hindu and a white woman! I've got a hunch we'd better stick around![112]

But more significant than the few painful presentations of racial stereotypes is the general lack of characters of color, at least on the Allied side of the conflict. Compared with future Captain America stories that would retroactively insert African Americans and other nonwhite characters into the World War II conflict, the Allied forces contemporary to the actual events depicted were exclusively white.

Nor were the 1940s Captain America comics particularly enlightened concerning gender roles, although Cap occasionally found capable help from Betsy Ross.[113] Most female characters served a more passive role, providing intelligence or merely getting in the way.

In *Captain America Comics* number 32, Cap and Bucky have an exchange that is representative of their general attitude toward women. After the two persuade the female leader of a guerrilla group to remain behind, they are captured and tortured. Then they see the "girl leader" (as the comic refers to her; her name is eventually revealed to be Joan) being led into the cellblock:

> BUCKY: For cryin' out—? Look, Cap! Look wha's bein' brought in!
>   Something tells me that dame ain't what she's—
> CAP: (Groan). Now I have to get her out of here also!
> WOMAN: I'm sorry! I became worried and thought that I could help
>   in some way! A Nazi patrol caught me before I even got half way!
> BUCKY: Hmm. Just like a dame to put her foot in it every time![114]

A similar scene is given in *Captain America Comics* number 49:

> STEVE ROGERS: It's the same girl! She's in trouble!
> BUCKY: Aw! Dames always are![115]

In general, Cap and Bucky appear surprised when a woman can handle a weapon, has valuable information, or comes to their rescue. In 1940s Captain America stories, female characters are often the foils used to get the heroes into compromising situations. A notable exception is Olga, a Russian dancer who turns out to be a "good fighter."[116]

Even in the Captain America stories when he takes Golden Girl as a replacement partner for Bucky, Cap hardly seems to treat her as the equal adult she represents. Even though Bucky often blundered into compromising situations (being captured in nearly every comic), Cap reprimands Golden Girl for trying to save him on her first mission.[117] And after she conducts solo detective work that results in Lavender's capture, Cap initially avoids her embrace but then rewards her by grabbing her and kissing her.[118]

The 1940s Captain America was not the liberal bastion of gender and racial equality that he would eventually become. The character does not seem particularly interested in challenging traditional conceptions of social norms. Characters in his comics seldom prove to be more than the labels that define them. Germans are Nazis, and there appears little room for consideration that German Americans could be on the side of right. Of course, given the wartime setting for the narratives, this finding is hardly surprising. Captain America does not spend much time questioning the role his patriotism has in shaping his worldview. The inner turmoil concerning his role as icon and agent of US policy that would characterize later incarnations of the character is simply not present in the 1940s version.

The patriotism of the 1940s Cap stands in sharp contrast with the considered rationalism of the Cap in later eras. The anti-Hitler Captain America served his purpose: raising awareness of the Nazi threat to American interests (at least as his Jewish creators perceived them), symbolically battling America's enemies and killing them, and providing an ideological justification for America's wartime tactics. With children at home and soldiers abroad making up the majority of the comic books' readership, it is easy to understand why Cap's stories were presented with such powerful and simple declarations about the relationships between American power and the rest of the world's nations.

It is also easy to understand why Cap had such a hard time appealing to the same audience in times of peace. The various attempts to modify his narrative—in particular the shift in his focus to crime (which is what other heroes such as Batman and Superman did in the postwar climate, but those heroes had fought crime initially and had skirted meaningful combat duty)—diverge from the elements that first made him popular. The anti-Hitler Captain America's appeal essentially died with the declaration of peace. Where readers found excitement in the brash wartime stories, they found irrelevance in a character draped in the American flag battling other Americans and solving crimes like a gaudy policeman.

Captain America would eventually become an international icon and a cornerstone of the Marvel Universe. To get there, his comic adventures demonstrate the process of history creation and revisionism, but, more important, they provide access to the underlying ideologies of the age in which they were popular because, as Jewett explains, they present "in mythic style the ideals that are widely felt but that are no longer articulated in more sophisticated circles."[119]

Yes, Captain America would have to evolve before he would find popular acceptance in postwar culture. And evolve he would, tracking developments in the culture he was designed to embody. But not before the "anti-Hitler" formula would be revived once again and applied with disastrous results to a new threat to the American way of life: the Communist bloc.

3

Commie Smasher! (1953–1954)

At the beginning of 1945, when it became apparent that World War II would soon be over with an America victory, superhero comic sales began to drop. By the end of the following year, superhero sales had fallen by one-third,[1] and some publishers began to turn to other story genres.

Timely Comics had already juggled between superhero stories and humor comics, and when the superhero craze appeared to slow, the company diversified its offerings by introducing romance titles for female readers such as *Tessie the Typist* (introduced June 1944), *Millie the Model, Nellie the Nurse,* and *Patsy Walker* (the latter three introduced in 1945). Superheroes were gradually phased out. As noted at the end of chapter 2, Timely creators made several attempts to adapt *Captain America Comics* by blending its superhero theme with romance, science fiction, and horror stories.

By 1949, Timely had canceled *Captain America Comics, Sub-Mariner Comics, Human Torch Comics,* and *Marvel Mystery Comics.* Or, rather, the company had transitioned those books into other genres. Because postal codes at the time made it more expensive to ship new publications than existing titles, Timely and other publishers began to rechristen the failing books. For example, Timely's flagship title *Marvel Mystery Comics* became *Marvel Tales,* featuring horror stories. Romance, crime, horror, science fiction, talking furry animals, and Western-themed comics soon displaced all of Timely's heroes.

Martin Goodman organized all of his magazines and comic book publications through a centralized distribution company, Atlas. As a result of this arrangement, with the Atlas logo appearing on most comic books during this era, comic fans came to think of Timely comics as "Atlas comics," though the creators working for Goodman still thought of their wares as "Timely comics" or, increasingly, "Marvel comics."[2]

The Golden Age of comics is considered to have ended during this period, though the boundaries of these ages are understandably under constant dispute. There does appear to be consensus that for Timely the Golden Age ended with the publication of *Captain America's Weird Tales* number 74, the last appearance of Captain America, although the character was featured in the following month's *Human Torch* number 35.[3] One final issue of Captain America's comic would be published, but he did not appear on the cover, nor was he featured anywhere in the book.

Without the global struggle that gave birth to them, superheroes were simply less relevant to a postwar public characterized as conservative and weary of reform.[4] The addition of the atomic bomb also contributed to their diminished appeal. As comics scholar William Savage explains, "In the flush of victory, some Americans saw the bomb as confirmation of several of the ethnocentric notions long held dear to the popular mind. The Bomb was clear evidence that God was on our side: His gift of the Bomb ranked right up there with the one involving His only begotten Son."[5] Superheroes in general and Captain America in particular had been designed to empower an American citizenry whose growing concerns about turbulent world affairs found resonance in the heroes' abilities to exceed prewar America's comparatively impotent tendencies. But, for many, the atomic bomb represented an awesome power, the power to destroy whole populations, next to which superheroes suddenly seemed less impressive.

National Comics (soon to be known as Detective Comics and later DC Comics) managed to preserve several of its heroes by moving its storylines away from political representation altogether in favor of lighthearted comedy and relational drama. Of course, Superman and Batman had begun their adventures before the war as civic crusaders and had been adapted to the global war superhero narrative in merely symbolic ways. Adjusting their narratives back to domestic concerns did not prove too difficult for their writers.

The Timely heroes, by contrast, had capitalized on the global nature of World War II and had embodied specific patriotic ideals that did not translate well to an era of peace. Captain America as mere crime fighter robbed the character of the brashness that had stirred up interest in the first place, or that brashness seemed inappropriate when employed against his fellow countrymen.

But the Timely superheroes would soon return, thanks in large part to revived interest generated by the wildly successful *Adventures of Superman* television series, which debuted in February 1953.[6] Superman had made the leap from comic books to radio dramas and television programs and had as a result created a new revenue stream of merchandising. Martin Goodman reportedly was able to interest television producers in a possible Sub-Mariner television series.[7] But it was determined that the show (and by extension the merchandising) would probably not be as successful without contemporary comic stories, so it was time to give the Timely heroes another try.

With *Cowboy Romances* (debuting in October 1949), Timely writers attempted to fuse two of the company's new editorial directions into one title. The first three issues did not sell well, so the title was changed to *Young Men*. Designed to present stories targeted to young readers (as opposed to Atlas's *Men's Adventures*), each comic presented a series of morality stories featuring youths, involving a mixture of school and dating stories, World War II stories, sports stories, and even spy stories (in which the bad guys are Communists).

The choice of World War II stories in lieu of contemporary Korean War stories might seem strange, but most publishers offering tales of war initially stuck to World War II settings. According to Savage, "From the perspective of the mid-1950s, World War II was a safer place for comic books to be—and perhaps a safer place for their readers. World War II was more satisfying to contemplate than Korea, because it had been a declared war that ended in clear victory. In the popular mind, ambiguity had not characterized the American response to World War II. An evil enemy had been decisively defeated. None of this could be said about Korea, a police action having no convenient resolution."[8]

However, in an effort to boost sales, Timely (which readers now considered Atlas) decided to give the Korean War a try. Beginning with issue 12, the comic changed its title yet again to *Young Men on the Battlefield*, offering Korean War stories through issue 20. The Korean War stories didn't quite resonate with readers the way World War II stories had, though. As Savage explains, "Comic books pertaining to the Korean War were pessimistic exercises, reflecting on the difficulty Americans had in working up enthusiasm for the sort of limited conflict the Bomb had supposedly rendered obsolete."[9] The title reverted to *Young Men* with issue 21 and began to portray hot-rod stories, supernatural stories, boxing stories, and war adventure stories. Struggling to find a successful niche, the comic became the perfect place to test a return to the superhero narratives of the previous decade.

The Commie Smasher Cap (1953–1954)

In *Young Men* number 24, each of Timely's "big three" heroes was featured in individual short stories, none exceeding ten pages. For each hero, a brief origin and an explanation for the postwar absence were provided.

In this comic, the heroes largely picked up on the formula that had made them popular in the 1940s: political relevance. The Human Torch (featured prominently on the cover of this first issue, probably because he among the three most resembled Superman, whose television success was the catalyst for the heroes' resurgence) sets the tone of the heroes' return. He reappears after several years missing and recounts his absence: he ended the war in grisly fashion by burning Hitler alive (a play on the knowledge of the leader's cremation).

> HITLER: OWW! The Human Torch has set me afire! But don't let the world know how I died! Tell them I committed suicide! ARGGG!
> HUMAN TORCH: Lying with his dying breath![10]

According to the new story, after the war the Torch battled crime until he and his sidekick, Toro, were captured by a criminal syndicate. The Torch was buried in the desert, only to be awakened years later by an atomic bomb test, which revived him and increased his powers.[11] He travels to Korea and finds Toro brainwashed by Communists. After Toro's conditioning breaks, the duo track down and foil a criminal scheme and destroy a helicopter with four crooks aboard, killing them all.[12]

The second story brought back Captain America and Bucky. Although the lack of credits in Atlas publications meant the loss of the identity of the writers of Cap's tales, John Romita was the artist who worked on nearly every Atlas-age Cap story (with early help from Mort Lawrence). Steve Rogers is now a history professor at the Lee Academy, and Bucky is one of his students.[13] The two hear that the Red Skull (who is working for "friends at the Kremlin") has taken the United Nations building staff hostage. Returning to action, Captain America and Bucky race to the scene and defeat their archenemy. The duo appeared in the next three issues of *Young Men* before Cap regained his own comic, *Captain America . . . Commie Smasher!* The run lasted only three issues (the duo also appeared in three issues of *Men's Adventures*, for a total of sixteen appearances in this era) before low sales led to cancelation.

While the run lasted, Cap sought out spies and agents who used duplicity to win battles of propaganda, much as he had during the World War II years. In fact, Cap's adventures in this period appear to be little different from his World War II exploits. His arch nemesis, the Red Skull, is somehow now affiliated with the Communists, and Cap employs the same tactics and cultural logic to oppose his foes that served him so well fourteen years earlier. However, he would ultimately receive a different reaction from his readers.

Cap continues resorting to violent acts to achieve his goals of peace. Nor does he shy away from homicide. In terms of his demeanor and attitudes toward violence, Cap acts as the previous incarnation of the character did, killing when necessary and even at times when not. In one story, he tricks a female spy into firing a weapon in an underground tomb, knowing she will be killed in the cave-in.[14] In another, after defeating a Communist spy, Cap pushes him into a burning fire and then gloats over the death.[15]

In the sixteen Atlas-era stories featuring Captain America, he and his allies commit actions that directly cause the death of at least one opponent in nine instances. Statistically, Cap picks up where he left off, amassing bodies at a slightly more regular rate (56 percent of his newer adventures are resolved with a violent act, compared with 44 percent of his Golden Age adventures) than he had during the war years.

That is not to say Cap's opponents act like Nazis. Unlike the Nazis, who were portrayed as boldly anti-American, the Red agents in these narratives express themselves in contradictory double-talk. An example from "The Man with No Face," a storyline from *Captain America . . . Commie Smasher!* number 77 in which Cap and Bucky visit New York's Chinatown to help Chinese Americans forced to make financial contributions to the Chinese government under threat of having their relatives at home executed, illustrates these contradictions. Lt. Wing, a loyal Chinese American, argues with the Man with No Face, a Chinese agent:

> MAN WITH NO FACE: We Communists are united in one purpose: we will lead the world out of chaos and into peace and plenty! After all, we are your friends . . . we are not the blood-thirsty killers you've been led to believe!
>
> WING: You lie! You are traitors, ready to kill anyone, anywhere to get power!
>
> MAN WITH NO FACE: That is not so! There is deep love in our hearts for all mankind! Even if we have to kill them to prove it![16]

And if the subtle cues aren't clear enough, the captions of Cap's comic make clear enough the view of communism from the editorial perspective: "Beware, Commie spies, traitors and foreign agents! Captain America, with all loyal, free men behind him, is looking for YOU, ready to fight until the last one of you is exposed for the yellow scum that you are!"[17] These portrayals of the Communist threat were hardly unique to the Atlas books. As Savage points out in his book about comic books of the 1950s, "Portrayals of the enemy conformed in most cases to the Red-Menace imagery established elsewhere in the comic-book medium. Communist officers, be they North Korean, Chinese, or Russian, were always brutal and inhuman and, if they held any rank above major, usually stupid."[18] However, Cap and Bucky encounter "Red threats" in the domestic sphere as often as they dealt with threats on the battlefield. Uncovering espionage rings, industrial sabotage plots, and even attempts to influence entertainment media is as integral to the "Commie Smasher's" campaign as direct opposition to Russian or Korean soldiers.

These elements were also not new to this incarnation of the character. Looking back at the story titled "The League of Hate" (August 1945) in *Captain America Comics* number 49, one sees a familiar kernel of conservative postwar ideology. In the 1945 story, Cap and Bucky uncover a Nazi plot in which American prisoners of war are replaced with maimed Nazi soldiers who use the Americans' uniforms and reputations to speak out against the war effort. When Captain America discovers the truth, he reveals the plot in a live radio broadcast, concluding: "Fellow Americans! This is our fanatical enemy! Dedicated to spreading hate! Pitting man against man! Race against race! And only thru united action by all freedom loving people will tyranny and oppression be utterly destroyed and mankind be rid of war and gain a lasting peace!"[19] This story, consistent with Cap's earlier conflict with the German American Bund, which led him to strike several Americans and servicemen who publicly spoke out against the war effort,[20] demonstrated the Golden Age character's willingness to fight struggles of ideology and usually with his fists instead of with verbal counterarguments. These tendencies continued unaltered in the Atlas era, with results that demonstrate just how damaging the patriotic fervor from World War II was to American society in the Cold War of the 1950s.

In his second "Commie Smasher" adventure, Cap is asked to guard the secret of a new atomic cannon the United States has built for the Korean War effort. Cap and Bucky recognize two Communist spies, and Bucky witnesses the abduction of Jim Slade, the designer of the atomic gun's firing pin. Cap and Bucky rescue Slade, but one of the spies turns out to be "the Executioner," who kills her husband and then herself rather than be caught. Cap, Bucky, and Slade close out the story standing on the firing range and watching a mushroom cloud rise in the distance:

BUCKY: Wow! What a sight!
CAP: A glorious sight . . . when it's on our side in the struggle for world peace![21]

Former Marvel editor in chief Roy Thomas describes the dialogue and visuals that compose this scene as iconic of its political age: "For better or for worse, depending on your politico-historical views, there is no better Cold War image in all of 1950s comic books."[22]

The third story takes Communist ideology head on as Red agents administer to Cap a "virus of evil" that causes him to turn against his country.[23] After delivering a speech full of Communist ideology, Cap destroys a base in Alaska and then travels to a Russian submarine, where he turns the tables and reveals he was faking. He and Bucky tamper with the sub, drowning all aboard.

There are several interesting details about this story. When Cap delivers the "traitorous" speech, he merely proclaims, "[A]lthough Russia and America are in a cold war, the Russians aren't so bad! They feed their people and give them every freedom!"[24] Such are the statements that cause Bucky to recoil in horror. Russians not being "so bad" is apparently enough to qualify as a traitorous statement.

After Cap and Bucky doom the Russian submarine crew, Bucky asks Cap why the "virus of evil" didn't work. Cap responds, "WE'VE got scientists, too . . . and the ones who gave me my strength also made me immune to such trash!"[25] The implication of the superiority of American scientific progress over that of the Soviets and other Communists would be a recurring theme throughout the run, just as trumpeting the superiority of American ingenuity over that of the Nazis and Japanese had been a staple of Cap's World War II dialogue.

The fourth anti-Communist story, presented in *Young Men* number 27 (cover-dated April 1954), finds Cap repeating the false brainwashing performance for the Red Skull. Pretending to succumb to torture, Cap feigns a state of shock and agrees to divulge secrets about America's defenses, leading the group on a wild goose chase that ends with their truck driving into a brick wall, apparently killing the Red Skull and his men.[26]

The following month Cap returned to his self-titled magazine, *Captain America . . . Commie Smasher!* number 76 (resuming the numbering from *Captain America's Weird Tales* number 75). In the first story, Cap and Bucky rejoin the army to help prevent the Communists from spying (why juggling this mission with military duties is advantageous is never discussed). Betsy Ross, who no longer appears to be Golden Girl or even blond, approaches Rogers for help in clearing her name as a suspected spy. Cap and Bucky discover that her photographer and editor are Communist spies gathering intelligence to start a new world war. They defeat the spies, and Cap burns the microfilm that Ross's editor had developed. Blake is despondent and cries out, "My film! My precious film!" Cap knocks him into the flames, saying, "If you're so crazy about your film . . . join it!" Looking over the burning house, Cap proclaims, "He died the way he wanted the free world to die . . . in flames!"[27]

The second featured story in the issue concerns Communist sympathizers' recruitment of Steve Rogers.[28] Of course, Rogers leads them along until he, as Captain America, is able to defeat the cell. In the third story, Captain America and Bucky infiltrate French Indochina to investigate radio broadcasts featuring Americans claiming that they are being treated well under communism and that America should stop fighting the Cold War. Cap pretends to be a Communist sympathizer but turns the tables after freeing the Americans from their drug-induced state, saying, "[Y]ou can tell the world the truth . . . REAL AMERICANS NEVER TURN RED!" The next panels caption reads, "Beware, Commie spies, traitors and foreign agents! Captain America, with all loyal, free men behind him, is looking for YOU, ready to fight until the last one of you is exposed for the yellow scum that you are!"[29] Just as in Cap's first run, the writers externalized the threats he faced to the reader's environment. It wasn't enough to read about Communist plots in comic books; those narratives were meant as an implied warning for the readers to remain diligent in their own interactions. In the final story of Cap's first 1950s issue, *Men's Adventures,* Cap and Bucky travel to Egypt to uncover a Communist conspiracy.[30] In *Young Men* the following month, they confront and defeat drug dealers in South Africa trying to smuggle in a "million dollars in dope," which was "enough to make the South Africans revolt! Another step in the world-wide rebellion by the Communists!"[31]

The following month *Captain America . . . Commie Smasher!* number 77 was released with three more Cap cases: helping a young blind boy whose father has been blackmailed into turning over a "midget atomic engine,"[32] the case described earlier involving the loyalty of Chinese

American citizens,[33] and a case in which Cap takes his first trip to Korea to prove that Communists are poisoning their own soldiers in United Nations prisoner-of-war camps to make the international organization look bad.[34] The latter case served as an interesting critique of communism on several fronts. As Cap sets out to deliver a vaccine, his plane is confronted by Communist warplanes. Rather than engaging them, he simply runs, claiming, "No Commie jet's faster than THIS baby . . . hang on Bucky!"[35] He survives several attempts to stop him as his opponents seek to protect their plans to sacrifice their own soldiers for their political cause: "We planted the poison in the food of our own soldiers in the prison camps, just so we could accuse the U.N. of mistreating them! We WANT them to die. As long as we can make a case out of it before the world . . . and Captain America's not going to spoil it for us!"[36]

Once Cap arrives at the Korean camps, he begins to administer the vaccine. The Korean prisoners appear confused about his intentions and attack him, forcing him into the unfortunate position of beating them. The sick prisoners quickly revive, and the healthy prisoners cease their attack and step away, their "heads bowed in apology." Cap muses: "Now if we could only teach them the rest of the real truth! . . . that their own masters are the REAL killers . . . and that the United Nations are the only ones who can cure what ails them . . . with freedom and democracy!"[37]

Also in that month Cap and Bucky again travel to Korea in *Men's Adventures* number 28. Escorting American prisoners of war through enemy territory, Cap, Bucky, and a shell-shocked private are captured. The disgruntled soldier finds his nerve and frees Cap, who fires into an ammunition dump, killing ten Korean soldiers. Cap confronts the Korean leader, Kag, and knocks him into the resulting blaze, killing him.[38]

In the final *Commie Smasher!* comic before cancellation, Captain America faces his most ideologically significant challenges. The first story in *Captain America . . . Commie Smasher!* number 78 brings him face to face with his first superpowered Communist foe, Electro (not to be confused with the later Spider-Man supervillain). After a long battle (including a scuffle on a giant typewriter), Cap intentionally kills Electro.[39]

In the second story, Cap and Bucky slip into China to recover a list of Chinese defectors. They play on the Chinese citizenry's superstitions by making a robotic dragon appear to come to life.[40] Cap catches the spy and chokes him until the man turns over the list, which Cap destroys. After the battle, Cap learns that the robotic dragon had actually come to life, fulfilling the prophecy that the Green Dragon would return to attack China's true enemies—the Communist regime.

The final story of Captain America's "Commie Smasher" career involves a Communist plot to use a youth celebrity idol to undermine young Americans' faith in the United Nations by bombing it. Cap recovers two bombs and saves the day. After the crisis has passed, he reveals that he suspected the celebrity was a Communist sympathizer because his rhetoric reminded him of someone:

BUCKY: Cap, when you said he reminded you of someone . . . who was it?

CAP: Hitler! Same words: "strong minds in strong bodies," and "play to win!" Americans play not to win, necessarily, but for the sake of good sportsmanship and fair play . . . which Nazis and Reds know nothing about at all![41]

In this way, Cap once again equates the philosophies of communism with the politics of Hitler's Third Reich. And once again, rather than engage the enemy's philosophy, Captain America recasts Soviets as Nazis and uses the justification from a previous conflict with a previous opponent to support a new conflict. But the jingoism that was so successful in the early 1940s failed to capture the attention and imagination of the readership in the 1950s.

Scholar Bradford Wright offers a possible explanation for this failure: "Comic book makers overestimated the size of the audience prepared to accept such naïve presentations of the Cold War. As the enormous popularity of crime comic books had already demonstrated, the postwar comic book market had not only grown, it had grown up. Even young people understood that the Cold War was not going to be won as quickly and easily as the comic book version of World War II."[42] By not engaging communism on its own terms and not fighting against Communist foes who actually appeared to be credible Communists, the comic book writers' efforts to engage politically relevant themes fell short. As Wright remarks, "The series offered no further discussion of Cold War issues beyond the message that Communists were evil, overweight, and poor dressers."[43]

Apart from the lack of ideological engagement with an enemy that Cap often demonized, the violence leveled at such an unknown opponent appeared to have little appeal for the readers of comic books. As Savage notes, this era of comic book stories was full of violent attitudes toward Communists: "American heroes, it seemed, were no longer required to play fair with their enemies. Rather, they fought fire with fire, in recognition of the dire consequences awaiting the free world if they should fail in any of their respective missions. Merely neutralizing Soviet agents—or, for that matter, Soviet armies—served no good purpose, given the stakes in the game; so homicide, and not infrequently genocide, became reasonable and acceptable undertakings for comic-book operatives."[44] Of course, such tactics were not new for Captain America. It would be difficult to suggest that his writers, having already portrayed Cap killing more than a million opponents in World War II, were led to increasing portrayals of violence by the spirit of the new age. More likely, other comic creators adopted the formula Cap had helped establish in the 1940s, leading to an amplification of the violence toward America's enemies. But this tendency toward violence ultimately proved unpopular with readers.

Stan Lee told Romita that the conservative writing had created a backlash among readers,[45] and each of the Timely/Atlas superhero books of the 1950s was soon cancelled. In many ways, superheroes became victims of their own persuasive ideology. Arguments about inequalities of social justice among classes lost some of their relevance when America exited the Great Depression, and all classes possessed greater access to wealth and resources. The war had also strengthened and broadened the scale of the federal government and institutionalized a standing military force recently proven more than capable of responding to and dealing with threats against American citizens or their interests.

With less visible injustice and with greater public infrastructure, the world seemed somewhat less scary and messiahs and saviors less relevant. In short, superheroes had much less to say to a status quo experiencing an influx of wealth (and, with the defeat of the Axis, an apparent age of justice). There was simply less that Americans needed "saving from." The American monomyth—which, as explained in chapter 2, is a formula that Captain America's stories helped institutionalize—capitalizes on the perception of "external threats" to American society as a "purified Eden." In a World War II setting, the "innocent nation" mythology allowed American heroes to be violent toward the "obvious" evils of the Nazi regime and Japanese military. But because the Korean War functioned according to the Cold War mentality (making it difficult to determine which of the two sides in the conflict was "obviously evil") as a direct threat to American culture, the superheroic formula failed to capture the same readership it had in the 1940s.

So the industry turned away from politics and away from social conflict. The superhero comics that survived followed this trend. The Superman presented in the comics of the 1950s and even in his televised adventures was neither a World War II veteran nor a cold warrior. Superman has often adapted his interests to serve the interests of the society in which his readers live.[46] But the Timely heroes reintroduced in the 1950s did not adapt much. Captain America in the 1950s was presented as a Cold Warrior in the spirit of his World War II adventures. The world had changed, but because Captain America had not changed with it, he was abandoned.

The Introduction of the Comics Code

It is probably just as well that Cap didn't resonate with readers at this time, for the comic industry was about to endure a crisis of politics that would shape the comic book formula for a generation. Comic books had traditionally been one of the few unregulated mass-media formats in America, probably owing to their fringe status within the culture. But World War II had recently demonstrated the power of propaganda (and comic books had participated in this demonstration), and as the hysteria over the emerging Cold War began to rise in tenor, the comic book industry entered a battle over cultural control and authority.

Though comic books had certainly been the objects of cultural concern earlier, the increase in the number of comic books published after the war seemed to some to correlate with a crisis over the youth culture in America. With many of America's fathers serving overseas and many of America's mothers entering the workplace, a new generation of youths had experienced a different upbringing from the previous generation. As fathers returned home, and as at least some of the mothers returned to the domestic sphere, a crisis of family culture became apparent. The correlation among the dramatic increase in comic book publication, the rising concerns about the activities of America's youth outside the home, and the concerns about whether America was engaged in a shadowy ideological war of ideas in 1947 planted the seeds that made comic books a convenient scapegoat.

Much has been written about the activities of psychologist Fredric Wertham and the series of assaults he made against the comic book industry. In 1948, Wertham was quoted in a *Collier's* article as declaring that "the time has come to legislate these books off the newsstands and out of the candy stores."[47] Attributing many social ills to the reading of comics, Wertham failed from the beginning to distinguish between different comics companies or comic titles, suggesting that "[t]he number of 'good' comics is not worth discussing, but the great number that masquerade as 'good' certainly deserve close scrutiny."[48]

Probably owing to the quiet discontent residing in the postwar American psyche, the article generated an unexpected flurry of attention, with many of the country's news publications weighing in. Concerned about public perception, the comic publishers attempted to create a self-regulatory body in 1948, but the effort failed. Several publishers (including Timely/Atlas) recruited education experts and child-development authorities to serve on their editorial boards, although these efforts also failed to diffuse the assault.

Other voices began to weigh in, including creators of other disreputable media formats. For example, in 1949 pornographer Gerson Legman published a book titled *Love and Death: A Study in Censorship* in which he argued that the violence in comic books was an expression of suppressed sexual urges.[49] Legman's premise suggested that because pornography was so tightly regulated, the resulting frustrations were channeled into violent tendencies. Regarding Timely/Atlas (which produced more horror and crime titles than anyone), Legman charged that its proclivity to violence was due to the fact that most of its staff was composed of homosexuals.

In 1950, Wertham appeared before the US Senate Subcommittee to Investigate Crime in Interstate Commerce, chaired by Senator Estes Kefauver of Tennessee. Kefauver had been elected as a progressive Democrat in a southern state by aggressively pursuing criminal activity. The hearings angered many publishers but ultimately did not lead to any regulatory reform. Wertham continued to write articles and books. He would get one more public chance to state his case when Kefauver helped form the Senate Subcommittee to Investigate Juvenile Delinquency.

Wertham testified at the hearings, implying that superhero comics encouraged boys to aspire to a homosexual lifestyle, as illustrated primarily by the supposed relationship between Batman and Robin, two bachelors living alone with a butler in a mansion, a "[w]ish dream of two homosexuals living together,"[50] and encouraged girls (based on the exaggerated bosom lines rendered in romance comics) to stuff their bras. EC Comics publisher William Gaines also testified and was ambushed, leading to a public-relations nightmare for the comic book industry.

Despite significant public attention and several other government hearings and attempts at legal regulation, Wertham became frustrated. He then penned his most comprehensive indictment of the comic industry yet, *Seduction of the Innocent*. Appearing early in 1954, Wertham's book rehashed his case against the industry, blaming the comics medium for rises in juvenile delinquency, sexual deviance, dyslexia, and even murder. Once again Wertham laid his charges at the feet of the entire medium: no qualification was made for those who avoided the violence under scrutiny or even those who had tried to reform.

Although Wertham's writing and the two rounds of Senate hearings did not lead to regulatory reform, the comic publishers decided to voluntarily self-regulate the industry to avoid potential external regulation. On October 26, 1954, all the major comics publishers (except Dell) officially became members of the Comics Magazine Association of America and developed the Comics Code Authority, which reviewed comics from member publishers and provided a seal of approval for those that complied with the code. Regulations included a ban on portrayals of crime that did not present it as "a sordid and unpleasant activity"; bans on profanity, nudity, seduction, rape, and sex; a ban on the words *horror* and *terror* in comic titles; and a prohibition on "[s]cenes dealing with, or instruments associated with walking dead, torture, vampires and vampirism, ghouls, cannibalism, and werewolfism." And just for good measure, the code proclaimed that "[i]n every instance good shall triumph over evil and the criminal punished for his misdeeds."[51]

Within a year, horror and crime comics disappeared, and comic book violence was toned down dramatically. Despite these changes, the following year saw thirteen states pass laws to limit sales of horror or crime comics, effectively banning books that no longer existed.

But the toll on the industry was costly. In 1950, the year before the horror trend began, approximately 300 titles had been published, with industry revenues estimated to be about $41 million. At the height of the medium's popularity in 1953, approximately 650 titles were published, bringing in an estimated $90 million. As a result of Wertham's efforts, the Senate hearings, and the institution of the Comics Code, the industry entered the 1960s publishing only 250 titles, and eighteen publishers had disappeared from the market.[52]

Of course, one of the great ironies of the Comics Code was the typical blind spot present in superhero comics: criminals were always to be "punished," but the heroes delivering the punishment were themselves performing criminal acts by using vigilante methods. Every time a hero such as Captain America or Batman causes blunt-force trauma to a villain (to say nothing of the more violent actions Captain America took during the 1940s and 1950s), that hero is committing assault and battery. And yet this righteous violence was (and is) somehow considered acceptable despite the ban on violence and the unacceptability of any celebration of criminal activity.

Even as the industry (and society) clamped down on comic book content, the American monomyth and superheroic formula remained an exception to the rules of regulation. Such omissions indicate the deep roots that superheroic vigilantism possesses in American popular culture. Patriotism may move in and out of fashion, but the acceptance of masked vigilantes beating on criminal elements has rarely, if ever, been challenged as a legitimate form of popular culture.

The Patriotism of the Commie Smasher Captain America

The Captain America of the Atlas era was extremely unpopular with most potential readers, so much so that when Marvel Comics revived Captain America in the 1960s, its writers created a "retcon" story—that is, a story with retroactive continuity, or the reinterpretation of "historical" material to change previously established facts in serial fiction—that made the 1954 Cap a different person from the Cap of both the 1940s and the 1960s.

Applying the formula from World War II to the 1950s Cold War environment had proven a disastrous choice. The patriotism that had served Cap so well in the 1940s worked against him in the 1950s. As *Captain America: Commie Smasher!* artist John Romita recalled, "Patriotism was a dirty word for a while."[53]

Joe Simon and Jack Kirby, the original creators of Captain America, also found this formula to be problematic for the Cold War environment. In the early 1950s, Simon and Kirby tried to re-create their success with Captain America by producing Fighting American, a carbon copy.[54] Like the Cap of the Atlas era, Fighting American fought Communists. In terms of sales, he fared even worse than the hero he was designed to imitate.[55] The 1950s were not generally a positive decade for superheroes, and even though the patriotic superheroes had played such a prominent role in the 1940s, they failed to resonate with a readership tired of struggles of international justice.

The superhero texts that survived—Batman, Superman, and Wonder Woman maintained an unbroken run through the decade—did so largely by adapting their narrative formulas to keep pace with changing tastes. National/DC Comics had maintained its own strict editorial codes since the early 1940s,[56] codes that prohibited much of the violent content that the Timely/Atlas books had used at the core of their narratives. The immensely popular *Adventures of Superman* radio and television programs breathed new life into the DC titles, eventually leading to film and television adaptations of Batman and Robin and a television series for Wonder Woman.

In the broadcast narratives and the comics that followed, the DC heroes increasingly concerned themselves with domestic issues. After the characters Lois Lane and Jimmy Olsen proved popular in the television narrative, for example, two new comic book series, *Superman's Pal Jimmy Olsen* and *Superman's Girlfriend Lois Lane* premiered and proved instantly popular.[57] Batman, who began his career running from the police, became such an establishment figure that he carried a platinum police badge. Instead of hunting down hardened criminals, Batman and Robin began to go up against zany villains such as the Joker, who became known for "acting like a fugitive from Looney Tunes,"[58] and began to juggle their crime-fighting mission with awkward romantic relationships with Batwoman and Batgirl.[59] For each of the DC heroes during this period, as much time was spent considering the ramifications of maintaining friendships and relationships as fighting crime, and little content resembling a critique of American culture or overt political statements appeared within the storylines during this period.

Timely/Atlas, failing to adapt its superheroic formula to satisfy changing tastes, moved on to monster and crime comics for the duration of the 1950s. But as the 1960s began and Americans' tastes again shifted, the superheroic formula would once again arise to capture the attention and imaginations of the comic book–reading public.

4

The Man out of Time
(1963–1969)

If attitudes toward the Cold War had killed the popularity of superheroes in the 1950s, the shifting attitudes in the 1960s would provide the perfect environment for a superhero renaissance. However, that reemergence seemed unlikely at the beginning of the decade. The Senate hearings, the voluntary institution of the Comics Code, and the collapse of the American News Company contributed to a major financial recession for the comic book industry.[1] Eighteen publishers folded, while others became much more limited and conservative about their offerings.

Television penetration was increasing, and under the confines of the Comics Code many publishers struggled to offer products that could compete with television and motion pictures for teenagers' attention, forcing publishers to focus on children. These conditions made superheroes a natural subject because the stories were easier to safely portray than crime or horror stories.

National Comics (DC) had thrived relative to its competition because it had integrated its own distribution system and still received revenue from its merchandising and television programs. Superman, Batman, and Wonder Woman maintained their unbroken publication streak, and because DC remained relatively solvent, it was able to experiment with new heroes. Editor Julius Schwartz updated and resurrected the Flash in *Showcase* number 4.[2] The Flash proved popular, and DC next revamped and reintroduced the Green Lantern in *Showcase* number 22.[3] More modern heroes followed, and DC soon launched a new team book to feature them: *The Justice League of America*.[4] Superheroes were suddenly making significant money again. The introduction of these heroes, after years of decline in superhero narratives, hallmarked the beginning of the Silver Age of comic books.

Timely/Atlas had not fared as well as DC Comics. At the beginning of the 1960s, Timely had dissolved its distribution center and had signed an agreement by which DC distributed eight Timely comic books each month.[5] The 1950s had been so bad that Stan Lee had downsized his entire staff and produced only reprinted stories, but he had recently hired back Jack Kirby and added new talent Steve Ditko. Lee began to focus on science fiction and monster stories (though still publishing romance stories featuring Millie the Model and Linda Carter Student Nurse as well as Western heroes such as the Two Gun Kid).

Timely publisher Martin Goodman purportedly heard about the success of *The Justice League of America* and asked Lee to emulate its success. Lee decided instead to deconstruct the superhero formula. Instead of iconic godlike beings, Lee desired to create superpowered characters "as real, living, breathing people whose personal relationships would be of interest to the readers."[6] Lee's heroes would be flawed and would not seek to hide their identities from the public: "I was utterly determined to have a superhero series without any secret identities. I knew for a fact that if I myself possessed a super power, I'd never keep it a secret. I'm too much of a show-off. So why should our fictional friends be any different? Accepting this premise, it was also natural to decide to forgo the use of costumes. If our heroes were to live in the real world, let them dress like real people."[7] Although he would later yield and reintroduce many of the traditional superhero conventions into his characters (the Fantastic Four would even by their third issue adopt team uniforms reminiscent of costumes), the superhero mold would forever be changed. Nevertheless, the basic ideologies of American Cold War mentality set the tone for each of Marvel's early heroes, addressing modern conceptions of the nuclear family, masculinity, teen culture, and playboy culture.[8]

The Fantastic Four would be the first of many such heroes. Their origin is born of the spirit of the Cold War space race: scientist Reed Richards has built a rocket and wishes to reach outer space. However, Ben Grimm, Reed's former college roommate and the mission's pilot, initially refuses to pilot the ship because of concerns that cosmic radiation will have negative effects on the crew. Susan Storm, Reed's fiancée, interjects, "Ben, we've GOT to take that chance . . . unless we want the Commies to beat us to it! I—I never thought that YOU would be a coward!"[9]

Ben is thus embarrassed into joining the mission, and so, accompanied by Sue's younger brother, Johnny, the crew sneak aboard Reed's rocket and blast off into space. Once the ship leaves Earth's atmosphere (making the four the first in space), cosmic rays penetrate the ship, altering the crew's genetic structure. After returning to Earth, the four find they have unusual abilities. Reed gains the ability to stretch, and Sue the ability to turn invisible; Johnny ignites into flame and possesses the powers of the Golden Age Human Torch (whose name he takes), and Ben becomes a rock-studded monster with great strength. The four pledge their abilities to help mankind.

True to Lee's intentions, the four heroes never attempt to hide their identities, allowing the characters to struggle with the pains of celebrity in addition to the obstacles of superherodom. Rather than constructing a secret headquarters, the team lives in the Baxter building, funded by Reed's patent royalties and the merchandising income generated by the group's incorporation.

As individuals, the characters display flawed personalities uncommon in previous superhero incarnations. Considered one of the most intelligent men on earth, Reed (Mister Fantastic) has a tendency to think aloud, often to his teammates' irritation. Sue (the Invisible Woman) not only possesses the matronly qualities one would expect from the only female member of a superhero group but also serves as a source of sexual conflict between Reed and Ben. Johnny Storm (the Human Torch), the lone teen member of the group, often acts impetuously and often does not consider how his actions affect others. Ben (the Thing), who resembles several of the Atlas-era monsters Kirby had drawn, is foul tempered, easily frustrated, and prone to jealousy.

Though the presentation of such "real people" was unprecedented in superhero comics at the time, it would appear that Lee and Kirby had merely transposed the narrative style of the nonsuperhero stories they had been writing into the conventional superhero genre. Reed Richards talks and acts like many of the scientists in the Atlas-era comics; Johnny Storm does not seem radically different from many of the teen characters presented in the hot-rod comics; Sue Storm seems pulled from the romance stories; and Ben Grimm does not seem too far removed from some of the more sympathetic monsters. In one comic, Lee and Kirby had managed to fuse the strengths of four of their previous genres together as a new style of superheroes. And that transfer would change the superhero genre forever.

In hindsight, the appeal of the new formula is easy to discern: by making heroes powerful yet humanly flawed, Lee and Kirby reintroduced to the superhero genre the "reluctant hero" characterization that lay at the heart of the American monomyth,[10] which had been missing since the conclusion of World War II.

Lee also revolutionized the process of creating comics. In what would eventually be called the "Marvel Method," he would provide a general synopsis (instead of a detailed script), and the writers and artists would simultaneously contribute to the layout of the comic and the dialogue. The purpose was to reduce Lee's workload to allow him to work on other projects,[11] but the result was that the artists and writers could work more closely together, often resulting in greater expressions of creativity.

In addition, Lee changed industry standards by printing writer and artist credits in the comic books (and eventually inking and layout credits, too). Marvel creators were characterized as part of the "Marvel Bullpen" and given colloquial nicknames (e.g., "Jolly Jack," "Swinging Steve") to make them more approachable to readers.

The success of *The Fantastic Four* was immediate, although Goodman was reportedly considering dropping the title in favor of a Western or war title until the sales figures arrived. Lee suggested he knew the book would be successful when the company began receiving significant fan mail for the first time.[12] *The Fantastic Four* was a hit, and as the letters revealed, the readership showed significant growth among young adults and college students.

The readers connected not just to the entertainment value but to the world-changing ideas the comics espoused. As one fan (and member of the Merry Marvel Marching Society) wrote, "[T]he M.M.M.S. would eventually take over the world. I don't know if the club would do that, but

I must say that your books could. And with your beliefs, I think it would be for the best. Your democratic ideas could help the poor people in communist countries even more than CARE or Radio Free Europe, if we could get them to the victims of such tyranny."[13] In *The Fantastic Four* volume 1, number 4, Lee began to publish and respond to fan letters to engage the newfound fan community. That issue also saw the reintroduction of the Sub-Mariner, albeit with a new twist.

The Human Torch discovers the Sub-Mariner living in a homeless shelter. The hero of World War II has no memory of his former life, but the Torch discerns his identity by comparing him to his likeness in a Sub-Mariner comic book.[14] The Torch drops Namor into the ocean, hoping the water will jog his memory. It does, but the Sub-Mariner quickly finds his home, Atlantis, deserted and concludes that atomic weapons are the cause: "DESTROYED!! It's all destroyed!! That glow in the water—it's RADIOACTIVITY!! NOW I know what happened!! The HUMANS did it, unthinkingly, with their accursed atomic tests!"[15] The Sub-Mariner returns to New York, announcing his intention to unleash his wrath upon mankind. The Fantastic Four defeat the Sub-Mariner, but his allegiances will forever be murky at best.

With the Fantastic Four and the Sub-Mariner gaining popularity (measured by sales and letter responses), in 1962 Lee decided to try for a third nuclear-irradiated antihero. Dr. Bruce Banner is a government scientist under pressure by the military to produce a new weapon of mass destruction: the "gamma bomb." Under General "Thunderbolt" Ross's impatient eye, Banner oversees a final test of the weapon when a young man enters the testing area. Asking his assistant, Igor, to halt the countdown, Banner enters the testing grounds to warn the youth, Rick Jones. Igor, later revealed to be a Communist spy, does not stop the countdown, and Banner is exposed to the "gamma radiation" released from the bomb's detonation.[16]

That night Banner transforms into a gray-skinned monster, referred to as "the Hulk," and battles Igor, who is captured by military police. From his prison cell, Igor reports back to his superior, the radiation-deformed Gargoyle, a Communist superscientist. The Gargoyle kidnaps the Hulk and transports him and Jones to the Soviet Union. The Hulk reverts, and

Banner offers to help the Gargoyle become a normal man with radiation therapy. The Gargoyle is returned to normal, and he immediately rises and addresses a portrait of a political leader on the wall: "It was because of YOU that I became what I was! Because I worked on your secret bomb tests! But it took an AMERICAN to cure me! And now—now that I am no longer a Gargoyle, I can defy you, and all you stand for like a man!"[17] The Gargoyle helps Banner and Jones escape to America and sets off a bomb, apparently killing himself along with several Communist officers. Aboard the escape rocket, Banner hears the explosion and explains to Jones, "It's the end of the Gargoyle! And perhaps . . . the beginning of the end of the red tyranny, too!"[18]

By the Hulk's second issue, the creature is inexplicably green instead of gray—Lee has since revealed the change occurred because maintaining a consistent gray was difficult with 1960s printing presses[19]—and in issue 3 the Hulk begins to transform during the day, no longer merely at night.

Lee's next hero would prove to be the company's most enduring and most popular: Spider-Man. Another bright individual, teenager Peter Parker, is bitten by a radioactive spider during a scientific experiment and absorbs the proportionate abilities of a man-size spider. Fashioning web shooters and a gaudy costume for himself, Parker initially tries to capitalize on his abilities for monetary gain, but when a criminal he refuses to stop kills his uncle, he rededicates his life to fighting crime.[20] Wearing a costume that covers every inch of his body (unusual for superheroes at that time) and drawn in a new eerie style by Steve Ditko, Spider-Man encapsulated the "antihero" spirit perfectly. Although he had been thrown into the last issue of the already canceled *Amazing Fantasy* series, his instant popularity would lead to the hero's self-titled series a few months later.

Spider-Man's teen angst and devotion to his late uncle's mantra ("With great power comes great responsibility") were reportedly drawn from Ditko's fascination with the "romantic realism" philosophies of Ayn Rand[21] and Lee's stated desire to present a hero "with all the problems, hang-ups and angst of any teenager."[22]

Among Lee's other irradiated heroes in this period was Daredevil, a superhero whose accident with radioactive waste robs him of his sight but heightens his other senses to superhuman levels.[23] And one of the more popular mainstays of the company's titles, *The X-Men*, portrayed a team of mutants who had presumably been born of exposure to atomic energy.[24]

But not all the new heroes gained their abilities from radiation. In 1962, Lee and Kirby also created the Norse god Thor, a hero of mythological origins.[25] Another nonradioactive science hero was created when Lee and Kirby redrafted the shrinking scientist Henry Jonathan Pym from *Tales to Astonish* number 27 into the superhero Ant-Man in *Tales to Astonish* number 35 after the sales of the first story proved higher than anticipated.[26]

Perhaps the most innately political Cold War hero was Iron Man, introduced in *Tales of Suspense* volume 1, number 39. Modeled on Howard Hughes,[27] Playboy industrialist Tony Stark visits Vietnam to inspect new portable mortars he designed. He stumbles into a trip wire, and the explosion sends pieces of shrapnel into his chest. Captured by the "red guerrillas," Stark is forced to spend his last days on Earth building weapons. Instead, with the help of a Vietnamese scientist who opposes the Communists, he builds a suit of technologically advanced armor that keeps him alive, and he defeats the Communists.[28]

Beginning with the May 1963 issues, comics began to appear with the identification "Marvel Comics Group" on the cover. That month Marvel put out another war comic, *Sgt. Fury and His Howling Commandos*[29] to replace *The Incredible Hulk*, whose first series ended after only six issues. Lee maintains that *Sgt. Fury* was a result of bet with Goodman when Lee boasted he could sell even a war comic in the emerging "Marvel style" without "Amazing," "Fantastic," "Mighty," or "Incredible" in the title.[30]

Set in World War II, *Sgt. Fury* allowed Kirby to return to his love of nostalgic war epics, albeit in the new Marvel style. The racially integrated cast of heroes acted like superheroes, pulling off incredible feats of strength and dexterity while liberating Jewish prisoners from concentration camps. Gabe Jones became the first recurring African American comic character in the first issue (or, rather, technically the second issue because the printer accidentally colored Jones as Caucasian in the first issue). The war epics renewed Kirby's interest in Captain America, although he struggled to find the new "twist" that would make the character compatible with the burgeoning Marvel Universe.

Lee's next project was to put together a team for the existing heroes (like DC's Justice League of America, the initial inspiration for the return to heroes). *The Avengers* volume 1, number 1, combined the absent Hulk with Iron Man, Thor, Ant-Man, and the Wasp (Ant-Man's female partner introduced in *Tales to Astonish* number 44) to oppose Thor's brother and god of mischief, Loki.[31]

The Avengers team has remained a consistent mainstay of the Marvel Universe ever since. Unlike Golden Age superhero teams, the Avengers lineup has regularly changed, allowing the creators great flexibility in story scope and scale. Nor have the changes always resulted in complimentary characters or personalities. For example, the original team suffered dramatic changes in their second issue together when Ant-Man reversed his powers to become Giant-Man, and the Hulk left the team in disgust.[32] Two issues later Captain America would be resurrected in the pages of *The Avengers* and quickly become a member and their leader.

The Man out of Time Captain America (1964–1971)

Working on *Sgt. Fury and His Howling Commandos* had given Lee and Kirby the nostalgic itch to bring Captain America into the modern Marvel Universe. But could a character created by the 1940s establishment offer a credible critique of 1960s American society? Lee had resurrected the other two Timely giants by adding interesting twists to their characterization. The new Human Torch had a completely different personality from the android of World War II. And although the Sub-Mariner was the same character, Lee had turned him into a villain.

Lee and Kirby began by testing the waters. In *Strange Tales* number 114, the Fantastic Four's Human Torch encounters someone he thinks is Captain America but who turns out to be his enemy, the Acrobat, in disguise (an interesting choice, given that the Human Torch was also the one who first encountered the Sub-Mariner). At the end of the story, Lee leaves the reader with a call to action: "You guessed it! This story was really a test!

To see if you too would like Captain America to return! As usual, your letters will give us the answer!"[33]

The response was favorable, and Lee and Kirby settled in to update the Sentinel of Liberty once again. While they considered, fate intervened. President John F. Kennedy was assassinated on November 22, 1963, and the news reportedly devastated Kirby.[34] As the nation struggled to make sense of the world in the wake of the assassination, Kirby decided to capture the mood with Captain America's story.

In *The Avengers* number 4, the Sub-Mariner encounters a tribe of Eskimos worshipping a frozen figure. Enraged, Namor hurls the icy idol into the distance. As it falls into the southern waters, it begins to melt, freeing the figure inside. The Avengers, pursuing the Sub-Mariner in their submarine, find the figure and bring it aboard. They quickly recognize their cargo:

GIANT-MAN: Who can he be? Why is he frozen solid?

THOR: Look! Beneath his tattered clothes—some sort of colorful costume!

WASP: Wait! Don't you recognize it?? It's the famous red, white, and blue garb of—Captain America!

IRON MAN: The Wasp is right!

THOR: Can this really be the famous shield of the once-mighty crime-fighter?

IRON MAN: And his face mask—with the proud letter "A" on it! It must be him![35]

Cap awakens, screaming for Bucky. He struggles for a moment, but then remembers that Bucky is dead. Cap recounts a story in which Bucky died when he and Cap tried to stop an explosive-filled drone plane from taking off and the plane had detonated, but Cap had fallen off, plunging into the icy ocean, where he began to freeze.

In this way, Lee and Kirby erased the last few years of Cap's World War II adventures, the mystery and crime adventures of the late 1940s, and the "Commie Smasher" return from Cap's continuity. In addition, killing

Bucky in this manner introduced a character flaw in the form of survivor's guilt that would plague the character the rest of his career.

From the initial return of Captain America, Lee and Kirby framed the hero as a source of wisdom from a golden era, trapped in a politically charged culture. The first nonhero Cap encounters after his recovery is a policeman, who bursts into tears at the sight of him: "And all these years—all of us—your fans—all your admirers—we thought you were dead! But you've come back—just when the world has need of such a man—just like FATE planned it this way. Forgive me, Cap, willya? I seem to have something in my eye!"[36] In his first Silver Age adventure, Cap winds up saving the Avengers and helping them battle the Sub-Mariner (the two oddly don't recognize each other). At the conclusion of the story, Cap is officially inducted into the ranks of the Avengers.

After the Avengers and the Fantastic Four skirmish with the Hulk (who feels jilted when Rick Jones becomes Cap's partner) and a quick mission against the Lava Men, Cap's history comes full circle as the Avengers face the Masters of Evil, led by Baron Zemo. Zemo, the (retconned) World War II villain responsible for Bucky's death, quickly becomes an obsession for Cap. As the two old foes clash in *The Avengers* number 6, Cap delivers the first of his "combat speeches": "Where is your braggadocio, NOW, Master of Evil?!! I still remember how you sneered at democracy . . . how you called Americans soft . . . timid . . . too spoiled to fight for freedom! You mocked free men! You boasted your contempt for liberty!! Feel my grip, Zemo! It's the grip of a free man! Look into my eyes, tyrant! They're the eyes of a man who would die for liberty! The world must never again make the fatal error of mistaking compassion for weakness!! And while I live, it WON'T!!!"[37]

This style of idealistic rhetoric in the midst of battle would become a common characteristic of each of Cap's 1960s battles against idealistic foes, in particular former Nazis (especially when Kirby was drawing the book). Zemo and the Red Skull would regularly wage this form of battle with Cap, in which each combatant would launch as much a battle of words as fists. Zemo would perish by his own hand during a battle with Cap in *The Avengers* volume 1, number 15, but not before Cap slips in an ideological point against him:

CAPTAIN AMERICA: I think you'll be safe now, lad! You were a
means to an end—I'm the one Zemo wants to destroy!
RICK: But Cap—you're all alone—and Zemo has weapons—men—
everything in his favor!
CAP: Not everything, Rick! There's one weapon we're armed with
which he can never possess! A thing called—Justice![38]

When Cap isn't moralizing on the battlefield, he is serving in the leader/
tactician role. Although Lee and Kirby had shortened his World War II
career to roughly four years before he fell into the icy waters of the Atlan-
tic, Cap somehow becomes the voice of experience and wisdom in the art
of war. He is presented as a leader who draws respect for "how quickly he
conceived a battle plan,"[39] as a "guy who's used to being obeyed,"[40] and
even as the "spark that lit their flame of glory."[41] Even when the Avengers
are trapped in future centuries, the leaders there yield to Captain America: "I shall follow your command, Avenger! For, there is no doubt—you
were born to lead!"[42]

This leadership would soon be put to good use. At the conclusion of
a conflict with the Masters of Evil in The Avengers volume 1, number 16,
all of the Avengers except Cap take a leave of absence. Before they depart,
they choose Captain America to lead a new team, comprising former villains Hawkeye, Quicksilver, and the Scarlet Witch.[43] The formation of the
new team puts Cap directly into conflict with his younger teammates (in
particular Hawkeye) as his values and leadership style create tension. Cap,
representing the 1940s generation, has trouble relating to the youth culture of the 1960s.

Even before Cap became leader of the Avengers, he tended to represent a conservative voice speaking to a progressive age. Although he
doesn't get the opportunity to express such views in every Avengers issue
(ensemble comics often make consistent individual character development difficult), little moments occasionally emerge, such as when the
Avengers express concerns after the Wasp is hit by a bullet while in her
reduced form. While Giant-Man rails against feeling helpless, Cap turns
to a more conservative mode of coping:

GIANT-MAN: Then we still can't know . . . we still must wait . . .
unable to aid her! All of us . . . helpless!

CAP: There's nothing left for us now except prayer![44]

Outwardly, Cap challenges his teammates to fight the good fight, espousing his 1940s values freely. But inwardly he wrestles with his lot in life. Feeling isolated from the alien culture around him, Cap longs to find a sense of belonging. He begins to brood. In a July 1965 issue, he asks, "How much longer can I go on this way—being a living symbol to millions—and yet, a frustrated anachronism to myself! Outside my window the world passes by—a world which I have still to find my rightful place—my own identity!"[45] Half a year later, he is still posing the same existential questions: "How much longer can I continue to live a life not truly my own? A life with no roots? As Captain America, I'm merely a relic of an almost-forgotten past . . . Yes, as Captain America, I wear the mantle of Avengers leadership! But, what of the man inside the costume? What of Steve Rogers?? Am I destined to go through life with no real identity of my own? Is Steve Rogers always to live in the shadow of Captain America?"[46]

Cap's adventures continued primarily in the pages of *The Avengers* (although he also made the regular guest appearances in other Marvel comics that all Marvel heroes were subjected to) until he appeared alongside (and in combat against) Iron Man in *Tales of Suspense* volume 1, number 58.[47] Beginning with the following issue, Lee and Kirby permanently added the character to *Tales of Suspense*, a book he would share with Iron Man until taking it over as a self-titled comic in 1968.[48] Cap's solo adventures gave the writers an opportunity to devote more attention to the character's personality and views.

Early in Cap's solo adventures, the writers established his opposition to communism by sending him on a rescue mission to Vietnam in *Tales of Suspense* volume 1, number 61. There he encounters Communist foes who display their inferiority to Americans verbally (in English, no less):

CAP: Is the Communist Fighting Man so weak, so unsure of himself that he fears one lone American?? Is THIS the much-vaunted power of the Viet Cong??

VIET CONG STRONGMAN #1: He has the temerity to mock us! Let
us attack him together!
VIET CONG STRONGMAN #2: Ah So! It matters not HOW we win,
so long as we crush the jeering American![49]

The early issues of *Tales of Suspense* and *The Avengers* contain several
such exchanges, and readers quickly complained about the use of Communists as villains.[50] Although Lee and Kirby defended their choice in
their responses to these letters, they quickly moved away from the Cold
War narrative. In *Tales of Suspense* volume 1, number 63 (cover-dated
March 1965), a new rendition of Cap's origin story appeared. Many of the
elements from *Captain America Comics* number 1 (the disguised shop
and shopkeeper, the Jewish scientist, the Nazi assassin, etc.) remained
consistent, but a few interesting changes were thrown in. One trivial
change involved the serum. Instead of receiving an injection (as he had in
the origins presented in *Captain America Comics* numbers 1 and 59) or a
series of injections (as in the origin story presented in *Young Men* number
24), Rogers now ingests the serum orally.[51] Another change involved the
name of the scientist: "Dr. Reinstein" (obviously modeled from "Albert
Einstein") becomes "Dr. Erskine" (Kirby would later admit he had simply
forgotten the original name).

A significant change involved the treatment of the Nazi assassin. In
Captain America Comics number 1, Rogers had purposely knocked the
man into a bank of electronics and then gloated over the corpse. In *Captain America Comics* number 59, Rogers merely struck the assassin (no
explosion occurred). In the new *Tales of Suspense* version, the assassin
begins by announcing his presence, yelling, "Down with Democracy!
Down with Freedom! The Third Reich shall live forever!" After Erskine
crumples, Rogers gets in one blow but then chases the assassin on foot. As
they cross the room, Rogers yells, "Stop you fool! You're running toward
the electrical omniverter! Look Out—!"[52] The assassin stumbles into the
machinery and is electrocuted.

This change was significant because it signaled a shift in Captain
America's attitude toward violence. The Anti-Hitler Captain America committed homicide (sometimes of many foes at once) in more than 85 percent

of his comics and 44 percent of his stories. The Commie Smasher Captain America killed foes in 56 percent of his stories. Until *Tales of Suspense* volume 1, number 63, Cap's Silver Age views on violence had been inconsistent. When Kirby drew him, he tended to kill minions on occasion (usually Nazis in flashbacks or Sgt. Fury stories). But he mostly stood by approvingly as enemies who perished did so as a result of their own efforts.

The origin story in *Tales of Suspense* volume 1, number 63, represents a major transition point in the direction of Cap's comic series. Avoiding the sticky political ramifications of the Cold War, the *Tales of Suspense* stories became a "flashback series," allowing Kirby and Lee to retell Cap stories from the 1940s. Although many of the stories were lifted directly from the 1940s series, Cap's persona was consistent with modern developments since his rebirth in 1964. Cap only occasionally employs lethal force against his opponents by using grenades[53] or even firearms,[54] and he appears less brutal than he was depicted in the 1940s series.

The "Man out of Time" Captain America was much less of a killer than his previous incarnations. Even stories directly lifted from the 1940s are reinterpreted to be less violent. For example, in the story continuing from his origin story, Cap and Bucky take great pains to disarm the Nazi troops they face (Bucky even stops one by pulling his cap over his eyes). Cap and Bucky destroy a Nazi submarine, but not until the crew are bound and gagged on shore.[55]

The response to the "flashback series" was not positive. By *Tales of Suspense* volume 1, number 68, Lee and Kirby were receiving letters requesting the 1940s story arc be terminated in favor of 1960s stories.[56] And so Cap's adventures returned to contemporary stories nine issues after his trip down memory lane began. The readers apparently objected to Cap's heavy-handed treatment of Nazi characters and his 1940s attitudes toward women, illustrated by the following exchange with a female member of the French resistance:

PEGGY CARTER: You were wonderful! I'll never forget these weeks . . . with Captain America fighting at our side!

CAP: I won't forget them either! But . . . you've got to leave the partisans! This isn't WOMAN'S work![57]

In *Tales of Suspense* volume 1, number 72, the flashback transitions into a story Cap tells the other Avengers. He remembers that the Red Skull had promised the rise of three sleeper devices on the twentieth anniversary of Germany's defeat. A note from Lee appeared on the final page of the comic telling readers the creative team had received numerous letters asking for modern Cap stories.[58] Cap would spend the next three issues battling these Nazi robots, and the Red Skull would make his first modern appearance in *Tales of Suspense* volume 1, number 79.

Cap not only made the transition to the present in deed but spent much of his emotional energy considering his struggle to adjust to the modern world. His brooding became a mainstay of his personal narrative. Even in the modern era, his resistance to the inclusion of female heroes and operatives left some readers stewing.[59] The writers used such cultural issues to define a "Man out of Time" narrative, an underlying theme of Cap's struggle to adjust to a new era. As Cap, he leads the Avengers and battles for justice. As Steve Rogers, he has trouble fitting in with the wonders around him: "But that was all an eternity ago—in the dead past—the forgotten past—the past that will live with me forever! Today, it's all behind me! This is a new world—a new age! An age of atomic power, space exploration, social upheaval—yet, an age over which the threat of war hangs heavy once again! And, so long as danger beckons, there is still a need for an old relic like Captain America! A need that must be met!"[60] He can't reconcile the two parts of himself: "All my life I've tried to find a place for Steve Rogers—but still he lives under the more colorful shadow of Captain America. . . . Perhaps it's Steve Rogers who's the legend—and Captain America who is the reality! Perhaps I was born to be a red-white-and-blue avenger—and nothing more! But there must be more to life than endless combat! Others have found a home—a family—why can't I? Or is Steve Rogers destined to walk alone forever—until the final battle—until he walks no more?"[61]

At times, his internal conflict sounds downright desperate:

Perhaps it would have been better if I'd never been rescued from that glacier—where I was in suspended animation for two decades! The world seems so changed—so different—I feel like a relic—a holdover from some dim and dismal past! Everything has changed! The cities are more crowded—more tense—with people racing about in vehicles we never dreamed of in the forties! But is it really progress? [Looking at newspaper announcing plans to visit moon.] We may one day be meeting strangers—on far distant stars—But we still haven't learned to live with our neighbors—in peace and brotherhood![62]

In this way, the writers justified using the 1940s values instilled in Captain America to critique the culture of 1960s America. Cap begins to voice his ideals in loud (and increasingly verbose) speeches. In private, his internal monologues bemoan the seeming lack of virtue in modern society.

In *Tales of Suspense* volume 1, number 95, Cap decides the hero biz is too complicated, reveals his secret identity to the world, and quits,[63] although he is quickly persuaded to come back. Cap's quitting when he becomes disillusioned with his mission would serve as a theme in the decades to come. Cap quits the Avengers again in the following month's issue,[64] but even after he resumes his personal mission, he does not rejoin the ranks. The Black Panther takes Cap's place in *The Avengers* volume 1, number 52.[65]

With the one hundredth issue, *Tales of Suspense* became officially titled *Captain America* (Iron Man also received his own publication). Lee and Kirby used the new popularity to begin a major conflict between Cap and his arch nemesis, the Red Skull. As Cap and the Skull lock horns throughout the epic storyline, they once again clash as much with words as with fists.

Captain America volume 1, number 101, sees the two battle amid the emergence of a fourth sleeper robot. As Cap and the Red Skull grapple and trade blows, they verbally assault each other's ideology:

THE RED SKULL: Men were born to be slaves! They're not worth your idiotic concern! Why should you care for them when they don't even care for each other? Look around you! The world is consumed by greed, crime and bigotry! Men are no more than animals, unworthy to—UNHH!!

CAPTAIN AMERICA: Tyrants have always scorned their fellow humans! But still the race endures—while the despots fall! And those who would grind us underfoot—can never hope to keep us from our eventual destiny!

SKULL: Can't you see?? You're an anachronism! You belong in the dead past! The world has no more use for idealism—!

CAP: It is YOU who are wrong!! The only TRUE REALITY lies in FAITH—and in HOPE! This world is still young—the future ahead—It's YOU who have outgrown the dream—YOU who are blind to the promise of tomorrow![66]

And so it is that what Cap once thought for himself (that his values are anachronistic) now becomes the heart of his ideological struggle. But the strength of Cap's newly reasserted conservative ideology would soon have consequences with the readership.

Cap mounts his next verbal assault against the Red Skull in *Captain America* volume 1, number 103:

CAPTAIN AMERICA: There IS no master race—and you know it! We're ALL human beings—All equal before our creator! Nothing you can ever do or say will change that!

THE RED SKULL: Equality! You fool—equality is—just a myth!

CAP: A MYTH, is it? Then America herself is just a myth—as are liberty, and justice—and faith! Myths that free men everywhere, are willing to die for!

CAP: It's tyranny which is the myth—and bigotry which is an abomination before the eyes of mankind! It's YOU who are the fool! For, humanity has come of age—and so long as love, not hatred, fills men's hearts—the day of the tyrant is ended![67]

The mention of "the creator" was becoming a symbolic source of conservative values for Cap. Two issues later he would take the religious references over the top:

BATROC: My so-great speed will take me to safety—while you stupidly risk your life for zee undeserving masses!

CAP: There was another who gave his life for the masses . . . many centuries ago . . . and though he was the wisest of all . . . he never thought of the humblest living being . . . as undeserving![68]

Fans would strongly object to the religious overtones and the conservative ideology in coming issues. But before they could weigh in (letter publication usually lagged nine or ten issues behind issue publication), Kirby would present Cap's origin yet again, filling in some of the contextual backstory.

In the origin story presented in *Captain America* volume 1, number 109, Steve Rogers receives the supersoldier formula from Professor Reinstein in the form of an injection, and then he is exposed to "vita rays" to activate the formula. As Reinstein fawns over his achievement, he frames Rogers as the perfect man (suggesting Kirby's messianic interpretation of the character). The Nazi spy shoots Reinstein, and Rogers knocks the spy into the equipment bank, killing him. As he strikes, he bellows, "Fascists have always misjudged free men! No man fights as well—as the one who battles to rid the earth of tyranny! And that shall be my purpose—my sworn dedication—for all the days of my life!"[69]

Here Captain America regressed closer to the form Kirby had originally had a hand in creating. But he would not remain in this state for much longer. Kirby would leave Marvel before the next issue, and Jim Steranko would take over the artistic duties for a couple of issues.[70]

As it turned out, the readers directly shaped the transition. Many of the young men and women (though there were fewer women) began to react negatively to the Kirby critique of their age. A controversy soon broke out in the letters section that would result in a remarkable transformation in the character. In *Captain America* volume 1, number 110, a letter from reader Albert Rodriquez described the Marvel Comics hero as a warmonger and criticized the editors for giving the character speech consistent with a "defender of the Establishment":

This magazine does not fit in with today's society. Cap ought to know that someday the world will be built on a pinnacle of peace and freedom. Cap believes the same way, but must he show it through violence and heroics? Of course, without this element there would be no Captain America. All I question is his reasoning, which is entirely out of date. This is a strong plea against war lovers and so-called patriots. One more thing. Get rid of that Living Legend of World War II deal. Who wants to be reminded of a shameful ideal? Aside from this, Cap is one of your best characters. It would fit the standards of today, though, if he were more liberal.[71]

The editors published the letter without response. Four issues later, three of the four published letters in *Captain America* volume 1, number 114, attacked Mr. Rodriquez's words, claiming his letter "made my blood boil!"[72] and "shocked me to the core!"[73] The editors took the opportunity to side with the outraged responders, and the argument should have died then and there.

It didn't. Over the next six years, the "Let's Rap with Cap" letters column presented more than sixty letters about the burgeoning "patriotism controversy." Published letters came from military personnel, politicians, social scientists, three future writers and editors of Marvel Comics, and readers from seemingly every walk of life. Before the conclusion of the controversy, the letters addressed such topics as the US military presence in Vietnam, McCarthyism, Watergate, and a host of other political issues.[74] The letter feud ran nearly eighty issues, long enough to involve seven comic writers and twelve artists, until the return of artist-writer Jack Kirby to the comic in the January 1976 issue drew enough attention from the discussion that it finally died down. The letter writers used argument, humor, symbolism, emotional appeals, and even threats to bolster their positions. The controversy centered on how a patriotic character designed to represent America should react to the changing cultural climate of the 1960s and 1970s.

The creative teams at Marvel paid close attention to the tone and volume of the debate. Cap's persona soon began to change in accordance with the prevailing sentiments expressed in the letter. Cap soon began to struggle mightily with his conservative 1940s culture. Within the comic narrative, a series of storied events shaped Cap's new social conscience. In *Captain America* volume 1, number 117,[75] Cap encounters and mentors the Falcon, Marvel's first African American superhero.[76] Cap's relationship with the Falcon would prove influential to his views and values in the coming months and years.

However, the most significant changes to the character would occur when Cap is working alone. Starting in *Captain America* volume 1, number 128 (cover-dated August 1970),[77] Cap decides he doesn't know enough about modern America and sets off on motorcycle—in the spirit of Dennis Hopper's 1969 *Easy Rider*—to "find himself."[78] Two issues later, Cap happens upon a university riot pitting college students against police officers. As he surveys the scene, he expresses confusion unlike the earlier values-laden "Man out of Time": "What can be happening up ahead? There's nothing but a college! COLLEGE! Of COURSE! I should have guessed! Judging from the noise I hear—it must be a student riot! Here's where I oughtta step in and make like a swingin' hero! But how do I know whose side to take? What the heck—the cops don't need any help—but these kids do!!"[79] After diffusing the standoff by rescuing the college dean, Cap decides to visit a local television station to make a public statement regarding the protest:

> I've been asked to speak to you today—to warn America about those who try to change our institutions—But, in a PIG'S EYE I'll warn you! This nation was founded by dissidents—by people who wanted something better! There's nothing sacred about the status quo—and there never will be! I don't believe in using force—or violence—because they can be the weapons of those who would enslave us—But, nor do I believe in an establishment that remains so aloof—so distant—that the people are driven to desperate measures—as in the case of a college dean who isolates himself from his student body![80]

This speech represents the completion of Cap's evolutionary political journey. The conservative patriot of the early 1960s, truly a man out of time, gives way to a "liberalized" Captain America. In *Captain America and the Falcon* volume 1, number 134, Cap and the Falcon become official partners,[81] and this relationship (among others) forces Cap to deal with race, gender, and class struggles that were contemporary to American culture in the early 1970s.

The Patriotism of the Man out of Time Captain America

Although Lee and Kirby made obvious initial strides in updating Captain America's ideology (some to conform to the spirit of the new Marvel narratives, some imposed by the Comics Code), the character seemed to fall out of favor whenever writers (Kirby in particular) presented Cap's ideological message too explicitly.

Once Kirby left *The Avengers* comic to pursue other projects, Cap seemed somewhat inconsistent when one compares his personality in *The Avengers* with his personality in *Tales of Suspense* and *Captain America*. Within the context of his leadership of the Avengers, Cap's values and moral code become a source of tension for the other team members. Although a central thrust of the stories in this era involved Cap's experience and wisdom serving as the critical factor in many Avengers victories, the interaction between Cap and Hawkeye (although other characters created similar tensions, Hawkeye served as a fulcrum for the voice of 1960s youth culture) presented a challenge to the authority of the older establishment.

The Avengers of the 1960s (in true Marvel style) concerned itself as much with the team members' flawed relationships as with the challenges presented by their missions. Captain America is a source of wisdom, but he also appears to regularly misjudge his teammates' capabilities, just as the older establishment struggled to understand the rising youth culture of the 1960s. The writers and artists involved with *The Avengers* appear to present Cap as occasionally wrong and occasionally right in his differences of opinion with younger teammates. Ultimately, he appears to be a guiding force, but one who must learn and adapt to the changing world around him if his advice is to be taken seriously or have relevance.

By contrast, within the stories of his own comic, Cap generally appears less flexible. This Captain America is morose, seeming to sit in his room nearly paralyzed with confusion and regrets. Between battle sequences (when he is forced to banish his thoughts in order to achieve the actions needed for conflict resolution), the character broods about his place in the modern world and whether his mission is anachronistic (this word appears with unusual frequency in his comic) to the changing values of modern society.

This tendency could be representative of how Kirby, one of many service veterans who returned from World War II only to see the evolution of the values he believed he fought for, felt like a "man out of time" himself. It is not too difficult to imagine a writer from the Greatest Generation struggling to understand the expressed resistance to his values coming from a youth culture that (at least from his perspective) possessed the voice for that critique because of the sacrifices made by those being critiqued.

This would certainly account for the increased focus on the World War II narrative, which may have been an attempt to inform a younger generation about the trials of the older generation or merely an attempt to allow Kirby to return to familiar ground when the readers of many Marvel comics raised concerns about the treatment of Communist characters. It would also account for the increasingly strong ideological speeches Cap delivers to foes such as the Red Skull. By resurrecting former Nazi villains for Cap to face (and argue with), Cap's writers appeared to be using the foil of fascism to justify and explore the values embodied in Cap, the representative of the older generation.

One gets the sense that Hawkeye, for example, would have little to say to the Red Skull. Hawkeye's concerns (which tend to focus more on the image and status concerns of the 1960s youth culture) do not diametrically oppose the Red Skull's fascism the way Cap's dogmatic libertarian views do. Nor does Cap bring the same passion (and certainly not the idealistic dialogue) to his encounters with the many other foes encountered by the Avengers.

The 1960s readers of *The Avengers* and *Tales of Suspense/Captain America* did not seem to react well to Cap's ideological speeches, commonly suggesting that they sounded like heavy-handed preaching, an oversimplification of a complex world, and a dangerous justification for continuing the policies and ideology that some of them saw as problematic. As Americans often do, the readers rejected the (stilted, from their perspective) lessons from history. The actions of a previous generation seemed less relevant than the actions of the generation active in the modern world. The historical ideologies of the previous generation were of little interest (and seemed irrelevant) in the face of modern concerns and issues.

The scope and scale of the letter column controversy were unprecedented in popular mass media, and the effect of the sentiments expressed through that medium on the writers was equally unprecedented. Expressing dissatisfaction with the presentation of patriotism by a hero created as the embodiment of American patriotism, readers not only rejected his initial ideology but also provided numerous suggestions for how to modify it to make Captain America's opinions about the values of American more acceptable to them.

The letters column controversy was cultural conflict displayed for all to see, resulting in the dramatic renegotiation of the character. Andrew Macdonald and Virginia Macdonald would later submit that the 1970s Captain America had evolved into a character that had "accurately caught the changing mood of the past thirty years."[82] But it was not a simple journey. The "Liberal Crusader" that would break new ground on political relevance in the 1970s looked extremely different from Kirby's brooding "Man out of Time."

5

The Liberal Crusader
(1969–1979)

The combination of the greatest economic expansion of the twentieth century and the birth of about eighty million children in post–World War II America radically changed the face of America youth culture. As the new generation grew into a prominent position of consumer power, its members began to exert their voices in support of new value systems and ways of thinking. Several key events are credited as signposts of the Baby Boomers' growing voice: the publication of Jack Kerouac's novel *On the Road* in 1957;[1] the launch of second-wave feminism; the March on Washington for Jobs and Freedom on August 28, 1963, which culminated in Martin Luther King Jr.'s historic "I Have a Dream" speech at the Lincoln Memorial; and the Berkeley student rebellions beginning in 1964. By the early 1970s, the young Boomers had been exposed to a renaissance of music, books, movies, and clothing. Comic book publishers, members of a conservative industry, were relatively slow to adapt to the changes in culture. But as the late 1960s came to an end, Marvel and DC Comics began slowly to change to accommodate their readers' evolving tastes.

Although the timeframe and characteristics of both the Golden Age of Comics and the Silver Age of Comics are fairly accepted, the third age of superhero comics, usually referred to as the "Bronze Age," was not begun by a singular seminal event. Rather, scholars and comic fans look to a series of smaller events that characterize the distinction between comic book trends of the 1960s and those of the 1970s. One event that many point to is the departure of Robin for college in *Batman* number 217.[2] Another was certainly (and more importantly for Marvel) the departure of

Jack Kirby from Marvel Comics at the beginning of the 1970s. Until that point, Lee and Kirby had been behind most of the innovative components of Marvel Comics, and when Kirby left for DC Comics, a new direction for Marvel was signaled.

Around this time, Marvel managed to leave behind the constraining distribution arrangement with Independent News, and as a result its offerings expanded dramatically, until the company led comic book circulation in 1972. The business was changing, as Marvel and DC began to move toward the direct-sales system that allowed them to ship to specialized retailers (such as the specialty comic books stores that began to crop up in many urban markets), resulting in more dependable sales and nonreturnable issues. Fans began to take precedence over casual readers, leading to a need for back inventories of previous issues to support the new emphasis on collecting comics.[3]

Even more important, by the beginning of the 1970s Marvel and DC had become corporate properties. Martin Goodman sold Marvel to the Perfect Film and Chemical Corporation, and DC became part of the Warner Communications empire. Both companies had become increasingly salient in the popular consciousness, and signs of this awareness began to emerge in the form of intertextual references and media coverage. Singer Jerry Jeff Walker released "The Ballad of the Incredible Hulk," Peter Fonda's character in *Easy Rider* was known as "Captain America," and a Herb Trimpe drawing of the Hulk appeared on the cover of the September 1971 issue of *Rolling Stone*.[4] The late 1960s saw animated cartoons and live-action television programs featuring Marvel heroes. All of this activity was designed to be synergistic with the comic narratives, at least according to a Stan Lee interview in 1968: "We realize that we are rather popular now. We appreciate it. But the thing that bothers me . . . corny as it may sound . . . we really are trying to elevate the medium. We're trying to make them [comic books] as respectable as possible. Our goal is that someday an intelligent adult would not be embarrassed to walk down the street with a comic magazine. I don't know if we can ever bring this off, but it's something to shoot for."[5]

But this market success also had another effect on the way comics were produced, according to Marvel editor Roy Thomas:

There was a time around '68 or so when Stan told me and Gary Friedrich—who was working there by then—that he didn't want things to
change in the books from that point on. We were to give "the *illusion* of
change," but then bring them back to the status quo ante. We weren't wild
about that, but it was Stan's decision. When you get something going just
right, you can become reluctant to meddle with it. Do you keep evolving
and hope your readers will follow you, or do you figure at some point
you've pretty much got the thing right? If you keep changing it, you may
end up undoing what you did right in the first place. It's hard to know.[6]

Of course, one character that couldn't simply return to the status quo was
Captain America. Having endured a dramatic shift in ideological outlook
in the late 1960s, Cap would continue to evolve throughout the 1970s.
And yet as his creators fleshed out new dimensions of his formula, those
tenets would form a new status quo that would serve as the foundation of
the character for decades to come. The 1970s were a time of exploration
for Captain America, but once the results of those explorations were complete, the character's past and future would be rewritten to ensure that his
history didn't conflict with the contemporary understanding of him.

The Liberal Crusader Confronts Racial Tensions

The transformation that began with a letters-column fight (and with a
cross-country motorcycle trip for comic book continuity) resulted in a
transformed liberal crusader who participated in what would become
a pattern of "relevant" comics in the 1970s. Bolstered by the increased
attention *Captain America* received, Marvel continued to explore Cap's
newfound social conscience throughout the 1970s. Much of this exploration occurred through Cap's relationship with the Falcon, the first African
American superhero, who first appeared in *Captain America* volume 1,
number 117,[7] and became Cap's official partner in issue 134.[8]

Although Marvel had previously made implicit statements about racism (for example, in the Sons of the Serpent story in *The Avengers* volume
1, numbers 32 and 33), the company had been slow to present African
Americans as superheroes. In commando Gabe Jones, Lee and Kirby had

introduced the first major recurring African American character in comic books in May 1963,[9] but it would be three years until the second such character, Dr. Bill Foster (who would eventually become the superhero Black Goliath) debuted in *The Avengers* volume 1, number 32,[10] followed a year later by *Daily Bugle* city editor Robbie Robertson.[11] Soon thereafter, the Prowler became the first African American supervillain in *The Amazing Spider-Man* volume 1, number 78.[12] Lee and Gene Colan (the writer-artist who would later create black characters Blade and Brother Voodoo) also prominently wrote a blind African American soldier into a Daredevil story concerning overcoming disability.[13] All of these characters preceded John Stewart (Green Lantern), DC Comics' first recurring African American character (and superhero), by at least two years.

The first black superhero (though not American), the Black Panther, was introduced in 1966 as an African king in *The Fantastic Four* volume 1, number 52,[14] but no dark-skinned heroes had followed until the Falcon's first appearance in *Captain America* volume 1, number 117. And according to a 1970 interview with Lee, Marvel approached even that three-issue storyline with caution, letting the readers weigh in before making him a permanent feature of the comic:

> I think we have a better chance with The Falcon. We've used him in three stories, then we dropped him, and I want to wait and see how the mail comes in. I'm hoping it'll be good and I'd like to give him his own book. I'd like to just make him a guy from the ghetto who is like Captain America or Daredevil. No great super-power, but athletic and heroic. And let him fight for the cause that will benefit his own people. I would have done this years ago, but again the powers-that-be are very cautious about things and I can't go leaping.[15]

The letters were glowing, however, and when the Falcon resurfaced, he was more than just a supporting character, instead playing a prominent role in Cap's narrative. In fact, the comic was retitled *Captain America and the Falcon* until issue 222. The two characters interacted with (and sometimes fought over) racial tensions presented through their experiences, in costume and out.

Seeking to increase his contribution to the public good, Steve Rogers soon sought employment as a New York police officer. Despite Cap's growing social awareness, Rogers himself remained a two-dimensional caricature, and the fact that he would seek fulfillment in another uniform speaks volumes about his lack of individuality during this period. The Falcon's alter ego (Sam Wilson) became a social worker, a position that often put him into conflict with more militant African American characters. The Falcon's role would often be debated among the supporting African American characters. Rafe, a streetwise militant, would routinely criticize the Falcon's associations with the establishment (primarily for not taking a more militant stance with his white partner), whereas others would take a more communal view of his identity politics:

> RAFE: Gimme a break kid! If that Uncle Tom Sellout's got his hash in a sling—you think I'M gonna give a good lump? Who needs that boot-lickin' jiver?
>
> CITIZEN: A minute of your time, there, brother. I think you got the Falcon figured wrong. He's done a lotta good for the neighborhood—somethin' I ain't seen your gang gettin' on too often. And besides—no matter what you think about him—the Falcon's still black.[16]

The Falcon himself, in his secret identity as Sam Wilson, would similarly be torn as his status and approach to authority often led to conflicts with his neighbors, most notably with Leila, a militant love interest. Leila, introduced in *Captain America and the Falcon* volume 1, number 139,[17] would serve to introduce the identity angst in Wilson that many African Americans experienced in the 1970s. As the Falcon, he serves society beside Captain America and is fiercely loyal to his mission; as Wilson, he serves his African American community by helping those in it to reconnect with the establishment; but as Leila's potential mate, he is continually challenged regarding his loyalty to his people, leading him to express frustration at his predicament: "Cap and Leila: my two extremes. Will my loyalty always be torn between them?"[18]

For her part, Leila is also torn between two worlds. She is attracted to Wilson but finds his trust in the establishment a challenge to her convictions. On many occasions, the two clash over how justice is best enforced in the African American community, and Leila often invokes associations of masculinity and manhood to spur the reserved Wilson into action:

> SAM WILSON: What more IS there? The cops are baffled, honey.
> LEILA: The COPS? You expect them to help US? Brother, where have you BEEN the last ten years? Forget them! What are YOU planning to do, MEESTER Wilson?
> SAM: I'll do what I've been doing, Leila—
> LEILA: —in other words—you'll do NOTHING! Seems like I've made a mistake about you, Sam Wilson . . . I used to think you were a MAN![19]

Of course, these appeals cause great tension for Wilson, who in his guise as the Falcon has already committed himself to his clandestine mission precisely because the authorities are unable to maintain an adequate sense of justice in Harlem (the motivation that compels most superheroes to put on a mask and punch villains in the first place). But the need to maintain his secret identity keeps Wilson in an awkward situation with Leila, for he cannot prove his "manhood" without revealing his dual identity. Heroes are often put under such pressure for dramatic tension, but Wilson's cultural need to express his masculinity as a member of the urban African American community (and to express it by taking action outside the established social authority) magnifies the internal struggle over his identity. In fact, he will eventually decide to jettison his secret identity. The secret identity would prove to be a particularly difficult burden for early African American heroes, whose identities as symbols of justice came into conflict with their identities as positive role models for their communities. DC's John Stewart would reject wearing his Green Lantern mask from the outset,[20] preferring to avoid exactly the type of identity crisis Wilson suffered throughout the 1970s.

Marvel writers such as Gary Friedrich produced Captain America stories that also confronted racial politics head on from within the partnership itself. As Cap struggles to be a friend and partner to the Falcon, he inevitably proves insensitive to the Falcon's sensibilities. After Cap and the Falcon calm a race riot (artificially created and manipulated by the Red Skull), Cap angers his partner:

CAP: Well, all's quiet for now—but who knows WHAT little something it will take to make them explode again!

FALCON: I don't think I like the way you put that, partner! They—WE—got reason to blow up! I got some value reassessing to do! I'll get in touch when I know where I stand![21]

The next such exchange places a great strain on their relationship:

CAP: I know it's tough playing the hero role . . . and being black can't make it any easier, but . . .

FALCON: YOU know? You know what it's like to be sneered at by your own people?! I got news for you! That's the trouble with you whites! You think you've got all the answers . . . when you don't even ask the right questions! On the day you realize that . . . then maybe you'll have the right to say you know how it is!

CAP: Okay . . . I guess I deserved that . . . ALL whites deserve it! But I think you're intelligent enough to know that anger and hatred won't help either side to reach that day of understanding!

FALCON: Won't it?! I've been thinking like you most of my life . . . and what has it gotten me?! My people call me Uncle Tom . . . and the girl I love won't give me the time of day! I don't know how that looks to you . . . but in my book, it makes me a failure!

CAP: That's not true! You've done a great deal of good here . . . not only as a social worker . . . but as the Falcon, too!

FALCON: Yeah?! Well if that's true . . . then how come I'm ashamed to show my face on the street?! But I'm gonna change all of that! I'm gonna be proud, baby . . . proud to be black . . . and proud to be me! And it's all gonna start right now! As far as you and I as a team . . . you can forget it![22]

Soon after the conclusion of the Friedrich plotline involving race relations in the urban ghetto, Marvel brought writer Steve Englehart onboard to keep the "relevant narrative" style going. Englehart had begun at Marvel as an artist assistant to Neal Adams but had recently transitioned to writing and was selected to fill in when Friedrich went on vacation. When Englehart took over *Captain America and the Falcon*, it was under imminent threat of cancellation. Rethinking the core identity of the Captain America character, Englehart decided to create political tension within the character, redefining the significance of his mission:

> Well, *Captain America*, to me, was a philosophy in a sense. . . . *Captain America* was clearly the book that had the least reason for existence. . . . [O]nce [Cap] got his own book, clearly, Stan had no idea what to do with it. It was just sort of bad super-hero stuff without a purpose or anything. But the problem wasn't just Stan. Everybody was having difficulty with a character who was supposed to be a patriotic example of America when the Vietnam War was going on and when people were very much up in arms about what America was doing, and so forth, and it was like nobody was able to wrap his mind around doing a patriotic character in a sort of anti-American time. . . . I could see [Cap] pretty clearly as a guy who exemplified the best that America had to offer, not what it *was* offering. And so right from the start, I was just doing this sort of philosophical take on this guy.[23]

Friedrich's story had blended together a world-order conspiracy, marrying an international conspiracy force that had ties with an American organized crime syndicate to a hidden organization of former Nazis. This level of intrigue and sophistication was not common in comic books at that time,[24] and Englehart built onto this style of narrative by having Cap fight a Cold War doppelgänger (the retconned 1954 Captain America) whose paranoid right-wing tendencies clashed powerfully with Cap's social conscience. In 1972, reimagining the Marvel continuity to reinclude the 1950s Captain America adventures that Lee and Kirby had omitted, Englehart crafted a story in which a separate individual had taken up the mantle of Captain America during the McCarthy era, but whose increasing paranoia had led to his capture by the government. A disgruntled FBI agent, angry at Nixon's decision to visit China, releases the 1950s Captain America to unleash the conservative voice on "the red tide."[25]

The 1950s Captain America and Bucky represent the worst attributes of their era. They encounter the Falcon first, whom they enrage by calling a "colored creep."[26] Once they have subdued him, the 1950s Captain America further distinguishes himself from the primary character by declaring, "Now we'll make him tell us where that mug calling himself Captain America is hiding—even if it means—TORTURE!"[27] In the course of their schemes, the duo express many objectionable attitudes toward African Americans and other races but also display an ideological fervor against the progressive spirit of the age, which leads them to target the modern Captain America as its embodiment.

In this way, Englehart was able to use two Captain Americas to bring two views of America into direct conflict and engage the conservative voice (through historical McCarthyism). As scholar Jason Dittmer explains,

> In this case, it is not just *Captain America* that is being "retconned" but it is the established national narrative of the United States. The original Captain America, representing the spirit and ideals of America, has been purified—connecting the 1960s liberal movement with the ideals of World War II, while marginalizing the perceived conservativism of America in the 1950s. In addition, it leaves ambivalent the relationship between America and communism, which for the young and liberal readership was not necessarily the biggest threat to the United States.[28]

The modern, liberal Cap confronts and soundly defeats the 1950s conservative Cap by playing on his hateful paranoia.[29] Though the doppelgänger is stronger, the narrative portrays him as inferior in several ways: his costume rips during the battle, his shield easily dents, he makes wild logical errors, his prowess is not on par with the original Captain America. In this way, the narrative asserts that the conservative fervor of the 1950s is a "cheap copy" of the earned patriotism of the generation that served in World War II.

Dittmer further explains in his analysis of the storyline how the story invoked ideological statements about the cultural conflict: "The retcon that created the character (as a separate entity from the 'real' Captain America) was intended to establish the continuity of American national identity from the wartime righteousness of the 1940s directly to the liberal idealism of the 1960s, excising the red baiting McCarthyism of the 1950s from both the continuity of the Captain America character and from the overarching national myth."[30] Though the modern Cap defeats his doppelgänger foe, he is visibly shaken by the confrontation, realizing that his fierce patriotism is not altogether different from that of his adversary. He laments that he isn't sure that had he been active during the 1950s, his attitudes would have been dramatically different from those of his foe. And of course, this is an ironic ideological element, for the characters were originally one and the same. Nor are Cap's attitudes in his original 1940s adventures quite so defensible as the reader is led to believe.

This 1950s retcon Captain America would later return as the leader of a neo-Nazi organization. Through the course of that story, the character would redeem himself by rejecting his paranoid and prejudiced ways and committing suicide, symbolically destroying the legitimacy of the conservative voice of the 1950s and purifying himself through the liberal multiculturalist values of the 1970s.[31]

Another of Englehart's stories involved a young conscientious objector named Dave Cox.[32] Cap's initial encounter with Cox causes him to wonder about the man's fortitude, considering his views as a conscientious objector, but after Cox is tortured by supervillains but doesn't betray his friends, he gains Cap's respect. This adjustment in attitude provides Cap with yet another opportunity to embrace the progressive values of his age, and he declares, "He has HIS way, and I have MINE—But Dave Cox is no coward! He was willing to die in order to protect us—without violating his beliefs! His beliefs . . . aren't the ones I was taught—but I guess things do change with time."[33] This framing explains how Cap struggles against the earlier conceptions of his own masculinity to incorporate a sentiment of constraint, which would be a mainstay of his presented character in nearly all future portrayals. A few issues later Englehart revealed in print that he was personally a conscientious objector who had been honorably discharged from the armed services, an admission that won him respect from several fans.[34]

Englehart's next two storylines would weave current events and fiction into a narrative that has long been considered one of the classic pieces of Captain America lore. In Englehart's "Secret Empire" story arc, Cap becomes the target of a slanderous advertising campaign produced by a conservative coalition, the Committee to Regain America's Principles (the implied acronym, CRAP, is never actually used). The Viper, a costumed foe who was once an advertising executive (invoking this history in perhaps the most amusingly indirect racial epithet of the series during a battle with the Falcon when he declares the hero to be a "fool . . . typical of your demographic segment!"[35]) initiates the slander campaign, justifying it with a cynical critique of the American public:

> VIPER: I'm ringing up my old partner at the ad agency. He's as crooked as I am, but he still plays the game of seeming honest. Hello, Quentin? Jordan Dixon—alias the Viper—here. Listen, sweetie-baby, I want you to start an ad campaign for me—the un-selling of Captain America! Sure—they sold the president through the media! We'll use the same techniques in reverse to convince the great unwashed that C.A. is a glory-grabbing vigilante, despoiling the name of America!
>
> EEL: You and your nutty ideas.
>
> VIPER: Wait and see, Leo. Never underestimate the power of advertising. For the majority of the public, "all they know is what they read in the papers"—or see on television! I've hawked absolutely worthless products with tremendous success, using the right method. This will work . . . [36]

The leader of the coalition bears more than a passing resemblance to H. R. Haldeman, who spent twenty years working for J. Walter Thompson in advertising.[37]

Throughout the next dozen issues, Cap and his colleagues hear the resulting advertisements largely as a background element of the comic narrative. Each appears written in the political advertising language of the day:

Good day, my fellow Americans. This is a man many of you know: Captain America. For years, Captain America has been a one-man vigilante committee, attacking anyone he deemed a criminal. Some were clearly such—but others were private citizens—men the recognized legal agencies had never molested! In fact, recognized legal agencies are hardly ever involved in Captain America's headlong pursuit of his individual concept of law and order. He is unwelcome, for example, at SHIELD. Who is Captain America? He wraps himself in our nation's proud flag, yet no one in our government is responsible—or will take responsibility for—his actions. Perhaps the reason for this lies in chemicals—which, many allege, created his unnatural abilities in a secret laboratory! Yet he continues to roam the streets, striking at will at those who displease him! He claims he does it for all America! YOUR America? <This public reminder paid for by the Committee to Regain America's Principles>[38]

As the propaganda campaign works and the public turns against him, Cap works to penetrate a secret society of conspirators and prevent them from taking over the US government. At the core of the conflict is the battle over truth and image.

At this point, reality collided with Englehart's story when the Watergate scandal rocked American politics. Taking his cue from current events, Englehart concluded the story in mid-1974 in *Captain America* volume 1, number 175, with Cap chasing the leader of the Secret Empire (Number One) into the White House. He corners the clandestine leader and unmasks him, only to discover to his shock that the leader is actually the president (the connection is merely asserted—Englehart never shows the character's face, only Cap's reaction), who commits suicide.[39]

The effectiveness of this representation led Max Skidmore and Joey Skidmore to reflect in a scholarly article a few years later that comic narratives (and the Secret Empire storyline in particular) serve as a reflection of the political conditions in which they are produced.[40] Englehart suggested in a recent interview that he hadn't set out to chase current events but that the events that unfolded during the Watergate scandal had compelled him to address them in Cap's narrative:

> [F]or people who weren't around then, it was very much like having this epic movie unfolding day by day. Every day there was forward motion in the storyline, there were new revelations, there were machinations, there were Senate hearings, and it really was the whole summer. So it seemed impossible to me that Captain America could not pay attention to it. . . . I started shaping a story which hadn't really started off in that direction . . . shaping it toward the whole thing where the president blows his brains out in the White House and Captain America is disillusioned, that America doesn't believe in what he believes in at the time. And then it just seemed obvious that he would give up being Captain America . . . it was like every story led into every other story, and there was no long-term plan.[41]

This presidential assassination led Cap into Englehart's next story arc, in which the hero, his faith in the US government shaken, spends an entire issue pondering whether he can continue to serve America in his official role. After speaking with several of his friends and colleagues, he ultimately decides to quit, a move Englehart claims he intended to address feelings of disenchantment and betrayal brought about by the Watergate scandal:

> [W]hen he quit being Captain America, that was sort of the culmination of all that stuff. He did stand for something better than America was. America had really gone off the track . . . it was a thing for him to really come to terms with—not for me, but for him—to come to terms with the fact that what he stood for, what he had signed up to be back in 1941 at the beginning of the greatest generation, had gone to the Watergate point, and so I thought it was worth doing an entire issue where he just talked about that.[42]

Cap would give up his patriotic identity for nearly a year before finding a way to restore his faith in America. Adopting a new identity as "Nomad" (a wanderer without a country), Rogers continues his liberal crusade for justice without the baggage of cultural history, but he is eventually jarred from this approach when a young gymnast who takes up the Captain America identity is savagely murdered by the Red Skull. Pondering this turn of events, Rogers, in his new identity, is afforded the opportunity to grapple verbally with the disenchantment of the age as he struggles to regain his faith:

I'll fight the Skull as the Nomad . . . but Captain America is dead! He died the day his ideals did! The Skull is looking for a ghost—a phantom . . . and a fool! C.A. lived in a DREAM world! He was born in 1941, a time when the America Dream filled all our hearts! We WILLINGLY went to war against the Red Skull's kind, because they wanted to destroy that dream! But now, with the White House suicide . . . and everything since . . . ! From the moment I returned to life in 1964, at the beginning of our Viet Nam war, I felt out of my time—but it took Number One [President Richard Nixon's alter ego] to make me see how wrong things had gone since I'd been away! The people who had custody of the American Dream had abused both IT and US! There was NO WAY I could keep calling myself "Captain America," because the others who acted in America's name were every bit as bad . . . as . . . the . . . Red . . . Skull . . . ! (silence) . . . every bit as bad as the Red Skull . . . and yet, I didn't want to know about those people! The Skull was okay to oppose, and still is . . . but Number One wasn't, because he was supposed to be on our side! Oh Lord . . . if I wasn't prepared for any and all threats to the American Dream, then what was I doing as Captain America? I'm not the poor, abused hero I've been telling myself I was! I'm not even a fool! I'm a failure! I thought I knew who the good guys and the bad guys were! I thought, as USUAL, that things weren't as complex as they are . . . and I couldn't understand how the good guys could put their faith in a man so bad! But my naiveté is MY problem—not America's! The COUNTRY didn't let me down—I let HER down, by not being all that I could be! If I'd paid more attention to the way the American REALITY differed from the American Dream—If I hadn't gone around thinking the things I believe were thirty years out of date—then I might have uncovered Number One, and stopped him, before it was too late! I guess . . . what I'm saying is . . . there has to be SOMEBODY who'll fight for the dream, against any foe . . . somebody who'll do the job I started—right! And God knows I can't let ANYBODY ELSE run the risks that job entails for me![43]

Resuming his role as Captain America, the hero once again prepares to go after the Red Skull. But he renews his mission with a new appreciation and understanding of his place in society:

> [B]eing Nomad was no mistake! Being forced into a greater awareness of corruption, deceit, and the madness of power was no mistake—even if the initial shock was almost more than I could bear. I did react more with my heart than my head—but it forced me into a great awareness of myself, as a man—and as a superhero, apart from the living legend I had become. I learned what makes me tick—something I could never have done while I was living my life trapped deep in a rut! I never intended to go back to being C.A., but it was only through stepping outside myself that I could gain a perspective on going back in! No, I may not have always made the best decisions—but nothing I did can be called a mistake! I've broken away from the blindness of the past, which can only mean a better future for both myself—and the country![44]

Having declared this sense of evolution, Cap returns to his public mission and is greeted by thousands of citizens who turn out to express their support of him, representing the resolution of the Nixon administration's cultural betrayals.

The following storyline (Englehart's last Cap arc) quickly returned to the problem of racial inequality in America as Cap discovers that the Falcon has a criminal past and may have been a plant by the Red Skull, who boldly claims, "After so many years, I knew you well, Captain America! I knew exactly what kind of man would most appeal to your sniveling liberalism:—an upright, cheerful negro, with a love of the same 'brotherhood' you cherish!"[45]

Nor was this the only racial undertone of the story, as Shield agents Gabe Jones and Peggy Carter begin an interracial romance, the first in a comic book among recurring characters. This fact enrages the racist Red Skull (who is, after all, a Nazi), whose obsession with the relationship nearly proves to be the distraction that undermines his plans: "Only one thing taints the joy I feel at this moment . . . a mere detail, of course . . . and yet . . . and yet I cannot chase it from my mind! That SHIELD agent, Gabriel Jones—that black schwein—with the WHITE WOMAN!"[46]

After a dispute with new editor in chief Gerry Conway,[47] Englehart quit Marvel Comics, leaving the series in the midst of this plot without resolving the Falcon's fate: "I was leaving that for the next writer to play with—was it true or was it mindf#ck?—so I have no idea what I'd have done with it. I know a guy like Sam Wilson was, in some circles, too good to be true—and in others, a legitimate good guy."[48] John Warner, Tony Isabella (who would later create Black Lightning, another iconic African American hero), and Bill Mantlo continued the arc as the Falcon faces legal charges for crimes committed in his former life. Suddenly saddled with baggage from his past, the Falcon (in his new "Snap" persona), who once stood for justice, becomes wary of the courts, claiming, "BULL! I may have been out of it for six years—but Snap Wilson remembers how white courts treat blacks, Mister! I'd rather bank on tryin' to escape!"[49] All of the capital and trust in the justice system for which Sam Wilson had argued is replaced with a stereotypical mistrust:

CAP: Why don't you ease up and let us try to help you!
FALCON: Yeah, huh? It ain't your neck, Cap! I hear they got the
    noose up a bit higher for all us basketball playing blacks!
CAP: Cut that kind of talk, Sam! It's not true and you know it!
FALCON: Look man—you're the one with America as a last name!
    Me—I'm just an ex-slave, fella—and this country ain't never
    done anything worth a plugged nickel for me![50]

The Falcon is found guilty of the charges in court and given a commuted sentence, but the damage was done. Fans reacted poorly to the retroactive origin given to the Falcon, expressing offense at the retconned criminal past and the notion that the first African American superhero was secretly an urban hood and could exist as a hero only because of an artificial scheme (and to some fans the sequence in issue 186 in which the Red Skull makes the Falcon squawk like a chicken came off particularly demeaning[51]). This sour taste further compromised the Falcon's popularity, which waned as the series continued. The hero who had once inspired some fans to see a positive role model for African Americans now became a representation of inequality:

> The Falcon's back story bombshell suggested a troubling dynamic about successful blacks. Even the most righteous black person may have hidden beneath their professional and cheerful veneer a corrupt alter ego informed by a black ghetto environment. Given that blaxploitation cinema frequently presented black protagonists with a criminal background that validated his/her status as an authentic antihero, the "Snap" Wilson storyline might have been an attempt to make the character edgy and relevant. This might address the source of the influence that informed the direction the character took, but it does not diminish the damage done to the Falcon to symbolically expressing a post–Black Power moral authority concerning racial inequality in America.[52]

Even after the Falcon had received wings and the power of flight (from the Black Panther, no less, legitimizing the empowerment from Wilson's ethnic roots), he still seemed to many fans to be living in the shadow of his supersoldier partner, a condition that served for some as an uncomfortable metaphor for the African American experience in America.[53] *Jack Kirby Collector* contributor Jerry Boyd, an African American, recently expressed his reservations about the character: "The thing that I disliked the most was his early 'I've gotta live up to Cap's training and trust' attitude . . . it may have been better if he'd acquired his powers/abilities independently of Steve Rogers."[54]

Englehart's contribution to *Captain America* received accolades from many sources. Fans in the letter columns praised the relevance of his storyline. Sales improved: when he inherited the title, *Captain America* was among the worst performers; his run catapulted the title into the bestselling series Marvel possessed at the time. The Convention of Modern Language Associations presented Englehart with a literary award. And his peers noted his influence.

Contemporary comic book writer Joe Casey explains that Englehart's style revolutionized the way comic book stories were written: "The way

Englehart wrote long-form comic books in the early '70s set the template for just about every super-hero writer that came after. . . . [H]is ability to craft long arcs that would start small and then build into a huge, dramatic crescendo and then scale back and start the whole process over again showed the rest of us how to maintain interest and energy on a series over a period of years."[55] Ed Brubaker, the much-praised author of the fifth volume of *Captain America,* recently suggested that Englehart's take on the character left a lasting imprint: "I think it was the genesis of the whole thing about Cap not serving the government, but the ideals of America, too, which has been carried over for decades now."[56]

Of course, Captain America was not the only Marvel hero to experience a progressive renaissance. In a three-issue arc in 1969, Spider-Man, in his secret identity Peter Parker, encounters a campus demonstration and makes waves with his friends when he declares that he won't join their ranks until he understands both sides of the issue under protest.[57] Two years later the company would publish three issues of *The Amazing Spider-Man* without the Comics Code seal in order to embed an antidrug message into the story arc,[58] one of the earliest efforts to address the topic in popular culture[59] and an effort that eventually led to the first major revision of the Comics Code.

During this time, DC Comics followed suit as Neal Adams and Denny O'Neil teamed up to produce a run on *Green Lantern/Green Arrow* that would grapple with "relevant" issues such as racism, poverty, governmental corruption, overpopulation, religious cults, and pollution.[60] Much as with the relationship between Captain America and the Falcon, the relationship between the duty-driven Green Lantern and the anarchist Green Arrow represents tensions between the political Right and the political Left in framing and discussing the social problems of the age.

Much of the socially relevant spirit in Captain America's narrative dissolved when Jack Kirby returned to the book in *Captain America and the Falcon* volume 1, number 193.[61] Reportedly not "particularly" wanting to take on his patriotic creation, Kirby refused to read the previous issues of *Captain America* written by others.[62] Assuming the writing and artistic duties, Kirby launched into an arc that tapped into the science fiction themes he had been pursuing in his contemporary work, culminating with an American Bicentennial–related conclusion in issue 200, which serendipitously coincided with a July 1976 release date.[63] (On the eve of the American Bicentennial, Cap and the Falcon thwart a plan to undo the American Revolution and return control of American society to a group of wealthy American elites.) This run was distinguished (or, perhaps more accurately, gained notoriety) by isolation: during Kirby's run, Cap rarely interacted with the rest of the Marvel Universe events or its characters. And when one of his early villains called "the Swine" seemed to resemble John Lennon, fans and Marvel creators alike began to grumble in the press about the series.[64]

For his part, Kirby tried to incorporate the racial tension between Cap and the Falcon, but the execution often came off clumsy, as in the following exchange:

> CAP: All kidding aside . . . I—I dreamt about my ancestor Steven Rogers. He fought in the Revolution, you know!
>
> FALCON: Hooray for him! Chances are that he owned a farm with a lot of singing black slaves!
>
> CAP: I can't really say, friend . . . He left a diary when he died . . . It remained in the family for generations . . . But, I don't recall reading anything about slaves!
>
> FALCON: Don't go on with that hero jive! Your boy had a stake in the revolution! My family still worked that farm . . .
>
> CAP: Probably true! Yet that was a time when men began to turn away from injustice! It took two hundred years, Falcon . . . but this country's grown up!
>
> FALCON: Jive! It's STILL trying, friend! I'll stake my life on that![65]

Where Englehart and Friedrich had presented a Captain America who was increasingly aware of his racial insensitivity, Kirby's Cap seemed more innocently defensive of the white status quo. And the Falcon seemed to revert back to a two-dimensional stereotype, such as when he ponders his plight on the way to defuse the Madbomb: "It's a cruddy job to be doing, in the very hour of America's Bicentennial Celebration!—An ironic deal for a black man, too!!—the direct descendant of a cotton-pickin' slave

. . . Perhaps, this is the very reason that a black man must do this job—so that slavery can never happen again! Not here—not anywhere!"[66]

Because of either the awkwardness of the creators who inherited him or the negative perceptions associated with the Falcon's origin, the character continued to decline in popularity. Within the narrative, he and Captain America slowly drifted apart. As Cap and his alter ego Steve Rogers slowly developed a personal life more consistent with the 1980s American culture, there seemed little room for the Falcon in his daily life. The Falcon would end the 1970s as a member of S.H.I.E.L.D. (Supreme Headquarters, International Espionage, Law-Enforcement Division), training superpowered agents[67] and interacting with Cap only in brief encounters. Even after several rehabilitation attempts, the first African American superhero still to this day doesn't seem to capture the fan popularity of black heroes such as Luke Cage and DC's John Stewart (the African American Green Lantern).

The Liberal Crusader Confronts the Feminist Movement and Social Causes

Besides the ever-present issue of race relations, the 1970s Captain America confronted other social issues. In a two-story arc spanning *Captain America and the Falcon* volume 1, numbers 135 and 136, Cap and the Falcon battle the Mole Man and his minions, who live beneath the surface of the earth. The mole people are stirred up because of a military project called "Project Earth Dig," an attempt to dig the "deepest hole on earth" for the purpose of disposing of America's atomic waste. After Cap falls into the hole, and he and the Falcon encounter the Mole Man, they return to the surface to warn the military off the project, and the general in charge of the project declares, "Maybe this is a lesson for all of us, gentlemen. We can no longer despoil the planet we live on—sooner or later, we'll all have to pay the price."[68]

Captain America also interacted with the feminist movement in several stories, though in embarrassing ways. The focus of this discourse was Cap's relationship with S.H.I.E.L.D.'s Agent 13, Sharon Carter. The younger sister of Peggy Carter (who herself had a brief romance with Cap as Agent 13 of Army Intelligence in the 1940s *Captain America Comics* stories), Sharon embodied the plight of the 1970s feminist—or at least embodied the view of 1970s feminism held by the all-male writers of the Marvel titles: she and Cap loved each other yet argued over who would need to quit his or her job to make their relationship work.

Although the 1970s Sharon Carter works for the world's most elite military agency, she displays troubling stereotypical traits. When Cap emerges from the "deepest hole in the earth" in *Captain America and the Falcon* volume 1, number 137, Sharon faints.[69] Whenever Sharon expresses intuition or caution, Cap often disparages her gender:

> CAPTAIN AMERICA: Safe? What are you talking about, Sharon?
> SHARON: I'm not sure! I just know I've got bad vibes! There's something wrong!
> CAP: You bet there's something wrong! The Falcon needs help—and he's gonna get it. This is no time to go feminine on me, honey.[70]

Sharon apparently holds a PhD in metaphysical psychology and heads up the S.H.I.E.L.D. Psych Squad, which Director Nick Fury describes as "hyped-up woman's intuition."[71] In *Captain America and the Falcon* volume 1, number 144, Sharon leads a new assault task force composed of female agents called the "Femme Force." As she and her fellow female agents complete an impressive test of their skills, Sharon addresses Cap:

> SHARON: RIGHT ON SISTERS! [to Captain America] If THIS doesn't make you a believer in the Women's Lib movement . . . I don't know what will!
> CAPTAIN AMERICA: Well . . . let's just say it makes me a believer in the SHIELD Femme Force . . . and let it slide at that![72]

Although Cap was transformed from a conservative on race relations to a race activist, he never quite seems to embrace gender equality in his 1970s stories. Perhaps he cannot be blamed, for the female characters who surround him never seem to evolve past painful gender stereotypes (and perhaps these portrayals are unsurprising, given the lack of female writers during this period), as when Sharon and one of her subordinates on Femme Force compete with each other to impress Captain America on a mission, even to the point of compromising the success of the operation.[73]

Revising the Greatest Generation

The new liberal values Captain America embodied would soon be projected on his past as Marvel editor Roy Thomas created a title called *The Invaders* that depicted the early wartime adventures of the original Timely superheroes. The concept was reportedly created when DC Comics writer Dennis O'Neil and Thomas conspired to create an informal crossover between the two companies.[74] Developing loose but recognizable character types based on the primary DC heroes on the Justice League roster, Thomas had the Squadron Sinister (later to become the Squadron Supreme) square off against the Avengers in *The Avengers* volume 1, number 70.[75]

In the following issue, Thomas needed another team of opponents, so he had the team face off with wartime versions of Captain America, the Sub-Mariner, and the original Human Torch.[76] Thomas had grown up reading Timely comics (when he was hired at Marvel, he represented the beginning of the first wave of fan-creators, individuals who had grown up as fans of the properties they were to eventually work on), and he soon began to lobby Lee for a new series based on the original heroes' adventures. The first issue brought the core members of the team together (the original three Timely heroes, plus Bucky and the Torch's sidekick, Toro) and retold Cap's origin, reconciling many of the conflicting details presented in previous renditions. For example, the scientist who invented the supersoldier serum had alternatively been referred to as "Dr. Reinstein" and "Dr. Erskine." Thomas reconciled the names by explaining that the name "Dr. Erskine" was a code name to mask the scientist's identity from Nazi spies. By now, several renditions of the origin either had Cap intentionally killing the Nazi agent who had killed Dr. Reinstein or made the assassin's death an accident, either because Rogers accidentally knocked him into electrical equipment or because the agent himself blindly rushed into the equipment. Thomas chose the latter form, having Rogers attempt to warn off the agent.[77] Thomas would also retell the origin story two years later in *Captain America and the Falcon* volume 1, number 215, and in that version Captain America appears to intentionally knock the agent into the equipment.[78]

But within the pages of *The Invaders*, Cap is no killer. Issue 15 establishes that Cap has been operating for about a year,[79] positioning the story in the first issue as one of Cap's first career missions, and from the beginning Thomas's Cap does not resort to lethal violence. In issue 18, Cap is very clear about this fact as he considers making an exception of Hitler, who has captured his teammates: "ON TO BERLIN! And, if Adolf Hitler has harmed Bucky—or ANY of the Invaders—by the time we reach them—then, for the first time in his life—Captain America will commit COLD-BLOODED MURDER!! THIS I SWEAR!"[80] Nor would Cap resort to torture, as he demonstrates in issue 3 when he stops the Sub-Mariner from beating information out of a Nazi U-boat captain:

> CAP: That's enough, man! Stop it! That's not the way we do things!
> NAMOR: But—he's a lousy Nazi—!
> CAP: And we're no better, if we start using THEIR methods—beating up defenseless prisoners! We're in this war, Namor, and we're going to win it—but let's make sure we're still the "good guys" when we do! Or else—we don't deserve to win![81]

Of course, these statements appear quite rich coming from the hero who in the original version of his World War II exploits tortured suspected agents, killed more than a million of the enemy, and struck civilians in the street who spoke in what he considered unpatriotic ways.

But just as Lee and Kirby had done in the early 1960s, Thomas carefully rewrote the vintage tales for *The Invaders*. Most of the title's plotlines were new, with Thomas introducing Axis supervillains such as Agent Axis (who evolved from the Golden Age "Man with no Face"), Master Man, Warrior Woman, the Shark, and others. New heroes included Union Jack (retconned as a World War I superhero returning to the field) and Spitfire. But many of the characters Thomas used had actually operated during the 1940s (the Red Skull, the Whizzer, Ms. America, the Destroyer, etc.), and

Thomas exerted great care to present selected stories and elements from that era that didn't contradict the new moral tendencies of the heroes, in particular Captain America. As the series progressed, the past increasingly came to reflect the political present.

The Patriotism of the Liberal Crusader

During the 1970s, the patriotism represented in Captain America's mission went through a strikingly visible transformation. Beginning the decade in an identity crisis in which the "Man out of Time" appeared to lose his bearings completely and took to the open road to discover himself, Cap emerged as a liberal champion of social justice, becoming a voice against racial discrimination, poverty, McCarthyism, government corruption, conservative propaganda, the abuse of the environment, and gender inequality (though the latter only in the most superficial sense).

But, of course, once Captain America became a liberal crusader, his new status created uncomfortable impressions about his past. One would expect that the social problems he began to recognize would impugn his sense of honor and duty for having defended a kind of freedom that did not extend to all citizens. However, Captain America was spared this indignity, for he does not seem to reflect on the culpability of his role in maintaining a collection of unjust social norms, even as those around him (in particular the Falcon) appear to arrive at this observation. Instead, he experiences yet another crisis of identity in which he begins to recover memories of his childhood that suggest he grew up a pacifist who went to college to avoid World War II and became Captain America only after his elder brother was killed at Pearl Harbor.[82] These memories would later be undermined as false implants, but within the narrative they served to suggest that Captain America's liberal spirit was not quite as recent a development as the long-term reader might have concluded at the time.

And, of course, the narrative presented in *The Invaders* supports the notion that Cap has always been an idealist, a peaceful man driven to restrained violence by the circumstances in the world (a classic embodiment of the American monomyth). To achieve this storyline, history is revised, blurred, and reconditioned to fit present understandings. As psychologist Frederic Bartlett observed, human beings naturally refine their history by altering details during recollection.[83] This reinterpretation process is what psychologists call "destructive updating" because the original memories of an event are often replaced by the newer interpretations formed of the events,[84] a process Maurice Halbwachs describes as "a reconstruction of the past achieved with data borrowed from the present."[85] And with those memories comes a rewriting of history, a purposeful reconstruction of the nature of the past in order to make it align with the understandings of the present.

How else could a hero responsible for using a weapon of mass destruction ("atom-water") to kill thousands of Japanese soldiers,[86] trapping and drowning an estimated one million Japanese foot soldiers,[87] boasting over the death of the Nazi agent who had killed his "father,"[88] and injecting an unconscious Nazi soldier with poison[89] claim that "for the first time in his life" he might commit murder?

Of course, Thomas was merely adapting Captain America to the conventions and spirit of the age, as Geoff Klock suggests is required for superheroes' long-term survival.[90] But with what effect? Although we will see in upcoming chapters that Captain America continued to evolve with each new era of American culture, it is certainly true that such evolutions began with a particular understanding of the character. And the new history codified through *The Invaders* would become the new standard for Cap's narrative: Americans don't kill, for we are the "good guys"; therefore, Captain America did not kill his Axis opponents in World War II. And this understanding of the character would become a central tenet of Captain America's identity: the 1980s and 1990s storylines would contain narrative tension around the necessity of terminal violence—tension created by the assumption that Captain America does not kill and does not use projectile weapons. And yet even a cursory examination of the 1940s Captain America comic books proves otherwise. To be fair to Thomas, writing about the 1940s narratives in the mid-1970s did bring another powerful variable into the mix: the Comics Code. The fact is that Cap's original adventures could not have been published in the 1970s because of the wanton violence contained in the plotlines. And yet it is also clear that Thomas (and Kirby before him in the mid-1960s) was not merely making implicit the violence that was explicit in the 1940s, for he had Captain America make strong and unequivocal declarations about his avoidance of mortal violence as a tool for justice. For the next two decades, it would be assumed that Cap doesn't and hasn't ever taken a life, for he is the ultimate "good guy."

6

The Hypercommercialized Leader (1979–1990)

The 1980s brought with them a new attitude about American culture. After the politically turbulent 1970s, the election of Ronald Reagan and the revival of the Republican Party brought a new mood to American society.

Within the walls of Marvel Comics, a culture change similar in nature was occurring. After Stan Lee stepped down as editor in chief to become the company's president, Roy Thomas held the post for about two years before he relinquished it to become an editor-writer. In the following years, a revolving door of four more editors in chief in as many years assumed and then abandoned the post until Jim Shooter took it and held it for nine years. Shooter, who sold his first story to DC Comics at age twelve, represented a second wave of fan-creators entering the industry (much as Thomas had represented the initial wave).

Unlike his predecessors, Shooter was interested in innovating on the business side of the company, and he quickly began to confer with Marvel president James Galton on a range of matters, including changing the way in which Marvel creators were compensated, launching concerted efforts to get Marvel properties on television and in feature films, and coordinating more tightly the way in which Marvel characters and stories fit together in the shared Marvel Universe.

An early shift occurred with the properties Marvel licensed from owners outside the company. After Martin Goodman's departure, Marvel had struggled to maintain profitability. Roy Thomas had found success licensing the adaptation of the *Star Wars* franchise in the late 1970s, which

Shooter later claimed saved the company from folding.[1] Marvel soon licensed other television and feature-film properties for adaptation, such as *Battlestar Galactica* in 1979 and *Star Trek* in 1980.

Profits increased, writers and artists began to receive more compensation, and soon Marvel's editorial staff and the number of publications expanded. Meanwhile, an increasing number of comic book specialty stores were entering the market, built around the business of selling back issues of comics, and Marvel soon began to shift to direct sales because comic stores were better than newsstands at promoting the books to fans. This arrangement in turn influenced the company's editorial decisions, as it began to produce certain books only for the direct sales market aimed more at comic book fans than at general readers.

Embracing the rising fan culture surrounding its products, Shooter began to push the company to produce resource materials to help fans perceive new layers of significance to the characters and stories, while making the management of the increasingly complex Marvel Universe easier for writers and artists. To do this, Marvel continued its tradition of embracing fan contributions to the construction of the shared universe.

The first prong of this effort arose from fan culture. George Olshevesky was a college student who had begun circulating indexes of the events and major character events found in his Marvel collection. The benefit of these documents was the communication of knowledge without the potential depreciation in value of one's collection: "Instead of having to pull out my collection to find out something, instead of having to handle all the different comics and risk damaging their condition and thus lowering their value, all I have to do is flip through a couple of the indices and I quickly get everything I want," Olshevesky explained.[2] When Olshevesky contacted Marvel Comics to obtain permission to disseminate the indexes to a wider fan base, Marvel offered to publish them as an official record of the Marvel Universe's event. Officially sanctioned, Olshevesky began to rework his index of *The Amazing Spider-Man*, which Marvel published in January 1976. He reportedly started with Spider-Man because of the character's tenure at college, which provided a baseline timeframe to begin building a calendar for the rest of the Marvel Universe: "If we know how many years Peter Parker spent in college," he stated, "then we know how many years passed for the Fantastic Four during the same interval, and for the Hulk and for all the other Marvel characters because, as I've discovered, the different comics more or less keep pace with each other. In terms of Marvel Time, they are all probably within six or seven months of each other."[3]

In all, a dozen indexes were produced, each containing a brief synopsis, extended notes, a chronological listing of the contents of each issue relevant to the character, cross-reference indexes listing appearances of prominent characters, and a cover gallery.

The second prong in the systemization effort was the creation of *The Official Handbook of the Marvel Universe,* a "kind of encyclopedia in comics format."[4] This initiative also grew with support from the fan community. Marvel writer Mark Gruenwald produced a three-page feature in *The Amazing Spider-Man Annual* volume 1, number 15, that compared Spider-Man's strength to that of other characters, creating an informal taxonomy.[5] Gruenwald encouraged fans to respond with comments and disagreements, and after the feature received more mail than any other comic, Editor in Chief Jim Shooter commissioned a "Super-Specs" book, which grew into the handbook. This serialized comic contained comprehensive files for each of the major characters in the Marvel Universe, including detailed background histories; first appearances; a ranking system for attributes and abilities; and physical characteristics. The result was a reference manual for fans and creators alike that allowed individual characters to be researched and compared with one another.

Shooter had longed to create a systematic record of Marvel heroes for himself and was reportedly concerned that with more than two decades of Marvel Universe history, many of the new readers might not possess enough context to relate to contemporary storylines.[6] The success of the index and handbook led Shooter to initiate the third phase in the effort: combining the research in both to produce a series titled *Marvel Saga,* which would place the Marvel stories in chronological context. As editor Danny Fingeroth explained,

> You'd have to be a full-time comics historian to really get the full picture. And you'd have to be a master storyteller to take all the information

about the full backgrounds and interlocking relationships of the characters that has emerged over the twenty-five "real" years that the Marvel
Universe has existed and weave them into a coherent, exciting storyline. . . . We will now have the full story—in correct chronological
order—of how the Marvel Universe came to be as it is today, incorporating facts from all 25 years of Marvel History. You could say that *Saga's*
a companion to *The Official Handbook of the Marvel Universe*, taking
the historical material printed ther [*sic*] and weaving it into the complex
tapestry that is the Marvel Universe.[7]

Marvel Saga interspersed a textual history with panels reprinted alongside original art from the earlier Marvel works. As Fingeroth said, "I think
it's important to show the art from these original stories. It's going back
to the source."[8] As a result, Marvel codified the history of its characters,
sorting through discrepancies in the various origins presented over the
years. This codification would have interesting results for fans of Captain
America, in particular those who had been reading the series since the
1960s, longer than some of the younger writers of *Captain America* had
been involved with the character.

Marvel also embraced the fan culture by launching a new fan magazine in 1983 titled *Marvel Age*, which purported to provide an insider
source of information about comic stories before the books were published
(as well as to combat some of the negative press levied by the other independent fan publications) and to provide fans with the information needed
to maintain their collections. As the first issue of *Marvel Age* explained,

There have always been comic fanzines (even before the Marvel Age
began). Fanzines to let you know what's happening, where it's happening, when, who's doing it, how people feel about it, and so on. Marvel
itself has even had a couple, but Marvel Age is the first Marvel-produced
fanzine available to all and sundry, at the inflation-fighting cost of 25¢,
that will tell you everything you want to know in the hallowed halls of
Marvel.

Will there be hype? Sure there will. When we have projects coming
out that we get excited about, we want you to know. We want to try and
transmit some of the enthusiasm that seizes us when exciting projects

come along, or when one of our current titles takes an unexpected twist, gets a hot new artist, or undergoes astounding changes.[9]

Not content with merely dominating the comic book industry, the company also created the division Marvel Press, which concentrated on producing full-color posters and portfolios by Marvel creators.[10] The company also licensed out characters for toys, clothing, and jewelry[11] and even formed a relationship with the game company TSR to produce the *Marvel Super Heroes Role-Playing Game.*[12]

This activity led to a series of projects in which the company created editorial content to support the popularity of action figures and toys. The first such project was G.I. Joe, a toy line the Hasbro toy company had decided to resurrect. Hasbro reportedly came to Marvel with the name "G.I. Joe,"[13] asking for a set of characters and a storyline that was "very military—but not a war comic book"[14] and that could be cross-promoted in a television cartoon to support its new toy line. Marvel creators complied, creating both the dossiers that were printed on the back of the action-figure packaging and the antagonistic terrorist organization Cobra to allow the team to engage in military actions not tied to a specific war context.

This work also resulted in Marvel's *G.I. Joe* series, which served to chronicle the property's narrative as well as to introduce new characters tied to upcoming toy offerings. In late 1984, Larry Hama, writer for the *G.I. Joe* series, explained the relationship between Marvel and Hasbro: "The people at Hasbro come up with the look—a character sketch of what they want to produce, a style. . . . Usually they'll give the character a working title like 'infantry man' or 'anti-tank specialist.' Then I create the name, background, training history, personality—all the stuff that makes him 'real.'"[15]

Another property that received this treatment was *Transformers*. Marvel chief Jim Shooter said he saw the narrative possibilities the moment he saw the toy line: "The Transformers caught my attention right away. Hasbro had already created the toy figures—fascinating robots unlike anything I had ever seen. I saw a wealth of possibilities for these imaginative figures, so I immediately contact Denny O'Neil to help me create a full history for them."[16] Both the G.I. Joe and Transformers property eventually resulted in television cartoons, creating an immensely profitable cross-promotion among the cartoon, comic books, and toys. A third popular toy line that enjoyed a successful television cartoon before Marvel added a comic narrative to its Star line of comics (created for younger readers) was He-Man and the Masters of the Universe.[17]

Although the merchandising and toy markets provided a new revenue stream and increased attention, the ties between the various companies also meant that the characters appearing as action figures and on television were treated conservatively. (Marvel had, by the early 1980s, spun off its own television cartoon offering, including the popular *Spider-Man and His Amazing Friends*.) As the cross-promotions brought new readers to the comic versions of the storylines, Shooter encouraged increasing caution and tighter editorial controls on story development to avoid unnecessary confusion.

Shooter asserted his vision most prominently in Marvel's own cross-promotion event, *Secret Wars*, complete with Mattel action figures and playsets. Originally titled *Cosmic Champions*,[18] the series transported most of Marvel's major heroes and villains to another universe in the multiverse, where they were compelled by a godlike being called the Beyonder to battle for an ultimate prize. The twelve-issue limited series (one of the earliest such series for Marvel) appeared in January 1984; was exclusively written by Jim Shooter, drawn by Mike Zeck, and inked by John Beatty; and was purportedly intended to "permanently alter the histories of everyone from Captain America to the X-Men to Spider-Man!"[19] Some of the changes were matters of minor character development, but some were more dramatic, most notably a costume change for Spider-Man. *Secret Wars* was the first series that brought so many Marvel characters into contact with each other in the same comic, requiring Shooter to regularly consult with all the Marvel characters' writers to keep continuity consistent.[20]

Secret Wars would become the best-selling comic title for several decades,[21] and Shooter would launch a follow-up saga, *Secret Wars II*, the next year. This time set on Earth, the nine-issue series directly crossed over with every Marvel title, resulting in a "forty-issue saga."[22]

Despite the success of these efforts, a segment of the superhero audience expressed critical dissatisfaction with *Secret Wars* and superhero comics in general. By now, many of the fans of the 1960s and 1970s were adults, and they (in particular those raised on the enhanced realism of Marvel comics) began to clamor for stories that better reflected the edgier spirit represented in other forms of popular entertainment.

Frank Miller had introduced fans to a grittier narrative style in his initial run on *Daredevil*, taking antiheroism to a new standard when the assassin/love interest Elektra is introduced in *Daredevil* volume 1, number 169, and then killed in number 181. The conflicting loyalties, moral ambiguity, and loss experienced by the central characters provided a strong contrast to the traditional superhero narrative, which was Miller's goal: "I feel that generally, in comics, the writers tend to make it too easy for the heroes to be virtuous. Since virtue and character are defined by conflict, I set out to test Daredevil's virtue. So I put him in situations where he has to do bad things to achieve good things."[23]

The run was well received by fans, and the stark violence and inner turmoil Miller's Daredevil experiences would soon become a defining trend of late 1980s comic books. Two graphic novels put out by DC Comics in 1986 (one a collected series and one available only as a graphic novel) signaled the beginning of the so-called Dark Age: Alan Moore's *Watchmen*, which served to deconstruct the superhero genre, and Miller's *The Dark Knight Returns*, an exploration of Batman's excessive vigilantism.

Marvel quickly embraced the trend with a violent Vietnam epic titled *The 'Nam*, a limited series, and then *The Punisher*, a regular series offering that artist Mike Zeck compared to Charles Bronson's *Deathwish* movies.[24] The connection between the new breed of superheroes and 1980s action movies was underscored by the publicity leading into the Punisher's regular series:

> He's big. He's mean. And if you're a criminal, you'd better watch out, because he might just be the last thing you ever see.
>
> Could we be talking about Arnold Swartzënegger [sic]? Nope. Chuck Norris? Uh-uh. Sylvester Stallone? Guess again. Clint Eastwood? Close, but no cigar.[25]

Tom DeFalco, the editor who succeeded Shooter, said in 1991 that he believed characters such as the Punisher (Frank Castle) and the X-Men's

Wolverine became popular because of the cultural mood of the 1980s: "[I] t's a way of dealing with society's frustrations. These days, people are upset with the way the law works, upset with politicians, upset with everything. They want to see someone actively solving problems instead of just talking about them. The characters that are popular are the ones people need at the time."[26] New publishers such as Image and Valiant also began to explore the dark themes, and most heroes soon acquired dark and violent tendencies, according to Mark Voger: "With conscience-deprived heroes indistinguishable from their adversaries, the Dark Age was typified by implausible, steroid-inspired physiques, outsized weapons (guns, knives, claws), generous bloodletting, and vigilante justice. While heroes of the Golden and Silver Ages depended solely on their wits and powers to vanquish their adversaries, heroes of the Dark Age were not above flaunting a weapons advantage. Their guns got bigger and bigger. It seemed the bigger the guns, the smaller the heroes' heads."[27] By 1989, the dark trend had become so pronounced that a *New York Times Magazine* writer observed, "[C]omics have forsaken campy repartee and outlandish byzantine plots for a steady diet of remorseless violence."[28]

Captain America did not succumb to this trend, although he was hardly unaffected by it. As the hyperviolence became increasingly popular, it appeared as though Cap's popularity began to slip. Although he had been consistently ranked as the second most popular Marvel hero behind Spider-Man during the 1970s according to *FOOM* fan magazine, in the 1980s the X-Men, X-Factor, and the Punisher dominated the top sales rankings recorded by *Marvel Age*. In fact, during the 1980s only one issue of *Captain America* (number 339) ranked in the top-ten list, and that issue contained a major mutant event tie-in.[29] What's more, when Marvel later expanded the monthly list to include the top-twenty books, *Captain America* volume 1, number 365, was ranked at number 17,[30] suggesting the series had never been among the top tier in terms of sales.

That's not to say the character was unpopular. Although the title's sales could not compare with the sales of the mutant and "dark" books, the readers of *Captain America* and *The Avengers* (which was also notably missing from the top ten during the 1980s) exhibited extreme passion about their hero. One fan, for example, wrote: "Cap's mag is one of the few that stirs my blood and thrills me to the core. Much to my wife's amusement, I actually cheer out loud when I read this mag."[31]

In fact, it may very well be that Cap's resistance to the "dark" trend served to endear him to his fans: "[Captain America's] values and morals are so upstanding and so inspiring (at least *I* think so) that I always feel good after reading an issue or two. Some comic-collecting friends of mine feel that when Cap delivers one of his fancy speeches, they'd rather turn the page. However, I would rather read on and 'listen' to Cap. His speeches are sometimes the highlight of his battles. His monologues about freedom and the American Way always make me feel proud to be a part of this country."[32]

The 1980s Captain America was heavily influenced by his environment. Whereas the 1970s had seen the character evolve from a "man out of time" into a "liberal crusader," the 1980s showed Captain America taking on some of the characteristics of his age.

The Individualist Consumer (1979–1990)

The Captain America of the 1980s became a moralistic icon and was noteworthy for the expressions of wealth and individuality represented through his narratives. Captain American himself began to be treated like a celebrity when citizens encountered him on the street in stories.[33] And his identity as Steve Rogers began to feature more prominently in the storylines. Prior to this period, Steve Rogers lived either in the Avengers mansion to perform his Captain America duties full-time or in barracks or rundown apartments while he served in the army or as a police officer.

But by the 1980s the alter ego, Steve Rogers, had become a focal point for character development. By issue 237, Rogers had become a commercial artist (mostly in advertising at first) and moved into a posh apartment building.[34] This new building housed a diverse group of middle-class tenants who would form a social circle to flesh out the character's personality. Rogers soon began to wear suits when not in uniform and appeared to fit in nicely with the consumer culture of the age. Fan letters expressed pleasure and relief that the writers were allowing their hero to enjoy the comforts of life.[35]

Far from the brooding hero of the 1960s and the cultural warrior of the 1970s, the 1980s Captain America/Steve Rogers appeared oddly at ease and began to exhibit some of the consumerist traits of the era: "I did lose a few decades of my life in suspended animation. I used to resent that a lot," he comments. "America had changed and I just didn't fit in anymore. I guess I wasn't ready to understand things like the Vietnam War and Watergate and all the rest. But I've grown up the past few years. And I've learned that Steve Rogers can take the mask off when he wants to. Someday, the Good Lord willing, I'll be able to take the mask off for good and settle down to a normal life—but only if I start planning for my future now."[36]

And yet the character did not completely transform into a stereotype. For example, Steve Rogers consistently struggles with his social role as an advertising illustrator, telling his boss, "[W]hen you think of everything that needs to be done in this country—how can you possibly justify the MILLIONS these people throw away trying to foist hamburgers on the American public!"[37] On another occasion, he offers the following critique: "I know that advertising plays an important role in America's free enterprise system, but I can't escape the feeling that our promotion of material things contributes to a consumer-oriented society—one that places more value on possessions than people."[38] Following this speech, Rogers quits his job and eventually decides to try his hand at illustrating comic books,[39] which he feels provides him a more relevant social role. In a twist of intertextual irony, Rogers gets an offer from Marvel Comics to draw the *Captain America* comic book. In the Marvel offices, Rogers has a conversation about the offer with the *Captain America* editor "Mike" (whether this is portrayal of real-life editor Mike Carlin is not specified):

MIKE: To tell you the truth, ol' Cap could really use a boost like your art might give him. Sales have been slumping lately, and there's even been talk about canceling the book.

ROGERS: You're kidding! I thought Cap would be more popular . . .

MIKE: I think he IS, but the creative team I've had just hasn't been portraying him right. That's why I want to shake things up a bit. The book still gets a lot of mail.[40]

For Captain America, the economic changes of the 1980s would be even more pronounced. In *Captain America* volume 1, number 259, Cap receives a customized motorcycle from someone he had helped[41] and later is given a customized van by the Black Panther.[42] Rogers also receives a check for almost a million dollars in government back pay, which he uses to build a national hotline infrastructure.[43] As Cap becomes more upwardly mobile, he becomes more physically mobile, expanding his experiences and operations to a national level. Although occasionally confronted by activists critical of US economic policy, Cap, it should be noted, never addresses economic disparity in any meaningful way.

The hero also appears to embrace the image-driven spirit of the age, and his personality and reputation increase in stature. As editor Mike Carlin suggested in the mid-1980s, "Captain America demands respect. . . . As the writer of Captain America, I have to put any humorous situations around him. He couldn't be the perpetrator or the victim. He gets respect from everyone around him."[44]

In a later interview, when Carlin critiqued a fan-submitted plot, he revealed further insight into his conception of Captain America. First objecting to Cap's being bested by a relatively inexperienced opponent— "Cap should rarely be touched in a fight"—Carlin objected more strongly to characterizations of specific behaviors: "In Marvel comics we don't usually say 'damn,' and Captain America definitely wouldn't. During the fight scene Cap picks up a *gun*. Now at least he doesn't shoot anyone [which would be '*way* out of character'], but he picks up the gun to hit the Russians with. He shouldn't have to hit them with anything, except maybe his shield."[45]

The 1980s creators of Captain America (each of whom appears to have modeled his portrayals as symbolic representations of idealized America) carefully defined him through his personal relationships, his leadership, his politics (or apolitical stances, as the case may be), and his resistance to the violent trends of the era. Although overlapping, each of these components contributed critical understanding of how these writers and artists understood an idealized masculine symbol of America, and so they are worth exploring individually.

Captain America's Relationships

With Sharon Carter dead, the only other personal tie Cap carried over from the 1970s was the Falcon. As mentioned in the previous chapter, the Falcon had been a central part of Cap's 1970s adventures. This relationship with Marvel's first African American superhero served to awaken a sense of racial justice in Captain America. Professionally, the two had been staunch partners until the Falcon's shady past was revealed and the two clashed over whether to trust the court system. As the 1970s ran out, the Falcon joined S.H.I.E.L.D. to help train superpowered agents,[46] and he began to be featured in small separate vignettes in the back of the comic that bore his and Cap's names. *Captain America and the Falcon* volume 1, number 222 (cover-dated June 1978), did not even feature the Falcon,[47] and the following month the Falcon was dropped from the title, which reverted to *Captain America*.

At first, it appeared as though the Falcon would branch out, initially teaming up with Spider-Man in *Marvel Team-Up* volume 1, number 71,[48] and then receiving a solo adventure in *Marvel Premiere* number 49.[49] But the hero didn't sell enough books, and he soon disappeared from sight.

Perhaps most embarrassing for Marvel and the Falcon, in *Captain America* volume 1, number 228, Cap rescues a black child from a potential calamity and is reminded that he had forgotten that the Falcon had gone missing eleven issues earlier. The realization is doubly embarrassing because the Falcon had not gone missing in number 217 and had appeared in subsequent issues. It appears the new writers didn't even remember where the Falcon was said to have been. Cap sets off to "find" the Falcon.[50]

Nor did the readers appear to miss the Falcon much. One black letter writer expressed concerns that he appeared able to identify more with Marvel's white characters than with the African American characters. Singling out the Falcon, he wrote: "I feel it was a mistake to team him up with Captain America. The amount of exposure and characterization that Cap needs will always prevent the Falcon from playing a bigger role than he does now. Since in the long run you will have to get rid of the Falcon, please do so now. I think the Falcon, properly handled, has the strength to carry his own book, but at the moment, both Captain America and the Falcon are being hindered by the team-up."[51]

The Falcon would surface in the pages of *The Avengers* when government liaison Henry Gyrich demands the hero be added to the roster to fill a racial quota. The Avengers (in particular Hawkeye, who is the Avenger displaced by the appointment) express their displeasure:

HAWKEYE: B-but why HIM—and not me? That bozo's only powers are flying and rapping with birds! He's not even an Avenger!

IRON MAN: Hawkeye is right, Gyrich! We can't risk the whole team on an untried member who might not be able to handle it!

GYRICH: I'm afraid you'll have to, Iron Man—since the Black Panther isn't available. If the Avengers are to be sanctioned by the government, they'll have to adhere to government policies—and that includes equal opportunity for minorities![52]

Captain America vouches for the Falcon as a "good man," though he makes no comment on the government policy. When he tracks down the Falcon to formally invite him, he similarly takes no stand on the question of racial justice in strong contrast to his rhetoric earlier in the 1970s:

STEVE ROGERS: It's not my idea, Sam. The government says we have to have more minority members. And if you don't join—the Avengers priority privileges will be suspended!

SAM WILSON: Oh, well then maybe I oughta change my name to "The Token," huh? Blast it, Steve! I've proven myself as a superhero! And I don't like being chosen to fill a quota!

ROGERS: I don't like it either—not one bit! But our backs are to the wall! Call it a personal favor, Sam? Please . . . ?

WILSON: Well, if you're going to play dirty and put it that way . . . okay, but I don't do windows![53]

In this way, Captain America becomes the appeasing white stereotype: accepting affirmative action because of governmental intervention, not because he "likes" the idea of his former partner (and closest confidant) joining the team. The Falcon, for his part, becomes obstinate, making parodied racial remarks to Gyrich.[54]

The Falcon's tenure on the Avengers is rocky. In each mission in which he participates, he demonstrates a lack of judgment or an inability to fulfill the role needed for the mission's success. Meanwhile, Hawkeye proves himself indispensable. Frustrated at his performance, the Falcon quits the Avengers in issue 194, signaling the failure of the affirmative-action policy.[55] So Marvel's first African American superhero is shown to be a burden to his fellow Avengers because of his own ineptitude and displacement by the better qualified but white Hawkeye.

Captain America's lack of involvement with the Falcon in the 1980s is a stark contrast to his relationship with the Falcon in the 1970s. Cap was, after all, the one who recruited and trained the Falcon and the one who consistently argued that the Falcon and he were equals not because of race but because of their common mission. Cap stands silently while Hawkeye accuses the Falcon of being underqualified because of his lack of power, a peculiar charge given that neither Cap nor Hawkeye has a superpower of his own and given that the team didn't object to the Black Panther, another unpowered hero. The hero who routinely steps forward and makes speeches about those misunderstood in society says little (only that Falcon is a "good man") to defend one of his closest friends. He weakly comments only that he "doesn't like" the policy, despite his earlier understanding of African Americans' plight in general and Sam Wilson's plight in particular only a few years earlier.

The Falcon would finally get his own limited series in 1983, written by Jim Owsley (Christopher Priest), an African American writer who would later write notable African American comic narratives such as *The Black Panther* and Valiant's *Quantum & Woody*. In the promotional materials leading up to the Falcon series, Owsley explained that he was attempting to get back to the Falcon's Harlem roots. Planning to explore the tension between the Falcon's superhero mission and his daily struggle as social worker Sam Wilson, Owsley said the book would address urban black culture. He wanted to use the series as an "opportunity to try to explode a few of the many ridiculous stereotypes some people have on entire segments of society."[56]

In that regard, the series lived up to its author's intent. The first issue depicted the Falcon breaking up a plot by a local (superpowered) slumlord to destroy his government-funded housing project to capitalize on the insurance.[57] The third issue explored the Falcon's origin when Wilson reveals that his path to crime had been related to his depression over the death of his father.[58] In that issue, the Falcon is forced to break a promise to a local gang leader, rupturing the uneasy trust he had spent years gaining. Once again he is caught between two worlds, neither of them fully trusting him. When he next encounters the Legion gang, one of the members calls him "Sammy Falcon, the Oreo wonder,"[59] and Owsley supplies a footnote to make sure his readers understand the implications of the term.

The primary plot involves a simultaneous battle with the supervillain Electro and a search for President Ronald Reagan, who was abducted by the Legion. Defeating Electro (without his wings), the Falcon confronts the gang leader and persuades him to talk to President Reagan. The gang leader releases Reagan and introduces his gang members, explaining how each of them has been affected by issues related to urban poverty. The following day President Reagan holds a news conference in which he announces the sponsorship of new legislation to address urban poverty.[60] The Falcon ends the evening by going on an interracial date with a young woman he had previously rescued.

This brush with political reconciliation apparently resonated with Marvel's creators, for soon Sam Wilson announces he plans to seek public office, first seeking to become a member of the local school board[61] and then campaigning for a seat in the House of Representatives.[62] A media scandal erupts over his superhero identity (which he renounces) and his criminal past. During the struggle for his identity, Wilson appears to dig deep within himself and rids himself of his "Snap" personality.[63]

Despite this personal growth, Wilson loses the election. His loss is attributed to the scandal of the former accusations brought against him (though long dismissed) and the fact that his constituency of poor African Americans did not vote in sufficient numbers to elect him. Once again, the stereotypes of the 1980s appear to be legitimized in the pages of a book, *Captain America*, that previously had fiercely battled over issues of race relations.

Falcon would continue to appear on occasion in the pages of *Captain America* but largely in increasingly superficial ways. The bond of friendship between him and Cap appears to continue to be strong, but their past and his race seem not to be factors in any of their adventures. After having endured so many identity crises, the 1980s Falcon devolves into a generic supporting character, and Captain America seems unmoved by the transformation.

Other nonstandard characters would play a more dramatic role in Steve Rogers's life. One of the earliest and most significant would be a love interest, Bernadette ("Bernie") Rosenthal. A Jewish glass blower, Bernie meets Rogers in *Captain America* volume 1, number 248.[64] She moves into Rogers's building, and the two are attracted at first sight. Unlike the shockingly timid Sharon Carter in the 1970s, Bernie is a strong female character and often takes the initiative in ways formerly reserved for male characters. In *Captain America* volume 1, number 267, it is Bernie who kisses Steve Rogers.[65] In the next issue, she tells him she loves him,[66] and he doesn't return the sentiment until issue 284.[67] Although the two become a couple, Rogers conceals his superhero alter ego from Bernie, but she figures it out on her own and confronts him.[68] In the course of their relationship, Bernie also winds up saving Captain America[69] and chewing out the formidable Nick Fury.[70]

But perhaps no action is more direct than her proposal to Rogers in *Captain America* volume 1, number 292.[71] He doesn't immediately answer, and two issues later she presses the issue:

STEVE ROGERS: I can't marry you.

BERNIE: WHAT?!

ROGERS: Let me explain, hon. The risks are just too—

BERNIE: You can stop right there! I know the whole routine! Don't you think *I* read comic books when I was a kid? [Feigns drama.] "Oh, Darling," the hero would sigh, "I cannot marry you for fear of what my arch-enemy, Hairless Harry, might do to you if he found out!" I didn't buy it then—and I don't buy it NOW!

ROGERS: But it's TRUE!

BERNIE: IT'S BULL![72]

As the conversation continues, Bernie counters each of Rogers objections and then kisses him until he relents and agrees to marry her. Fans reacted overwhelmingly positively to Bernie's take-charge portrayal. As one wrote, "Bernie's sure the woman for Cap! Either her inner strength and spirit matches [sic] his, or else some of his has rubbed off on her!"[73]

In truth, the two characters couldn't have behaved more differently. Bernie (particularly when written by writer J. M. DeMatteis) served not only as a "liberated" female character but also as the perfect foil for reconciling Cap's mission with his personal life. While Cap's devotion to his work at the expense of his personal concerns is all-consuming (like the stereotypical 1980s male, it would seem), Bernie forces him to take enjoyment in his downtime. While he fears the consequences of commitment (in terms of both her personal welfare and the potential effect on his career), she pushes him into every step of their relationship and shows him that renouncing his martyrlike devotion to his work actually makes him a more whole person.

Once Mark Gruenwald took over the writing duties, the relationship between Bernie and Steve would take a series of twists. Losing her glass-blowing shop, Bernie begins to study for the law exam.[74] When she receives excellent scores, she decides to attend law school at the University of Wisconsin–Madison.[75] As she prepares to move out and Rogers decides to move back to Avengers mansion, one of the other tenants asks him if he intends to join her. He responds, "The academic life is not for me,"[76] perhaps a humorous jab at his 1950s occupation as a schoolteacher (who was later retconned to be a separate individual, not Steve Rogers). Although they suggest the engagement is still intact, they will soon drift apart. Bernie and Steve thus experience the quintessential 1980s breakup as competing occupational interests put too much distance between them to sustain their relationship.

Fans who wrote in about the separation appeared to connect personally with the breakup. Several reported feeling touched by the sense of loss and regret on both sides. As one fan wrote, "The emotions those two felt were real and heart-rending. I know, I've been there. It is this quality of treating your characters with respect and humanity that sets CAPTAIN

AMERICA singly and the Marvel Universe as a whole, head and shoulders above your competition."[77]

Another personal relationship that would touch the life of Steve Rogers was that of Arnie Roth, a short, overweight, bald man who is a childhood friend of Rogers.[78] Although it is never explicitly stated, the storylines strongly imply that Roth is gay, a fact that Rogers appears to accept without comment. As Cap, Rogers struggles to save Michael, Roth's "roommate" but is unable to prevent him from becoming critically injured.[79] Michael dies, and at his funeral Roth once and for all forces Rogers to leave behind the guilt and regrets he has carried with him since his revival in the 1960s:

> ROGERS: Blast it, Arnie—This would never have happened if not for me. I seem to leave a trail of death and misery in my wake. It's like a curse! Bucky, Sharon, Michael, you, Bernie . . . How many other victims that I've forgotten over the years? Will I ever have a normal life? Will this madness ever end?
>
> ARNIE: It'll end when you LET it end, Steve! Can you hear yourself? Do you see what you're doing? This is MY time—MY grief—but you're so wrapped up in self-pity, in a pattern you've been following for decades—you won't even let me mourn! No, we've got to stand at Michael's grave and feel sorry for poor Steve Rogers! Well, there's nothing to feel sorry ABOUT, Steve!! You say you want a normal life, but tell me: what's NORMAL? If you think it's an idyllic existence without pain or suffering—then you're chasing a dream! Blast it, Steve, you're a hero . . . a legend! More than that, you've got a career, friends—and a woman who loves you and accepts you for what you are! Stop blaming yourself for the world's ills and grab hold of what you have![80]

Cap would have an opportunity to repay the favor when in *Captain America* volume 1, number 296 (cover-dated August 1984), Baron Zemo and the Red Skull kidnap Roth, torture him, dress him in ridiculous clothing, and force him to sing a humiliating song while Cap looks on:

ARNIE ROTH: A funny song, isn't it, Steve? A funny song—about a funny little man. A pot-bellied, bald-headed wretch—who doesn't know a thing about REAL, HUMAN LOVE. I'm a strutting freak. No wonder the Nazis wanted my kind—the weak, the MISFITS—locked away in the concentration camps with the other pariahs! I'm a menace to society—a disease! And you star-spangled idiot—you call me FRIEND! Wh-what does that say about YOU? Most people simply hate men like me . . . yet you always treated me w-with respect. C-compassion. WHY? Is it because . . . YOU'RE ONE OF US? Is it because, deep inside, under all that macho bravado, you're really a sorry excuse for a man . . . like me? Wh-what kind of man are you h-hiding underneath that chain mail?

CAPTAIN AMERICA: Arnie—listen to me: no matter what words they force out of your mouth, you know the TRUTH! You are NOT a freak! You're as good and decent a man as I've EVER KNOWN! . . . They can't corrupt your love for Michael with their lies any more than they can corrupt my love for Bernie! Do you hear me, Arnie? THEY'RE the pariahs! THEY'RE the disease![81]

Soon after this story arc, Roth would quietly move away. But while he was in Steve Rogers's life, he added context and depth to Rogers's character. Physically, he couldn't have resembled Cap less (as was likely the point), but the loyalty and devotion Rogers showed Roth demonstrated his unqualified acceptance and belief in freedom. It would be nearly eight years before Alpha Flight's Northstar would become the first openly gay superhero,[82] but "coming out" would be a trend of the 1990s, not the 1980s.

Cap's masculinity would receive challenges from the opposite end of the spectrum through his interactions with Nomad. A new Nomad (the third to take that name, with Rogers himself having been the first) appears in *Captain America* volume 1, number 281—Jack Monroe (the retconned 1950s Bucky).[83] In the following issue, Monroe assumes the Nomad identity to mount a rescue mission for S.H.I.E.L.D,[84] and soon he becomes Captain America's regular partner.

As Cap mentors Nomad, he is confronted by the masculinity and traditional values of the 1950s. On one of their first outings, the duo encounter an instance of domestic violence. After Cap disarms the husband, he relents his assault on the man at the wife's pleas. Nomad comments that the world seems more complex, and Cap responds: "The world's not really more complex, Jack. We've just stopped looking at the things in black and white terms. One thing you're going to have to learn . . . FAST . . . is that the American Dream we've both sworn to defend—is often times light years removed from the America reality! These are strange times we're living in, HARD times. And people aren't so easily pigeon-holed into good guys and bad guys. You've got to learn to trust your instincts as much as you trust the flag!"[85]

Jack also receives a healthy dose of conservative work ethos from Bernie (before she moves away) as he struggles to balance his nighttime activities with the demands of a regular occupation:

BERNIE: Oh, and Jack, if you ever hope to find a job—I wouldn't stay up late every night and then sleep until noon. Bye.

NOMAD (thinking): . . . I wonder how long she's been thinking of me as a slacker? Hmmn, maybe I am. I have been living in Steve's apartment for a couple of months now—not paying rent, mooching off him for food and pocket money, probably getting in the way of his and Bernie's privacy. I guess I really haven't been trying all THAT hard to find a job. Just trying to measure up to Captain America's standards as a sidekick has been tough for me—Maybe that's what's been bugging me about my relationship with Cap lately. How can I expect him to treat me like my own man when I'm not even paying my own way in the world? I really ought to do something about that. Maybe I haven't been lucky job-hunting 'cause my expectations have been too high. I ought to take any job I can get as a start! Yeah! I'll show Miss Bernie Rosenthal a thing or two. When she gets back tonight, I'll have myself a job . . . NO MATTER WHAT![86]

The job proves unmanageable for Monroe, and Nomad soon dissolves the partnership with Cap because he can't live up to Cap's example and wants to set out on his own.[87] It will eventually be revealed that his physical enhancements are unbalancing Nomad, making him increasingly aggressive. But once again the conservative values of the 1950s confront Cap, and once again he works to counteract them with modern sensibilities. Where Nomad shows aggression, Cap often shows mercy. When Nomad feels insecure in his manhood, Cap appears to be the model of solidarity, even as he faces many of the same challenges.

Another character that would challenge Cap's character is Rachel Leighton, a.k.a. Diamondback. First appearing as a member of the Serpent Society in *Captain America* volume 1, number 310,[88] Leighton finds herself attracted to Cap during combat and passes up two opportunities to kill him, one in *Captain America* volume 1, number 313, and the other in *Captain America* number 315.[89] Finding herself alone with Cap in one of the Serpent Society's flying saucers, Diamondback tells Cap her origin and then makes her move:

DIAMONDBACK: [W]hen I laid eyes on YOU in that Jersey shopping mall, know what I said to myself? I said, now here's a man who could be a good influence on me—here's somebody worth goin' straight for. So how about it, Cap? How'd you like to throw away your inhibitions and let me show you a real good time?

CAP: Sorry, Diamondback. I don't take that kind of thing lightly.

DIAMONDBACK: Who said anything about love? Let me reword my proposition, Cap—either you promise to let me have my way with you or I'll let this saucer crash!

CAP (thinking): She grabbed the ignition key!

DIAMONDBACK (dropping the key into her tunic): That is, unless you want to search me for the key—which might be a lot of fun, too! Well . . . ?

CAP: My decision is . . . NO DEAL. I don't believe you're willing to throw away your life on something so fleeting as a few moments of pleasure.

DIAMONDBACK: You—COLD FISH![90]

Leighton would later call on Cap when the Serpent Society has been infiltrated by the Viper,[91] and over the course of a few adventures she would become a partner and eventually a 1990s love interest.

Unlike Bernie Rosenthal, whose assertiveness embodies liberated womanhood, Leighton's forwardness is depicted as an offensive kind of aggressive sexuality. Although clearly less physically vulnerable than Bernie, Leighton has to work hard to earn Cap's trust because of her earliest actions toward him. Through Leighton, Cap is placed in compromising situations that the stereotypical 1980s male would likely fantasize about. Against her wiles, Cap proves himself incorruptible and seemingly sexually pure (although the limits of the physical aspects of his relationship with Bernie are never portrayed).

Finally, Steve Rogers forms lasting character traits through his relationship with Tony Stark, the invincible Iron Man. In the 1980s, Stark succumbed to alcoholism, losing his status as a hero, his company, his wealth, and many of his relationships. In *Iron Man* volume 1, number 172, it is Captain America who tracks down Stark and saves him from a fiery death.[92] During this encounter, Cap reveals to Stark that his own father was an alcoholic and that, based on that experience, he knows Stark cannot be helped until he is ready to start living. In this moment, Cap not only affirms the tenet of 1980s conservative notions of personal responsibility but also reaffirms Stark's personal autonomy, a view that would become a strong trend in Cap's 1980s attitudes.

The relationship would take another turn in the late 1980s when the two came to blows over the role of their mission as it relates to authority. Iron Man, on a crusade to rid the world of technology stolen from his company, defeats and immobilizes government agents wearing suits of armor based on his designs. Cap confronts him, but Iron Man attacks Cap from behind when his guard is lowered.[93] The two battle a second time in this decade in *Captain America* volume 1, number 341.[94]

Iron Man has often served as a contrasting personality for Captain America. In the 1970s, Iron Man's conservative tendencies, growing from his industrial-capitalist origins and corporate dealings, strongly contrasted with the liberalism displayed by Cap. But by the 1980s it took Iron Man's conservatism to reveal the nuanced idealism Cap displayed. The two

Avengers would eventually repair their relationship, but the breach (as well as the earlier rescue) would wind up providing deep context for the two men's conflict during Marvel's 2006–7 Civil War event.

Captain America's Leadership

Although Captain America's natural leadership ability had been referenced as early as in the 1960s Avengers stories, the 1980s narratives cemented leadership as an enduring component of the character. The premise that appeared to justify this leadership was Cap's experience in World War II. However, within his comic's continuity, the roots of this leadership are not as obvious on second glance, particularly when one considers that he is supposed to have operated for roughly four years (the vast majority of this activity on his own or with Bucky, if his Golden Age exploits are to be taken at face value) and then is frozen on ice for several decades. Of course, the late 1970s and 1980s narrative drew on the assumption that Roy Thomas's *Invaders* series took precedence over the original stories, and in that series Cap has operated as a de facto leader of a team of superpowered freedom fighters for his entire war career. This experience would appear to have (retroactively, it seems) prepared Cap for his Avengers leadership, which was a necessary plot device to explain why Cap was suited to lead the small team of untried Avengers when all of the founding members quit the team in *Avengers* volume 1, number 16.

Although *The Avengers* continued to attract a loyal following into the early 1980s, the book's sales could not compete with the mutant books. And so it was that *Secret Wars*, the first comic series to feature most of the Marvel heroes at once, served to establish Captain America's reputation for leadership, a trait that would become another enduring part of his identity for years to come. It is hard to remember that before 1984 most of the Marvel characters had not interacted on a familiar basis. *Marvel Team-Up* had been a mainstay publication for years, but Spider-Man was the constant of that work, and his status as a loner meant that the larger teams did not have the opportunity to interact except through the occasional temporary plot crossover.

The X-Men, in particular, had operated largely outside the purview of hero teams such as the Avengers and the Fantastic Four. In fact, although Cap had interacted with the X-Men in the 1970s, he had not come into contact with them since the renaissance that brought in the characters who had launched that franchise's immense popularity—Wolverine, for example.

From the moment of the various hero teams' arrival on the Beyonder's Battleworld, however, Cap assumes command of the hero forces, a fact that some of the older characters establish as natural:

CAP: Be Ready for anything! Form a circle! I've got the twelve o'clock position! I want an Avenger at two, four, six, eight and ten with eyes peeled! MOVE! Iron Man! Keep your radar working!

WOLVERINE: Good at giving orders, ain't he?

HULK: Yes he is! Maybe the best![95]

Once the heroes get a lull in the action, they have a brief discussion over who should lead. The Wasp, though technically serving as Avenger chairwoman, defers to Cap's experience. The heroes appeal to Reed Richards of the Fantastic Four, who argues he is too distracted by the separation from his pregnant wife to lead effectively. The Hulk is approached, but he suggests Cap would be a better choice. Cap appeals to Charles Xavier of the X-Men to lead, but Professor X solidifies the sentiment that Cap is the best choice:

CAPTAIN AMERICA: What about you, professor? You read minds! That could come in handy!

PROFESSOR X: I'm also good at reading hearts—no man in existence equals your courage, Captain America!

WOLVERINE: What a minute! He's the least of us! He can't do anything! I won't follow him—!

THOR: I will! I am a prince of the gods! I do not pledge my allegiance to many of mortal stature! This man I will follow through the gates of Hades![96]

Wolverine and the rest of the X-Men would prove to be Cap's biggest doubters, an attitude consistent with the themes of distrust of authority in their own book. The US government had proven itself time and again to be the enemy of mutantkind, and Cap's uniform serves as an impediment to easy trust.

Not that the X-Men are the only critics of Cap's authority. Other heroes (outside of the Avengers, who never question Cap's orders) at times question Cap's decisions but often with an Avenger in earshot to reaffirm Cap's authority:

CAPTAIN AMERICA: Iron Man, Torch, Thor—! Patrol the fortress perimeter in a spiral pattern! Make sure we have a secure
area within a one-hundred mile radius! The rest of us will
take turns on watch here! I'll need two details—one to check
for suitable quarters, and one to find a mess hall—and food if
there is any!
HUMAN TORCH: Do you guys think Cap's handling this right?
IRON MAN: Does Doctor J play roundball, junior?[97]

For his own part, Cap's rhetoric becomes excessively militaristic and pragmatic. Although his comrades are overwhelmed by their alien surroundings, Cap rarely appears shocked or flustered. Once he arrives on the scene, he begins to use military jargon, and most dialogue from him is expressed as tactical analysis. He serves to rally his troops and tries to weave them into a collective fighting force: "We have five of our foes captured and imprisoned! We hold the edge—a big edge! I figure they'll gamble on one desperate, all-out attack . . . probably as soon as the storm breaks! But if we're ready! If each of us does his duty and pulls his weight, our advantage in strength will guarantee victory!"[98]

Nor do these efforts go unnoticed. When Cap asserts his authority, particularly when he barks orders at other heroes (heroes who have, after all, rejected the status quo authority to put on masks), a character will mutter or think about how Cap's behavior, although unacceptable from others, is somehow justified by an intangible credibility:

HUMAN TORCH: Thor's down! With his hammer out of the fight–!

CAPTAIN AMERICA: Don't think about it! Do exactly as I told you! Our attack must be perfectly coordinated! That thing's "gun" must be silenced—at any cost!

THING: Boy, I love that kind of talk!

TORCH: Good shot, Cap!

CAP: So it DOES have weak points! Okay—hit him! I'm counting on you!

THING (thinking): Somethin' about that guy—you just can't let him down![99]

Nor are these attributes lost on the supervillains in the conflict. Although Cap, as Wolverine points out, is among the least powerful of the heroes, both hero and villain alike recognize his ability to rally and coordinate the heroes' efforts. In a battle between several enemies and Cap, the Hulk, the Thing, Spider-Man, and others, Cap is the priority target:

DR. OCTOPUS: Cut down that star-spangled fool first! With him dead, the rest will be easy pickings!

CAPTAIN AMERICA (thinking): We're in trouble! We're tired . . . battered!

CAP: Fall back! Give ground, but return fire! Keep slugging! Slow 'em down–! Once we blunt their initial thrust, on my order, dig and in and HOLD![100]

Ever the reluctant hero (and a perfect exemplar of the American monomyth), Cap at times relies on the praise and affirmation from others:

CAPTAIN AMERICA: You know, Reed . . . I—I can't help but think that if I'd done things differently . . . maybe the Wasp wouldn't have died! I . . .

MR. FANTASTIC: Don't torture yourself, Cap! What could have happened . . . did! No one could have led us better or more wisely than you![101]

As noted, one group from which Captain America does not receive initial support is the mutant community of heroes, in particular Wolverine. The *Secret Wars* narrative introduces a flashpoint for the heroes to quarrel over: the inclusion of Magneto among them. In his struggle against humanity, against which the X-Men define Professor X's more humanitarian approach to human–mutant relations, Magneto has committed acts of terrorism and killed humans, a fact that makes his presence alongside superpowered humans difficult to accept. (For most of the Battleworld conflict, the X-Men fight alone as a third independent force.)

Although Wolverine had previously opposed Magneto, he finds himself defending the former villain in *Secret Wars* because the two are mutants. This defense is naturally directed at Captain America as leader of the human heroes. As such, Wolverine and Cap clash over Magneto's past:

> WOLVERINE: What you don't understand, Cap'n, is that we mutants are at WAR! Always have been, always will be! You, with your high-falutin' ideals—you're the champion of the American Dream, fighting for liberty and justice—but only for your own kind! For HUMANS . . . for regular Americans! But you just stand by while mutants are being persecuted, don't you? When have you ever fought for OUR rights? Some of the God-fearin' Americans you protect HATE mutants—and when they come after us, it's a lot like how the Nazis went after the Jews! Xavier wants us to hide . . . to try to help humanity . . . earn acceptance . . . fit in! But when they're threatenin' you and yours, it's easy to play it like Magneto did—! Fight back—! Take the offensive—! Drive 'em into the sea if you have to . . . Now, though, Professor X has convinced Maggie to lay off . . . stop taking the expedient route . . . stop using noble ends to justify violent means . . . an' still you won't lay off! Sort of makes me wonder if Magneto was right.
>
> CAP: Nothing justifies terrorism . . . or murder!
>
> WOLVERINE: Terrorists! That's what the big army calls the little army! I used to have some respect for you . . . [102]

But Cap and Wolverine will settle their differences. When an attack by villain forces damages the foundation of the heroes' base, Cap puts himself at risk to free villain prisoners from the detention center before the structure's collapse. In the midst of the confusion, he encounters Wolverine, and the two work together to save the lives of their common foes. As they work, Wolverine expresses a grudging respect for Cap, which represents the last confirmation of Cap's reputation and leadership status among the major Marvel heroes:

WOLVERINE: Don't take this wrong . . . but you're a better man than I gave you credit for! I'm an attacker an' you're a defender— but we're both soldiers! I'm beginning to think you got room in your high-falutin' ideals for all people . . . don'tcha–? Even if they're mutants!

CAP: Some of my best friends are people![103]

Of course, Cap's foes continue to recognize these qualities, even an omnipotent Dr. Doom, who, having stolen away the godlike powers of the Beyonder, launches an overwhelming attack against the heroes. Captain America rallies his troops and manages to break through to Dr. Doom's inner sanctum. As he enters, Dr. Doom observes, "Ah . . . Captain America! If one among your group could get this far, it would, of course, be you!"[104]

By bringing together the players of the Marvel Universe and having each (either immediately or reluctantly) acknowledge Captain America's reputation as a leader more worthy than even the most powerful and talented among them, the characters involved in *Secret Wars* convey upon him an enduring status and reputation for leadership and integrity. He, in effect, becomes the standard by which other heroes' morality will be judged.

Although some of the fan magazines were critical of the promotional nature of the series (the two most common complaints cited a lack of innovation and the commercial aspects of tying in action figures and coloring books), *Secret Wars* set new standards for comic books sales, and the letters collected and published in *Marvel Age* number 20 appear to indicate its generally favorable reception. Readers also seemed to approve of Cap's depiction, and some letters specifically pointed to the recognition of his leadership as a strength of the series.[105]

"Worthiness" would also be considered synonymous with "perfection," an attribute reinforced in the sequel, *Secret Wars II*. In that series, the Beyonder comes to Earth to better understand the human condition through experience. After observing from afar, the Beyonder chooses to replicate Captain America's form for himself because he views it as the "ideal template" of humanity.[106]

From the mid-1980s forward, Captain America would be idealized as "perfect" and "moral," with his leadership abilities rarely called into question. In that regard, he represented the new incarnation of the "innocent nation"—powerful, wise (though young), and idolized by peer nations.

Captain America's Politics

Although Captain America represented the image and spirit of 1980s America, his politics were hardly Republican, although they were influenced by the Republican manner. Despite his continuing to hold the liberal views he gained from his 1960s and 1970s adventures, his expression of his political views in the 1980s was much more measured and cautious. The character prone to lecture the Red Skull in the 1960s and to moralize out loud with the Falcon in the 1970s seemed rather mute in the 1980s. As a result, many characters within his storylines (as well as readers and fans reading those stories) naturally assumed that with Cold War patriotism becoming increasingly en vogue, Captain America would be a Reagan Republican.

One fan, reacting to Cap's attitude shifts in 1980, wrote a letter that praised Cap's return from liberalism ("transient morality") and his embrace of conservatism to become the "rock-ribbed, John Wayne–style symbol of American solidarity."[107] The letter drew an extended response from writer Roger Stern, who took up the rest of the letter column to explain how he and Roger McKenzie approached Cap's political views:

> Cap is not quite the rock-ribbed conservative you imagine him to be.
> As a matter of fact, he's probably about as dead-center in the political

spectrum as one can get. (Iron Man is probably a bit more conservative than Cap, coming as he did from a good, old-fashioned entrepreneurial-capitalist family.) Steve Rogers/Captain America grew up during the worst economic depression in the recorded history of the world. Steve's boyhood saw the growth of America's labor unions, social unrest, and— yes—campus demonstrations. If anything, Steve Rogers probably grew up as a New Deal liberal! Otherwise, he'd have gone stark-raving mad when he saw what the world was like after his many-decades sleep.

Stern also argued that Captain America stood as a symbol for the "American Dream" rather than the contemporary body politic, a claim many writers would make to distinguish the hero's sense of patriotism from any specific policy or social outcomes. As Stern argued, "[A]nyone who thinks the American Way comes anywhere close enough to the Dream is living in a fool's paradise. . . . [Cap] can teach us a lot about where we've been and where we're going. And maybe, just maybe, he'll make us all *think* a little along the way."[108]

Stern also referred to a "forthcoming" storyline, and in *Captain America* volume 1, number 250, he presented Captain America as a candidate for president of the United States. Although Cap is an unwitting nominee, he briefly considers the pros and cons of becoming commander in chief (and receives much encouragement from his peers in the superhero community as well as from individuals in his personal life). Ultimately, he decides against it, announcing at a campaign rally:

The presidency is one of the most important jobs in the world. The holder of that office must represent the best interests of an entire nation. He must be ready to negotiate—to compromise—24 hours a day. To preserve the republic at all costs! I understand this . . . I appreciate this . . . and I realize the need to work within such a framework. By the same token—I have worked and fought all my life for the growth and advancement of the American Dream. And I believe that my duty to the DREAM would severely limit any abilities I might have to preserve the reality. We must all live in the real world . . . and sometimes that world can be pretty grim. But it is the dream . . . the hope . . . that makes the reality worth living. In the early 1940's, I made a personal pledge to uphold the dream . . . and as long as the dream remains even partially unfulfilled, I cannot abandon it! And so I hope you can understand— that I cannot in all fairness be your candidate! You need to look within yourselves to find the people you need to keep this nation strong and, God willing, to help make the dream come true![109]

The "Cap for president" plot device seemed primarily to give him an opportunity to deliver this speech. Cap's speech making was hardly new, but whereas most of the "Man out of Time's" speeches came during battle against an ideological opponent, and the Liberal Crusader's speeches came alongside the Falcon or other friendly challenges to the status quo, the Captain America of the 1980s would find himself delivering formal speeches on stages and on television. The celebrity status given to him by the public allowed for these opportunities, though Cap usually took advantage of them after some crisis of identity or perceived misconceptions portrayed through the plot.

Roy Thomas, whose use of Cap reinvented the way future writers would conceptualize the character, further fragmented the character's pre-Marvel history. In the origin story presented in *Captain America and the Falcon* volume 1, number 215, Thomas explained that after Cap's disappearance in 1945, President Truman asked the Spirit of '76, another of Thomas's patriotic creations, to take up the mantle.[110] After this hero perished in combat, yet another of Thomas's heroes, the Patriot, took up the mantle. This approach allowed Thomas to reconcile nuances of the Golden Age stories with the mainstream Marvel continuity, using these other men to frame the divergences in continuity caused by Lee and Kirby's decision to revive Cap as if the late 1940s and 1950s adventures had not occurred.

Captain America Annual volume 1, number 6, further explicated these attempts at historical reconstruction by bringing all three of the Golden Age Caps—the original, Spirit of '76, and the Patriot—as well as the 1950s Commie Smasher together in a single adventure.[111] In the context of this story, in which Cap first learns of his successors, it is established that the Spirit of '76 served as Cap during at least some of the *Invaders/All Select* period and that the Patriot took over for Cap during the period in which Golden Girl replaced Bucky in the late 1940s. Although Thomas and DeMatteis dramatically rewrote Cap with respect to his morality and attitudes toward violence, the additional Caps were introduced to preserve established continuity and to separate Cap's history from the use of atomic weapons against Japan.

This reconciliation between the modern Cap and the Golden Age Cap did not mean the character would continue in the tradition of the 1970s Liberal Crusader. In *Captain America* volume 1, number 267, Cap begins to walk the noncommittal line he would tread throughout the 1980s. In one story, he delivers an inspiring speech in a school auditorium, only to be confronted by an angry student who challenges him: "Let's talk about the American reality—about unequal distribution of wealth—about poverty, frustration and death!"[112] The young man pulls a gun and fires on Cap, who takes him down. In police custody, the boy continues his accusations: "[Y]ou're the symbol of everything that stinks in this country. Yeah—you're the shining example who says 'You can be what I am if you only try!' It's the American success sickness: strive to BE something—scramble to the top of the heap. But you know only one in ten thousand is going to make it! So what about the rest of us? What about the failures?"[113] This confrontation leads to a conflict with a costumed villain named "Everyman," whose exploits represent a populist cry against the establishment, with Cap as its symbol. During the conflict, Cap considers his own journey, that it "took time for me to become aware of the huge gap between the America dream and the American reality."[114] After defeating Everyman, Cap considers the cultural implications of the clash and observes, "There's such a mood of renewed patriotism sweeping the land that it's easy to forget the dark underbelly of the American dream."[115]

The American dream would make Cap idealistic about his moral code. In the next issue, for example, as Rogers and Bernie exit a theater, he wonders aloud, "Despite the fact that he did some good along the way, this 'Indiana' Jones character was . . . well, he was essentially AMORAL."[116]

This heightened morality would lead Cap a few issues later to take down a steroid ring in wrestling, thereby making a stand in the war on drugs.[117] Neither Cap nor anyone else in the story examines the fact that his own physique was the product of an artificial substance that might be considered similar to steroids, despite the fact that the serum is mentioned. In fact, many of the Marvel characters were used to promote social causes in the 1980s, and Cap was featured on a 1989 poster sponsored by the FBI in which he says, "Drugs destroy lives. Join the FBI and me in our battle against drugs." And in early 1990, Cap would appear in a special FBI issue titled *Captain America Goes to War against—Drugs.*[118] Once again his own origin story is not critically examined, nor is the apparent hypocrisy of using a hero who owes his physical prowess to an artificial substance as the official FBI spokesman for the war on drugs.

One issue with which Cap routinely involves himself in the 1980s is freedom of expression. The 1980s Captain America passionately advocates freedom of speech for all Americans, even going so far as to defend the speech rights of neo-Nazi groups (who deny the Holocaust that he himself witnessed). As Steve Rogers, he argues with Bernie, his Jewish girlfriend, "I agree that these neo-Nazis are a vile breed—but, if we deny them their rights, where do we draw the line? Who decides which beliefs are acceptable and which aren't? A free society has to allow ALL ideas—both noble and ignoble—freedom of expression!"[119] As Cap, he continues by chastising a Jewish activist, "Don't you realize that, in your attack you've attacked your own freedom as well? The freedom that guarantees ALL ideas—both noble an ignoble—the expression that is imperative if our society is to survive!"[120] Throughout the 1980s, Cap often finds himself in such situations: his symbolism is thought to imply a particular view, and he is called to refute the assumptions about his views.

One big challenge to Cap in the 1980s (and back-handed critique of the Reaganesque moralizing in this decade) comes from the Coalition for an Upstanding America, which begins a Morality in Media campaign that will use Cap's image as a symbol of American morality.[121] In the April 1983 issue of *Captain America*, Cap reacts negatively to seeing his image used for this campaign:

CAPTAIN AMERICA: Who the devil ARE you people?

PUBLICITY DIRECTOR: The coalition represents a group of concerned citizens—men and women of considerable wealth—who have banded together to speak out against the erosion of moral values in our country today . . . most notably in the mass media. We're not kooks or religious fanatics, Captain—we just CARE. We'll be using our dollars to wage war against immorality! Our ad campaign will reach the hearts of the American people . . . let them know that we can be their voice! We've got two major boycotts planned . . . a new cable network almost ready to go on the air . . . Bennett advertising doing the brunt of the P.R. work . . . we're an idea whose time has come, Captain—so what do you say? Are you with us?

CAP: Son, Captain America represents ALL the American people—their highest dreams, their grandest ideals—and no select group—however right—or wrong—can claim me for their own![122]

Later, Cap ponders his own struggle for morality and idealism and tries to reconcile it with his concerns about the campaign:

> There's something about the coalition that gets my hackles up. I can't say I disagree with their goals. Having seen this country fly apart in recent years—I understand the fire that drives men to want to improve our lot—to see a return to a better—more decent—time. But it's their methods that leave me cold. What happens to the individualist in a land where morality is wielded like a club? Where decency is dictated by those with the loudest voices—and greatest wealth? Sure I've done my share of moralizing. I seem to have developed a penchant for high-flown speeches the minute I put on these red, white and blue longjohns! But I've always tried to steer clear of the line between sharing ideas—and ramming them down people's throats![123]

Later in the story, the committee's "moral message" is revealed to be a construction of crass capitalism: "Let's face it Hargrove—we're going to make a fortune off of this coalition thing! People today are such frightened little mice that it's almost the duty of enterprising men like us to exploit those fears. Lord knows if WE didn't, someone else would!"[124]

Thus, the writers of *Captain America* offer an indirect critique of the rising Republican tenor of moral superiority through a character who, at least on the surface, appears to embody it. The message is clear: images can be deceiving, and the goal of this morality movement is to mask fiscal opportunity with social conservatism.

But, of course, Cap doesn't fall for the ruse. Perhaps because he is so sensitive to the meaning of his own image, he is often suspicious of those who argue for a superior morality, even as he exhibits one of his own. Humility appears to be the key difference between Cap and his ideological opponents, a humility the authors seem to suggest was increasingly missing from American society in the 1980s. Cap's humility would also be on display as he accounts for America's treatment of the native population it had displaced.

Such situations allow Cap to question the rising wealth and privilege in American culture without having to intellectually confront the wealth that he has amassed in each of his identities. Cap always manages to frame himself as standing between the corruption of the powerful and the plight of the downtrodden, although he himself appears to have vast resources and power at his disposal.

On Christmas Eve 1984, Cap is confronted by Black Crow, a supernatural Native American who seeks to create a confrontation with Cap to rectify the injustices of America's past:

> Look around, my brother, at the world you embody! A world of concrete and metal that smothers the land and strangles the soul! Then ask me why—if you dare! On this night so sacred to your people—the night when the spirit of your America is at its peak—retribution shall be mine! When you die, Captain—the sins of your fathers die with you! The scales will have found balance—the restless spirits of my people will have found harmony once more! And in that harmony, the past and present can merge . . . become transformed . . . and this land we love so can birth a future worthy of BOTH our peoples! Such is the will of the Earth Spirit! Such is our destiny![125]

The Black Crow knocks Cap from atop the Brooklyn Bridge and assaults him with his mystical powers. Cap summons his will to live and fight on but then kneels humbly before his opponent. The Black Crow laughs, embraces Cap, and declares "the Earth Spirit is pleased."[126] The closing caption says it all:

CAPTAIN AMERICA: Her past was born of dreams and blood; savage nobility—and civilized barbarism. Her present is equal parts violence and ideals, unfathomable despair—and unfathomable hope. And her future? Perhaps the seeds of her future . . . have been sown tonight.[127]

This confrontation could not be more different from Cap's original conflict with Native Americans in *USA Comics* number 16 from 1945, in which Cap and Bucky caused an entire tribe to perish as Cap claimed it was "best," for the savages were "madmen—dedicated to murder!"[128] This time Cap shows humility—a humility born of innocence. Of course, the earlier story is not mentioned, and the writers probably were not even aware of its existence.

This connection between America's past and present does more than merely reconcile the spirits of the two ages, but the Black Crow would play an important role in Cap's next adventure. As issue 300 approached, DeMatteis launched into a long story arc that brought Captain America into mortal combat with the Red Skull. Artificially aged by an administered poison, Cap battles the decrepit Skull, who succumbs first. As Cap nears death, the Black Crow appears to him, and the two converse as images of US history engulf them:

CAPTAIN AMERICA: Am I dead?
BLACK CROW: No, my brother—you still cling to life!
CAP: I am seeing things . . . visions of America! What do they mean?
CROW: You are the embodiment of America. The panorama of the country's history dwells within you. That is why you must not die. You must keep on fighting to make the American Dream a reality . . .
CAP: But the poison—!
CROW: The poison is stronger than any man. But the spirit within you—the spirit of America—is stronger than any poison!
You cannot win this battle by will alone. You must surrender yourself to the spirit of America!
CAP: Surrender? I don't know how!

CROW: Let me help you, my brother. Trust in me, your friends, in all Americans!
CAP: I'll try.[129]

The sweeping rhetoric here captured readers' imagination. As one wrote,

> Page twenty alone would have been worth the price of the comic. It's the most philosophical comic book page I've ever seen. Could the poisons in Cap's veins somehow be related to the poisons within America today? In short, I thought it was a really beautiful, heart-rending picture.
>
> Thanks for one of the best comics ever published. If the end of this era gives way to the beginning of one as good as "Das Ende," I might just be tempted to start buying CAPTAIN AMERICA again.[130]

The following year, 1985, Mark Gruenwald, who had been editing *Captain America* during the three-year DeMatteis run, decided to take over the writing duties. Expressing a love for the character, Gruenwald took up the entire letter-column page of *Captain America* volume 1, number 306, to flesh out how he saw the ideological "essence of the character" as the embodiment of the American Dream:

> I believe Cap, the self-made man, is one of the few original, basic ARCHETYPAL heroes in all comics! Here is a man who has not had greatness bestowed upon him by accident of birth—he worked for it and continues to work for it to this day! Here is a man who does not battle evil out of guilt, neurosis, hatred, sense of obligation, or sense of destiny—he battles evil for sheer love of freedom and justice! Here is a man who does not just accept responsibility for himself, but for the society that has fostered him—a man who realizes he is a symbol to his fellow man, and constantly strives to be worthy of that trust. Here is a man who does not give up, who has confidence in his own resources and abilities, trust in the ideals by which he lives, and faith in the innate goodness of human nature. Captain America has been called the ultimate human fighting machine . . . the super-soldier, but these tags miss the point. It's not that he fights, or how good he is at it—it's WHAT HE FIGHTS FOR that counts. Captain America IS a man of action. He sees a wrong

and will immediately try to right it. But he will only use force when met
with force.[131]

The assertion that Rogers had made a choice and that the choice he made
reflected the American value of "freedom" would become a canonical
truth of the character from that moment forward. This choice also relates
to the hero's stance on the use of violence to achieve his mission goals.
Captain America's restraint would become a mainstay of the character,
defining his masculinity as one permanently in the throes of restraint
and defining him as a figure who refuses to cross over that boundary of
righteous violence so consistently present in the American monomyth
framework.

A few years later Gruenwald expanded on his personal feelings about
the character: "I believe that there are good characters and there are bad
characters, and furthermore, there are good characters and there are perfect characters—perfect archetypal characters. . . . Our best one, as far
as an all-around character that really works, is Captain America. I love
Captain America because of his thematic basis. He's an embodiment of
American ideals."[132] The characteristics Gruenwald described appear to
be somewhat connected to the feelings about America at the time. As the
1980s progressed and American citizens began to move away from the
uncertainty of the 1970s, a new spirit of patriotism grew, a spirit based on
the security from attack, military dominance, and seemingly endless cultural capital. As one fan wrote, "One of my favorite experiences is to pick
up a brand new issue of CAPTAIN AMERICA and sit down comfortably
to enjoy the adventures of one of the greatest heroes of all time. Cap is the
best that Marvel has to offer. Maybe it's because he is, in the truest sense
of the expression, a protector of the people."[133]

As Cap continued to rise in popularity (at least among his somewhat
narrow audience—that is, narrow when compared to the popularity of
other Marvel books of the era featuring mutants and symbolic resistance
to the status quo), Gruenwald continued to make most of Cap's cultural
conflict related to his status as a symbol and concerns about free speech.
In one instance, Cap feeds false information to the press in order to trap a
serial murderer. As the trap is set, Cap shows just how idealistic he is about

his views of the freedom of the press (and how much he worries about what those around him think of his integrity):

> CAPTAIN AMERICA: You know, sheriff, this is the first time I've deliberately interfered with our nation's free press by tampering with the truth. Mirage may have relatives who are hurt by this misinformation.
>
> SHERIFF: Come ON, Captain. If it'll help catch a mass murderer, don't you think it's worth it?
>
> CAP: Yes. This was my idea, after all. I just want you to know that I don't take lightly what I asked you to do.[134]

After several letters arrived asking the writer about the character's reaction to court cases connecting the practice of flag burning to freedom of expression, Gruenwald wrote an extended essay on the subject in *Marvel Age* number 84. "A flag is a materialistic thing," he mused, "with abstract connotations."

> For Cap, these connotations are all of America's greatest virtues, virtues which include freedom of speech. But Cap is savvy enough to know that not everyone shares his view of America's ideals. He would even grant others the freedom to let the American flag represent other things than those which it represents to Cap. And if the person disagrees with those which the American flag represents to him or her, would Cap grant the person the freedom to publicly express that disagreement through the public act of burning the flag?
>
> ... To sum it all up, Captain America, as I understand him, has a deep and abiding love for his country, the symbols of his country, and the ideals that those symbols stand for. But perhaps the foremost of those ideals is freedom, and Cap would not advocate abridging a person's freedom of speech or symbolic activity even if he found the content of the speech or symbolic act personally repugnant.[135]

This explicit commentary seems consistent with the implicit inferences embedded in Cap stories from the era. One of the important narrative developments of the decade was the extension of Cap's operations to areas outside of New York City. Although the hero had largely operated in New York City (with the occasional trips to Washington, DC, in the 1970s and extensive travels on missions with the Avengers), he remarks, "This entire country of ours is my concern," in response to a letter sent to Marvel Comics from a farm in Ohio and printed in issue 311.[136]

As noted earlier, through a mix-up involving his back pay as an army officer in World War II, Rogers receives a government check for nearly a million dollars, which he then uses to establish a national hotline to allow Americans to call him directly. The launch of the hotline gives the hero another opportunity to hold a press event, and hundreds of citizens crowd into a convention center for the chance to see their hero. Gruenwald supplies the mood: "As Captain America strides deliberately to the podium, he grins uneasily, concerned that the cheering crowds do not see him as a celebrity, like a movie star, pop singer, or sports figure. For his fame is a mere byproduct of his mission to give America an enduring symbol of its highest virtues—Freedom, justice, dignity, and opportunity for all. He hopes that the acclaim is for the things he represents, not the man who represents them."[137]

At the event, Cap is attacked by a new ideological opponent. Calling himself Flag-Smasher, the villain attacks Cap, burns the American flag draped behind him, and takes the crowd hostage to ensure he gets a chance to speak. Flag-Smasher then delivers a critical speech about the dangers of patriotism in society, with predictable results from the 1980s American crowd members:

FLAG-SMASHER: I am NOT against America in particular! I am against ALL countries . . . I am against the very concept of countries! I believe all men are brothers, sprung from the same primal parent. Tribalism, ethnicism, nationalism—these are all latter-day concepts that in our nuclear-powered world have become outmoded and dangerous! They make people think they are all different . . . special . . . better than other people. THIS IS WRONG! All men are EQUAL. No better or different than anyone else! When you say "I'm an American," what you're saying is that you are separate from anyone who cannot make a similar statement. Every nation fosters the idea that it is better than all the others! This is what has brought us to warfare with our fellow beings—what has brought us to the brink of nuclear destruction!

If we were to erase national boundaries and accept the essential unity of all mankind, the world would be a better place! Earth should not be divided into nations! WE ARE THE WORLD—not a bunch of different species!

CAPTAIN AMERICA: Look, Flag-Smasher, I cannot fault you for wanting to see the world a better place—so does EVERYBODY here. But does your desire for peace and unity justify your acts of violence and terrorism? The people you've injured with flying glass—you expect them to heed your words and ignore your deeds?!

CROWD MEMBERS: Get real, creep.

You tell 'im, Cap!

If you don't like America, take a hike!

Go back to Russia, ya commie!

FLAG-SMASHER: What? I'm not a communist. Weren't you people listening? I hate what the Soviet Union stands for as much as I hate what America stands for!

CROWD: Flake off!

Get out of the country!

FLAG-SMASHER: What ARE you people? WAR-MONGERS? You like feeling superior to Italians and Swedes and Poles and Africans—? You want to see this planet torn apart because of petty abstractions—? You pathetic fools![138]

After patiently allowing Flag-Smasher to speak his mind, Cap uses the opening created by his opponent's outrage—with the apparent effect of symbolically allowing the marketplace of ideas to consider and reject his foe's views before he acts—to knock him unconscious. Thus, Cap embodies the will of the Americans around him, who even at the risk of physical harm voice their judgment upon the attack on their culture. Members of the crowd ask Cap to respond to the comments Flag-Smasher uttered, and he comments, "I believe my opponent was wrong. There is nothing harmful about having a sense of national identity or ethnic heritage. America is made up of a multitude of different ethnic groups, each of which has had its own part to contribute to American culture. Be proud of your heritage, but never let your pride make you forget that beneath it all, we are all human beings who have the same wants and needs and deserve the same respect and dignity. At least, that's how I see it."[139]

The confrontation predictably generated a string of letters. Some praised the introduction of an ideological foil against which Cap could inspire and defend measured patriotic sentiments. But others (identifying with Cap's Liberal Crusader framework) dissented, arguing that the dichotomy appeared uneven. As one reader commented, "Cap is patriotic and the 'good guy,' and Flag-Smasher, who is against nationalism (as am I) is the 'bad guy.' You didn't even try to give each side an equal chance."[140] Another echoed the sentiment: "At the risk of being tarred and feathered, I must say I almost found myself rooting for Flag-Smasher. *Almost*. . . . Although his ultimate goal is virtuous (we should stamp out prejudice and unfair separatism), all his means are distorted by an unrealistic understanding of the problem."[141]

A few issues later Cap again clashes with the Flag-Smasher. This time, the two are isolated, giving Cap the opportunity to respond to the nationalistic charges brought against him, saying, "I'm not a knee-jerk patriot. I DON'T believe in my country, right or wrong. I support America in its concept, its essence, its ideal. Its political system, its foreign and domestic policies, its vast book of laws—I am NOT America's official advocate of any of that. What I represent are the principles that America's politics, laws and policies are based upon—freedom, justice, equality, opportunity."[142]

Once again, these challenges seemed trite to the readers, and Gruenwald's next opponent for Cap was a new costumed hero, the Super-Patriot.[143] Self-promotional and egotistical, the Super-Patriot represented the new spirit of the 1980s America without Cap's guiding wisdom and experience. Publicly taunting Cap, the Super-Patriot stages false conflicts and public-relations events designed to diminish Captain America's stature, sending a clear signal that the most efficient way for a 1980s superhero to succeed is contingent upon his peers. In their first direct clash, the two battle fiercely, with Cap narrowly avoiding defeat.[144] Having failed to beat the Super-Patriot, Cap begins to doubt himself, wondering whether his values (seemingly reflective of his battle prowess) are sufficient for the new era.

Gruenwald next brought Cap into direct conflict with the government to flesh out the tension between the hero's love of country and his disapproval of government officials' abuse of power. First, Cap confronts a new supersoldier, whose drug-induced rage has turned him into the Ramboesque character that some fans began to clamor for Cap to become in *Daredevil* volume 1, numbers 232 and 233.[145] Cap soon faces another such soldier, G.I. Max, whose creation represented the conflation of corrupt corporate interests with the military-industrial complex.[146] In both cases, Cap's martial victory over a physically superior opponent reinforces his status and moral authority. The source of this moral authority is technically not explained, for Cap himself was augmented with artificial substances provided by the military. And yet the lack of explication did not seem to bother the readers and fans. The image of Cap's authority, claimed by the successful use of his fists, was persuasive enough.

Perhaps the biggest challenge and statement concerning Cap's individuality came during a story arc that occurred between numbers 322 and 350 of *Captain America* volume 1. A government commission, manipulated by Cap's nemesis, the Red Skull, orders Cap to return to official military service. Rogers responds by relinquishing his government-owned name, uniform, and shield:

> To return to being a mere soldier would be a betrayal of all I've striven for, for the better part of my career. To serve my country your way, I would have to give up my personal freedom and place myself in a position where I might have to compromise my ideals to obey your orders. I cannot represent the American government, the president does that. I must represent the people. I represent the American Dream, the freedom to strive to become all that you dream of being. Being Captain America has been MY American Dream. To become what you want me to be, I would have to compromise that dream . . . abandon what I have come to stand for. My commitment to the ideals of this country is greater than my commitment to a 40-year-old document.[147]

The government selects another man—John Walker, the Super-Patriot, no less—to become the replacement Captain America, but he proves less capable despite superior strength and endurance. On his second assignment, the new Captain America kills a downed opponent in cold blood.[148] The John Walker Captain America represents the ultimate action-hero archetype presented in popular films of the era. Stronger and more brutal, this Cap does not shy away from violence the way the original Cap does. Fan reaction was mixed, although some felt a less-perfect Cap was a better representation of 1980s America: "Steve Rogers has remained a paragon of 20th century knighthood, while the American people have been morally crumbling. Steve Rogers has stood for principles, principles that the American public has been abandoning. Thus a new Captain America may be in order—Steve Rogers represents a dream, a dream of freedom and justice, etc., but only a dream. Johnny Walker is more of a mirror of the real thing: powerful, determined, yet ethically shaky (to put it mildly) and with no clear sense of direction and purpose."[149]

For his part, Steve Rogers endures yet another soul-searching exercise at this point. Although he believes the lack of presidential support is a sign of his irrelevance to the culture, those around him, the friends and colleagues who form his social identity, disagree:

> STEVE ROGERS: Look, the commission was hand-picked by President Reagan, one of the most popular presidents in history. The president must be aware of what happened. It must be okay with him!
>
> BERNIE: I wouldn't make any assumptions about what the president knows, Steve![150]

Though the Iran–Contra scandal broke during the story arc, Gruenwald continually insisted that his portrayals of President Reagan and his administration were not influenced by these specific events. Rather, he said government corruption and ineptitude were general trends of the era. "There seems to be a certain amount of carelessness, not paying attention to details [in the Reagan administration]."[151] Gruenwald also said the book was on the verge of cancellation when he took over and that he manufactured the identity crisis to redefine the character with the goal of attracting new readers.

He certainly gained attention (if not sales), though not the kind he had originally imagined: "I got some of the worst hate mail of my career. . . . And what was funny about a lot of this was they would say, 'Dear Marvel, I'm not a regular reader of Captain America, but how dare you replace Steve Rogers as Captain America?' And I say if you're not a regular reader, that's why we replaced him. So many of these people admitted that they weren't regular readers, that they'd lost interest in the character, yet now they were up in arms because we were playing around with the status quo of someone they had lost interest in."[152]

After his friends persuade him to get back into the action, Rogers assumes a new identity ("the Captain") and continues his mission to uphold and defend his particular notion of justice. Now readers had to contend with two heroes exhibiting different values. As the Captain (Rogers) saves the president from terrorists,[153] Captain America (Walker) witnesses his parents' murder at the hands of vigilantes and begins to leave in his wake an impressive body count.[154]

As the commission struggles to discipline Walker and figure out what to do with Rogers, now incarcerated because it perceived his action to save the president as an assault on him, President Reagan makes another appearance, definitively clarifying his relationship to the decisions:

PRESIDENT RONALD REAGAN: Why wasn't I informed about your replacement of the original Cap?

DOUGLAS: Er, when you granted the commission its discretionary powers, sir, I thought you did not want to be burdened with the details of our functions.

REAGAN: Don't you think that something as noteworthy as the substitution of our nation's premiere super hero warranted my attention? You would not believe the mail the White House has received since you announced it. Half the people wish the new man well, the other demands to know what happened to the original! Well, what happened to Steve Rogers, Douglas?

DOUGLAS: We had to fire him, sir. In our judgment, he could no longer do the job required of him.

REAGAN: I see. So where is he now?

MEMBER: Actually, sir, he's currently being held for questioning in connection with the assault on you.

REAGAN: You mean the night of the snake riot? My memories of that night are so vague . . . but one thing I do recall is a masked man saved my life! If that was Steve Rogers he should be given a medal . . . not imprisonment! What can I do to expedite his release?

MEMBER: Uh, nothing, sir. We'll take it from here.

REAGAN: Good, good. I hate to see an old soldier like him being treated shoddily. Carry on, gentlemen! As for YOU, young man, I expect to hear great things about you. It's a proud tradition you are upholding.

WALKER: I know, sir.[155]

Rogers is released and embarks on a final mission in which he defeats Walker in battle, confronts the Red Skull and vanquishes him, and exonerates himself in the eyes of the government. The commission reverses its decision with the ultimate stated affirmation of Steve Rogers's individuality: "While it's true that the government owns the name, the uniform, and the shield of Captain America," admits Commissioner Valerie Cooper, "the majority of us decided it is you, Steve Rogers, who made the name, uniform, and shield mean something!"[156] Individuality is confirmed to be the chief value of heroism.

In the course of this arc, Rogers completes the classic American monomyth. Forced to abandon his mission, he is also forced by circumstances into reluctant action. Granted a new costume and shield, he resumes his mission, but without his reputation. He eventually comes into conflict with his successor (the man who made him question his status) and defeats him in battle. He saves society and is awarded his old uniform and shield.

All of this activity occurs without Rogers's having compromised his politically neutral stances or his idealistic zeal. Throughout this story and the 1980s, Captain America maintains his reputation for integrity. Although a corrupted bureaucracy wrongfully infringes upon his "rights," his self-sacrificing righteousness and uncompromised individuality serve to help him overcome these obstacles. In this sense, he represented the ideal model for surviving the excesses of the 1980s American culture.

It is also interesting to note that the process of regaining his stature is framed as one of purification. For example, in *The Mighty Thor* volume 1, number 390, the Captain is able to lift Thor's hammer, a feat impossible for any but those who are "pure in heart and noble of mind."[157]

In the letter debate about the new Cap and the "firing" of Rogers, one reader described at length his thoughts about the identity crisis, illustrating several dimensions of the story's cultural significance to readers:

Rogers has often espoused that he stood for the American Dream rather than [for] any particular ideology or political system, and yet the "American Dream" he cherishes encompasses not only Americans but freedom lovers everywhere. As such, it conflicts greatly with his identity *as* Captain "AMERICA." That name and his physical representation reflects his country, but the man himself seems to have reached a grander plateau, as close to godhood as a mortal can aspire to (witness THOR #390) and still be human. In short, he is Marvel's equivalent of Superman, with the very important difference of genuinely being a man of Earth.

Some may say that this makes him too bland a character, one who is too noble, too heroic. I say, what's wrong with that? There are too many Rambo clones in the comics nowadays and we need characters like Steve Rogers to counter-balance them and offer a more positive view of what someone with potential can achieve. And, of course, it's up to Mark to delineate his human side so we don't lose touch with him (as has happened in the past with the Man of Steel).

Contrast this with John Walker, someone who still has a long road ahead of him, who is still unsure of his motivations, unflagging (no pun intended) in his loyalty to his country (though it appears he has begun to question things more and more), and uncertain (lacking?) in his moral convictions and true sense of justice. Limitless story possibilities there![158]

Of course, the difference in politics was not the only point of comparison between the two heroes. The Rogers/Walker saga largely served to critique Rogers's advocacy of restraint against the rising trend toward violence in action-hero media during the 1980s. As Walker served as the allegory for the hypermasculine hero, killing his enemies in bouts of righteous rage, Rogers served to counter this trend with an increased restraint of his own potential for violence. Together, the duo's struggle against each other (both by comparison and in direct conflict) represented a conversation about vigilantism and the relationship between superheroes and the authority within society.

Violence in Captain America's Mission

Although the Captain America character—at least the 1940s Simon and Kirby version—had originally been created to espouse violence, the modern Cap's tolerance of violence lessened over the years. By the 1980s, the threshold was so low that his origin was reimagined to suggest that Steve Rogers had originally been a pacifist and decided to join the war effort only when his brother perished in the attack on Pearl Harbor.[159]

When contrasted with the increasingly dominant archetype of the violent hero, such as the Punisher, Cap struggled to maintain his nonviolent methods. In their first meeting, the Punisher tells Cap he admires him but warns him not to interfere with his lethal mission. When Cap argues that the mobsters the Punisher hunts have rights, the Punisher asserts that criminals lose their rights the moment they commit a crime. Cap then delivers the line that forms the basis of the superhero moral code (at least, after the Comics Code): "[I]f you fight on their terms, you're no better than they are!"[160]

The Punisher rejects this logic and delivers a part of his own superhero code: "If you're not with me, you're against me!"[161] But Cap continues to battle the Punisher, and as the conflict progresses, he once again makes a familiar (and fantastic, considering his past) claim: "I was doing this before you were born, Punisher—and no second-rate hood is about to stop me now . . . no matter how much fire-power he has! That's something you should learn, Punisher. Oh, I've handled a gun a few times in my career, but I've never willingly taken a life . . . and I never will!"[162] But even this historically sanitized Captain America has killed on select occasions, as he did when battling the vampire Baron Blood in *Captain America* volume

1, number 254.[163] Locked in a death struggle and knowing that innocent lives are on the line, Cap realizes he must use his shield to behead a monster, but he continues to resist the need to kill:

> CAPTION: Cap struggles valiantly, but he can feel Baron Blood's strength slowly growing, as the sun sinks in the west. And he knows, it is only a matter of time before the monster wins! It is then that he recalls Lord Falsworth's words . . . "There is only one way to totally destroy a vampire!" And in that moment, he knows what he must do!
>
> CAP: No . . . oh, no.
>
> CAPTION: The deed is horrible to comprehend. But he knows he has no other recourse!
>
> *Chuk!*
>
> UNION JACK: BLOODY–![164]

Roger Stern and John Byrne, who would create the presidential nomination storyline, put their stamp on the hero by producing yet another origin story in celebration of Captain America's fortieth anniversary in 1981. *Captain America* volume 1, number 255, would soon become the definitive origin story (for example, when later in 1986 *Marvel Saga* number 12 gave an official account of Cap's origin, the issue reprinted more content from Stern and Byrne's version than from Kirby's or Steranko's).[165] Gone is Steve Rogers's early pacifism and the brother who died in Pearl Harbor, but his artistic talents are still present. This version portrays Rogers intentionally knocking the Nazi assassin into the electrical equipment. New additions include Captain America's initial adventure and a scene in which he receives his circular shield from President Franklin Delano Roosevelt. Even with the pacifism removed from his origin, Cap's attitude toward terminal violence remains intact, and he would again make references to having never willingly killed anyone. He even, through arguments with Nomad, manages to critique the violent tendencies of the age:

> CAPTAIN AMERICA: The way you hit that kid, you're lucky you didn't KILL him! Nomad, you've got a super-soldier serum

coursing around inside of you that makes you far stronger than the average man! And that means you've got an obligation to use that strength judiciously! That isn't the Red Skull over there! That's your common, garden-variety robber! For all we know, he's some mixed-up kid who's never tried a stunt like this before!

NOMAD: But the gun—! He was shooting at that man! He—

CAP: Then you disarm him and take him down without using undue violence! It's not our job to flex our muscles—to see how hard we can hit and how many bones we can break! If you want to prove your manhood then I suggest you–

NOMAD: I've got a suggestion for you, mister! GET OFF MY BACK!!![166]

But once Gruenwald took over *Captain America*, he was unwilling to let these values remain unchallenged. Cap soon found himself tracking down a vigilante calling himself the "Scourge of the Underworld." Much like the Punisher's, Scourge's mission involves killing those who have broken the law (except that the Punisher seems to hunt members of the mob, whereas Scourge hunts supervillains). And he is remarkably efficient, killing nineteen villains in *Captain America* volume 1, number 319, alone.[167] Gruenwald was searching for a way to remove many of the minor villains that fans didn't take seriously, and Scourge was the result. "I guess I've killed more characters than anyone else," Gruenwald once claimed.[168]

Cap does track down the vigilante in *Captain America* volume 1, number 320, and after he captures him, the two argue about Scourge's mission:

SCOURGE: The only difference between us is when *I* go after a menace to society, they don't cop a plea and go back on the streets in 3 months to a year. The problems I solve stay solved.

CAPTAIN AMERICA: What gives you the right to play judge, jury and executioner?

SCOURGE: I DON'T play judge and jury. Every person I've killed has been convicted of a crime. Go ahead and check. The American system of justice is far too lenient. I have to compensate for it.

CAP: You HAVE to, eh? Who told you to?

SCOURGE: Don't patronize me, Captain. No one told me to. I'm not crazy. I don't hear voices. I decided to do this for the same reason any of us vigilantes decides to.[169]

Much as the Punisher represents the moral justification for violence, Scourge represents the pragmatic justification and a natural extension of the superheroic formula to solve a social problem. Cap continues to oppose both justifications (relying exclusively on his fists and shield) but finds himself in the next issue directly confronting the implications of his morality. On a mission to free American hostages in Switzerland, Cap confronts a team of terrorists. As he mounts his assault (in disguise as one of the guards), a terrorist opens fire on the crowd of hostages, and Cap is forced to gun him down to save them.[170]

As Cap ponders this decision, he reflects on his values, once again framing his career as bloodless: "I believe that guns are for killing, and killing is the ultimate violation of individual rights—the ultimate denial of freedom. I NEVER carry a gun. I have never taken another person's life. Until three hours ago."[171] The shooting weighs on Cap, and he begins to wonder if he still has what it takes to perform his duty. Finally, in *Captain America* volume 1, number 323, he decides to appear on national television and explain his actions to the American people:

My fellow Americans. Certain people whom I consider friends have advised me against doing this. They told me to maintain a low profile and let the incident that has gained me so much notoriety lately quiet down. But that's never been the way I do things. I've always tried to be straightforward and honest in my dealings with everyone, especially you, the American people. So today I'd like to tell you about the shooting incident. It's true, I DID take the life of that terrorist. I profoundly regret having done so, but at the time I could see no other way to save numerous lives without taking one myself. My attitude towards killing remains unchanged.

I believe killing is morally wrong and that my actions should not be condoned or sanctioned by anyone. I am willing to go to Switzerland

and stand trial for what I did if the Swiss authorities so desire. I am also willing to accept any penalties or restrictions our government may see fit to impose.

What I ask of you is that you understand that I do not take lightly what I did, nor do I advocate murder as the solution to any problem. I also ask that you forgive me for letting you down. Since becoming Captain America, I have done my best to live up to the ideals that our nation embodies. I like to think that I've done a pretty good job at it, too. But I am only human, and even I can fall short of my ideals at times. But what I think is more important than how often you succeed at something is how hard you strive for it. I may not always succeed at being the example of all that is good in America, but I promise to never stop trying.[172]

Although Cap's writers had effectively reinvented the character—from a hero who had intentionally killed millions in the 1940s, using guns, grenades, and even poison, to a hero who feels the need to address the nation via television after his "first" shooting of an opponent—the long-term fans struggled to accept the transition. Letters poured in that challenged the claim that Cap had never intentionally taken a life: "I don't get why Cap was so shook up about killing somebody. I mean, didn't he kill anybody during World War II? He and the Invaders couldn't have gone that far behind German lines just using their fists!"[173]

The *Captain America* editors mounted a defense:

As far as Cap killing during WWII, here's the scoop. Neither Cap nor the Invaders ever carried *guns* behind enemy lines during the War. They were never actively engaged in combat with the Axis *militia*, but concentrated their efforts against Nazi super-agents and their leaders. All this is to say that Captain America never sought to kill anyone on the battlefield. It probably happened that soldiers who shot at Cap were hit by their own ricocheting bullets, but that's not the same as Cap shooting someone. We cannot deny that Cap was at the center of a lot of bloodshed during the Big One, but he himself never intentionally shed another man's blood. The Ultimatum incident in Cap #321 was the first time Cap *intentionally* took someone's life. All clear?[174]

In that response, by limiting Cap's World War II body count to Axis soldiers "hit by their own ricocheting bullets," the creative team effectively discarded Cap's actual Golden Age history and codified Roy Thomas's retcon *Invaders* narrative written in the 1970s in its place. The image of history became the recognized history.

Not all readers objected to the portrayal. Several letters praised it. For example, in the following issue one reader stated that "[a]s an individual who strongly believes in non-violent political opposition and non-killing criminal opposition, I was glad to see that Cap was truly disturbed by the fact that he had to kill someone in order to stop him. Cap knows that killing criminals makes him no better than the terrorists themselves."[175] Such letters not only supported the establishment of a revisionist historical continuity but also undermined the original Captain America monomyth formula. Through the lens of the present, the creative team and some of the readers reconstrued the past to fit the mood of later sentiments about violence and the contemporary ideology of war. World War II, instead of being a gritty conflict (granted, portrayed in a jingoistic manner in the original comic books), literally became a superhero narrative, with all the thematic and moral implications of the American "innocent nation" frame.

But once again not all readers accepted this revisionist frame. More letters criticized the revision, including one that presented a content analysis of Captain America's Silver Age violence to reject the character's evolution:

[I]n #322, he says he has never taken a human life! That statement is patently absurd. Is Cap suffering from selective amnesia? . . . Here's a quick rundown of what Cap's been depicted as doing to the enemy during the war. TALES OF SUSPENSE #63: Cap forces Dr. Erskine's killer into a bank of machinery, killing him, and later destroys a Nazi submarine. . . . TALES OF SUSPENSE #67: Bucky blows up a roomful of Nazis with a grenade, then kills a platoon of Nazis with a burp gun. SGT. FURY #13: Bucky shoots Nazis with a handgun. CAPTAIN AMERICA #100: Cap holds off hordes of Zemo's men with a high-powered pistol. CAPTAIN AMERICA #109: Cap and Bucky toss grenades at Nazis, killing them all. Cap even says, "As long as I live, I'll dedicate myself to fighting . . . to destroying the enemies of liberty!" Captain America #112: Bucky fires a machine gun at the Nazis. Cap also fires a pistol at unseen foes.

. . . I don't expect this letter to be printed since Marvel is in the process of "revising" its history. But I had to get this out in the open.[176]

By presenting a content analysis of Cap's actual narrative history found in comics, this reader's letter demonstrates the uneasy relationship that long-standing fans have with a permeable text. As the Marvel creators repositioned Captain America's stance on violence, the change became evident to those who still possessed the older comic narratives, and that dissonance drove some to object to the changing status quo.

In response to this letter, the creative team back-pedaled and struggled to support their view of the character's history: "Gee, Pierre, we frankly don't know where you get the idea we're revising history—has there been some kind of history-altering crisis we didn't hear about? We may make new revelations about old events now and then or (in the case of MARVEL UNIVERSE and MARVEL SAGA) have to decide which of two conflicting past accounts is closer to the truth, but wholesale revisions? Not that we know of."[177] By invoking *The Official Handbook of the Marvel Universe* and *Marvel Saga*, the editors appealed to the accepted authority of Marvel continuity. But from where did these authoritative sources originate?

Before Mark Gruenwald became the writer for *Captain America*, he was the editor and writer of *The Official Handbook of the Marvel Universe*. As such, the reference material contained in those volumes is a product of the herculean editorial effort of the same individual whose stories now drew the critique from readers. Thus, in a sense, the editors of *Captain America* responded to criticism of Gruenwald's portrayal of Captain America by referring the reader back to the character bible assembled and written by Gruenwald.

Marvel Saga, however, is an unusual text in itself, one that bears brief exploration. As mentioned earlier, Marvel editor in chief Jim Shooter intended *Marvel Saga* as a primer for new readers, a way of catching up on Marvel history. Danny Fingeroth, who served as the series editor, explained why he and writer Peter Sanderson drew from original materials to craft their historical narratives: "I think it's important to show the art from these original stories. It's going back to the source."[178]

By framing their editorial selections and revisions (which were needed to sort through conflicting accounts through the years) as drawing from the "original stories," Fingeroth and Sanderson presented *Marvel Saga* as a codified and official history of the Marvel Universe and the characters that exist within it. So how did this effort portray Captain America?

The series begins not with the Golden Age Timely heroes, but with the dawn of the Silver Age Fantastic Four exploits. To frame the historical context of the events in these stories, a brief three-page history is presented. Precisely one panel features Captain America, and this portrayal places him in the context consistent with *The Invaders* narrative, not with his Golden Age incarnation.[179] Thus, according to *Marvel Saga* ("The Official History of the Marvel Universe"), Cap's Golden Age history is lost, and what remains is a historical image reinterpreted through the editorial lenses of the Marvel writers of the 1970s and 1980s.

Cap's own Silver Age story would be portrayed in *Marvel Saga* number 12, picking up at the point of the hero's icy recovery by the Avengers. Roughly half the book is devoted to Cap's recovery and origin, and it is here that the Stern and Byrne rendition of this story originally presented in *Captain America* volume 1, number 255, is codified as definitive. Although the *Marvel Saga* creative team included original artwork from Jack Kirby and Jim Steranko, the Byrne artwork is privileged. When considering the various portrayals of how Steve Rogers dealt with the Nazi assassin who had just murdered Dr. Erskine, Sanderson presents the following narrative: "Justly angered, the transformed Rogers knocked Kruger into the vita-ray power source before the Nazi could kill him, too. Struggling to free himself, Kruger grabbed hold of its high voltage terminals and electrocuted himself."[180] So Marvel once and for all absolves Captain America of the Nazi agent's death. Though Rogers is "justly angered," he is not responsible for the assassin's death (it is difficult, however, to reconcile the text with the image of the event given in the artwork). The remainder of Cap's story is presented in the framework that the 1980s creators and writers had become familiar with: Cap doesn't kill and is a hero of the highest ethical and moral integrity when it comes to resolving violent conflict.

These conflicts and the resulting codification of Cap's revisionist history serve to critique the rising violence in American culture in the mid- to late 1980s. Through his struggles with and against the violent antiheroes and terrorists portrayed in his 1980s narratives, Captain America acknowledged the growing acceptance of violence in American culture while firmly adhering to his values and moral code.

And yet it should be pointed out that even these "moral" distinctions are products of the American monomyth. Captain America uses physical blunt-force violence to subdue criminals and those he disagrees with (provided they "draw first," in the spirit of the Western cowboy version of the monomyth). He throws an unbreakable metal shield at villains and routinely knocks them unconscious. It is a general concession of the superheroic formula that a righteous beating is an acceptable form of social engagement, but somehow for Captain America in the 1980s using the gun that his cowboy counterparts brandished (and that several of his fellow Marvel heroes used at that point and that many more would use in the 1990s) is "extreme violence." And, of course, the "ban on guns" controversy ignored the character's own historical use of wartime weapons in his original narratives.

Race in 1980s Captain America Narratives

Despite the fact that *Captain America* had broken the African American race barrier for heroes and featured the lion's share of the early attempts to consider race relations from a civil rights context, the 1980s narrative seems largely silent about race by comparison. The marginalization of the Falcon, formerly an equal partner with Cap (in both fact and title), into an occasional supporting character removed much of the racial tension from Captain America's adventures. Although Cap interacted with positive role models for other races and ethnicities (Jewish characters such as Bernie Rosenthal received expanded portrayals; the Black Crow brought Native American discourse into a few storylines; and so on), African Americans were not portrayed much, at least not remotely approaching the frequency with which they had appeared in Cap's 1970s storylines.

However, one footnote to the racial portrayal of African Americans concerns the introduction of the new partner for Captain America (John Walker), an African American character first called "Bucky" and later renamed "Battlestar." The name change resulted from a cultural conflict between writer Gruenwald and readers.

Lamar Hoskins was originally presented as one of three supporting characters for John Walker in his role as Super-Patriot. Calling themselves "the Buckies" (a stretched acronym standing for "Bold Urban Commandos"), the three men wore derivative uniforms resembling Captain America's in an effort to discredit Captain America by staging criminal activities and having the Super-Patriot confront and defeat them. Once Walker became the new Captain America, Hoskins was outfitted with a version of the uniform worn by Bucky Barnes, Cap's original teen sidekick during World War II. After his initial appearance in the uniform, readers—in particular African American readers—began to voice their outrage at the character's portrayal. The following exchange illustrates the conflict:

> It's bad enough that there are very few black superheroes and the ones that *do* exist are very honorable indeed, but to go and blatantly stir up controversy is beyond anyone's intelligence. And to add insult to injury, having the "new Cap" say to him something to the effect of "well, no one's going to mistake you for the old one." C'mon gentlemen, I think you can do better than that.
>
> . . . Last thought, did it ever occur to you that this event slams the very name and meaning of the book itself? Would the ex–Captain America take on a black Bucky? . . . (ask the Falcon).[181]

The editor responded, referencing other complaints Marvel had received about Hoskins and providing insight into the insensitive nature of their oversight:

> When it occurred to us to give the new Cap a new Bucky, we chose the black member of the Bold Urban Commandos (Buckies) for no other reason than it seemed the most innovative choice. Yours is hardly the only letter we've received regarding our casual decision, so we now realize we have indeed inadvertently stepped on a few toes. Firstly, writer

Mark Gruenwald turned a ghastly shade of purple when someone first informed him that in some parts of the country, "buck" is a derogatory name for a black man. It seems Gruenwald had never heard that particular expression in the Midwest where he'd grown up, and sure wishes someone had pointed it out to him *before* it got into print.

The editors also argued that the theme of the story arc was the struggle to live up to another's image and defended Hoskins's lack of objection to the name "Bucky" as part of the portrayal of a character "who is not the most enlightened black character in comics (they can't all be—that would be unrealistic)."[182]

But other letters appeared in subsequent issues, and the discourse provided insight into the race relations of the era, as readers expressed their dissatisfaction with additional aspects of the character portrayal:

I am a Black American from Chicago's south side, and I was totally appalled by the events portrayed in issue #335 of CAPTAIN AMERICA. . . .

If CAPTAIN AMERICA has to have a Black partner, why must his name be "Bucky"? Are you gentlemen aware of the discriminatory implications of such a name? Why is "Bucky" portrayed as the "donkey's tail," meaning why hasn't he any backbone whatsoever? In this issue, he knows how people will react to him in a town like Custer's Grove, Georgia, but still he adapts an OKI-DOKE attitude toward the whole thing, and actually tries to wander around town alone, asking nosy questions!

Not only is "Bucky" portrayed as a literal black ass, but how does he help fish out villains? By posing as a fast-talking pornographer who's only one step from looking like a stereotype pimp! Is this the image of the Black hero these pages will portray from now on? I find it utterly tasteless and infuriating, as would anyone with even an ounce of morality.[183]

The letter also strenuously criticized the lynching of this character, which the letter writer argued invoked the troubling history in American race relations.

To address the increasing number of objections, the *Captain America* creative team incorporated the dispute into the comic narrative. While on assignment at a government prison, Hoskins is pulled aside by an older African American guard for a discussion:

> VAULT GUARD: [A]ppreciate seeing another high profile black super hero and can imagine how proud you were to get the job—but what kind of name is Bucky?
> BUCKY: That's the name of the original Cap's original partner.
> GUARD: I know that. A young white kid who died forty years ago. You ask me, that's not a fitting name for a black man who's the same age as Cap, and has the same power as Cap, and is bigger to boot!
>
> Not only that, in some parts of the country, "buck" is an offensive term for a black man. You ask me, I think the government stuck you with that name to keep you in your place.[184]

This discussion causes Hoskins to approach a member of the Commission on Superhero Affairs regarding the historical and racial implications of his superhero name. Mortified, the government provides Hoskins with the new identity "Battlestar" and a uniform more similar to that of his partner.

Other than this embarrassing chapter in the history of African American superheroes (and the disappointing reduction of the Falcon's involvement in Captain America's adventures), the Captain America of the 1980s remained largely silent about matters of race. Like most controversial social or political issues, Cap at times expressed strong ideological sentiments in private, but these sentiments rarely led to public statements or expressions. Like much of the American population, Captain America appears to have internalized his opinions about social injustice or the need to reform (other than, of course, the need to stand against criminal activities and threats to the status quo). In contrast to his outspokenness in each of his earlier eras, Captain America remained relatively mute in the 1980s, just at a time when his symbolism appeared to convey powerful messages beyond his control.

7

The Superficial Icon
(1990–2002)

Capitalizing on the popularity and iconic status of the character, Marvel produced a superficial image-heavy expression of Captain America in the 1990s. Several industry and cultural changes influenced this trend.

On the industry side, the animation and licensing successes on third-party properties (such as *G.I. Joe: A Real American Hero* and *The Transformers*) of the early 1980s had proven a boon to Marvel, so much so that the company had been purchased by New World Pictures in late 1986.[1] However, in its first annual reports after acquiring Marvel, New World immediately cut the third-party arrangements to concentrate profit margins: "Marvel Productions will de-emphasize the production of animated programming based upon licensed characters and concentrate on the development and the production of programming based upon existing and newly created characters fully owned by Marvel, rather than third-party licensors, to benefit from the licensing, merchandising, publishing and other ancillary revenue streams which can be generated by character exploitation."[2] This decision would encourage conservative editorial directions for many Marvel comic books as the company began to increase its focus on holding the image of its characters in a recognizable stasis to reduce confusion among the readers, viewers, and toy collectors approaching them from different experiences. Comic books became a vehicle to promote characters and products, preventing the creators from writing stories that would result in significant changes. The summer of 1989 signaled this shift as the company embarked on a fourteen-issue annual crossover series titled *Atlantis Attacks*. Creative talent from so many different titles quarreled over the treatment of their characters, resulting in a convoluted storyline that confused readers and led fans to react negatively.[3] But the New World deal had signaled the mere beginning of struggles between Marvel's editorial divisions and its corporate owners. New World sold the publishing arm of Marvel in 1989, and Ronald Perleman gained controlling interest for a reported $10 million, touching off the corporate power struggle that would put the company in headlines throughout the 1990s and would ultimately lead it into bankruptcy.[4] Under Perleman, Marvel went public and further diversified its product line, selling trading cards based on the Marvel Universe characters and stories. In 1992, Marvel acquired the sports card company Fleer and created Marvel Studios, a corporate unit dedicated to handling Marvel's film and television projects. Ensuring that Marvel properties were consistently recognizable and attractive to a wide range of consumers suddenly became increasingly important.

Because of the multimedia nature of the properties, the scripting of characters such as Captain America became much more conservative when the corporation began to measure new story offerings in terms of brand appeal and cross-over product opportunities. Fan consumption itself was changing, and some of those changes led to different demands from comics in previous eras. When the direct-sales system put comics into specialty stores, one of the largest immediate benefits for the publishers was that the product was purchased upfront and could not be returned. Comic book stores would then place the remainders into bins to be sold in the future to collectors seeking out missing issues or past items of interest. The comic-collecting activities that had grown up largely in the 1970s and 1980s exploded in a wave of intense comics speculation in the 1990s as comic books began to be seen as investments for future resale. At the height of this frenzy, media reports noted that nonreader speculators were purchasing large numbers of comic books purely for their economic value.[5]

Marvel jumped to capitalize on this trend. The publication of *Spider-Man* volume 1, number 1 (which should not be confused with volume 1, number 1, of *The Amazing Spider-Man*, debuting in March 1963), resulted in three million copies sold (a record at the time), driven by the release of several variant covers to give collectors an incentive to buy more than one copy and the artwork of hot young artist Todd McFarlane, which compensated for a relatively mediocre story.[6] The impetus for the new series was, in turn, "to create a new series that could then easily be collected as trade paperbacks."[7] This kind of strategy—emphasizing artwork and collectability, creating content to fit into future modular products, and cross-promoting the varying content products—quickly built up a star system among comics creators and most particularly among artists.

Chaffing under the rigid status quo imposed on Marvel characters by the company, seven artists left Marvel to form Image Comics, a company that allowed creators to own and control their creations. The loss of talent hurt Marvel's creativity, and the company soon began to rehash variations on generic plotlines and focus more on artistic updates of familiar themes than on original stories. *Captain America* writer Mark Waid described the period as one in which the various remaining creators in the company were "invariably acting out of fear rather than confidence."[8]

Marvel acquired the comic book distributor Heroes World in 1994 in a bid to gain greater control over comic distribution. However, this move led other major publishers to make exclusive deals with other distributors, and the resulting upheaval resulted in a crisis for the comic book industry as the increased production and distribution costs resulted in higher prices at a time when comic book sales began to decrease dramatically. Labor disputes in professional hockey and baseball led to a sharp fall in the sports card market. Marvel's comic sales slumped: the company lost a reported $400 million, and in December 1996 it filed for bankruptcy,[9] which would bring about an end to the first volume of *Captain America* with issue 454.[10]

In order to protect some of its core properties (among them Captain America and the Avengers), Marvel temporarily outsourced them to the studios of Rob Liefeld and Jim Lee, two of their departed employees who had helped start up Image Comics, and the duo revamped the characters and created new lines of continuity. This arrangement lasted only a year, and the characters were returned to their original Marvel continuity.

In the new narrative, the outsourced heroes "died" in the Marvel Universe, sacrificing their lives to defeat a world-threatening villain named Onslaught.[11] However, the heroes really survived and were rebooted into a new universe of continuity. In this "pocket universe," the Avengers are a government-funded force,[12] an idea that would later be explored in the *Ultimate* Marvel stories and eventually become a premise of the Marvel Studios film franchise.

In Cap's second series, he receives a new origin and narrative context. The primary alteration would revolve around his ever-changing relationship with the government. At the conclusion of his World War II career, Captain America finds himself at odds with President Truman over the planned use of the atomic bomb. After Cap declares his intention to speak publicly against the bomb, Truman conspires with Nick Fury to place Cap in suspended animation to get him out of the way.[13] When Rogers awakens and recovers his memories, he has an understandable distrust of the US government, which serves as the motive for his insistence on serving the American Dream instead of the establishment's policies.

Though Liefeld experimented with several aspects of Captain America's motivations, backstory, and even costume, he had a falling out with both Marvel and Image,[14] and Jim Lee took over the book and quickly returned the character to the formula and form he has possessed since the late 1980s.

Marvel Entertainment Group merged with Toy Biz in 1997 to form Marvel Enterprises, which ended the bankruptcy, and the missing heroes returned to mainstream Marvel continuity. The third volume of *Captain America* reintroduced him to the Marvel Universe, but he again was subjected to formulaic and superficial retreads of previous narratives, as in much of the last stretch of the first volume: Cap renounced his uniform for a new identity for political reasons in *Captain America* volume 1, numbers 450–53 (as he had done in volume 1, numbers 332–50); he wrestled with the intersections of his mission with political operatives claiming endorsements in volume 3, number 13 (as he had in volume 1, number 280); he faced the Red Skull over control of the cosmic cube in volume 3, numbers 14–17 (as he had in *Tales of Suspense* volume 1, numbers 79–81, and *Captain America* volume 1, numbers 114–19); he entered prison to uncover corruption in volume 3, number 23 (as he had in *Tales of Suspense* volume 1, number 62, and *Captain America* volume 1, number 260); he confronts racism alongside the Falcon in volume 3, numbers 25–27 (as he had in *Captain America and the Falcon* volume 1, numbers

143–44); and he faced a new supersoldier with a personal grudge against him in volume 3, number 33–38 (as he had faced John Walker in *Captain America* volume 1, numbers 323 and 350).

The Antiviolent Crusader

To illustrate the Captain America complex, Robert Jewett and John Shelton Lawrence select a story from the third volume of *Captain America*:

> [Since his origin] . . . Captain America has allied himself with many causes, always adding a selfless muscular component, whether in battling against Cold War enemies, post-Watergate presidential villains, or industrial magnates who pollute air and water. In the eerily prescient issue of April 1999, Captain America had to confront his nemesis, the Red Skull, in New York City. Skull had raised the temperature of the city to a lethal level in January and then introduced a ravenous hunger in the dying New Yorkers. This was his opening gambit in a campaign to gain control of the earth. The cover of the issue featured the good Captain and Skull in vicious hand-to-hand combat—"for the fate of the world."[15]

Delving into the storyline, the authors point to the conflict's resolution, when, after arguing with other characters about taking the Skull's life, Cap relents and impales the Red Skull, killing him. The authors conclude that, the resistance to violence overcome, "[t]his elaborate effort at restraint in the use of force—suppressing his own aggressive instinct—places Captain America in the heroic tradition of the American cowboy killer, the man of purely innocent intention who draws second in the gun battle but shoots more quickly and accurately than the dastardly foe."[16] The story in question does contain the elements the authors describe, but a closer reading presents elements more complex than the typical American monomyth formula.

The Red Skull had previously died in a conflict with Cap over the cosmic cube, a device that would allow its wielder to alter reality according to his or her whims. At the conclusion of that conflict, the Skull had appeared to gain the upper hand, but Captain America had thrown his shield, which struck the cube and shattered it. The resulting explosion appeared to consume the Skull, leaving behind only a burned shadow of the villain on the wall.[17] The newer series, however, inserted an intervention by the time-traveling character Kang the Conqueror (secretly the time-traveling Michael Korvac), who resurrects the Skull in the hopes that the Skull's victory in the contemporary era would ensure a future conquest for Kang himself. In the course of the resurrection, Kang/Korvac experiences the Skull's mind and exclaims: "Over the millennia, I have been characterized as EVIL by those who, I now realize . . . have no concept of the word's TRUE MEANING. Until now, not even I knew the depths of Skull's DEPRAVITY . . . and for the first time, I wonder if I've made a ghastly mistake . . . in unleashing the GREATEST EVIL the world has EVER KNOWN . . . !"[18]

Captain America is given a prelude to the Skull's dominance by the Watcher, a supreme being charged with observing and recording galactic history. The Watcher (again secretly Michael Korvac) reveals the coming consequences of the Skull's victory: "This is the America of the Red Skull. A nation populated by two hundred seventy million slaves . . . and one dictator. There is no liberty anymore. There is no justice. Every freedom you or any soldier has ever championed is now meaningless . . . forgotten like a dream burned away by dawn's harsh sun."[19]

As Cap struggles to comprehend the coming apocalypse, the Watcher tells him it is ultimately Captain America's fault for not "terminating" the process by which the Skull (already omnipotent because of the residual power of the cosmic cube instilled in his form during his resurrection) would gain access to omniscience by summoning the starship of the world-eating Galactus. It is at this point that Cap begins to make the argument for reticence in the use of violence:

CAPTAIN AMERICA: "Terminate." An interesting choice of words.
    Are you asking me to kill the Skull?
WATCHER: You are a soldier, Captain . . . and the coming war
    for freedom in the face of Skull's galactic totalitarianism will
    be an unwinnable war so huge and climactic that even I can-
    not stay silent and uninvolved. There is no cube to knock from

the Skull's hand, not this time. You have seen tomorrow. To
eradicate the Skull before he can attain infinite knowledge
is earth's—reality's—only hope. To that end, I allow you your
choice of weapons.

CAP: So I can save the world through pre-meditated murder. No
thanks. I'll find another way.[20]

In the following issue, Captain America's S.H.I.E.L.D. agent partner
and occasional love interest Sharon Carter picks up the objection:

SHARON CARTER: Don't get all high and mighty with me, Rogers!
You've spilled blood before in war! You're a soldier!

CAPTAIN AMERICA: Different times, different circumstances.
Taking a life is always a last resort. I won't accept that there's not
another way.[21]

In the end, Cap concedes the debate by transforming his electronic shield
into a sword and impales the Skull from behind, killing him.[22] This act,
the death blow delivered following the long debate of resistance, signifies
for Jewett and Lawrence the invocation of the American monomyth, the
framing of vigilante justice as a necessity forced by evil villains against the
righteous savior figure's desires.

However, a few other factors should be considered in light of this conclusion. First, it should be noted that the authors of the story in question
titled it "A Tale of Morality and Failure: Extreme Prejudice." Contrary to
the celebration or promotion of the righteous killing frame, the comic
authors appear to have presented Cap's actions as a failure of morality,
not a moral justification of killing. Within the narrative, Cap is urged to
kill by the premonition of circumstances, the advice given by a seemingly
all-knowing (and neutral) entity, and the admonition of one of his closest
confidants, yet still he argues against using terminal violence. When he
decides to kill the Skull, the decision is the culmination of the story of
failure, not success.

Second, the reaction from readers should be considered. In the ensuing issues, several letters appeared concerning the act of killing, almost

exclusively from a critical stance. Three representative passages illustrate the act's reception among readers:

> I was shocked when Cap stabbed the Red Skull through the heart. At first, I thought, "Hey, now . . . Cap killing? No way. There's always another way." But then I thought, "Wait a minute. This is Mark Waid. He knows Cap better than any CAPTAIN AMERICA writer I've ever read. This'll all work out." And I'm sure it will.[23]

> I don't know if I buy Captain America so heartlessly killing the Red Skull. Yeah, Cap was a soldier during World War II, and I'm sure that as a soldier, killing is part and parcel of the job, but he's moved beyond that. Wartime is different. Cap now lives in a time and place where killing is an absolute last resort, and I'm sure he could've thought of a different way out of this Red Skull mess.
>
> . . . Cap killing the Skull is . . . well . . . out of character in my opinion.[24]

> [W]hen faced with a situation where the only information he had told him that there was only one way to survive, one way to save the world, he made the truly hard choice; the one that meant violating his code of ethics, his code of being, to save the greater good. Captain America became a murderer. He walked up to the Skull, fully aware of what he was doing, and plunged a sword through his back. . . . What makes matters worse; not only is Cap a murderer, but he is a liar as well.
>
> . . . And a world where Captain America can turn his back on what he represents is a world that much darker for us all.[25]

Finally, it is worth pointing out that Cap stabbing the Skull was not the resolution of the story, but the midpoint. After the Skull falls, Cap realizes that the Watcher has been Michael Korvac all along and travels to the future in the following issues to do further battle. At the conclusion of that struggle, Cap is returned to the present and appears there just as he flings himself at the Skull: he alters his energy sword into a staff and strikes the Skull without killing him.[26] He then is forced into a longer physical confrontation that ends when the Skull unwittingly defeats himself.

Contrasting with the use of the term *failure* in the title of issue 17, the title of issue 19 depicts the resolution as a "triumph of will,"[27] which is how Captain America's victories are generally framed when he outsmarts or outmaneuvers his opponent to overcome long odds without resorting to using brute force. Even regarding this victory, which leaves the Skull's fate ambiguous, some readers expressed appreciation: "The story element I appreciated the most, however, was Cap's own acknowledgement that he hoped the Red Skull survived. For the first time in my recollection, rather than leave it up to future writers to explain how the villain escaped certain death, through Cap's own exposition, we know how the Skull survives this encounter. You cannot know how much I admire Cap's concern over even the most evil of men. No matter how desperate the situation, it seems that Captain America always chooses life. A true hero, indeed."[28]

Other readers, however, were not satisfied with the story's conclusion, suggesting that Cap had not lived up to his reputation because he did not warn the Skull about the impending danger: "Captain America does not lie. Is not speaking the truth a lie in itself? When the Red Skull went into the antimatter engine, he wouldn't have paid heed if Cap did tell him the truth, so the same thing probably would have happened. The Red Skull would have seen it as a pathetic ruse on Cap's part, being the megalomaniac he is, and would have done so, anyhow."[29]

And still others found the story superficial and rote when considered overall: "a major letdown. . . . the readers were given a six-month Red Skull storyline that offered no new insights into the Skull or Steve Rogers. The storyline was basically the Red Skull committing various cartoonish, over-the-top villainous acts while reminding the reader how 'eeevviiil' he is[.] Not impressive, and not deserving of half a year's worth of stories."[30]

In fact, Captain America's views toward violence throughout the 1990s would have made a killing act an extreme outlier. The decade's first major opportunity to display Cap's objection to lethal methods came at the end of the "Galactic Storm" story arc. After the Avengers are dragged into an interstellar conflict and witness the deaths of millions of sentient beings, they discover that the culprit, the Supreme Intelligence, is within striking distance. Several Avengers decide to exact vengeance, a decision that splits the team down the middle. Captain America leads the debate, arguing against the assassination and concluding, "We are not judge, jury and executioner. It is as simple as that."[31]

Other Avengers join his resistance and voice their objection, including the young Quasar, who exclaims, "[W]e're the Avengers . . . we don't do things like this!"[32] But the rival faction is not dissuaded. Iron Man leads this faction on the quest for vengeance, and the Supreme Intelligence falls under the assault. When the heroes return, Cap hangs his head and slinks back to the team's ship. The story next picks up in *Captain America* volume 1, number 401, when Cap calls for a vote for his removal as the Avengers' leader. Iron Man responds that no one wants that and chalks up the dispute to a disagreement over "what constitutes appropriate conduct in a time of war."[33]

The irony (Captain America is the only hero in the room to have fought in a war) is apparently lost, and Cap demands that all Avengers report for a lecture (by him) later that evening on "Superhero ethics." When none of the faction that participated in the assassination shows up, Cap cancels the lecture and broods:

> Seems like my style of professional behavior is out of fashion, at odds with this increasingly violent society. Maybe guys like the Punisher, Cable, and Wolverine are the answer to the kind of threats America faces today. Maybe bad attitudes and lax moral codes are the only way to make headway.
>
> The values I've striven for my entire career seem so . . . untenable in this present clime. But without them, what am I?[34]

Cap does repair some of the relationships, but the dispute itself remains unresolved. As the 1990s progress, Cap routinely defines himself against the industry's trends, as when he observes to Iron Man, "The 'younger generation' worries me, sometimes . . . they're so much more impulsive and violent than we ever were."[35] This critique is limited mostly to such private discussions. Cap does serve as an example for others, but usually without commentary or confrontation (unlike in the 1980s). One exception to this early 1990s trend is Cap's confrontation with Americop, a superpowered police officer who judges on the spot the criminals he has detained and executes them. When Cap first comes into contact with Americop, he bellows, "How DARE you take the law into your own hands?" and eventually declares, "You're not a lawman—you're a self-appointed vigilante meting out your own warped version of justice! The presumptuousness of your kind sickens me!"[36]

Of course, this is an unusual statement coming from someone who also takes the law into his own hands and is also technically a vigilante. But the objection is framed specifically around the use of terminal force. Cap does not necessarily object to Americop's efforts or even to the blunt-force trauma he and Cap dish out to those they pursue. He objects to the taking of life, an action he himself once undertook with regularity.

Cap gets an opportunity to explicate the personal root of his philosophy of violence when he visits the villainous Crossbones in prison: "I have this theory that no one is beyond redemption. That's why I'm so big on preserving life—even the lives of those who try to kill me. As long as a person's alive, there's hope he may redeem himself."[37] However, a later storyline (by different creators) places the rationale at the heart of his symbolic and communal identity. Stripped of his uniform and citizenship, Steve Rogers finds himself on a clandestine mission with Sharon Carter to prevent a global conflict. As they approach a foreign military base, Sharon takes aim at a guard, and Rogers's reflexes manage to divert her shot. He angrily confronts her:

STEVE ROGERS: What is wrong with you? You took deliberate aim!
SHARON CARTER: Well, DUH. The Moldavarians are our enemies, remember? WHAT? That's not the way American troops act? Well, you're not an American anymore, remember?
ROGERS: That's not the point. And thank you. NO. KILLING.[38]

This example displays some of the interpretive confusion about Cap's morality. Carter seems to locate Cap's refusal to kill in his American identity, a position that Rogers quickly rejects. But he does not explain his own rationale, nor does he take the opportunity to address why so many conflicting assumptions are made about a hero who routinely strikes criminals in the head with an unbreakable metal shield but thinks using guns or knives is immoral.

Such questions would remain unexplored because Marvel soon ended Mark Waid and Ron Garney's run of *Captain America*. Turning over a selection of its core characters and titles to the creative forces in the Image Comics network, Marvel allowed these properties to be rebooted and reinterpreted for a year while it again sorted out financial trouble.

In terms of his views on violence, the new Captain America seemed to be as dogmatic in his nonlethal tendencies as his previous incarnation. In one of the first adventures with the reimagined Avengers, Captain America declares, "The Avengers don't kill their enemies. At least, not on my watch. Any of you have a problem with that?"[39] And later he declares to Thor, "[W]e avenge wrongs. We don't commit them."[40] But the expression of his views reached new dimensions with respect to his opinion regarding the use of strategic violence at the close of World War II. Reframing his narrative, the young creators presented Cap in conflict with President Harry Truman over the planned use of the atomic bomb. When Truman explains that the decision has been made and orders Captain America's silence, the hero responds: "I cannot and will not, in good conscience, support this decision. One of the founding principles upon which this great country was based—is the freedom of speech. You did what you thought was necessary to bring this horrible war to an end. I disagree with you. And we can stand here until tomorrow morning—and I will still disagree with you. I won't have any part of it."[41] This decision winds up being the impetus for Cap's long freeze when the government puts him out of commission to assure his silence.

When Cap and the other heroes return from the "pocket universe" into mainstream Marvel continuity, Cap finds himself the focus of public adoration, an international icon. As a result, his every action and opinion are of interest to the public, and Marvel creators took pains to reestablish his virtue. For example, in the premiere issue of the new nostalgic series *Captain America: Sentinel of Liberty*, Waid and Garney present a story retconned in the 1960s in which Captain America and Agent 13 (Sharon Carter) pursue a renegade S.H.I.E.L.D. agent. Carter conceals a termination order from President Clinton. When Cap discovers the deception, he confronts Carter, who defends her actions:

SHARON CARTER: You've never hesitated to do what your country has asked of you. For as long as anyone can remember, you've been the perfect soldier . . . but never an assassin. You don't kill—not in cold blood. When I saw that you were suddenly being asked to choose between duty and conscience . . . I decided to spare you the burden. I'm a soldier, too . . . Steve. There are times I HAVE to kill. I'm not proud of it . . . but my job gets dirty. Sometimes, the only way I can keep going . . . is to know that there's still one man out there who can always do the job clean.

CAP: You have no moral problem with killing this man in my stead?

CARTER: I have a personal problem. I'm afraid it might change how you feel about me.[42]

As this scene reveals, by the late 1990s Cap's attitude against killing is not merely personal but socially imposed. Sharon Carter, in her "wetworks" role, justifies the practice of clandestine assassinations to create plausible deniability for the public symbol of American values. This attitude not only provides insight into the peculiar fusion of military objectives and public politics inherent in policing the world as a lone superpower but also directly expresses a justification for the "innocent nation" mythology: covert immorality is a necessary part of maintaining the illusion of the nation's innocence.

The dichotomy in the functional relationship between Captain America and the various agents of S.H.I.E.L.D. is representative of the myths about the US military originating during the Reagan era. Throughout 1980s popular culture (e.g., films such as *Delta Force*, *First Blood*, and *Navy Seals*), references to covert forces' "dirty deeds" were contrasted with the "clean" and wholesome activity of the elected public servants and traditional military units (taking lives while in uniform is justified when American monomyth frames are presented by way of justification). Before the war on terror, Americans were comfortable enough with the knowledge that US Special Forces would occasionally get their hands dirty so long as the mainstream political and cultural America could maintain a "clean" image. Lawrence and Jewett argue that this narrative dichotomy led many Americans to accept the Iran–Contra scandal without outrage, likening Oliver North's actions to those of a Western vigilante hero or a hero in the vein of John Rambo or Chuck Norris.[43]

In the America before September 11, 2001, the world was presented as a scary place where dirty actions are sometimes necessary, but the idealistic symbols of America must remain above the violent actions needed to impose order. And the Captain American of the 1980s and 1990s, like the culture he represented, refused to get his hands dirty, even if it meant allowing the killing to be done by secret government agents.

In several other ways, in the 1990s Captain America critiqued aspects of his own narrative. After a battle with longtime foe Batroc the Leaper, Cap muses:

> I wasn't defending my country. I wasn't fighting to protect the innocent. I was brawling because some idiot came gunning for me. What a pathetic waste of time.
>
> Earlier, I was beating myself up for letting things happen rather than making them happen. Could I have found a better example? I fought a battle I've fought a dozen times before . . . and it did nothing to make the world a better place. This wasn't a heroic act. It was just a wrestling match . . . with just as little at stake.[44]

Nor does Cap take lightly those euphemisms and metaphors that invoke images of military conflict in everyday experiences:

> War. I regret her use of that term. Just as I regret people describing football games and wrestling matches as war.
>
> I know war. As lethal as this is, war is something far, far worse. True war is about death and suffering. About horrible misery inflicted on the human body and spirit by fellow men. It's about living like an animal in the rain, muck and mire. It turns proud cities into battlefields resembling alien landscapes more than communities of men, women and children.

The focus of war is mass death. Kill more of the enemy than he can kill of you. Bucky and I saw the carnage firsthand on the beaches of Normandy, the deserts of Africa and the freezing woods of Germany.

Once the process starts, once war is declared—no one is spared the savagery. I saw men . . . boys, actually . . . die far too young in the defense of their country and the ideals of freedom held dear.[45]

The criticism that physical conflict serves little purpose and is a "waste of time" (and is often overdramatized in "war" rhetoric) was an unusual critique for that era's superheroes.

One of the stereotypes of 1990s comic books narratives is that they involved the escalation of violence, increased use of firearms, and rampant portrayals of violent vigilantism. The 1990s Captain America, however, largely resisted those trends and was even used by his writers to critique them, such as when he interrupts a young man's attempted theft of comic books:

STEVE ROGERS: A Captain America comic—may I see it?

SHOP OWNER: Uh . . . yeah. Just don't take it out of the bag.

ROGERS: These comics are about heroes. People who do good
things for the sake of other people. How can you read these and
get the idea that it's all right to steal from others?

KID: Who reads 'em? I just collect 'em so I can resell them when
they're worth a lot of money!

ROGERS: I see. How about you? Do you read them?

OWNER: Of course I do! I love super heroes—they're at the cutting
edge of the counterculture! I wish I knew some of them personally! I'd have the Punisher break this punk's hands or Wolverine
carve the word "thief" on his forehead!

ROGERS: Those heroes are your favorites?

OWNER: Yep! The more violent they are, the better I like them! The
better they sell, too!

ROGERS: Do you want to press charges?

OWNER: Nah . . . the law will let him off anyway. That's why the
best heroes take the law into their own hands.[46]

The shop owner's commentary precisely expresses the tenets of the American monomyth. Not trusting the police to be able to deliver justice, the shop owner prefers vigilante justice with harsh consequences, meted out by self-appointed heroes who consider themselves above the law. Though Captain America shares the superheroic mission, he appears troubled by the extremes to which many of his contemporaries resort and by the appreciation those actions draw from such heroes' admirers.

Above all, Captain America represents the restrained use of force, though it is clear he relishes the opportunity to use his power from time to time. When he engages Protocide, a competitor supersoldier, and the two exchange initial blows, Cap exclaims, "That . . . hurt. I like that. It frees me—from having to hold back!"[47] The idea that Cap maintains continual restraint on a daily basis exemplifies the discomfort of the nation he represents: after the country was built into a superpower to combat a powerful foe, frustration and self-doubt emerged when that opponent disappeared and America was left the world's sole superpower. Captain America still has his enemies in the 1990s, but it is clear that his purpose is in perpetual question, and the uneasiness he feels with his own abilities is often on display.

However, Cap also appears to see himself as something of a democratic force. After stopping a rogue S.H.I.E.L.D. agent from firing a nuclear missile at the United States to "effect change," Cap bellows, "If you don't like the way America does things, there's a way to change it. It's called the vote. As soon as people cross into violence—I step in."[48]

But those moments when the United States is under direct threat are the few moments that Cap's mission seems so clear, even to himself.

The Masculinity of the Post–Cold War Captain America

In addition to raising questions about ongoing foreign policy, the end of the Cold War also presented significant questions about national identity among the populace.[49] This identity crisis was reflected in popular media in various ways, but often shifting the threats from the nation to the family and concerning itself with the threats of moral decay in lieu of nation-state othering.[50] The lack of boundaries resulting from the absence of the

Cold War adversary led to the presentation of symbols of failed masculinity in the face of feminine forces.[51] Whereas during the 1980s the hard action-hero body had served as an idealized representation of Reagan-era politics,[52] the 1990s brought a softer and more vulnerable kind of action hero.[53] These differences played out both with respect to physical confrontations and in criticisms of the previous era's presumptions of hypermasculine narratives as perceived through the lenses of hypomasculine or feminized perspectives.[54]

This trend showed up most literally in *Captain America* volume 1, numbers 387–92, an arc titled "The Superia Stratagem." Captain America and the mercenary Paladin wind up on a cruise ship full of female supervillains. After a prolonged battle, they are overpowered and placed in a laboratory to undergo "[f]eminization treatment."[55] With the help of two female colleagues, they escape, but to avoid detection they are forced to don their rescuers' costumes. Superia, the arch villain masterminding the gathering, has selected a cross-section of women she believes to be the pinnacle of her gender and plans to sterilize the rest of the earth's women with a chemical rocket. Her plan involves creating a female-led utopia by making reproductive ability a scarce commodity: "Those of us who remain fertile—that is, the 10,572 women here within Femizonia's hermetically sealed environment—will suddenly become humanity's most precious and vital resource! In order to even survive, the world will have to capitulate to our every demand! Think of the tremendous political power we will soon acquire! The power to control the destiny of the human race!"[56] The cross-dressed Captain America thwarts the plan by picking at Superia's inferiority complex until she loses her temper and lashes out in rage, destroying the integrity of Femizonia's protective boundary.[57] The rocket is intercepted, the crisis averted, and Cap and his colleagues are rescued.

The story arc presents several troubling stereotypes of feminism as a militant and coercive method of dominating men. Superia herself is presented as the ultimate militant feminist: "Men . . . are beasts, savages, brutes! They are far inferior to us and yet by force they've held sway over the civilization we share since ancient times! It is time for a change. It is time society rectified itself. It is time the world were ruled by those most fit to rule."[58] In the course of the story, her attempt to emasculate Cap can be seen as the ultimate threat to his gender. Not content to challenge him verbally or even physically, Superia presumes that once Captain America is female, he will simply side with his enemy because of his newfound "superior gender." And yet, in the end, it is Superia's temper that leads her to commit an irrational act that directly thwarts her master plan (two more stereotypes of women). When Cap goads her into irrationality, her true motive is betrayed as a desire to prove her gender's superiority instead of the rational goal of world peace to which she had earlier alluded. (The plight of the rest of the world's women in the plot—sterilization—is also disturbing.)

In this period, Captain America's narratives also engaged in hyper-masculine critique by reimagining core assumptions of earlier versions of the text, such as when the more realistically flawed soldiers in issue 41 of *The 'Nam* consider how absurd the Captain America narrative (and other war texts such as John Wayne's films) are when compared to their own more realistic experiences.[59] Captain America himself critiques elements of his narrative from previous eras, such as when he reconsiders the pros-pect of leading youthful sidekicks into battle during World War II: "When I look back at it all now, it seems miraculous that Bucky survived as long as he did. Amazing, in fact, that ANY of our junior counterparts survived. In fact, viewed with the clarity of hindsight, it seems pretty irresponsible of us to have had kid partners at all. We were adults. We knew what we were doing. But Bucky, Toro, all those kids who called themselves the Kid Commandos . . . [.]"[60]

This particular renegotiation represents the first time Cap criti-cally considers his own earlier texts. Previous intertextual conflicts were resolved either by ignoring the past continuity (such as when Captain America writer Mark Gruenwald claimed in *Captain America* volume 1, number 322, that Cap had never previously shot someone, thus disavow-ing the entire 1940s and 1950s comic book continuity[61]) or by framing that criticism through allegory (such as when Cap battled the 1950s version of himself in *Captain America* volume 1, number 156[62]).

In the 1990s, Cap's narratives also began to explore his personal rela-tionships, particularly with women, as in the entire issue devoted to Steve

Rogers's date with Rachel Leighton, the reformed villain Diamondback, who served as Captain America's partner for a time.[63]

Perhaps no critique was as extensive as the exploration of Captain America's bodily vulnerability. Superhero bodies serve as "the paradoxical vector of an aggressive masculinity as well as the locus of the characters' limitations,"[64] so it is only natural that a deconstruction of Captain America's body would occur during the 1990s, given the perception of the dualistic nature of masculinity itself: "The closer we come to uncovering some form of exemplary masculinity, a masculinity that is solid and sure of itself, the clearer it becomes that masculinity is structured through contradiction: the more it asserts itself, the more it calls itself into question."[65] One of the more interesting changes concerned some key renegotiations of Cap's body. In *Captain America* volume 1, number 372, Cap confronts one of his employees, who has confessed to drug use. When Cap declares he has a zero-tolerance policy, the employee wonders aloud whether the supersoldier serum that created Cap's physique could be considered a performance-enhancing drug. Cap responds, "That's . . . uh, different."[66]

Cap comes into contact with an airborne narcotic that contaminates his system, and to recover he must have the serum from which he draws his powers removed from his body. His blood is later filtered and purified, but he decides not to allow the serum back into his body, lest it send the wrong message to society. In later stories, the serum is again present in his blood, but no explanation for the discrepancy is offered.

Later in volume 1, Marvel writers had Cap's serum begin to deteriorate.[67] Faced with the prospect of ceasing his crime fighting or having his body shut down from chronic fatigue, Cap proves unable to restrict his activity. As he deteriorates, he dons first a utility belt, then a suit of armor before finally expiring (though at the moment of death, his body apparently disappears, so his colleagues find only his empty armor,[68] an odd parallel to a messianic resurrection story). And sure enough, Captain America would be resurrected (and in perfect health) in issue 445 of that volume.[69]

In terms of his physique, Captain America was drawn as the epitome of human musculature throughout the 1990s, but the presentations would be particularly dramatic during Rob Liefeld's handling of the character.

Superhero comics had always lent themselves to exaggerated physique in artwork, and Marvel had taken this exaggeration to a precise science:

> Note that the superhero is larger, with broader shoulders, more muscular arms and legs, a heavier chest, and even a more impressive stance. There's nothing weak-looking about the fellas next to Captain America, but a superhero simply has to look more impressive, more dramatic, more imposing than an average guy.
>
> Perhaps the most important single point to remember is that you should always slightly exaggerate the heroic qualities of your hero, and attempt to ignore or omit any negative, undramatic qualities.[70]

Already known for his exaggerated human forms, Liefeld brought a straining intensity to Captain America's frame, veins stretching across tight muscles even when the character seemed in a relaxed pose. In particular, one piece of promotional art would for Liefeld's critics come to define his run, a depiction of the Avengers Captain America with a physique so muscular that his pectorals look like female breasts. Even Liefeld eventually conceded some of his art was unfortunate: "Yeah, I drew a couple jacked-up images of Cap that tainted my initial offering of him—the big-breasted Cap I drew will follow me forever in infamy."[71]

But to consider only the male form would miss other important socially constructed dimensions of masculinity,[72] in this case Cap's relationship to the government and his community, his engagement of the political issues of his day, and his attitudes toward violent acts.

Captain America the Icon

Given Marvel's emphasis on capitalizing on its characters' collectability and image in the 1990s, it is fitting that the Captain America of that era would be so self-conscious about his status. In the waning issues of the first volume of Captain America, Rogers's colleagues repeatedly tell him that his status demands a certain gravitas and decorum, particularly when it comes to his dating life. When Diamondback asks Black Widow how the other Avengers consider her (Diamondback), the Widow replies:

"The truth? Well, they don't know you like I know you, of course . . . but some of them don't think you're worthy of the special status Cap gives you. He's such an icon of righteousness, while you—like many of us—are just a reformed criminal."[73] A few issues later Black Widow brings these concerns directly to Cap: "Face it, Steve, you're an icon. The Avengers hold you to a higher standard than they do anyone else. I guess Rachel doesn't fit their idea of who an icon would consort with."[74]

During this period, Cap takes a new crop of young patriotic heroes under his wing. One of them, Free Spirit, soon expresses her hero worship: "Captain America's been one of my life-long idols—right up there with Mother Teresa and Michael Stipe! It was the freakiest of circumstances that I happened to run into him down in Mexico yesterday, and got a chance to experience his greatness close up . . . As God as my witness, I'm not going to stand by and do nothing when I have the chance to repay him for being such an inspiration to me! I just hope I've got what it takes to help him!"[75]

Not only his colleagues show such adoration, but the general population in the Marvel Universe soon begins to follow suit, particularly after his return from the pocket universe. As a reporter narrates, "Even before his apparent death, he was revered. The news of his resurrection, however, has transformed him in the eyes of many worldwide from man to icon . . . certainly adored, perhaps even worshipped by some. Does he know this? Does he realize in what awesome regard he is now—more than ever before—held? If so . . . what impact will the ascension from hero to idol have on the man behind the mask? Only time will tell . . . [.]"[76]

For his part, Cap appears uncomfortable with the attention: "God, this is wrong. Captain America should be a symbol OF the people . . . not FOR the people. I never asked to be an action figure. Being a soldier doesn't automatically make me G.I. Joe."[77] Waid and Garney explained their approach to these issues in the letters column of the second issue in volume 3:

We've seen this guy revered as if he were the president, deferentially being called "sir" and given the best seat in front of the TV. Then there have been the folks who have tried to "humanize" the character, giving him a day job, insecurity about his clothes; that sort of thing. So which is the "right" way to do go? Cap the icon or Cap the "gosh-shucks, I'm just happy to be here" fellow? Maybe a little of both.

More than any other character, Steve Rogers very much is the essence of Captain America. Take away that union suit and the ideals, beliefs, and personal motivations of Steve Rogers would remain unchanged. As Mark Gruenwald so effectively pointed out during his run, you can put the suit on anybody, but it's the man that makes the clothes (how's that for a mixed metaphor). And what is it about this guy that makes that so? Steve Rogers represents the very best in all of us, the full potential that you, the mailman and the Fuller Brush Man all have to help others the way we help ourselves, not lie, and basically take that moment to make the world around us a better place. He believes that in helping others he is ultimately helping himself. If he could just get Dr. Doom and the rest of the gang to see that, then the world would be a lot better off and they, too, would be much less tortured. In effect, Steve Rogers is the epitome of selflessness and the model of a person without the self-destructive tendencies that do us in every day.

Of course, people like that are few and far between, both in the real world and in that next best thing, the Marvel Universe. The other Avengers have always seemed to look up to him, world leaders appear in awe of him—heck, even leaders of alien worlds seem to think he's A-OK (what's up with that?). And how does Cap feel about all this adoration? Does he develop a god-complex? Have his costume refitted for a bigger head? Make Jarvis polish his shield for him (not that that's an issue anymore—hee!)? No way! Sure, Steve's the kind of guy who was born modest, but his humility stems not just from his humble beginnings, but [from] the fact that he honestly can't wrap his brain around this whole hero-worship thing in the first place. To him, the concept of Captain America isn't about expert combat training or having a flashy costume—it's about doing the right thing. In fact, if everyone stopped cheering him on long enough to start doing the right thing themselves, we'd all be better for it. Of course, the world doesn't work that way, and Cap still hasn't figured out how to deal with being a celebrity. At least, that's our take.[78]

The struggle with status would lead Cap to question his own mission, given America's drifting focus in a post–Cold War era. In a televised speech to the nation, he provides some exposition on his conflict regarding his function in society:

I have to be honest. Americans aren't sure what I represent, because, lately, I've had doubts myself. In the past, I've said I stand for the American Dream . . . the American Way. But those terms are becoming harder to define with each passing day. This country doesn't know what it is anymore. We're all wondering what our role will be in the dawning of a new millennium . . . so let me lay down my role, once and for all.

Captain America is not here to lead the country. I'm here to serve it. If I'm a captain, I'm a soldier. Not of any military branch . . . but of the America people.

Years ago, in a simpler time, this suit and this shield were created as a symbol to help make America the land it's supposed to be . . . to help it realize its destiny.

Ricocheting from super-villain duel to super-villain duel doesn't always serve that purpose. There's a difference between fighting against evil and fighting for the common good.

I'm not always able to choose my battles . . . but effective immediately, I'm going to make an effort to choose the battles that matter. Battles against injustice . . . against cynicism . . . against intolerance.

I will still serve with the Avengers. I will continue to defend this nation from any and all threats it may face. But as of today, I am not a "super hero." Now and forevermore . . . I am a man of the people.

Together, you and I will identify and confront America's problems. Together, we will figure out what we are . . . and what we can be. Together we will define the American dream . . . and make it the American reality![79]

This struggle for focus would lead Rogers to consider himself a regulator of politics, such as when he says to Sharon Carter, "Lately I wonder . . . shouldn't Cap be doing more about ineffective officials?"[80] Dragged into a political campaign, Cap discovers one of the candidates is taking campaign contributions from Advanced Idea Mechanics (AIM), a criminal organization. Fearing that if he goes public without evidence, it might hurt the candidate he favors because of the appearance of bias, Cap instead privately shames the offending candidate for accepting the funds and decides to campaign for the candidate he supports, but as Steve Rogers, not as Captain America.

Captain America also has quite a bit to say about the failures of the press to serve as a watchdog against growing corporate corruption:

> The press is one of the last bastions of truth in this country. We depend on the First Amendment to guarantee it. You and I both know it is less and less often than the press accurately serves the public. Rather, it's the special interest groups—like Roxxon—that seem to control exactly what the public is exposed to. Not the real truth, but their version of it.
>
> Real truth doesn't come easy. It's your commitment to delivering that truth that benefits us all.[81]

This speech, delivered to a *Daily Bugle* reporter, concerns Cap's frustration that the events he has experienced have often not been accurately reflected in the press coverage. The reporter pushes back, explaining that without verification and sources willing to go on the record, nothing can be done except to stay within the provable facts. The two men argue but ultimately resolve to continue the imperfect struggle toward an elusive goal of truth.

The 1990s Captain America also dealt with racism in a couple of different ways. In *Captain America* volume 3, numbers 25–28, Cap and the Falcon battle a neo-Nazi militia in Idaho, a group led by the Hate-Monger (a clone of Adolf Hitler).[82] Though the heroes are victorious and defeat the neo-Nazis, the Hate-Monger escapes, and nothing significant is done or said about the problem of racism in America other than a side note about its status as "one of the biggest" problems facing America.[83]

Within the pages of *The Avengers*, racism would be approached from the opposite angle when special-interest groups lobby to have an African American hero added to the Avengers' roster for the sake of diversity. Captain America responds indignantly, "This is ridiculous. The Avengers have NEVER made race a factor in our memberships—we may not have any black members at the moment, but—[.]"[84]

Of course, the Avengers did actually make race a factor in previous memberships, most notably in *The Avengers* volume 1, number 183, in which the US government ordered Captain America to recruit the Falcon as a member to fill a minority quota slot.[85] In fact, in ensuing issues that plot from twenty years earlier (1979) played out in similar fashion, with a federal liaison arguing for a new member to be added over some existing members' objection.[86] The African American hero Triathlon would eventually be added to the membership to satisfy the Avengers' critics.[87]

Captain America also confronted homelessness in the 1990s. The first occasion is when he encounters one of his former partners, D-Man, who has just freed himself from a manipulative homeless community leader's influence.[88] Though the two men discuss the situation, no plan of action is presented to deal with the problem of homelessness and the exploitation of the vulnerable.

Cap would take a different tack a few years later when he discovers a homeless family living in his dwelling.[89] Compassionate to their plight, Rogers allows them to stay and even helps one of the children get a job with a local law firm.

Though Captain America would confront salient political issues of his day, his actions (if any) are usually constricted to the physicality of the immediate moment. He rarely acknowledges the policy implications of the problems he faces, nor does he do much to approach problems from a systemic level. Captain America's politics can be largely summed up as progressive but tied directly to his overarching narrative of rugged individualism and willpower.

When confronted with a challenge from his former sidekick Nomad in *Captain America* volume 1, number 421, and Nomad claims to have been forced into Nazism by his father's political views, Cap responds:

> Okay, say it's true. Your father is a Nazi. So what? That doesn't automatically make you one. Do we all inherit the sins of our fathers?
>
> My father was an alcoholic, a wife-beater, a quitter—does that make me the same?
>
> No! Each of us makes our own destiny. We have the capacity to rise above the failings of our parents! Each generation has the chance to go beyond the accomplishments—good or bad—of the previous one![90]

Such statements underlie the central ideology of Captain America's masculinity: self-made men can determine their own destinies with enough hard work and will. So although the 1990s Captain America faced many of the same political problems he had faced in the 1970s, he dealt with them purely from an individualist level, leaving others to do the same.

The 1990s era of Captain America narratives can largely be characterized as an era of superficial considerations for a celebrity icon. That narrative in part stemmed from the politics of the age, but it also emerged from the creative forces framing the character, most notably Mark Waid. In his farewell column in the final issue of the first volume of *Captain America*, Waid illuminated his own passion and fandom for the character of Captain America:

> I have been waiting to write CAPTAIN AMERICA every day of my life since I was twelve years old. He was my favorite Marvel hero—a strong-willed man of action who fought injustice armed only with a shield. No heat vision, no power of flight, no cool car or Batarang. Just an indomitable will and an ability to Always Find A Way. He was the hero who could be me . . . and still could, if only Cap'n Crunch and Diet Coke were the chemical foundations of the super-soldier serum.
>
> The thing I love most about Cap is that he's The Man With The Plan, always three steps ahead of the crisis. Some readers have commented on how little I have shown of Cap's thoughts. That's because he's always three steps ahead of me. More often than not, writing Captain America has been a frantic race to keep pace with the man as he torpedoes through the plot like a living, breathing super hero with little time or patience for his chronicler. John Williams 1941 blaring in the background (the official Waid/Garney soundtrack, by the way), I wheeze to keep up, typing like a maniac, trying to keep him in sight as he surprises me at every turn.[91]

Chapter 5 described the era in which comic fans first began to contribute to the creation of their beloved texts, and chapter 6 illustrated how that influence was magnified when the second wave of fan-creators entered the industry. The tendencies of yet another new wave of fan-creators are one reason why the 1990s are remembered as an era of excess. As Waid illustrates, his own interaction with Captain America strongly influenced the way he presented Captain America texts, which would in turn influence others. Waid's lifelong fandom, evidenced by his extreme displays of fan activity and the integration of the Captain America text into other facets of his life, position the hero as an icon worthy of the celebration inherent in Waid's treatment. In particular, the notion that Waid wouldn't write internal dialogue for the character because he struggled to keep up with the character (no matter how tongue-in-cheek the statement may be) represents the granting of a transcendent status to the character by the creator, revealing a relationship not commonly observed in previous eras.

However, this adoration by a creator who grew up loving the character whose stories he wrote might also account for the declining relevance of Captain America toward the end of the 1990s. When the text becomes an end in itself, it is easy to see how such an insular creation process might struggle to be seen as relevant to those outside the adoration dynamic. However, external events would soon provide a new context for Captain America to reestablish his external relevance as America experienced terrorism and a resurgence of the military-industrial complex.

8

Captain America's Responses to the War on Terror (2002–2007)

As demonstrated in previous chapters, the character of Captain America has endured significant renegotiation over the years to maintain his relevance amid changes in contemporary culture, in this way providing an indirect snapshot of American cultural development. As American society has evolved and adapted to new challenges, the character's history and motivations have also evolved. These evolutionary changes document the necessity of reinventing American myths to avoid engaging derogatory elements of American history and yet to preserve a sense of narrative continuity. Perhaps no transformation of Captain America is as culturally significant as the transition from the superficial icon of the 1990s to the soldier responding to the events of September 11, 2001 (9/11), followed closely by his role in Marvel's Civil War event.

In addition to the physical destruction and loss of life, the 9/11 terrorist attacks challenged several fundamental beliefs concerning the American character. Because most Americans, distanced from the complex realities of global politics by simplistic story frames, could not fathom US foreign policy as anything but just, such a vicious and unexpected attack created a period of cultural dissonance. How America would respond to this dramatic assault to our citizenry had the potential to form how Americans thought about their nation's place in the world for a generation.

Scholars John Shelton Lawrence and Robert Jewett critique superhero narratives built on the vigilante and personal vengeance found in American

Western motifs to reinforce a national monomyth in which heroes engage in extralegal redemptive activities without participating in the constraints and responsibilities of citizenship. The pair's second work specifically portrays the influence of the Captain America complex in the formation of an aggressive foreign policy in response to the terrorist attacks of September 11.[1] In their work, they identify six characteristics of the Captain America complex shared by Christians, Jews, and Muslim jihadists:

1. A belief that righteous anger is blessed by a deity, which absolutizes zeal and eliminates normal restraint.
2. The conception of opponents as members of a malevolent conspiracy, originating from a realm of absolute evil, and thus the view of any compromise as immoral.
3. The actors in the conflict are framed as either good or evil.
4. Righteous violence is redemptive, but the opponent's use of violence is senseless and unjust.
5. To be defeated is to abandon faith itself.
6. The defeat of the enemy will usher in an age of peace.[2]

The form of dualism found in Jewett and Lawrence's Captain America complex is consistent with the American monomyth at the root of American superhero narratives.

However, the character for whom the complex was named had already endured a striking evolution over the years, and each of the Captain America complex characteristics would eventually be challenged in the narrative of the fourth volume of *Captain America*.

Captain America: Soldier in the War on Terror (2002–2006)

Although Captain America began his career as a military officer, in the 1980s and 1990s he was more superhero than soldier. From the time of his resurrection in 1963 until the end of the twentieth century, Cap fought many villains and criminals with skill and agility while largely managing to avoid killing his enemies. Although the 1940s Captain America had often resorted to killing his opponents, a central tenet of his narrative since his 1963 revival is that he doesn't kill (and as of the mid-1980s has never killed). As documented in chapter 7, S.H.I.E.L.D. special agent Sharon Carter proves ready to kill to keep Cap from killing because she needs "to know that there's still one man out there who can always do the job clean."[3]

The terrorist attacks on the World Trade Center and the Pentagon disrupted this uneasy balancing act, for the villains, according to the American monomyth framing, succeeded in an act of mass murder on American soil (America itself serving as the helpless community under attack), bringing into question whether the American system of justice was capable of responding to the attack or bringing the foreign villains to justice. In other words, the 9/11 attacks so perfectly fit within the framework of the American monomyth that frontier or superheroic forms of justice seemed an appropriate response. Reactionary voices began to call for military action in the name of righteous vengeance. Two days after the attack, conservative commentator Ann Coulter wrote:

> The nation has been invaded by a fanatical, murderous cult. And we welcome them. We are so good and so pure we would never engage in discriminatory racial or "religious" profiling. . . . We know who the homicidal maniacs are. They are the ones cheering and dancing right now.
>
> We should invade their countries, kill their leaders and convert them to Christianity. We weren't punctilious about locating and punishing only Hitler and his top officers. We carpet-bombed German cities; we killed civilians. That's war. And this is war.[4]

Marvel's initial response to the terrorist attacks occurred in a special issue of *The Amazing Spider-Man* volume 2. In issue 36, which shipped in early November 2001, Marvel Universe continuity screeches to a halt as Spider-Man and other major Marvel characters react to the aftermath of the attack on the World Trade Center. The comic opens with Spider-Man lamenting over Ground Zero just as the second tower has fallen. After reacting in shock at the sight (and at the rebuke of citizens crying out, "Where were you?!"), Spider-Man reflects on his horror: "Only madmen could contain the thought, execute the act, fly the planes. The sane world will always be vulnerable to madmen, because we cannot go where they go to conceive of such things."[5] Spider-Man soon joins other Marvel heroes in the rescue operations. Heroes assist firefighters and police officers in digging through the rubble, and Spider-Man repeatedly speaks of them as the "true heroes"; even Marvel villains are positioned as more human than terrorists when some of them show up to show their support (Dr. Doom is actually shown tearing up at the sight, despite his own history of attempted mass destruction). Captain America is present, and Spider-Man, in his struggle for answers for why the attack occurred, reflects on Cap's unique perspective: "He's the only one who could know. Because he's been here before. I wish I had not lived to see this once. I can't imagine what it is to see this twice. I just can't imagine."[6]

In an interview with a *New York Times* reporter, Marvel editor in chief Joe Quesada spoke about how carefully the company sought to address the issues surrounding the events of September 11 and the war on terror: "You don't want to single out religions. We are not doing the jingoistic comics you saw in the '40s with Captain America saying, 'Take that, you Hun!' But we have to communicate ideas. Our comics are about good triumphing over evil."[7]

One reviewer praised the effort but then expressed his own mixed feelings at the treatment, writing: "In the end, this issue is like a cold, sobering dose of reality, into a medium that has thrived on its ability to deliver incredible amounts of destruction, without touching on the idea of massive fatalities."[8] This response appears to exemplify many readers' responses and reviews posted on comic-related websites.

The same month *The Amazing Spider-Man* volume 3, number 36, appeared, Marvel released the forty-eighth issue of the third volume of *Captain America*. Issue 48 quickly wrapped up the existing story arc's hanging plot and ended with a memorial service for Cap's fallen partner, Bucky. Issue 49 would wrap up the hanging thread from the series' exploration of Captain America's love life (Steve Rogers loses his relationship with Connie Ferrari, Captain America woos longtime love interest Sharon Carter). The fiftieth and final issue in the volume contained six stories. In the fourth story, "Relics," Captain America is killed when he valiantly disarms a nuclear weapon that would have destroyed New Jersey.[9]

In the remaining two stories, the public hears of Captain America's death, begins to mourn, and holds a funeral for him.[10]

This death is never explained in Marvel continuity. Captain America did not disappear from the ongoing *Avengers* titles, nor did his appearances in other comic book series diminish. Cap's next solo appearances were in two gritty miniseries, *Captain America: Dead Men Running* and *The Ultimates* (discussed in detail later in this chapter). Neither appears to be intended as a contribution to mainstream Marvel continuity. Once the terrorist attacks of 9/11 occurred, Marvel writers and editors seemed to have been unsure how to handle a character who had routinely become associated with the country's fighting spirit, so they wrapped up the book by killing him. Perhaps the "death" was only metaphoric because the coming fourth volume represented a dramatic shift in the character.

It is likely that a shift in representation was in the works before the terrorist attacks provided a forum for response. The superhero metaphor, as it had so many times before, once again dipped in popularity, and Captain America's own sales had once again slumped due to a lack of relevance among many in Marvel's readership. In the conclusion to the first edition of *Comic Book Nation*, scholar Bradley Wright wrote in early 2001 about the damage that the industry and cultural excesses of the 1990s had done to the comic book medium:

> Comic books are losing their audience not because they have failed to keep up with changes in American culture but because American culture had finally caught up with them. Throughout their history, comic books thrived as a uniquely exaggerated and absurdist expression of adolescent concerns and sensibilities. But those qualities no longer made them unique. America at the turn of the twenty-first century has a pervasive consumer culture based largely on the perpetuation of adolescence. Young children acquire tastes in entertainment and fashion formerly reserved for their elder siblings, while middle-aged baby boomers go to rock concerts and buy designer athletic shoes once thought only appropriate for teenagers. In a media culture preoccupied with youth, commercials for investment firms look like music videos, televised sporting events look and sound like video games, and network political coverage can sound like the plot for an X-rated film. Is there

a place for comic books in an America that has become a comic book parody of itself?[11]

The fourth volume of *Captain America* would redefine and reestablish the superhero formula, largely by deconstructing it. By incorporating the events of 9/11 directly into the storyline, the authors of the fourth volume presented Captain America as a soldier who refused to accept the dualistic approach to the enemies offered him in the new war on terror. In this way, Captain America himself actually resisted the Captain America complex that otherwise gripped America's foreign policy, and he became one of the few early critiques of the moralistic language presented by the Bush administration at a time when other media were far less willing or able to challenge suppositions about the identity and nature of America's enemies in the war on terror.

Confronting the War on Terror

As the launch of Captain America's fourth volume of comics approached, writer John Ney Rieber and artist John Cassaday were still working on the first storyline of the series when the terrorist attacks on the World Trade Center occurred. Delaying the planned opening stories, the creative team instead developed a controversial story arc that placed Cap directly into the post-9/11 environment.[12] The superhero's flashy fantasy elements were boiled away until only a gritty, jaded soldier remained. It should also be noted that the artwork for the fourth volume *Captain America* took on a realism that had been rare in Marvel comics before that time. In fact, most Marvel books would soon adopt a more realistic style as the company wrestled with adapting its narratives to more realistic settings.

After an introductory montage of the terrorist attacks, the story opens with Steve Rogers at the World Trade Center, desperately digging and sifting through ash, searching for survivors.[13] He refuses multiple requests to take a break (including orders from his superiors), finally yielding after dusk. On his way home, he encounters a Muslim youth threatened by a group of angry New Yorkers. Cap defends him and provides a symbolic example of strength in the face of adversity.

Seven months later Cap is deployed to deal with a terrorist infiltration of Centerville (the state is purposely never mentioned). A terrorist named Faysal al-Tariq holds the town's population hostage to raise Americans' awareness of the role the town's bomb-manufacturing plant plays in the death and injury to his people. To prevent the detonation of a weapon that would kill two hundred civilians, Cap kills al-Tariq with a vicious blow to the head. Fearing international tension over the situation, Cap unmasks on national television and claims personal responsibility for the death.

The removal of a superhero's mask is a highly significant action. Jewett and Lawrence argue that the masked identities that superheroes assume are the instrument through which vigilantes circumvent the law to deliver justice to the innocent.[14] They claim that according to the American monomyth, unlike Joseph Campbell's monomyth, the savior hero does not reenter society at the conclusion of the story. The Western hero moves on; the superhero maintains his or her secret identity. This anonymity allows the hero to continue to operate outside the law while delivering his or her higher standard of justice to society.

By removing his mask and taking personal responsibility for his actions, Captain America breaks with the American monomyth and enters society. In subsequent stories, he moves into a rough Brooklyn neighborhood and allows both of his identities to remain accountable to his neighbors and society at large. Unlike previous Captain America narratives, the post-9/11 Captain America will not be a faceless symbol of his country. By revealing his identity, he removes from his arsenal the primary weapon that both sides in a "war on terror" really have: anonymity. Cap's unmasking serves as a statement that faceless action is an escape from personal responsibility.

During the altercation with al-Tariq, Cap recovers electronic "cat" (Casualty Awareness Tracking) tags from the dead terrorists that had previously been established to be the same worn by American military intelligence officers. Cap confronts several heads of US intelligence agencies, demanding to know the connection, but he gets few answers. However, the fact of a vague connection between the US military-industrial complex and the terrorist forces it hunts is clear.

Cap next travels to Dresden, Germany, to follow a lead. En route he strikes up a debate with a German woman about the American war on terror:

PASSENGER: It's so confusing to the rest of us—your allies that you ignore. It changes every day. Who you're fighting. Where you're fighting—What the great evil is it that America must destroy today. I don't think you know why you're fighting . . . I don't think you know what you believe.

CAP: I believe . . . that on September the Eleventh, 2001—a psychopath murdered almost three thousand defenseless human beings in an attempt to trigger World War III. Ninety percent of the casualties of World War I were soldiers, fraulein. But half the people who died in World War II were civilians. Half of sixty-one million. I know why I'm fighting, fraulein. I don't want to see World War III.[15]

In Dresden, Cap confronts the terrorist leader behind the CAT tags (which are revealed to be part of a plot to kill American soldiers en masse). During the confrontation, the nameless terrorist justifies his actions and taunts Cap: "Guerrillas gunned my father down while he was at work in the fields—With American bullets. American weapons. . . . You know your history, Captain America. Tell your monster where he's from. . . . You can't answer me, you mean. You played that game in too many places . . . The sun never set on your political chessboard—your empire of blood."[16] Cap savagely beats the terrorist leader but appears to stop short of actually killing him. Rather, he delivers the limp form to the authorities.

In the next story arc (the original Rieber and Cassaday storyline), Cap is called on to confront a rogue intelligence agent who is terrorizing citizens in Florida. Inali Redpath, who is Native American, seeks to recover the land stolen from his people centuries earlier. In an attempt to convince Cap to join him, he exposes the hero to a powerful hallucinogen to encourage recall of his own past. Cap experiences a series of memories that call his history into question. He remembers the US government intentionally incapacitating him near the end of World War II and freezing him to prevent him from interfering with the use of atomic bombs to end the war. When he had shown signs of unwillingness to kill as US warfare policy demanded, Cap's own government had removed him from the war effort. This theme resonates throughout the arc, as the government continually pushes Cap to use lethal force. In one scene, Cap confronts Nick Fury, and Fury reacts with a statement about the new need to reconcile America's new role in the war on terror with Captain America's history:

> CAP: [W]hy can't you seem to understand my choice to live by my rules?
>
> FURY: Because your "rules" mean living with blinders on, pal, and they always have. Trying to recapture a past that never existed. Ever since 9-11 you've been challenged to be something you don't want to be and it's making you nuts.[17]

In this way, Fury alludes to the mythological past Americans construct when they refer to World War II as a just war. The allusions to the firebombing of Dresden and to the use of atomic weapons (of which Cap conveniently has no personal recollection) underscore the dark underbelly of modern warfare in contrast to the "glorious war" framing that Americans usually employ when discussing World War II. These allusions are not accidental. In the response to the 9/11 attacks, President George W. Bush frequently used terminology and framing that alluded to World War II.[18] The president even reportedly wrote, "The Pearl Harbor of the 21st century took place today" in his journal the day of the attacks.[19]

By invoking some of the less honorable moments of the "Great War," Captain America continually confronts the fallacy of the American "golden age" while also invoking the paradoxes within his own continuity. Just as Marvel Comics later sanitized Cap's World War II actions by assuming he did not take lives (despite the fact that the 1940s comics show otherwise), Americans often reimagine the history of World War II as a time of glory and honor.

Historian Howard Zinn challenges this revisionist view of World War II in his critique of Tom Brokaw's book *The Greatest Generation*:

> I refuse to celebrate them as "the greatest generation" because in doing so we are celebrating courage and sacrifice in the cause of war. And we are miseducating the young to believe that military heroism is the noblest form of heroism, when it should be remembered only as the tragic accompaniment of horrendous policies driven by power and profit. Indeed, the current infatuation with World War II prepares us— innocently on the part of some, deliberately on the part of others—for more war, more military adventures, more attempts to emulate the military heroes of the past.[20]

Cap's desire to maintain his own innocence is directly connected to his desire to protect those who are innocent. Like the terrorists in the first arc of the fourth volume of *Captain America*, Redpath justifies his actions against those who are innocent by linking their lives to the horrors of the past: "No one's innocent, Steve. By the laws of this very government— whether they want to accept it or not—every American is complicit in the darkness that this country spreads across the rest of the world—simply by paying taxes."[21] Cap neutralizes the agent but is forced to cope with the fact that the next foe he faces is financed and supported by the US secretary of defense. Cap learns that the US government is manipulating him, trying to encourage him to use lethal force.

Next, the US government taps Cap to serve on a military tribunal being held for a foreign antiwar activist charged with supporting terrorist activities against America. Traveling to Guantanamo Bay, Cap is confronted by the military's treatment of enemy combatants and the growing awareness of disenfranchised citizens who feel abandoned and neglected by their nation. While on this mission, Cap throws a military general into the ocean for mistreating detainees, his act a clear statement of his position on the detainment at Camp X-Ray in Guantanamo Bay and perhaps on the Abu Ghraib scandal, which gained public attention during that portion of the volume's run.[22]

Although the earliest portion of the 2002 arc forces Cap to endure and cope with the events of 9/11, his experiences ultimately serve to critique many aspects of the US war on terror. Struggling with issues of national accountability, attitudes toward foreigners and foreign cultures, as well as the American military culture's growing jadedness, this Captain America explores what it means to be an American in the post-9/11 world. Although his ideals ultimately emerge intact, his experiences during this period leave him troubled and uncertain. This state of mind appears to undermine the righteous certainty needed to sustain the American monomyth: because superheroes operate outside the law, they need to be sure their actions are just—certainty about one's mission of justice is what separates hero from villain.

Following the introduction of the 2002 version, several critiques appeared about the portrayal of Cap in the post-9/11 storyline, most notably Michael Medved and Michael Lackner's *The Betrayal of Captain America*. In this white paper, which received much coverage in the conservative press, the authors accused Marvel Comics of bowing to liberal influences, changing decades of tradition for the purpose of a "new understanding" of the character's patriotism.

Even a superficial survey of the Cap literature raises challenges to such claims. Although his 1940s characterizations could be construed as possessing conservative attributes, Cap certainly left them behind when transformed from the "Man out of Time" into the "Liberal Crusader" in the 1970s (as chronicled in chapter 5 of this volume). Clearly, one should not make claims about long-standing narratives without at least superficially consulting the body of literature in question.

Although not a "new understanding," the fourth volume of *Captain America* offers general critiques of each of the tenets of Jewett and Lawrence's Captain America complex. When pushed to allow righteous anger to increase his zeal and eliminate his restraints, Cap flatly refuses to compromise. His tactics in large measure remain unchanged (even the assassination of al-Tariq is later found to have been committed remotely by someone other than Cap). Captain America does see his opponents as members of a malevolent conspiracy, but he suspects from the beginning that his own government is complicit in that conspiracy or, at the very least, that the war on terror is made up of competing conspiracies. Cap mistrusts his government only slightly less than he mistrusts those he faces on the battlefield.

This version of Captain America rejects the "good versus evil" framing by both sides of the conflict. Rather, he fights for the protection of "innocents" on both sides of the war on terror. The innocence of civilians is questioned by friends and foes alike, but Cap refuses to allow passive complicity to justify violence toward civilians. His critique of the Dresden bombings reaffirms that his view of innocence is not driven by a society's politics or ideology. In that respect, Cap's view of humanity is global, and he refuses to adopt the nationalistic mindset sweeping the United States after the 9/11 attacks. When pressed about his patriotism, he at one point responds, "A country's only as good or bad as the people who run it."[23]

Cap still seems to see the redemptive value of violent force but continues to reject the killing of his opponents as redemptive (and the series even retcons this view to the moment of his "birth" in the laboratory[24]). Cap never disputes whether his opponents have cause for their anger but rather argues that blind hatred cannot be redemptive because it exposes innocents to additional suffering and loss. The character's faith appears to be more closely tied to the idealism represented in the American Dream than in the military success or political realities of the American institution. In that context, he does not see defeat as an abandonment of faith. Rather, he sees the escalation of violence and the suppression of the world's innocents as a greater compromise to his faith in the American Dream. Nor does he seem to believe that his victories will usher in an age of peace. He seeks to represent eternal vigilance against threats to innocents or to the American values of liberty, justice, and freedom. He presents himself as a jaded warrior who clings to the hope of furthering American ideals. He knows he faces enemies within his own country as well as from the outside world, but he finds purpose in making the world better (while acknowledging that America's golden age never existed nor is likely to exist in his lifetime).

The Captain America narrative tends to draw the most attention in moments when American cultural values are under scrutiny. Readers from all perspectives appear to identify with the hero, probably because he rarely takes specific stances on specific political issues. He reserves his strongest objections to broad challenges to the philosophic ideas of freedom and equality and the belief that every person can live a just and productive life.

Cap's popularity and relevance paradoxically appear to resonate most with fans when the nation is involved in a direct challenge from other nations or world bodies. Without a doubt, some of Cap's finest moments, according to many fans, occurred during his initial World War II run and in the fourth volume of his comic, which was written immediately after the events of September 11, 2001.

Within the pages of *The Avengers*, Captain America engages in similar critiques—most notably in the "Red Zone" story arc presented in *The Avengers* volume 3, numbers 65–70. This story portrays the heroes reacting to a deadly red mist that drifts across the American Midwest, killing almost instantly those it touches. As the Avengers strive to help the citizens caught in the cloud's path, they receive significant interference from the US government, and it is later discovered that the cloud's origin was the accidental deployment of an American bioweapon.[25] The Red Skull is the architect of the crisis, posing as Secretary of Defense Dell Rusk.

This version of the Skull does not seem bent on restoring the ideology of Nazi Germany. Rather, the Skull declares he has adopted the modern version of the American Dream but argues that "[f]reedom must feel fear. And fear leads to control. I was wrong about this country. This wonderful 'United' States of America. It has all the resources already in place. It already has the right attitudes laced within. They just need to be exploited. To become the perfect nation—America just needs a little push in the RIGHT direction."[26] In a clear allegory for the fear-mongering related to the 9/11 attacks (and the seemingly dubious connection between those attacks and the 2003 invasion of Iraq), the Red Skull explains his plans: "The Red Zone continues to extend. And only I hold the key to stopping it. Perhaps tomorrow. Perhaps in a month. When I feel there is enough fear and enough terror spread throughout this great country . . . When I know I will have no problems in persuading the President to launch a nuclear attack against the aggressor nation his Secretary of Defense's investigation will root out. Only THEN will I bring this disease to a halt."[27]

Of course, the Avengers ultimately defeat the Skull's plan, but not until after thousands of Americans have died or are affected. At the conclusion of the conflict, Captain America has a brief discussion with President George W. Bush. As the two men prepare to part ways, Cap confronts the president:

> CAPTAIN AMERICA: I want to be clear on one thing, Mr. President. If there are any other bio-weapons labs in our country—I trust they are being shut down.
>
> PRESIDENT GEORGE W. BUSH: We're already in the process of finding that out. And if we make a mistake of any kind again—I trust that you will be there to help us correct it.
>
> CAP: You have my word, sir.[28]

In the Marvel Universe, superheroes serve as a check on the Bush-era US government. In fact, government itself (at least under the Bush administration) is positioned as a potential source of threat to the populace itself, with superheroic savior figures serving to safeguard the public against threats, including the potential threat posed by the US government itself.

The Ultimate Neoconservative

It should be noted that even as the 2002 Captain America emerged, Marvel launched an additional Captain America narrative. Seeking to create a series of narratives that more closely tied into their film properties, Marvel Comics had created a second line of comic books based on their core properties. In October 2000, Marvel launched *Ultimate Spider-Man*, a comic that retold and updated the classic Marvel storyline with an eye to contemporary aesthetics and narrative style outside the continuity of the mainstream Marvel Universe. Marvel knew that the intertextual nature of comic book movies would lead new readers (in particular young readers) to their comics and anticipated a certain amount of confusion when a young reader tried to reconcile the basic elements of the movie narrative with the complexities of the comic narrative.

Spider-Man posed a particularly difficult challenge for new fans. Whereas the movie *Spider-Man* began with the character's origin and portrayed the exploits of a teenage hero,[29] the comic book's current volume in 2002 had long passed this era. The Spider-Man portrayed in Marvel Comics was in his midthirties, was married to supermodel Mary Jane Watson-Parker, taught at his old high school, and was involved in storylines that challenged his sense of adult responsibility.

Began as an entry point for new fans, the *Ultimate* imprint quickly gained support among existing fans through intertextual humor and carefully linked stories that held the *Ultimate* narratives to a higher level of relevance to each other than in the mainstream Marvel Universe. A striking example of this intertextual contrast can be found in *Ultimate Marvel Team-Up* volume 1, number 2. As Spider-Man confronts the Hulk for the first time, he makes many humorous intertextual references. When the Hulk looms over him, the hero looks up and mutters, "Hey, listen, man . . . Don't make me angry. You wouldn't like me when I'm angry."[30] This line, famously repeated every week in the opening credits of the 1978 *Incredible Hulk* television show, rewards longtime fans of Marvel entertainment properties while remaining accessible to newer audiences.

Set apart from the mainstream Marvel franchise, the stories told in the *Ultimate* comics carefully juxtapose established iconic history with new configurations of narrative intended to create meaning through intertextual tension. Through these books, Marvel writers and artists were able to deconstruct many tenets of the Marvel superhero genre, challenging the notions of secret identities, superhero team dynamics, the relationship between superpowered heroes and the military-industrial complex, the rationale behind costume design and use, and even the psychological implications of possessing superpowers.

Following the success of the *Ultimate Spider-Man* and *Ultimate X-Men* books, in 2002 Marvel announced the upcoming launch of *The Ultimates*, a book based on the mainstream *Avengers* property. From the beginning, *The Ultimates* was written with political and social commentary in mind. Contrasting the book with the mainstream *Avengers* title, writer Mark Millar described it as "an exploration of what happens when a bunch of ordinary people are turned into super-soldiers and being groomed to fight the real-life war on terror."[31]

In another interview, Millar explained his approach to the comic's politics: "[The] *Ultimates* is a pro–status quo book. If anything, it was kind of a right wing book, like Rush Limbaugh doing super comics. It was like, 'Hey superheroes should all be on the government payroll and go out there and fight the war on terror,' you know?"[32] In contrast, the storyline in *The Ultimates 2* would evolve into a stinging critique of the status quo at a time when popular support for America began to wane, but in both books the American establishment is reflected most strongly in the Nick Fury characterization as well as in Millar's portrayal of Captain America.

In direct contrast to his liberal mainstream Marvel counterpart, the Ultimate Captain America is first and foremost a soldier. Frozen in the 1940s and released in a post-9/11 world, Ultimate Cap maintains a conservative mindset consistent with the stereotypes popularized from the earlier era of American culture. Like his mainstream counterpart, Cap struggles to adjust to the dramatic changes that occurred in American culture while he was frozen. Unlike his counterpart, Ultimate Cap clings fiercely to his social and religious values. In *Ultimate Extinction* volume 1, number 2, this struggle manifests itself when the heroes find themselves facing the likely destruction of Earth:

CAP: Do you believe in God, Nick?

NICK FURY: Don't all good soldiers believe in God?

CAP: I asked one of your specialists if he believed in God. He laughed at me. Where I came from, everybody believed in God. And if someone asked too many questions about God, it was because they'd gone nutty from reading too many books. God was there. God loved us. That was the whole deal.

God gave us a sense of what's right, and strong arms to fight evil for him.

It's not a big world, and there were enough of us to stand under God and take on the evil in it, see?

. . . But there aren't enough of us, are there? It's an evil too big for me to hit. I never thought there'd be such a thing. I can't do anything.

. . . Yesterday I was a "super-soldier." Today I don't even know if I still believe in God.[33]

Through such portrayals, Mark Millar and Brian Hitch (as well as the other Ultimate Marvel creative teams) explored traditional American military culture: if God is at the center of all political and military action, then what happens when God's champions face defeat? Fortunately for Ultimate Cap, he is often spared such defeats in the end.

However, Cap's 1940s morality does not lead him to be overly idealistic. In mainstream Marvel continuity, Captain America is idealistic to a fault: he refuses to use firearms; he often refrains from striking an unsuspecting opponent from behind; and he strives never to kill his opponent. Ultimate Cap shows no such compunction: he is a pragmatist when it comes to using force, is fiercely defensive of conservative values, is short on words, and often relies exclusively on his physical prowess to resolve disputes. In his first confrontation with the Hulk in *The Ultimates* volume 1, number 5, Ultimate Cap immediately kicks the monster in the groin and later kicks a defenseless Bruce Banner in the face.[34]

Ultimate Cap doesn't hesitate to strike immobile opponents when he feels an advantage can be gained:

CAPTAIN MAHR VEHL: Captain, do you have a thing about kicking people when they're down?

ULTIMATE CAP: No, Captain—I always figured that was the best time to kick 'em.[35]

In contrast to the more liberal mainstream Marvel character, Ultimate Cap routinely carries weaponry consistent with a wartime soldier (automatic weapons, small arms, hand grenades, etc.) and often amasses a large body count on missions. Taking life is acceptable if it removes a threat. When approached by X-Men mentor Charles Xavier in *Ultimate War* volume 1, number 2, Cap proves unmoved by appeals to save the villainous Magneto's life: "No deals, soldier. I couldn't care less about any of that new age junk or why he didn't put this monster to bed when he had the chance."[36] Between the portrayal of Ultimate Captain America and the portrayal of the Ultimate Nick Fury (drawn to resemble actor Samuel L. Jackson and drawing on the brutish humor often displayed in Jackson's work), the US government in *The Ultimates* world is the epitome of the neoconservative ethic: arrogant use of power and ruthless pragmatism to subdue those with other perspectives.

The Roots of Neoconservatism

Scholars, public intellectuals, and political operatives hotly contest the precise definition and origin of neoconservatism. However, many of these voices agree that the movement (or "tendency") arose in resistance to the American leftist counterculture of the 1960s and that it has had an influence on recent Republican presidencies, most notably that of George W. Bush.

Fusing portions of the rhetoric from the 1960s New Left movement with the common man's more plainspoken rhetoric, one of the goals of neoconservatism has been "to make criticism from the Right acceptable in the intellectual, artistic, and journalistic circles where conservatives had long been regarded with suspicion."[37] According to Irving Kristol, the "acknowledged godfather of neoconservatism," there are three central tenets of neoconservatism: (1) a low-tax, pro-growth approach to economics that entrusts market viability to the actions of individuals; (2) a concern about the waning civic and cultural mores of American democratic culture; and (3) an expansive foreign policy that seeks to export democracy to other societies while resisting cooperative international authority structures.[38] The foundation of these neoconservative tenets assumes "the incredible military superiority of the United States vis-à-vis the nations of the rest of the world, in any imaginable combination," and seeks to maintain (and appropriately use) this strength to further the advancement of American values.[39]

Ira Chernus argues that the root of neoconservativism is a fear that American counterculture has and will continue to undermine the authority of traditional values and moral norms. He explains that because neoconservatives tend to hold a view of human nature that defines individuals as innately selfish, they worry that a society with no commonly accepted values based on religion or tradition will end up in a type of individualistic cultural civil war. To resist this outcome, the neoconservative holds strength as America's most important social value and, by extension, fears that weakness will lead to moral confusion and anarchy.[40]

These views also heavily influence neoconservative foreign policy. As neoconservative writer Charles Krauthammer writes, "States line up with more powerful states not out of love but out of fear. And respect."[41] David Brooks adds that in this view "[e]very morning you strap on your armor and you go out to battle the evil ones. It's more important to be feared than loved."[42] Neoconservatives were sharply critical of the post–Cold War military reductions of the 1990s and a perceived lack of willingness to use military force to support America's strategic interests.

After the 1991 Gulf War concluded with Saddam Hussein still in power, neoconservatism began to be identified with the desire to revisit Iraq and remove Hussein with military force. A 1998 open letter to President Bill Clinton arguing for the removal of Hussein was signed by dozens of political operatives who would eventually play key roles in the Bush administration and the 2003 plan to invade Iraq a second time.[43]

Rogue regimes appear to be a particular concern, and to deal with these threats the neoconservative favors military might (and even preemptive action) over international law and diplomacy. In an essay written before the invasion of Iraq, William Kristol and Robert Kagan summed up the neoconservative doctrine of strength:

> A strong America capable of projecting force quickly and with devastating effect to important regions of the world would make it less likely that challengers to regional stability would attempt to alter the status quo in their favor. It might even deter such challengers from undertaking expensive efforts to arm themselves in the first place. An America whose willingness to project force is in doubt, on the other hand, can only encourage such challenges. In Europe, in Asia, and in the Middle East, the message we should be sending to potential foes is: "Don't even

think about it!" That kind of deterrence offers the best recipe for lasting peace; it is much cheaper than fighting wars that would follow should we fail to build such a deterrent capacity.[44]

The Ultimates' Critique of Neoconservatism

Ultimate Cap's reactionary mentality (and that of several of his teammates) was reportedly a conscious choice on Millar's part. The writer claimed that he was in the midst of the first issue of the original series when the 2001 attack on the World Trade Center occurred.[45] Taking inspiration from life, Millar framed the story as a response to recent violent attacks (although the characters never confront al-Qaeda or make more than passing reference to the 9/11 attacks).

Although many of its members are civilians, the Ultimates team is a military unit funded and supported by the US government as a Special Forces branch of the military. As the characters struggle to adapt to their changing roles in society, the comic considers the superhero team's public versus private dimensions. Unlike traditional government-supported programs, the Ultimates are marketed and merchandised through private corporations. This arrangement (as well as the cooperative funding arrangements made with researchers Tony Stark, Henry Pym, and Bruce Banner) demonstrates the fusion of industry and government consistent with neoconservative philosophies of society. As private industry overlaps with publicly funded initiatives, the narrative explores the paradox of celebrity in American culture. The Ultimate leaders often emphasize the image of protection rather than the reality. Privacy, secrecy, exposure, publicity: all interact as plot devices in *The Ultimates*.

The characters appear very aware of their celebrity status and revel in the attention. In an amusing scene in *The Ultimates* volume 1, number 4, the team members sit around discussing which actors would best play them in a movie about them (Brad Pitt is mentioned for Captain America, Samuel L. Jackson for Nick Fury, Johnny Depp for Tony Stark, Matthew McConnaughey for Pym, Steve Buscemi for Bruce Banner).[46] This scene plays heavily on the intertextual humor generated by the fact that many of these actors served as role models for Brian Hitch's artwork. Speaking about the inspiration for *The Ultimates* portrayal of Nick Fury, Hitch said he and Millar "always knew that it had to be Sam Jackson. The idea of a high ranking black officer came from Colin Powell, but there would never be anyone cooler than Sam Jackson. That would be who we would cast if we were making the movie."[47] Other examples of postmodern humor are at times overt and at other times subtle. When Captain America is found adrift in the ocean, Tony Stark tells Nick Fury, "It's like something out of Joseph Campbell's book, General Fury. A country's greatest hero coming back in the hour he's needed most? I'm just glad I've got fifty percent of the merchandising rights."[48]

The evening gala scene celebrating the public launch of the team has several examples of subtle intertextual humor. As Tony Stark hits on a female reporter, the reader might notice that she bears a striking resemblance to Lois Lane and is accompanied by two men who resemble Clark Kent and Jimmy Olsen.[49] In addition, when President Bush makes his first appearance, he politely but firmly refuses an offered tray of pretzels.[50]

Such moments reward the observant viewer without distracting from the primary storyline in any way. Many moments play on the juxtaposition of ironic elements of context, such as when former fiancé Gail Richards and Bucky Barnes praise Cap for being decent compared to other heroes, despite his more ruthless tactics:

> GAIL: Congratulations on saving everyone, Steve. Sharon's two youngest watch the Hulk video every day after we pick them up from school. It's just nice to see them watching somebody decent for a change after Spider-Man or one of the horrible X-Men.
>
> BUCKY: Yeah, seeing you drop that tank on his head and kicking him in the stones, it seemed like I was nineteen years old and back in Normandy again, buddy.[51]

Perhaps the most significant of these juxtapositions involves the many subplots generated by the metaphors implied through the supersoldier program itself. The supersoldier race (resulting in the creating of "persons of mass destruction") is a race among nations, among corporations, and even among individual scientists. In this storyline, the original supersoldier, Ultimate Captain America, was created in the 1930s in response to an extraterrestrial terrorist threat (the Chitauri or Skrulls) that was propping up the Nazi forces.

In fact, the *Ultimates* narrative reframed the Allied forces' wartime efforts as opposition to this alien species, even justifying the use of the atomic bombs in Nagasaki and Hiroshima as an attempt to contain the extraterrestrial threat. America has always been involved in a "war on terror," whether the populace was aware of this fact or not. Volume 1 of *The Ultimates* involves the buildup to a contemporary confrontation between the heroes and the alien species, a black-and-white opponent in a war on terror.

From America's perspective, there are two justifications for developing, stockpiling, and mobilizing "persons of mass destruction." First, the government is engaged in a secret war on terror that simply cannot be won by conventional means. Because the military is allowed to protect the nation behind a veil of national security, the Ultimates prove able to defeat the extraterrestrial menace.

The second rationale for the supersoldier efforts is reminiscent of the deterrence element of neoconservative foreign policy. In several moments of dialogue, Nick Fury uses the classic appeal to strength favored by neoconservative intellectuals, such as the following exchange with President George W. Bush:

PRESIDENT BUSH: Is he as strong as you expected, General?

FURY: Stronger, sir.

BUSH: Is he smart?

FURY: Tactically off the scale, Mister President. There's genuinely nobody in existence I'd rather have leading this team when they're out there on the field. Add this Thunder God guy to the mix plus all the other Super-Soldiers Banner can create from Cap's blood and I don't see anyone acting up for quite a while. Do you, sir?

BUSH: No, I don't, General Fury. No, I don't.[52]

The appeal to strength also creates a need to avoid admitting responsibility for mistakes, even when those mistakes lead to the loss of life. When Bruce Banner becomes the Hulk and kills more than eight hundred people in a mad fury, the Ultimates are forced to bring him down. They succeed, but when it comes time to provide details on the conflict, Fury and Betty Ross decide to hide the government's involvement in the creation of the Hulk.[53] By hiding the truth from the public, the Ultimates maintain their appearance of strength and integrity, and it is often argued throughout both books that the appearance of strength is an essential component of the Ultimates' mission.

However, by the second volume Millar and Hitch began to shift the book's tone away from the black-and-white certainty of fighting extraterrestrials who are trying to destroy the planet to a more "gray" narrative. Millar explained he thought the book should be "a little more political given that we live in more political times."[54]

The second series opens with Ultimate Cap infiltrating Iraq to liberate American hostages in clear violation of the ban against the use of "persons of mass destruction" outside of the continental United States. This decision causes a rift with Thor, a Norwegian national who often serves as the tempering voice of conscience for the team.

According to Millar, the shift in tone and the choice of locale were not accidental:

> [B]y the time "Ultimates 2" came along, we started to see a different tone. We were all saying, "Well, these guys are in Afghanistan, you should be trying to get them." But the Bush administration and the cronies started to go for Saddam instead, who had nothing to do with it. No ties with Al-Qaeda at all. The rest of the world was starting to see it as not such a black and white situation, and I think "Ultimates 2" . . . was all about shades of grey. It was like, the most powerful nation in the world using these superpowered characters in a way that might not be as innocent as it seems. It was the abuse of the superheroes.[55]

President George W. Bush makes several appearances throughout the series, though rarely as the executive power directing the military strategy.

It is clear that in the world of *The Ultimates,* the military-industrial complex runs largely unchecked. In fact, at several points in the narrative, characters refer to military intelligence classifications by how many levels above presidential scrutiny or governmental "top-secret" clearance the material is.

Thor expounds on this view when he reveals his opinion of the American presidency in *The Ultimates* 2 volume 1, number 2:

> GROUPIE: —I said I love that piece in your book about America thinking it's the new Roman Empire, but why have you stopped mentioning the President by name, Thor? Why don't you personalize it anymore?
>
> THOR: Because blaming him for what they're doing is like blaming Ronald McDonald for the hamburgers. He's just their front man. I doubt they even let him into the meetings.[56]

Dissent is also not a value espoused by the government or the military. Among the heroes, Thor plays the voice of the dissident. Whereas the others follow orders and don't concern themselves with the implications of their actions, Thor consistently offers a social critique of American culture and military might, appearing on television shows (*60 Minutes* in *The Ultimates* 2 number 3) to warn Americans about the dangers of imperialism: "Forget this little street theater they're numbing your brains with. Our primary concern should be the rumors of The Ultimates being deployed in Syria and Iran. Because that's what's coming up if we don't get our act together, Bob. This team wasn't put together to stop burglars and bank robbers."[57] For speaking out, Thor's very identity and origin are attacked. Reframed as an enemy, Thor is accused of being a traitor and is confronted and defeated by the rest of the team. Once his voice is removed, the team begins regular incursions into Middle East, disarming military threats to the American status quo and causing worldwide concern that the United States is establishing an expansionist empire.

Even incarcerated, Thor continues to critique the situation as he tries to open his teammates' eyes to their manipulation by the military. These interactions serve as metaphors critical of the culture of fear that neoconservative officials use to justify preemptive actions to disarm rogue nations. An exchange between Thor and Tony Stark in *The Ultimates 2* number 7 illustrates this critique:

THOR: This is why you're going to lose, Tony . . . the tighter you squeeze, the more they'll just slip through your fingers.

TONY: And when did I become one of the bad guys?

THOR: Around the same time you took part in that pre-emptive strike against a Third World country.

TONY: A Third World country with nuclear weapons.

THOR: I think you'll find that the only nation that's ever used nuclear weapons against other human beings is the one you pledged an oath of allegiance to.

TONY: Oh, stop being an idiot, Thor. These people were targeting neighbors at the same time they were reassuring us they didn't even have a weapons program. What would you have done in our situation? Crossed your fingers?

THOR: They've got you, haven't they? All they have to do is say "nuclear weapons" and Tony Stark just falls in line like the rest of them. Do you think that's how they'll get you to invade all their other target countries? Supposing they decide China's a threat a few years down the line?

TONY: Now you're just being ridiculous.

THOR: I used to think you were the smart one, Tony.[58]

Through these events and conversations, Millar and Hitch use the team as an allegory for the American people and their fears regarding the implications of the American actions in Iraq. Millar pointed to how his own concerns about the expansion of US military action in the world served as inspiration for the story:

My feeling is that over the next year some kind of incident will happen or be arranged that prompts a nationwide call for the draft and pre-emptive strikes on Syria, North Korea, Iran and all the world hot spots.

This isn't such a conspiracy theory here in Europe. Many mainstream politicians are very skeptical of what's happening and worried about even the short-term consequences for the world. In the name of oil, this administration is stirring up a hornet's nest and, even though I'm a huge optimist, I think we're heading for some kind of Armageddon. I just can't see a good way out of this situation and, after decades of seeing Britain try to deal with the IRA, I know you don't defeat terrorists by killing their families. My own belief is that there'll be a couple of nuclear attacks in the States, the multinationals will move elsewhere, the American economy will completely collapse and make the 30s look like the 80s and the Middle East will be occupied by drafted teenagers from your home town. But don't get me started. I hope I'm completely and utterly wrong.[59]

But the critique of direct military action is not the only criticism embedded in *The Ultimates*. The creators also present commentary about the nature of force and the proliferation of power in an international setting.

As Nick Fury struggles to justify the expense of billions of federal dollars, the team initially proves its mettle by stopping the Hulk (but not before more than eight hundred civilians are killed in the melee). Ironically, the Hulk was accidentally created when his alternate identity was a government employee working in pursuit of the supersoldier serum. Most of the heroes and villains in the Ultimate universe are products of the search to re-create the supersoldier formula given to Captain America, including the Hulk, Giant-Man, Spider-Man, and nearly all of Spider-Man's foes. The search for a supersoldier results in the proliferation of superpowered beings (which in turn justifies the increased investment in additional efforts to create supersoldiers to defend against threats from these "persons of mass destruction").

In addition, the successes in the creation of the Ultimates team members lead other nations to begin their own "super-persons" programs. The European Union fields a covert team. Several countries are rumored to be experimenting with gene manipulation and human augmentation. Nick Fury demonstrates he is perfectly aware of the situation, explaining it to Ultimate Cap in *Ultimate Six* number 5: "Captain, you, like the atom bomb, are one of the greatest success stories in the history of war. And ever since, like the bomb, every country with a Petri dish and five dollars has been scrambling to not only repeat you . . . but to improve on you and stockpile you."[60] However, this proliferation creates a state of hypocrisy in American society as the government is forced to ban human genetic manipulation even while it is funding several projects that attempt to create government supersoldiers through gene manipulation. Even the Ultimate Captain America is unsettled by the realization of this double standard.

The international supersoldier proliferation comes to a head in the second volume as the Ultimates face the invasion and occupation of America by a team of foreigners called "the Liberators," featuring superpowered agents from China, Russia, North Korea, and Syria. These agents justify their actions as an effort to halt the increased aggression by the United States throughout the world. In this manner, the existence of the Ultimates creates the very threat they were assembled to guard against. But as one exchange between Loki and Colonel Abdul Al-Rahman (a Middle Eastern Captain America) from *The Ultimates* 2 number 9 illustrates, the foreign team is less motivated by aggressive tendencies and more concerned with the geopolitical implications of the neoconservative call for preemptive action in the world:

> LOKI: All this carnage must be very satisfying after everything the Americans have done to your country, eh, colonel?
> COLONEL ABDUL AL-RAHMAN: I didn't come here for revenge, Loki. I came here to lead this international collective because America's plans simply had to be curtailed. The world is a safer place now that this new Roman Empire has been restrained.[61]

The Roman Empire frame is used to describe America's war on terror mandate throughout volume 2. Once the Liberators have secured the major metropolitan areas of the United States, they begin to dismantle American symbols of power. As Liberator forces knock the Statue of Liberty into New York harbor in *The Ultimates* 2 number 9, Colonel Al-Rahman films the destruction and narrates: "We told you to stop making super people, America. We told you not to interfere with cultures you cannot understand. This is what happens when your ambitions outstrip your capabilities. The empire takes a fall."[62]

It is telling that only one of the four team deployments in the two volumes of *The Ultimates*—the Chitari invasion—is fought against an opponent whose origin is independent of the Ultimates' existence. The other three conflicts (with the Hulk, with Thor, and with the Liberators) occur as a direct result of the military buildup that created the team. This fact is not lost on the remaining heroes in the team, who, after defeating the Liberator forces at the end of the second volume, declare their independence from the American establishment and operate exclusively from private funding sources.

The Patriotism of Ultimate Captain America

A close reading of both volumes of *The Ultimates* (and the derivative *Ultimate* titles in which the Ultimates appear) provides an interesting perspective on the supposed outcomes of neoconservative philosophy. Patriotism's connection to hypermasculinity in this context becomes a negative force, at least as portrayed by *The Ultimates* series authors. Although many conflicting subtle statements are woven throughout the series (and many of these statements rest in the context of comparisons to the mainstream Marvel narratives), a few dominant themes emerge:

1. *Cultural value systems tend to close minds and isolate communities.* Captain America struggles mightily in his attempts to adjust to the twenty-first century. His inability to accept changes to contemporary culture and to approach people where they are leads to miscommunication and misunderstanding, which in turn lead to unnecessary conflict.

At different points in the series, Captain America alludes to "survival instincts" that have been programmed into him during his transformation. Claiming that these enhancements allow him to adapt to the present day, Cap becomes surlier and more brutish as the narrative progresses. He appears to have less and less tolerance for those different from him, and on two occasions he physically confronts teammates whom he perceives to have acted inappropriately and seriously injures one of them.

This tendency causes problems for the team as a whole, and as each character fights for his or her personal views to be validated, key facts and snippets of information are missed, leading to the surprise invasion's early success.

2. *Preemptive military action most likely leads to the creation of enemies and increases a nation's chances of being attacked.* Each of the Liberators has a personal motivation for joining the attack, but most of them either are reacting to the Ultimates' behavior in invading and disarming their home country or are working to prevent their country from receiving such a visit.

The narrative leaves little doubt that the surprise invasion would not have occurred without the more aggressive US policies in the rest of the world. Strength would appear to create resistance, not subservience. Hitch and Millar seemed to have joined the chorus of voices a few years after 9/11 who were suggesting that US involvement in other cultures (pursuing American interests to the detriment of others) causes many threats to America to emerge in the first place.

Although not explicitly connecting the Liberators' invasion to 9/11, the rhetoric surrounding the toppling of the Statue of Liberty is consistent with the justifications given for terrorist attacks on the United States. *The Ultimates* narrative suggests that aggressive policies do not actually make a nation safer but rather build up resentment among people who would care little about our civilization otherwise.

3. *Building up military strength for its own sake leads to a proliferation of national threats, both domestically and internationally.* As stated earlier, many (if not most) of the heroes and villains in the Ultimate Marvel Universe exist because of the pursuit of the supersoldier formula (in fact, in *Ultimate Origins* it is revealed that even that universe's mutants are the result of military experiments to create supersoldiers[63]). This pursuit would appear to have created more supervillains than heroes as well as the environment that led to the Hulk's Manhattan rampage and other collateral events.

In the analogy between "persons of mass destruction" and "weapons of mass destruction," the series considers the paradoxes inherent in America's establishment and enforcement of weapons policies on countries while continuing to develop increasingly deadly weapons of its own. Beyond the obvious hypocrisy is the cold implication that the introduction of larger and larger numbers of weapons will result in larger numbers of weapons and weapons knowledge on the black market, which other countries may use. In addition, the stockpiling of American weapons appears to encourage more rogue nations to seek counterbalances to American power. This critique flies in the face of the neoconservative notion of deterrence.

4. *The pursuit of power will lead many individuals to corruption or gross misjudgments, even when their intentions are pure.* Each of the characters in the *Ultimates* narrative plays an interesting role in questions of power and responsibility.

Nick Fury plays the exemplar neoconservative: always pragmatically compromising ideals to work within the reality of the power politics before him. Captain America often blindly follows orders, even when those orders put the country in danger. The competition among several of the characters leads to jealousy, which not only clouds the individual team members' judgment but also allows the entrance and manipulation of agents in league with the Liberators. Clearly, a central tenet of *The Ultimates* narrative is that the pursuit of power, even in the name of defense, often makes itself a self-fulfilling prophecy.

Power creates as many threats as it protects against, suggesting policy initiatives' karmic effect. By choosing to impose brute force to support unilateral policy initiatives, America stands to reap what it has sown.

And yet each of these critiques presented in the Ultimate Marvel Universe stands in contrast to the reactive text presented in the mainstream Marvel Universe. Using these two narratives, Marvel responded to post-9/11 concerns from both ends of the American political spectrum. The moral angst felt by the mainstream Marvel Captain America is offset by the violent hypermasculine passions experienced by the Ultimate Cap.

Race and Gender in the Ultimate and Mainstream Marvel Universes

The Ultimate Universe books are noteworthy for the general lack of regard they have for issues of race. Nick Fury, America's "Top Cop," is portrayed as an African American, but little is made of his race, save when Captain America doubts Fury because of his own 1940s preconceptions of race in the military.[64] The exception comes in the *Ultimate Origins* series of 2008, in which Nick Fury is shown to have been enhanced during World War II in a prototype experiment intended to create Captain America.[65] Although it is not explained that Fury was chosen because of his race (the portrayal more likely suggests that his selection was at least in part owing to his military incarceration for theft), the portrayal is strongly reminiscent of the mainstream continuity's *Truth: Red, White, and Black* series (discussed later in this chapter). Certainly, Fury's reception of the supersoldier serum was intended as a test, for his transformation clears the way for the serum to be administered to the intended recipient: Steve Rogers.

As far as gender portrayals, the era stretching from 2002 to 2007 possessed few significantly provocative female characters. That's not to say that female characters did not appear in the titles featuring Captain America—far from it. Rather, in the insular post-9/11 narratives, gender does not seem to play a large role in the female characters' performances. Notable exceptions include the consummated sexual relationship between Captain America and longtime love interest Sharon Carter[66] and the insanity of the Scarlet Witch as she aims to destroy the Avengers (which has more to do with her motherhood role). Even in *The Ultimates* universe, typically strong female characters such as the Wasp are portrayed as motivated by identity issues other than their gender. For example, the Wasp's insecurities come from her status as a mutant instead of from her gender.[67]

Race also appears to take a back seat during this era. The Falcon, who had all but disappeared from issues of *Captain America* and *The Avengers*, received a treatment from Christopher Priest, an African American author who had received high praise for his revitalization of Marvel's Black Panther character. Priest's series *Captain America and the Falcon* volume 2 was received with mixed reviews because the "Avengers: Disassembled" story arc occurred during its run, leading to much confusion about several points in the plot. Unlike in their previous experiences, in this series Captain America and the Falcon do little to confront issues of race through their partnership.

In 2003, Marvel published a comic series titled *Truth: Red, White, and Black*. Drawing on the historic revelations of mistreatment of African

Americans, author Robert Morales penned a retcon origin of Captain America that suggests the supersoldier serum had been developed by administering early versions of it to unwilling African American servicemen. Though the story was originally intended to exist outside Marvel continuity, Morales explained that Marvel decided to make it official.[68]

The series posits that after Steve Rogers became Captain America, two platoons of African American soldiers are administered trial versions of the lost serum. Only a half-dozen survive the trials, and all but one are soon killed. The remaining soldier, Isaiah Bradley, steals Captain America's uniform for his final mission to liberate the Schwarzebitte concentration camp. He fulfills the objectives of his mission but is captured by Nazi forces. Eventually escaping, Bradley is incarcerated by his own government for the theft of the Captain America uniform, and his identity is disavowed until Captain America happens upon the story by accident.

Rebecca Wanzo describes the patriotism represented by the prototype supersoldier in *Truth* as "melancholic patriotism."[69] Though victims of outright racial discrimination in the army, the African Americans fight for a freedom they will likely never possess themselves. As Wanzo explains, "If Rogers' transformed body represents US democracy's ability to transform its citizens into ideals, black Captain America Isaiah Bradley epitomizes not only the failure of US democracy to work equally for all citizens but also the ways in which the fantasies of US democracy can be built on the backs of those it uses and then discards."[70]

Poignant moments of the series include when Bradley is confronted by the horrors of the concentration camp but realizes that his own treatment by the US government has not been dissimilar to the Nazis' mistreatment of Jews.[71] Bradley is also confronted by Adolf Hitler and offered equal treatment for his race if he assists the Third Reich in the overthrow of America, but Bradley refuses.[72] The series culminates in Captain America's uncovering a dark history of the relationship between the US and German governments that tie his own origin as a supersoldier to racism and the eugenics movement.[73] He seeks out and finds Bradley, now debilitated from his neglect and abuse by the US government, and makes amends.

The Renegade Civil Warrior (2006–2007)

In 2005, Marvel introduced a fifth volume of *Captain America* comic books, authored by Ed Brubaker. Building on the uncertainty of the 2002 series, Marvel creators led Cap through a series of stories that reframe the death of his young partner, Bucky. Instead of dying in the blast that sent Cap into suspended animation, Bucky was merely injured according to Brubaker's retcon. Rescued by a Soviet submarine, the lad was subjected to intense mental conditioning and turned into a Cold War assassin.

As Cap chases down and confronts his former partner, he again is forced to reexamine his assumptions about his place in the world. The simple truths in his past are once again replaced with complex half-truths and shaded perspectives. It is this Cap who helps launch the Marvel *Civil War* narrative.

The origins of *Civil War* reside in tragedy. The careless exploits of a group of teen heroes in Stamford, Connecticut, result in an explosion that claims the lives of 612 civilians, 60 of whom are children.[74] Fear and resentment of costumed heroes follow, leading the country to debate the role of vigilantism in society.

In the wake of the controversy, Congress hurriedly passes the Super-human Registration Act, a piece of legislation requiring every masked hero in America to register with the government, receive proper training, and join a coordinated police effort run by governmental agencies. The heroes' responses quickly divide the superhero community into two factions: those who support registration and those who resist its enforcement.

Captain America is approached by acting director of S.H.I.E.L.D. Maria Hill with orders to prepare to help the government hunt down any heroes who do not meet the Registration Act requirements:

CAP: You're asking me to arrest people who risk their lives for this country every day of the week.

HILL: No, I'm asking you to obey the will of the American people, Captain.

CAP: Don't play politics with me, Hill. Super heroes need to stay above that stuff or Washington starts telling us who the super-villains are.

HILL: I thought super-villains were guys in masks who refused to obey the law.[75]

This exchange leads to a physical confrontation between Cap and S.H.I.E.L.D. agents. Cap escapes and goes underground to lead a resistance movement of superheroes who refuse to register. But as he reflects on his actions, he realizes this conflict proves to be just as much about how American culture has developed in recent years as it is about how costumed heroes should behave:

Drawing made me happy. Why did I stop? Oh yes, because people *need* Captain America. No. *YOU* need Captain America. *Steve Rogers* needs Captain America. They don't need anything. That's the point of all this. *They* want super heroes to be controlled by the government. They want to be puppets to a corporate shill structure. Like everything else on the planet. They don't see that we're all that's keeping them truly protected and free. What do you expect from a society that gets all its news from late-night comedy shows? Of course they don't care! Everything is a punchline. Everything is just—no. It's not true. They care. They just care more about themselves than they care about the world the live in. They want to be comfortable, not safe. They don't want to fight for their freedom. They want someone like me to fight for it for them . . . [.][76]

Cap's former partner, Bucky, provides a similar analysis as he contrasts his first contemporary Christmas with the seasonal spirit he remembers from the 1940s:

My first year back in the world . . . really back . . . and this is what they call Christmas?

No . . . this isn't Christmas. We may be getting this weak excuse for snow . . . and decorations may be around the city . . . but the spirit is gone. It's like someone knocked the wind out of America . . . and everything important went with it. But they just go through the motions, because no one knows what else to do. But you see in their eyes . . . they're scared. There's another war going on all around them. But they aren't involved . . .

They can't be. Because this war is fought by gods, not men. That's what it must feel like . . . like the way it must've felt like in 1940, when the Torch fought Namor and they blew up and drowned half the Bowery. Helpless.

And it's hard to feel anything else when you feel helpless.[77]

Because of his recent emergence from his own decades-long slumber, Bucky Barnes serves the same role that Captain America did in the 1960s. His voice is one of cultural critique as he compares the modern America he finds with the America of a previous generation. At several points in the narrative, he expresses concern regarding the culture of fear that has gripped the US citizenry, perhaps never so clearly as when he considers the treatment of Cap after the Civil War ended: "He was like that sainted can-do-no-wrong big brother. The guy you can't help but look up to . . . because you just KNOW you can never be that good . . . that graceful under pressure . . . or that strong in the face of horror. But they've all forgotten that . . . all they care about is their fear . . . [.]"[78]

For Captain America, the Civil War is about a conflict of ideals, not law. He had already revealed his identity to the public, had already received military training, and had long coordinated his efforts with governmental forces when needed. Sharon Carter, S.H.I.E.L.D. agent and former flame, tracks him down and asks him why he's opposing a law he has already complied with, giving him an opportunity to articulate his objections:

> CAP: I accept these things. Not gladly, but I accept these things. Because Captain America is who I am . . . and I understand what comes with that. But not everyone is like me. Not everyone is willing to risk what I have . . . should they be denied the right to make that choice?
>
> CARTER: Maybe . . . yes. Because they're risking other people's lives every time they jump into a firefight. And because it's against the law. And the rule of law is what this country is founded on.

CAP: No . . . it was founded on breaking the law. Because the law was wrong.

CARTER: That's semantics, Steve. You know what I mean . . .

CAP: It's not semantics, Sharon. It's the heart of the issue. The Registration Act is another step toward government control. And while I love my country, I don't trust many politicians. Not when they're having their strings pulled by corporate donors. And not when they're willing to trade freedom for security.[79]

With discourse like this, Captain America offers a social critique of emergency legislation such as the USA PATRIOT Act. Though some in our culture (like Iron Man in *Civil War*) argue that the government should be allowed broad powers in moments of cultural conflict, others (like Cap) believe that those in power can never be trusted with too much information about the citizenry.

Cap carries this argument further in a parlay with Iron Man, who leads the government's efforts to enforce registration:

CAP: The Registration Act takes away any freedom we have, any autonomy. You don't know who could get elected. How public sentiment might change. I'm old enough to remember Japanese-Americans being put into camps because they were judged potential threats to national security.

IRON MAN: That's your problem, Steve. Always looking at the past. I look at the future. It's what I do. And believe me when I tell you that your way is a lot more likely to get us put in camps than mine.[80]

This exchange connects the two sides of the contemporary American political scene. Iron Man's position can be identified with the conservative and neoconservative voice: security must be established at all costs, and dramatic changes to society's power structure are justified because those enacting such changes are good, trustworthy people. In addition, public opinion is touted as a justification for social change: "Cap, please. I know you're angry. I know it's an enormous change from the way we've always worked. But we aren't living in Nineteen Forty-Five anymore. The public doesn't want masks and secret identities. They want to feel safe when we're around, and there's just no other way to win back their respect."[81]

Because the government (or, in the narrative, the superhero community) is held accountable for failures of security, it seeks empowerment to enable more effective tactics against the threats faced. Owing to the emergence of the culture of fear created by tragic events (Stamford in the narrative, the September 11 attacks in reality), critical debate is dismissed by claims that the "world has changed." Iron Man's view is a pragmatic critique of the problem of securing a free culture in the modern world.

Captain America, in contrast, represents the liberal critique of power in society. He argues on several occasions that power cannot be centralized because of the potential of future abuses. To bolster his claims, he continually draws on historical abuses of power in American society. For him, the freedom of the citizenry (even the superpowered citizenry) to operate without governmental interference is more important than ensuring security.

Although the conflict in the storyline is often physical, the cultural argument is represented especially by the inner turmoil felt by Spider-Man. In the *Civil War* books, Spider-Man takes on the role of the soul of the nation, and Iron Man and Captain America struggle to convince him that each one's respective position is more consistent with the needs of twenty-first-century America.

Spider-Man is initially persuaded by Iron Man's appeal to order, law, and security. He reveals his identity to the American public and becomes the registration forces' chief enforcer. This choice brings him into direct conflict with Cap and the superhero resistance. In their first skirmish, Spider-Man manages to capture Cap's shield but decides to leave it for him as a message:

> When he finds it, I hope he understands the message—that the shield represents the country and the laws of the country decide who's right. Even the laws we don't like. Even the ones that suck. Cap thinks in terms of right and wrong, but this isn't a matter of right or wrong, moral or immoral. It's legal vs. illegal. At least, that's what I tell myself

in the middle of the night, when I wonder what the hell I'm doing here. I'm legal. I'm registered. I'm authorized. And as I feel this whole situation starting to unravel all around me—I just hope to God that I'm also right.[82]

Even as Spider-Man symbolically argues with Cap, he struggles with the reconciliation of law and morality (often codified in the narrative by claims of "what's right"). This juxtaposition is at the heart of the questions raised by the *Civil War* narrative: How does Lawrence and Jewett's Captain America complex, which represents the American narrative tradition of outlaw heroes whose morality compels them to vigilantism when the established officers of the law prove inadequate, fit into a post-9/11 world? Where does individual morality fit into the social need for security?

For his part, Iron Man's response to Cap is to portray Cap's ideals as unrealistic in the modern world, and Cap in return sees Iron Man as someone who can justify any means to his ends:

IRON MAN: You're the perfect man. You live by ideals and standards that are . . . more than outdated. They're impossible for anyone but you. And when you're confronted by the shades of gray, when people inevitably disappoint you because people are flawed, you do what you've always done when the going got tough. You dig your heels in and fight even harder. Never mind whether you can win. Sometimes I think you'd rather go out in a blaze of glory than face reality.

CAP: You know, even after all these years, that's one of the things about the modern world I've had the hardest time adjusting to. All the damn **psychobabble**. What's right is what's right. If you believe it, you stand up for it.[83]

Iron Man's discourse represents a common theme in neoconservative argumentation: civil liberties and individual freedom are fine and good in times of peace, but times of conflict require a culture of force and order. At the heart of Cap and Iron Man's disagreement is the individual's role in society and where social power should be located.

Spider-Man's opinion eventually changes as he witnesses the effects of the Superhuman Registration Act on individual freedom. He battles Iron Man and escapes. Seeking to join the resistance, he meets Cap, and the two make amends. Spider-Man asks how Cap, as a representation of the country's spirit, can resist the country's laws. Cap responds by quoting at length from Mark Twain's essay "My Country Right or Wrong," written as a response to the Spanish-American War. "For in a republic," Twain wrote, "who is 'the Country'?"

> Is it the Government which is for the moment in the saddle? Why, the Government is merely a servant—merely a temporary servant; it cannot be its prerogative to determine what is right and what is wrong, and decide who is a patriot and who isn't. Its function is to obey orders, not originate them. Who, then, is "the country"? Is it the newspaper? Is it the pulpit? Is it the school-superintendent? Why, these are mere parts of the country, not the whole of it; they have not command, they have only their little share in the command. They are but one in the thousand; it is in the thousand that command is lodged; they must determine what is right and what is wrong; they must decide who is a patriot and who isn't.
>
> In a monarchy, the king and his family are the country; in a republic it is the common voice of the people. Each of you, for himself, by himself and on his own responsibility, must speak. And it is a solemn and weighty responsibility, and not lightly to be flung aside at the bullying of pulpit, press, government, or the empty catch-phrases of politicians. Each must for himself alone decide what is right and what is wrong, and which course is patriotic and which isn't. You cannot shirk this and be a man. To decide it against your convictions is to be an unqualified and inexcusable traitor, both to yourself and to your country, let men label you as they may. If you alone of all the nation shall decide one way, and that way be the right way according to your convictions of the right, you have done your duty by yourself and by your country—hold up your head! You have nothing to be ashamed of.[84]

To this exhortation, Cap adds his own stance: "Doesn't matter what the press says. Doesn't matter what the politicians or the mobs say. Doesn't matter if the whole country decides that something wrong is something right. This nation was founded on one principle above all else: the requirement that we stand up for what we believe, no matter the odds or the consequences. When the mob and the press and the whole world tell you to move, your job is to plant yourself like a tree beside the river of truth, and tell the whole world—'No, you move.'"[85]

This response deeply affects Spider-Man, who joins the resistance. Cap's speeches and rhetoric provide a rallying point for the resistance forces. His fighting skills are considerable, but his determination and assurance serve as the conscience of those who fight beside him, as Spider-Man explains: "All I know . . . is that now that the final battle has started, I can't stop . . . won't stop . . . until and unless HE stops. And he won't. He'll never sacrifice what he stands for. Not as long as he's alive."[86]

However, this charisma is not used to interact with the press or the citizenry. Cap limits his influence to those who serve alongside him, appearing to have little faith in the public or American institutions. These attitudes are explicated when the Black Panther visits Cap and tries to persuade him to change his tactics:

CAP: Speak your piece, T'Challa. Why did you come here?
BLACK PANTHER: To convince you there's a better way to win this war than fighting.
CAP: Politicians talk—and get nothing done. I'm a soldier.
PANTHER: You're Captain America. The living symbol of this country. You could change the hearts and minds of the public—if you talked to them.
CAP: How many more heroes need to die while we wait for opinion polls to change?[87]

Cap's apparent lack of faith in and use of American institutions and political structures in turn creates a rather one-sided view of the conflict for the American citizenry. Throughout the conflict, Iron Man and the registration forces are featured in the media, but access to Captain America or his forces is restricted to the few brave journalists who defy convention and seek alternative viewpoints.[88]

Instead of fighting Iron Man's media strategy with one of his own, Cap resolves to confront the Superhuman Registration Act primarily by waging a guerrilla war. He uses his resources and considerable tactical knowledge to free many of the heroes detained by the government and eventually provokes an end-game conflict that puts his forces in position to win the war.

However, just as he is poised to deliver the decisive blow, Cap ceases his efforts when he realizes the scope of the damage to property and bystanders caused by the heroes' conflict.[89] Horrified at the fight's consequences for civilians, Captain America removes his mask, surrenders, and is incarcerated. He then decides to continue his fight within the court system but is assassinated before he gets the opportunity to voice his argument to the justice system.

Although Cap never seeks out publicity, he has several opportunities to explain his motives to journalists covering the conflict. In conjunction with the *Civil War* books, Marvel produced *Civil War: Front Line*, an eleven-issue series chronicling two reporters' struggles to unwind the prevailing issues of the conflict.

After the conclusion of the physical conflict, Captain America grants an interview in which he explains his rationale for waging the civil war: "I believe in the fundamental freedoms accorded us by our Constitution, Ben. I believe we have a right to bear arms, a right to defend and a right to choose. I have sworn an oath to defend America from external forces, and from within. If that means standing against the government, rejecting a bogus law passed by my own superiors, then I suppose that's what it means . . . I saw the possibility of a Registration Act as a basic violation of our rights as Americans."[90] Once again, Cap argues that civil liberties should transcend security and that the ideals of American culture are more valuable than the laws or policies of the state. Journalist Sally Floyd challenges Cap:

CAP: I did what I thought was right for America.

FLOYD: Let me ask you something, sir: do you know what MySpace is?

CAP: I'm not sure I understand the relevance of the question, Sally—

FLOYD: No. You just don't understand the question, sir. I'm trying to illustrate a point here, so bear with me. Do you know who won the last World Series, or who was the last America Idol? When was the last time you actually attended a NASCAR race? When was the last time you watched the Simpsons or logged onto YouTube to watch a stupid video? Answer? Exactly, never. You hold America up as some shining beacon of perfection but you know next to nothing about it.[91]

She lays it all down for him: "Your problem is that you're fighting for an ideal—It's all you know how to do. America is no longer mom and apple pie . . . it's about high cholesterol and Paris Hilton and scheming your way to the top. The country I love treats its celebrities like royalty and its teachers like dirt. But at least I walk its streets every day, at least I know what it **is**. You've **broken** that country, Captain America. What are you going to do to **fix** it?"[92]

Floyd argues (as several voices in the most recent rendition of Cap's comic have argued) that Captain America's idealistic struggle doesn't hold significance for postmodern America. Iron Man appears to second that voice, although Cap gets an opportunity to rebut:

CAP: Do you think the fact that I'm in **here** [in jail] means **you** won?
IRON MAN: Uh, yes.
CAP: We maintained the principles we swore to defend and protect. You sold your principles. You lost this before it started. Do you actually think the fact that you know how to program a computer makes you more of a human being than me? That I'm out of touch because I don't know what you know? I know what **freedom** is. I know what it feels like to fight for it and I know what it costs to have it. You know compromise. "Man is the only animal that deals in that atrocity of atrocities, war. He is the only one that gathers his brethren about him and goes forth in cold blood and calm pulse to exterminate his kind. He is the only animal that for sordid wages will march out and help to slaughter

strangers of his own species who have done him no harm and with whom he has no quarrel . . . And in the intervals between campaigns he washes the blood off his hands and works for the 'universal brotherhood of man'—with his mouth." Do you know who said that? Go find out. BECAUSE HE WAS TALKING ABOUT YOU!! **YOU** made this war!![93]

For Captain America, defeat means compromising one's ideals. If the Registration Act is viewed as an analogy for the PATRIOT Act, Cap sees the infringement on civil liberties as the greater evil. Emergency situations call for extraordinary effort, but maintaining the principles of American culture should be the highest priority.

Soon after this exchange, Cap is scheduled to have his day in court. As he is transported to the federal courthouse where he is to be tried for treason, he is shot multiple times. He expires on the way to the hospital, setting up a story arc called *Fallen Son: The Death of Captain America*, wherein the characters in the Marvel Universe begin to cope with the death of idealism represented by the loss of Captain America.

Putting the Civil War in Context

Marvel's *Civil War* narrative strives to re-create the environment of muted discourse that occurred in the weeks and months following the terrorist attacks of September 11, 2001. In the narrative, the Stamford disaster (in particular the death of so many children at a school) makes rational discourse impossible. When a national tragedy occurs, the impulse to "rally around the flag" privileges the voice of conservatives (and neoconservatives) and the government in the culture.

This privilege is derived from the "culture of fear" that can be created by opportunistic politicians and public figures when society is threatened. Several scholars and social critics have addressed these issues, perhaps most prominently Barry Glassner, Frank Füredi, and David Altheide.[94] These works suggest that in times of tragedy or extreme threat the voice of the government is difficult to counter or critique because dissent is perceived as a challenge to the society at large.

Ira Chernus argues that the root of neoconservativism is a fear that American counterculture has undermined and will continue to undermine the authority of traditional values and moral norms. He explains that because neoconservatives tend to hold a view of human nature that defines individuals as innately selfish, they worry that a society with no commonly accepted values based on religion or tradition will end up in a type of individualistic cultural civil war.[95]

To resist this outcome, the neoconservative holds strength as America's most important social value and by extension fears that weakness will lead to moral confusion and anarchy.

Captain America seems to understand this concept, which might explain his reticence to use news media to address the nation. Both he and his former partner Bucky perceive the American people as fearful and uncritical in their discernment.

This uncritical tendency echoes the chill felt through the journalism industry in the wake of the events of September 11. Syndicated columnist Ellen Goodman reflected on the behavior of the press less than three months after the attacks: "When terrorists struck on September 11, there was only one side. No editor demanded a quote from someone saying why it was fine to fly airplanes into buildings. No one expected reporters to take an 'objective' view of the terrorists. . . . Being neutral on terrorism was as absurd as being neutral on lynching."[96] This attitude, common among journalists (and liberal critics) in the aftermath of the attacks, explains why little dissent was offered over the passage of the PATRIOT Act or over specific announced initiatives in the war on terror. Criticizing the government's position in a time of war can be interpreted as aligning oneself with the enemy.

Nor are journalists and social critics unjustified in their reluctance to speak truth to power. In times of cultural stress, the American public has demonstrated a lower tolerance of dissent. In the aftermath of the attacks, at least two small-town journalists were dismissed for what were considered politically incorrect expressions, and the ABC program *Politically Incorrect* lost advertisers, was pulled from some ABC affiliates, and was eventually canceled when host Bill Maher described US military policy as "cowardly."[97]

Thus, it must not seem reasonable to many social critics (or, in this case, to Cap as their symbol) that voicing concerns about social policy changes to the public is wise, given that rational debate is unlikely to occur. When this environment of fear emerges, critical arguments are marginalized or forced to work outside the political system to exact change.

What makes the *Civil War* narrative such an effective allegory for contemporary America is encapsulated in Tony Stark's vision of the coming conflict: "At first I thought we'd be fighting a war against evil. But that's just that holier-than-thou attitude that **we're** always the good guys and who **we** fight is bad guys. But in a war there are no good guys and there are no bad guys . . . There're opposing forces."[98] Democratic governance is about balancing opposing perspectives, but the culture of fear encourages the reduction of disagreements into conflict frames that define opinion holders as "good" or "evil" depending on the popularity of their subscribed beliefs.

The irony of Iron Man's words emerges through his actions: he sees heroes as morally ambiguous yet allows his version of "right" to be trumpeted as "good," whereas Captain America's relative silence in the media discourse must appear to some as "evil" (or at the very least misguided). The ability to voice one's position in times of crisis would appear to be regarded according to social morality.

Ultimately, dissenting voices are largely ineffective in times of social crisis because they are perceived to be part of the external threat and therefore not trusted. And critics cite concerns that even if a dissenting critique were to penetrate the manipulation of social control, it might cause great damage to the society.

As a result, critical voices are squelched in times of conflict. The *Civil War* narrative concludes with the voice of civil liberties constrained and then silenced through assassination.

Historians will likely debate for ages to come whether the legal and social reforms passed in response to the 2001 terrorist attacks were for the benefit of American society or the world at large. Unfortunately for those who value the tenets of a democratic society, those debates will almost exclusively occur as a retrospective exercise. Although Marvel's

Civil War portrays the events of 9/11, the war on terror, and the passage of the PATRIOT Act through superhero allegory, the themes represented in its books capture the mood of their age to inform the present readership and to serve as an artistic expression of the age for future generations to consider.

9

The Death and Rebirths of Captain America (2007–2014)

The death of Captain America in 2007 not only left a void in the Marvel continuity but also generated a large amount of political discussion as pundits and writers struggled to impose meaning on the media coverage of the assassination of a patriotic superhero. Liberal bloggers framed the event as a damning indictment of Bush administration policies and the death of the American Dream.[1] "On paper he was offed by a sniper's bullet," one commentator argued. "But in reality it was the toxic state of Bush and Cheney's America."[2]

Arnold T. Blumberg, a comics scholar, claimed Cap's assassination demonstrated Marvel's pro-government leanings, vindicating Iron Man's stance in the conflict (and by extension, the Bush administration's policies).[3] Conservative pundits and commentators agreed; one anonymous blogger wrote, "I think his death symbolizes the left's betrayal of their own country, their constant desire for appeasement and their defense of those that would destroy us."[4]

Captain America writer Ed Brubaker explained that during his run Captain America's actions had often been interpreted through the lenses of a variety of political positions: "What I found is that all the really hard-core left-wing fans want Cap to be standing out on and giving speeches on the street corner against the Bush administration, and all the really right-wing [fans] all want him to be over in the streets of Baghdad, punching out Saddam."[5] Dan Buckley, president and publisher of Marvel Entertainment, claimed there was no overt political agenda in the assassination: "It seemed a little radical when it was first brought up.

But sometimes stories just take you places. . . . We as publishers and as creative people knew where the ending was going to go for a long time. We knew people might not like it, but I think we delivered a compelling story that made everyone think.[6]

Intentional or not, Marvel's *Civil War* series and the assassination of Captain America, particularly when considered alongside John Ney Rieber and artist John Cassaday's depiction of Captain America's response to 9/11, came to represent a critique of America in the Bush administration era. Captain America's death came to be viewed as the death of liberty, either rightfully so (from the left) or wrongfully so (from the right).[7]

Other concerns likely influenced the timing of Captain America's death and the circumstances of his reemergence. Those concerns revolved around the forthcoming motion pictures that would present Captain America to a broader public. The Captain America that would again pick up his shield in 2011 would look different in many ways from the one who died in 2007, and most of those changes appear to have been the result of a series of renegotiations of the character during the period in which he was dead or inactive.

After the success of Marvel Studios' film *Iron Man*, Marvel Entertainment announced four new movie projects on May 5, 2008, including *Iron Man 2*, *Thor*, *Captain America: The First Avenger*, and *The Avengers* movies.[8] The formal announcement of a movie featuring Captain America, made while the character was dead according to the comic book narrative, suggested to many that a resurrection would be imminent. As with comic books, the shifting tone of American political discourse surrounding the election of Barack Obama affected the tone of Marvel Studios' projects, including *Captain America: The First Avenger*. Said Marvel Studio president Kevin Feige at the time of the election, "The idea of change and hope has permeated the country, regardless of politics, and that includes Hollywood. Discussions in all our development meetings include the zeitgeist and how it's changed in the last two weeks. Things are being adjusted."[9] The success of the Marvel Studios films and the 2009 purchase of Marvel by the Walt Disney Company for $4 billion[10] appear to have changed the priorities of Marvel's content creation. To understand the significance of such a change, it is important to understand how Captain America has been adapted to film and broadcast media in the past.

Throughout the publication history of Captain America comics, Timely/Marvel engaged in various attempts to license the narrative to film and broadcast media. The first successful adaptation was the fifteen-episode serial released by Republic Films. Filmed in Pasadena in November 1943, the first installment hit theaters on February 5, 1944.

The Republic Films serial was produced for $222,906, 22 percent over budget, the most expensive of Republic's serials,[11] and was directed by John English and Elmer Clifton. Republic had already adapted other comic book properties for film, including Fawcett's *Captain Marvel* and *Spysmasher*, and the divergences incorporated into the Captain America serials from the comic book suggest the script had actually originated as a treatment of Fawcett's *Mr. Scarlet*, whose plot and characters are more consistent with the serial than the content found in *Captain America Comics*.

In the Republic serial, Captain America is the masked persona of District Attorney Grant Gardner. Facing a mysterious nemesis called "Scarab," Gardner begins an investigation into the "purple death," a rash of connected murders. Changing into the star-spangled garb of Captain America, Gardner uses a mixture of gun violence and fisticuffs to battle the henchmen of Scarab's criminal organization. Possessing no obvious superpowers or strength, Captain America uses brute force to bring criminals to justice. In his first adventure, he shoots one of the first henchmen he meets. Gardner later shoots two more henchmen in his civilian guise before switching into his uniform and throwing yet another henchman out the window to his death. The frequency of violent ends appears roughly consistent with the content of *Captain America Comics*, except most of Cap's comic book adventures occur in a theater of war, whereas the films are set exclusively in US settings. This level of action and violence was not unusual for action serials: "In the serials, a fight wasn't realism and violence—it was excitement and action,"[12] though the fights that appeared in *Captain America* were particularly noteworthy and considered the "apex of the traditional action film fight, in the opinion of many cliffhanger enthusiasts."[13]

Serial fans' reaction to the Republic serial over the years has been generally favorable,[14] but the reception of fans familiar with Captain America has been less generous. As one critic wrote, "After viewing this mediocre serial, one can only wonder why the rights to this great comic book character were purchased if only to be misused in such a manner."[15]

Captain America was also featured in two live-action television pilots, produced after Frank Price of Universal Television saw a Hulk T-shirt on his son and acquired the live-action rights to the twelve heroes of his choice for $12,500.[16] *Captain America* premiered in 1979. A former marine who is exposed to the Full Latent Ability Gained (F.L.A.G.) formula in an attempt to save his life, Steve Rogers gains the enhanced strength and abilities consistent with the comic book hero. Directed by Rob Holcomb, fresh off a stint directing *The Six-Million Dollar Man*, the show established Captain America as a wandering hero.

During the era following the New World acquisition discussed in chapter 7, a low-budget Captain America film was produced by Marvel Enterprises, the 21st Century Film Corporation, and Jardin Film. Attempting to capitalize on the success of the 1989 success of *Batman* produced by Warner Bros., *Captain America* was released directly to video through Columbia Tri-Star Home Video; it was one of several failed films based on Marvel properties during the early 1990s.

What increases the significance of the current offering of Marvel films is the coordination that occurs in the marketing, promotion, and even the generation of new content. Rather than merely licensing out Marvel properties for other media corporations to adapt or incorporate, the MVL Productions LLC wing of Marvel Studios (and Disney) maintains a closer degree of editorial control over Marvel's characters than in years past.[17]

As a result, where previous Captain America films have struggled to adapt the comic hero to the constraints of the film medium, Marvel now appears to be simultaneously adapting the comic narrative to its filmography as it adapts its characters to film. For example, following the 2008 success of *Iron Man*, comic book portrayals of Tony Stark began to exclusively feature the character with a goatee similar to that worn by Robert Downey Jr. in the films rather than with the moustache worn by the historic comic book character.

In the Avengers and Captain America narratives, such changes became more explicit. Though the Marvel Studios films present an African American Nick Fury (played by Samuel L. Jackson, who had originally served as the model for the Nick Fury character in Mark Millar and Bryan Hitch's *The Ultimates*), the mainstream Marvel character was a white World War II veteran. To address the likely confusion moviegoers might have when they encountered the comic book narratives, Marvel produced a limited series titled *Battle Scars*. In *Battle Scars*, African American army ranger Marcus Johnson is targeted by supervillains and later discovers he is the son of Nick Fury.[18] When Johnson is captured alongside his father by a villain named Orion, his eye is gouged out.[19] He mounts a one-man rescue operation and defeats Orion and is established at the end of the series as "Nick Fury Jr." and joins S.H.I.E.L.D. with his former service mate and friend Phil Coulson.[20] As a result, the new Nick Fury in the mainstream Marvel Universe now resembles Samuel L. Jackson, and Agent Phil Coulson (popularized in the Marvel Studios movies) makes regular appearances in Marvel comics.

This shift in the presentation of the Nick Fury character occurred with careful timing. *Battle Scars* number 6 hit comic store shelves on April 25, 2012, just before the premiere of *The Avengers* in theaters on May 4. The change strategically brought the comic experience into closer alignment with the film narrative. As *Battle Scars* writer Christopher Yost explained, "There is a great value in having new readers, people who come in after seeing the movies, and being able to pick up a comic that has the characters they recognize."[21]

This logic was also behind the launch of a new comic titled *Avengers Assemble*, which first appeared on comic store shelves on March 14, 2012. Set in the mainstream Marvel universe, the book pulls together a team of Avengers comprising Captain America, Iron Man, Thor, the Black Widow, Hawkeye, and the Hulk for an ensemble adventure, guaranteeing that moviegoers could find an Avengers comic book that resembled the configuration of characters in that summer's movie.[22] Though the Marvel continuity is preserved, the storyline finds intertextual reference points with the film, such as when Hawkeye and the Black Widow exchange a kiss,[23] even though those characters had not been romantically involved with one another for decades in the mainstream Marvel continuity.

The film version of Captain America drew heavily from both the mainstream and *Ultimate* versions of the comic character but also added new elements. In the film, Rogers does not kill the Nazi assassin present at his origin, but that agent (now of the organization Hydra) commits suicide by ingesting poison. To explain the introduction of the hero's uniform, the movie initially places Cap in a propaganda role before he enters combat, which represents a new contribution to the story. Positioning Hydra as the primary foe of World War II instead of the Nazis was a change (after all, the comic book version of Captain America was specifically created to punch Hitler), as was placing the Red Skull as the originator of Hydra (which in the comics had been positioned as an ancient secret society).

Rather than jingoistic patriotism, the movie Cap's motivation is that he simply doesn't like bullies, and his humility and compassion are his enduring traits. Scholar Anthony Mills argued that the movie portrayal of Captain America breaks the monomythic role because of the character's restraint and his devotion to equality regardless of status.[24] However, the film version also maintains his position outside of society, so that he interacts only to leverage violent action to battle the injustice (bullies) he sees. Furthermore, the equality Mills mentions appears mostly among his own superheroic colleagues, who themselves represent an external savior force. It is difficult not to see even the movie version of Captain America as representative of the American monomyth, if a gentler one than some of his predecessors (or, indeed, some earlier versions of himself).

The Postmovie Comic Book Captain America

After the release of *Captain America: The First Avenger* in the summer of 2011, the comic book version of Captain America's narrative and appearance would begin to shift to mimic elements of his movie adventures. For example, in the first issue of the fifth volume of *The Avengers*, Captain America dons an armored uniform that is more reminiscent of the Marvel Studios film attire than of his traditional comic book uniform.[25] In the first issue of the sixth volume of *Captain America*, references are made to Hydra's involvement in World War II,[26] even though Hydra had originally never made an appearance in Cap's World War II adventures.[27] Perhaps the most notable changes to Captain America were the appearances of gun and weaponry in both his historic flashbacks and contemporary adventures.[28] Though the original 1940s portrayals of Captain America featured guns and artillery use consistent with wartime comics, the more modern comics presented Captain America as never having used guns. But when the trailer for *The First Avenger* was released, it featured a scene with Cap using a handgun,[29] and the character indeed uses firearms repeatedly during the film.

This last transition would occur slowly, while the mainstream character was dead, and mostly through retold stories of Cap's wartime adventures. The period of the character's absence from comic books, starting with his death in *Captain America* volume 5, number 25 (May 2007) and ending with his resurrection in *Captain America: Reborn* number 6 (May 2010) represented a period of great reconfiguration of his story, his character, his history, and even his appearance. Through retconned historical tales, reimagined contemporary narratives, time-traveling epics, and alternate-universe tales such as *The Ultimates* and the kid-friendly *Marvel Adventures* series, 338 comics featuring Captain America appeared in the two years in which the character wasn't even alive in mainstream comics continuity.

In general, the sentiment expressed throughout the time Cap was dead was one of loss and regret. When asked about the effect the assassination had on the Marvel narrative, Brubaker explained, "It has a big effect. People on both sides of the registration issue unite in mourning this hero. Even if you didn't agree with him about registration, you didn't want him gone."[30] And yet within that loss existed the politics of blame, represented by elements such as the news media broadcasts Thor experiences a year after Cap's death:

> TELEVISION COMMENTATOR: One life that changed the world, both in the ways he lived that life, and the way in which he gave it. Captain America, killed one year ago today. As a nation

assesses the impact of that legacy, and the conflict that brought
an end to one of the most—

COMMENTATOR 2: And typically, the conservatives who most
insisted he be brought down are now hiding behind his memory
to avoid being held responsible for—

COMMENTATOR 3: More of the usual stupidity from the loony left
who have taken a symbol of American might and turned it into
an ad for the politics of surrender—

COMMENTATOR 4: Martha Stilton, of Newark, New Jersey, sued
several network news operations for millions on the grounds that
their coverage of the shooting of Captain America traumatized
her and her children—[31]

Many of the comic books during this period can be considered reactionary or mourning books, comics in which characters struggle with Captain America's death and his absence. The first was *Civil War: The Confession*, a story told in two parts, the first immediately after Captain America's death and the second immediately after his surrender. Though Iron Man had expressed his position at length to Rogers before he died, he concludes the first story with the tear-filled confession that despite considering himself right on the issues, he felt "it wasn't worth it."[32]

To get more of such reactions, Marvel published a five-issue miniseries titled *Fallen Son* in which each issue dealt with key characters' reactions as representative of one of the five stages of grief (denial, anger, bargaining, depression, acceptance).[33] Thor, who himself was not alive at the time Captain America was assassinated, conjures Cap from the dead and engages him in a discussion.[34]

Various heroes are forced to confront their reactions to seeing Captain America, such as when the 1940s team the Invaders are brought forward in time and join forces with the Avengers,[35] when a Skrull masquerades as Cap,[36] and when the 1950s era Captain America briefly makes an appearance.[37] In each case, characters are forced to deal with the shock of seeing Captain America seemingly alive, after which they privately express regret and then internally brood on what Cap's loss means.

Other specialty books, such as *Mythos: Captain America* and *Captain America: White*,[38] presented new re-creations of the 1940s Captain America adventures, and a new series of one-shot issues titled *Captain America: Theater of War* was dedicated to telling the stories of "the dark days" of Captain America's early career. Though Brubaker's Captain America series had established a more realistic and gritty view of the violence of war through flashbacks to Captain America's wartime adventures, it was the *Theater of War* books that began to normalize the images of Captain America wielding firearms during his wartime conflict[39] while also establishing the idea that Captain America's fighting spirit is present in all American wars (shown as a shadowy image of Cap transposed over each of America's major military conflicts), from the battles during the American Revolution[40] to the conflicts involving modern American soldiers.[41] Another miniseries titled *Captain America: The Chosen* describes a noncanonical death-of-Captain-America story in which the hero, whose body is breaking down, uses technology to enter the mind of a soldier in Afghanistan, Corporal James Newman, to inspire him to Herculean feats of bravery.[42] In the course of the story, Cap retells his origin story to Newman, establishing that he was selected for the Project: Rebirth experiment because of his unwavering humility,[43] which would be a key component of the plotline in *The First Avenger* movie. In addition, Cap directly reveals that when the Nazi assassin was dispatched, it was because Rogers had "lost control," thus establishing a death more consistent with the original version presented in *Captain America Comics* volume 1, number 1, not the accidental death that was portrayed in subsequent origin stories.[44] *Captain America: The Chosen* concludes with Captain America expiring as he saves the president, leading the unnamed president to ask, "How will we ever get along without him?" and Newman to explain his own bravery as having "a little bit of him in all of us."[45]

Such stories, arguing for the consistent need for Captain America in American society, dovetailed with the mainstream Marvel stories during that period, which grappled with the question of whether someone other than Steve Rogers should carry on the mantle of Captain America. In the issue of *Fallen Son* titled "Bargaining," Tony Stark offers the role of

Captain America to Clint Barton, Hawkeye, who decides he cannot agree with Stark about what Captain America should mean.[46]

Even those characters tangentially related to Captain America struggle with their identities, such as Patriot, a young African American member of the Young Avengers, who begins to question his own association with patriotism given his dislike of American policies, but he is convinced through a discussion with Captain America's former partner that his mission should continue as one that would provide inspiration.[47]

The Punisher, often framed as the Vietnam era's Captain America, experiences a short period of calling himself Captain America. Incensed at the prospect of another man wearing a uniform reminiscent of Captain America's to promote national socialism and lead a group of like-minded individuals,[48] Frank Castle dons a uniform that combines his death's head logo with Captain America's star to defeat the racist group.[49] Castle later meets with the Winter Soldier—Captain America's original partner, Bucky Barnes—and gives him the costume as well as the key to the locker where he stashed Captain America's mask, which he retrieved at the conclusion of the *Civil War* series.[50]

The most significant of the "replacement" stories tells how the Winter Soldier himself adopts the Captain America mantle for a period. Leading up to the Civil War storyline, writer Ed Brubaker had presented a storyline that resurrected the long-dead Bucky Barnes but had done so by creating a significant retconned backstory portraying Barnes as a hyperviolent combatant in contrast to the more restrained Captain America. In the fifth volume of *Captain America*, Barnes's established 1940s origin is instead an artifact of propaganda, and Cap's sixteen-year-old partner is portrayed as a brutal fighter, there to do "the things I couldn't," explains Cap. "I was the icon. I wore the flag . . . but while I gave the speeches to troops in the trenches . . . he was doing what he'd been trained to do . . . and he was highly trained."[51] This text, transposed above visuals of Barnes leaving a large body count through clandestine assassination techniques, reframes the young boy sidekick as a publicity misdirection intended to mask a ruthless killer.

In Brubaker's retcon, the death of Barnes near the end of World War II results in the young man's body being recovered by Soviet agents. Through intensive mental conditioning, Barnes is given a new identity as the Winter Soldier, a mysterious Cold War agent responsible for the assassination of foreign officials, the disruption of international affairs, and the destabilization of the Middle East in the 1980s.[52] Captain America recognizes Barnes and in the course of a confrontation uses a cosmic cube to restore Barnes's memories.[53] Distraught at the realization of who he is and what he has done over his career, Barnes flees and begins to work with Nick Fury.

In the original 1960s canon, Barnes's death had served as the character flaw for Captain America by giving him nearly crippling survivor's guilt. When Barnes returns, this long-standing tension remains but is transformed into Rogers's sense of responsibility for his former young partner. The two men have several adventures together, and it becomes clear that Barnes himself struggles to live up to the example set by Rogers.

After Cap is assassinated, Barnes steals the hero's shield from Tony Stark to prevent another hero from assuming the role of Captain America.[54] But then Tony receives a post mortem letter from Steve Rogers and honors its wishes by offering the role of Captain America to Barnes, who reluctantly accepts.[55] The Barnes Captain America debuted in *Captain America* volume 5, number 34, a controversial debut even before the comic was released because of the prominent presence of a handgun in the promotional images.[56] Without the supersoldier serum that gave Steve Rogers his fighting edge, Barnes relies on his more brutal tactics and weaponry to combat the more powerful enemies he faces.[57]

In 2010, a political controversy arose surrounding the portrayal of Tea Party activists in *Captain America* volume 5, number 602, in which Barnes and the Falcon are tracking down William Burnside, the repeatedly retconned Captain America from the 1950s, who has resurfaced as the leader of a domestic terrorist organization called the "Watchdogs" in Boise, Idaho.[58]

The Watchdogs were originally introduced in *Captain America* volume 1, number 335 (September 1988), as a paramilitary right-wing group in Georgia that clandestinely burned down local businesses they thought violated conservative morality (those engaged in pornography, abortion, sex education, and the teaching of evolution are specifically mentioned) and even murdered those who confronted them.[59] The contemporary group was now led by William Burnside, the individual who had served as Captain America in the 1950s before becoming unstable and losing a confrontation with the original Captain America in *Captain America* volume 1, number 156 (discussed in chapter 5).[60]

The controversy arose around a panel portrayed on pages 15 and 16 of *Captain America* volume 5, number 602, that features activists' protest signs resembling real-life signage observed in media coverage of Tea Party events, including messages such as "Stop the Socialists," "NO GOVT IN MY MEDICARE!" and "Tea Bag the Libs before They Tea Bag YOU!"[61] Even though the accompanying dialogue by the Falcon differentiates between the Watchdog terrorist group and the protestors—"So I guess the whole 'hate the government' vibe around here isn't limited to the Watchdogs"—Tea Party activists pounced on the portrayal, accusing Marvel of taking political sides:

Bet you didn't know that when you were indulging your right as a citizen to protest your government that you were a dangerous white supremacist that wants to destroy the country, did you? Bet you didn't realize that your reverence for the U.S. Constitution was a subversive thing to do, did you? And I'll also bet that you never imagined that you'd scare the little blue panties off of Captain America!

Nice going Marvel Comics. Thanks for making patriotic Americans into your newest super villains.[62]

Well now, we can add comic book hero Captain America to the list of those who are casting a suspicious eye toward Tea Party activists; yes, the same Captain America who fought Nazis and the uber-villainous Red Skull. In a recent issue of Marvel Comics' Captain America series, the ultimate red, white, and blue hero is busy investigating (obviously at great peril) the latest threat to national security . . . you. Forget about Islamic terrorists and all that 9-11 stuff. The real danger to the Obama, hopey-changey socialistic utopia is none other than you. And, Captain America is going to do something about it! By the way, Captain America also thinks you're a racist.

This seemingly innocuous Captain America comic is, in reality, a grossly effective weapon of the leftists, for it captures the hearts and

minds of children. It injects them with their message in the most insidi-
ous of ways, by associating those ideas with what children love: heroes
and the fight between good and evil.[63]

Its [*sic*] good when your enemy exposes themselves for the trash that they
are. Marvel comics, race baiting smear merchants who would rather see
your daughter as a prostitute than a patriot. It would seve [*sic*] them right
for their kids to end up in an Acorn whorehouse.
    Lucky for these losers Marvel was not always this way otherwise
we would not be talking about it today. The lefts [*sic*] motto should be
crap on the ones who brung ya. Really there is no lower type of person.
Marvel comics, too crappy to wipe your arse with.[64]

The jihadi loving libtards are perverting Captan America to show people standing up for liberty as being evil. The progressives have killed
million [*sic*] of people so far and intend to kill way more. It seems they
are transforming old symbols of liberty into tyrannical propaganda.[65]

Apparently Marvel has Captain America on the trail of evil, racist Americans who are then depicted at what definitely appears to be a tea party
protest. Way to go Marvel. There must be some comics fan out there
who can give them hell. Or just quit buying their comics.[66]

Right-wing icon Glenn Beck also picked up the controversy,
complaining,

He's Captain America. If he's waving American principles, I'm cool
with that. But even Superman isn't doing that anymore. If you saw the
last movie, they changed truth, justice and the American way to: truth,
justice—-and that's it.
    Where is this hatred for America coming from?[67]

The most consistent objection appeared to complain about one sign
in particular: "You'll note that one of the signs says, 'Teabag the libs
before they teabag you,' as if a tea party protester would ever use the liberal media's insulting and scatological term."[68] However, a cursory image

search revealed photographic and video evidence that the specific sign in question was indeed seen at Tea Party events.[69] Despite the accuracy, in response Marvel issued an apology and vowed to alter the offending sign in future reprints of the issue.[70] In addition, Brubaker disavowed authorship of the sign in question, and Marvel editor in chief Joe Quesada offered an in-depth explanation to absolve the writer of blame:

> The book was getting ready to go to the printer, it was on fire already from a deadline standpoint, but the editor on the book noticed that there was a small art correct that needed to get done. On the first page featuring the protestors, the artist on the book drew slogans into the protest signs to give them a sense of reality and to set up the scene. On the following page featuring the protestors again, there were signs, but nothing written in them. From a continuity standpoint, this omission stood out like a sore thumb, but was easily fixable. So, just before the book went to the printer, the editor asked the letterer on the book to just fudge in some quick signs. The letterer in his rush to get the book out of the door but wanting to keep the signs believable, looked on the net and started pulling slogans from actual signs. That's when he came upon [the offending sign] and used it in the scene and off it went to the printer. Unfortunately, to make the deadline, the work wasn't double-checked thoroughly, and it was printed as is, which is where we as an editorial group screwed up. We spoke to the letterer, and he was mortified at his mistake and was truly sorry as he had no political agenda. He was just trying to do his job, but ultimately the onus falls on me as E-i-C. All that said, we caught the mistake two weeks ago, after it was printed and removed the sign from the art files so that it no longer appears in future reprints of the title or collections. So, while the crowd protesting has nothing to do with the villains in the story, we in no way meant to say they were associated with the Tea Party movement, it was a simple perfect storm of screw-ups. It happens, we're human.[71]

In response to such explanations, some fans in return criticized Marvel for apologizing.[72]

Barnes and the Falcon would defeat the 1950s Captain America and the Watchdogs in *Captain America* volume 5, number 605.[73] Barnes would next face an in-text political conflict when Baron Zemo discloses Barnes's identity and leaks to the press details of his exploits as the Winter Soldier, including references to his prior assassinations of American officials while under Soviet control.[74] Barnes would face a trial in which he is convicted, though the judge would commute the sentence to time served.[75] Barnes would continue to serve as Captain America until he is seemingly killed by the new Red Skull in *Fear Itself* number 3.[76] It would later be revealed, though, that Barnes survived the attack and resumed his clandestine career as the Winter Soldier.[77]

During the stretch between the death of Steve Rogers in May 2007 and his return in May 2010, the Marvel continuity suffered through a "Dark Age." In the aftermath of the Civil War, the heroes who had aligned themselves with Captain America remained underground, while Tony Stark's forces consolidated their power. However, the *Secret Invasion* story arc would change the status quo, as the revealed infiltration and subsequent militant invasion by the alien shape-shifting Skrulls would oust Stark from power and hand the amassed might of the military-industrial complex over to the seemingly reformed Spider-Man villain Norman Osborn.[78] This turn of events would lead into Marvel's next event story arc, *Dark Reign*, in which Osborn secretly substitutes supervillains for superheroes and uses his status to consolidate power through a series of carefully orchestrated actions and events, all managed for favorable media coverage. Osborn would eventually decide to invade Asgard without presidential authority, which would set the stage for the return of Captain America and a restoration of a semblance of the pre–Civil War status quo.

Steve Rogers's restoration occurred in a series of stages that helped narrow the gap between the comic figure and the newer traits emerging from the character's movie version. In *Captain America: Reborn* number 1, it is discovered that "deceased" Cap is floating through his own history, reliving his life's experiences.[79] This journey not only allows the reader to review many of Cap's battles and accomplishments but also presents key changes to several. For example, in the retelling of his origin story, it is reaffirmed that Cap intentionally threw the Nazi assassin into the equipment that killed him.[80]

Captain America is physically resurrected in issue 4, but his body is under the control of the Red Skull's mind.[81] As Rogers's body is used to battle the Barnes Captain America, Steve Rogers battles the Red Skull for control within his own mind.[82] He succeeds and then leads a collection of Marvel's heroes to defeat the Red Skull's remaining forces.[83] In *Captain America: Who Will Wield the Shield?* number 1, Rogers tells Barnes after the battle that he would prefer not to resume his role as Captain America but ultimately leaves the decision up to President Barack Obama.[84]

Osborn's siege of Asgard presents the opportunity for Rogers to return to active duty in the Marvel Universe—a story arc told in the series *Siege*. Osborn arranges for a manufactured crisis resembling the Stamford explosion that had set off the Civil War in order to implicate an Asgardian god as an enemy of the state. When Thor arrives to intervene, Osborn's Dark Avengers attack and subdue him. Rogers sees the media coverage of Thor's struggle and is shown in the final panel of the event comic book in his Captain America uniform with a clenched and shaking fist.[85]

This turn of events allows Rogers to follow the American monomyth archetype of the reluctant hero. Upon his physical return, he chooses not to resume his mission and even asks the president not to call on him unless the need is dire. But when he sees his friend mistreated by a group of supervillains, his righteous anger builds and compels him back into action. Cap organizes the superhero community into a response force and leads them against Osborn's forces. President Obama, incensed that Osborn invaded Asgard without permission, throws his support and authorization behind Captain America's forces.[86] Cap's forces prevail, Osborn is captured, Barnes is reaffirmed as Captain America, Rogers is promoted to "America's Top Cop" to replace Osborn, and the Superhero Registration Act is repealed.[87] A subsequent adventure involving Captain America, Thor, and Iron Man even leads to forgiveness between the two prime movers of the Marvel civil war.[88]

However, *Siege* represents one more troubling text among a series of troubling texts when one considers the role democratic structures and governance play in the resolution of the conflict. *Siege* begins with Osborn, as master controller of the military-industrial complex, unilaterally deciding to make the country safer by invading Asgard against the president's explicit directives. The executive branch's loss of control of its own security apparatus is what causes the conflict. Nor does the administration appear to have an effective plan of action to counteract Osborn's efforts but instead appears relieved that Captain America rallies an informal collection of heroes together to combat the threat. When it appears that effort will be successful, the Obama administration throws its support behind Captain America and provides minor military support.

It is clear in the event-driven Marvel Universe that the representative government is reduced to having to choose between two superpowered vigilante forces. Even when the government attempted to regulate and control the administration of superhero force, that force was unable to prevent the Skrull infiltration and invasion, and the second force actually went rogue and engaged the nation in a martial conflict against the elected government.

And how does the administration improve its lot? It hands the reigns of the same security apparatus to Steve Rogers, apparently hoping that the third attempt will prove more successful than the previous two. Of course, within the text, the difference between Rogers's efforts and his predecessors' is his ability to unite and inspire his forces. Where the previous security forces divided their time between hunting rogue heroes, providing normal security, and responding to supernormal threats, Rogers is able to bring the rogue heroes into the fold and leverage them in a variety of relationships to the establishment (though all without any real oversight or civilian control).

To perform this duty, Rogers allows Barnes to serve as Captain America on the Avengers, and Rogers himself instead leads a hand-picked team of heroes, the Secret Avengers (whose motto is "Run the mission. Don't get seen. Save the world"), assuming the role of a superspy: "I know when I called on all of you to join this team, I told you what our mission was . . . stealth tactics and preventative intervention. We go where we're needed and perform surgical strikes."[89] During this phase of his career, Rogers's struggles to adapt his superhero mission to managing the military-industrial complex can be read as a loose allegory of the Obama administration's struggles to enact its campaign promises. For example, Rogers expresses impatience and frustration with his inability to shut down the 42 Prison, the prison existing in an alternate dimension outside the United States— an established allegory for the controversies of enemy combatant detainment at Camp X-Ray in Guantanamo Bay, Cuba.[90]

One of the threats that the Secret Avengers face involves the hacking of government databases and the disclosure of the identities of secret agents and sources of information across the globe. The man responsible argues in support of his actions in a way parallel to the tone of those who supported Wikileaks, the antielite sentiments of the Occupy Wall Street movement, and the charges of the neglect of the nation's returning veterans:

> I can imagine a lot of people are going to be calling me a traitor right about now. And I bet a few more will be asking why I did this. First thing you should know is I love my country. I dedicated my life to serving it, and I don't regret that for a second. Even now, knowing what I know.
>
> I fought in Afghanistan and watched a lot of my brothers die . . .
>
> Then when I got home, all I saw was a bunch of people fighting over who gets to be in charge of keeping us "safe"—and none of them doing a very good job of it. Just ask Broxton.
>
> I don't give a damn if people call themselves "good guys" or "bad guys." The way I read it, they all do the same things. And they just keep doing more and more of it, without asking anyone, without wanting to be held accountable to anyone.
>
> I think it's time the rest of us had our say, too. So this is our message. When all of you who appoint yourselves our protectors break the public trust—when you put yourself above the law and above what's just—we'll be right there. We have a right to know what you do in our name.[91]

Rogers tracks down this individual, who wears one of Rogers's previous costumes (the Captain), and the man delivers an impassioned criticism of Rogers:

> You remember when you wore this uniform, don't you? Government cronies told you to do Captain America their way or walk. You walked. Became the Captain instead.

You were taking a stand against corruption back then. Now look at you. Turns out they got what they wanted in the end, yeah?

All they had to do was give you a little power. All those years of that "holier than thou" act, then they put you in charge and here we are—our government in bed with a bunch of terrorists, murderers, and despots, most of 'em selling each other out to get ahead. Secret Avengers teams that don't answer to anyone but you—

YOU SOLD US OUT! We deserve to know what's going on—the people have a right to—[92]

Rogers interrupts the speech with a punch to the jaw, beats his opponent to the ground, and, while he recovers, responds:

Now—are you ready to listen, or do I have to hit you a few more times?
. . . This job I have now—this job I fell into, really—there's shades of gray to all of it. And what you said before might even be true—in a different time, I might be the one fighting to end something like this. But if I ever start really questioning myself, and whether or not I'm fit to do this, I remember—I, and the people I stand with, good and bad, faults and all—no matter how right we believed we were . . . we'd never let people die just to prove our damn point.

Now I don't know if that's enough for you, or for the rest of the world, but for the time being—It'll have to do.[93]

This confrontation perfectly represents a particular challenge to American masculinity posed by twenty-first-century warfare. The Secret Avengers, for all their power, are helpless when they realize they cannot possibly save all of the exposed intelligence sources in time. Instead, they focus on saving one particular source but still fail. Impotent, the team members express their frustration physically. Furthermore, when Rogers confronts the culprit, his reaction is telling. Interrupting the man's speech with a punch, he beats the man to the ground and then speaks over him. When confronted with an intellectual argument supporting antielite equality (democratic values), Rogers exerts his superior physicality to silence his critic. This assertion of masculine force illustrates a crisis of masculinity in modern conflicts in which access to information is often more important than physical prowess. In that moment, Rogers becomes the bully that he normally wears a costume to oppose.

Secrecy and the control of information would continue to be a dominant theme in *Secret Avengers*, but this concern also presented itself in other aspects of Rogers's mission. Originally objecting to the existence of the "Illuminati" gathering, Rogers eventually joins the group and pledges to keep its secrets.[94]

Not all of Rogers's colleagues are comfortable with the need to control information. When rogue supersoldier Nuke begins to kill foreign nationals, S.H.I.E.L.D. imposes a media blackout. While Captain America battles Nuke in an attempt to lessen the negative images that would be presented of Nuke's actions, Falcon tracks down a lone reporter named Samantha Chan who has taken photographs of the carnage. The two debate the competing interests of national security and freedom of the press:

> FALCON: I'm on strict orders—I need that camera.
> SAMANTHA CHAN: WHAT?! I'm an American journalist! I don't give my camera over to some clown in tights!
> FALCON: A clown in tights who saved your life? A clown under direct orders from S.H.I.E.L.D.?
> CHAN: Yeah? Who cares? We didn't elect S.H.I.E.L.D.! Some clandestine organization that thinks it operates above the law—but they AREN'T the law. And they sure as hell aren't the law here.
> FALCON: I'm just trying to save lives, not get into a debate on freedom of the press.
> CHAN: But that's where you find yourself. But I tell you what, "super hero." You want my camera? Take it. Make a choice. Do you believe in freedom of the press as a fundamental rule . . . or only when it's convenient to those in charge? What are your principles, Falcon? And how far away from them will you go to uphold them?[95]

Falcon relents and lets Chan keep the camera and film. When the photos appear on the front page of the *Daily Bugle*, Cap admonishes Falcon, who appears unmoved.

During his superspy period, Rogers's tactics also show a tendency to compromise to more expedient methods. For example, when called into a personal confrontation with John Steele, Rogers "cheats" by having his teammates attack when he proves unable to take Steele alone.[96] His teammates, in particular Black Widow and Moon Knight, tend to use lethal force when encountering opposition.[97]

For all his bravado, Rogers continues to wrestle with his new role. When he encounters Thor, the two talk of his frustrations:

> THOR: You don't seem yourself, Captain.
>
> CAPTAIN AMERICA: It's been . . . a rough patch.
>
> THOR: Are you still the head of world security?
>
> CAP: Yes.
>
> THOR: And the Avengers and all that entails?
>
> CAP: Yes.
>
> THOR: I know there is a contradiction here but hear me out. As much of a leader and a military man as you are, there is also a side of you that has a more . . . rebellious streak. I believe that is the term.
>
> If I may . . . you are always at your best when you buck the system. And if that is true, how can you be at your best if you are the system itself?[98]

Rogers would soon begin the transition back to Captain America, yielding his spy operations to the new Nick Fury. When he refuses to entertain an Illuminati discussion about whether a planet should be destroyed to save Earth, the Illuminati wipe his mind, and he is forced from the group.[99]

The Many Faces of Captain America

Even within the more traditional confines of Steve Rogers's role as Captain America, the adjustments to his narrative continued to occur. In the seventh volume of *Captain America*, his origin is shifted once again. Reemphasizing that Rogers is a first-generation American and that his parents were Irish immigrants, writer Rick Remender created a new motivation within Rogers. Rogers fights to prove himself to be unlike his father, who succumbed to abusive rage and ultimately abandoned his family, and to be resistant to such failure (doing so as an American because the core difference between Rogers's character and that of his father seems to be Rogers's belief in the American Dream).

A character cannot be handled by so many creators and in so many series at once without contradictory texts emerging. One such contradiction involves Captain America's view toward violence, one of the core concepts undergirding his masculinity. An underlying tension in the recent *Uncanny Avengers* series revolves around a difference in attitudes toward terminal violence. When Cap discovers that Wolverine killed while affiliated with the Avengers, he becomes angry and bars him from the team: "Allowing Wolverine membership was a mistake, and not one I plan to continue making. We're not going to go off and kill these twins, no matter what they've done. That's not the Avengers—NOT EVER."[100] However, this attitude seems hypocritical: Ed Brubaker had recently portrayed Captain America himself killing foes, and his Secret Avengers teammates have killed on multiple occasions. But when Rick Remender and Brian Michael Bendis write Captain America, they tend toward the restrained hero who doesn't tolerate terminal violence. During the conflict between the Avengers and the X-Men, Red Hulk sneaks off to attempt to quietly kill Cyclops because he knows Cap won't condone assassination.[101] And in Remender's Captain America title, Cap's enemy Jet Black admires him because of his restraint: "I've never seen a creature like him . . . never felt the unrest his form stirred within me. More than just his physical beauty, there is a powerful allure to his temperance and mercy . . . Compassionate yet powerful."[102]

However, certain traits appear to be present within Captain America no matter which creator is handling him: his uncompromising purity and his ability to judge the character in others. When given the opportunity to use the Infinity Gauntlet, an item that grants the user near-unlimited power, Cap is able to do so without giving in to personal temptation.[103] Similarly, when he has the opportunity to wield the Ultimate Nullifier, a device that would allow him to erase foes from existence, Cap shows restraint in using it, leading Galactus to note, "You faced the lure of ultimate power, and you did not give in to corruption. In my eons of life, it is a rare sight indeed."[104] When he encounters Vengeance, a demon with the power to magnify the corruption in an individual until it consumes them in flame, no corruption is found in Captain America.[105] And even when the Red Skull uses mind manipulation that causes humans to kill even the mutants to which they are in committed relationships,[106] Captain America is able to resist the same impulses because "he is no ordinary man. This is Captain America, his resolve unwavering. Skull's hatred finds no grip on his noble heart . . . [.]"[107]

Captain America is usually charged with determining who will serve on a given team of Avengers, and, as such, his reputation for judgment is renown:

> NOVA: So I wanted to ask how you felt when he asked you. Or was I the only one who stood there with his mouth open?
> SPIDER-MAN: I think everyone spazzes out for a sec when they get the call. All I could think was "why?" I'm a solo guy, not a team player. I guess the only why you need to know is . . . Cap thinks you're right for the job.[108]

When Cap entrusts his former opponent Jet Black to help a vulnerable population despite her loyalties to her father, it is Sharon Carter who soothes her self-doubt: "Steve says you won't let that [the murder of innocents] happen and he's NEVER wrong about a person."[109] This faith in the intrinsic good in people appears to be a core component of Captain America's patriotism, the trust in others to live up to the American Dream, in which he has ultimate faith.

Recent Captain America stories contain several key challenges to the American monomyth. The first comes from former Avenger Simon Williams. When asked to rejoin the Avengers, Williams not only declines but challenges the premise of the team's existence at all:

> SIMON WILLIAMS: And I am telling you: putting the Avengers back together is a terrible idea.
> STEVE ROGERS: How can you say that?

WILLIAMS: Because—hey, maybe it's one of those things you can't
see when you're right in the middle of it, but once you step back
it couldn't be more clear. From my point of view . . . the super
hero civil war, the mutant Decimation, the Skrull invasion, Norman Osborn, they have—they all have one thing in common . . .
they are all the Avengers' fault.

ROGERS: Oh, Simon, how can you say that?

WILLIAMS: Steve, how can you not?

ROGERS: The Avengers stopped—Those were threats that the
Avengers put a stop to. The Civil War—fine. That was a different
story, but all the others, Simon, we stopped them.

WILLIAMS: . . . I know you can't see it yet, Steve, but I hope to God
you figure it out before it's too late. Free yourself from this. Don't
be part of the problem.[110]

Rogers also receives a critique of his national devotion from his
adopted son, Ian:

[O]f all the nations of your home earth, what makes America so important that you stand ONLY for it? Why would a noble man choose only
one section of the homeworld to protect? Perhaps you imagine your
nation to be vastly superior to all others?

Perhaps it is hubris. The exclusionary arrogance of a fascist pig!
Champion of the status quo! A pious mercenary, protector of an elite
nation built by slaves! You are no champion of truth and justice—you're
just a delusional guardian of the rich and greedy![111]

To neither critique does Rogers mount a passionate defense, apparently
comfortable to allow his actions to speak for his position. The same is not
true when Cap faces Nuke, who justifies the homicides he has committed
by arguing for the defense of American honor against foreign enemies:

CAPTAIN AMERICA: Patriotism taken too far is fanaticism. No matter who you are where you're from.

NUKE: These filthy foreigners made us look bad.

CAP: Foreigners aren't your enemy, son. I'm the son of immigrants.

NUKE: W-what?

CAP: When I was a kid it was my father's people, the Irish, who were looked down on. Called filthy foreigners. Discriminated against. Is that the xenophobic America you want? All religions, all nationalities, we all want the same thing. To see our children grow strong. To provide safety for our families. To live in quiet times. Peace, son. Isn't that why we became soldiers? To fight for a peaceful world?[112]

As in eras past (since his 1970s liberalization, anyway), Captain America's patriotism is more focused on the universal rights of man as expressed through the American Dream than on a position championing the specific cultural or political goals of the United States.

However, as his narrative evolves, Cap's sense of historical perspective begins to become dislodged. In a flashback to his childhood, his mother is portrayed instilling in her son a sense of adaptability through forgetting: "In order to grow you must let go of the past . . . Inside that small frame is a big, strong heart. A good man. A strong heart will take you further than any physical strength. A strong heart means you'll never quit . . . You'll always maintain the optimism of this great nation . . . Life is too short to allow yourself to become trapped in one chapter. You learn what you can, you stand up, and you move forward."[113]

In the course of the same issue, as Cap struggles to cope with the loss of Sharon Carter, he collects all of his World War II memorabilia and burns it.[114] This act shows a significant shift in the character's personality. In fact, the very "Man out of Time" theme so common in Cap's narrative involves his inability to move past his losses: the loss of his mother, the loss of Bucky, the loss of his era, and the occasional loss of faith he suffers when the contemporary political establishment or culture fails to live up to his Greatest Generation expectations. In fact, Cap's usual method for moving beyond a cultural moment is having a new writer pick up his book and change the history he cannot forget. How this newfound attitude will play into Cap's future adventures remains to be seen, but the concept of cultural forgetting is a core trait of the American monomyth.

Conclusions: Considering Superheroic Masculine Patriotism

The Captain America narrative reinforces the notion that one can use experience and willpower to compensate when one lacks knowledge or other potential advantages. Because Cap usually relies on his vast experience to face and successfully defeat more powerful foes, he affirms a core American myth that hard work will persevere over greater power or resources. Though his superb physical conditioning originated from artificial means, his prowess and agility give him an advantage, and the intense training and dedication to refining battle technique are a central part of the character's lore.

The later incarnations of Captain America command respect from enemies and allies alike. Comics scholar Arnold Blumberg calls Captain America "the moral center of the Marvel Universe. . . . He provides the center for what is correct, the ideals, for what is best for America."[115] His code of honor and his honesty are above reproach, and the confidence with which he carries himself exudes an air of power coupled with innocence, a view consistent with how many Americans see their country in respect to others in the world.

By contrast, the original Cap of the 1940s is a brute owing to different expectations from his military readers engaged in a war. The fact that later Cap stories attempt to claim that Cap has never used firearms or killed in the course of his career shows just how far we Americans can stretch our myths when needed, but the recent move back to conform to the film narratives shows how elastic a rebound the long-term fans will accept. This particular form of retcon, expunging past violent tendencies, is not uncommon for long-standing characters, but the conceptualization of a supersoldier who served in World War II without taking a life does stretch the imagination, as does the reversal of this frame.

However, the current attempt at retroactive continuity runs precisely the opposite direction, reaffirming that Captain America did use firearms, did take lives on occasions, and did engage in wartime activities alongside soldiers. This shift has occurred through the various retellings of Captain America's origins, placing elements of restrained violence at key moments. But, in effect, this act of reframing Cap's continuity also appears to place the continuity of the 1980s and 1990s on shaky ground. What are readers to make when reading stories that claim Captain America made it through the whole of World War II without taking a life? Or that he has never carried a firearm? Or what should readers make of the 1980s story in which Captain America has an internal struggle about whether to kill the vampire Baron Blood in *Captain America* volume 1, number 254.[116] Or when in *Captain America* volume 5, number 601, they read an accounting of Cap and Bucky killing several vampires during World War II?[117] It would appear that there continue to be many Captain Americas to choose from, depending on the point of entry to the text. This problem is also why this book considers Captain America an open text.

It is also telling that such transitions occur mostly through a death and rebirth cycle, sometimes literally but most often figuratively (as when a new writer takes over the book and presents a new origin story for the character that reconfigures his identity without explicitly acknowledging the changes). Americans are well known for their antihistorical tendencies, preferring to express philosophy through literary conventions.[118] Rather than critically investigating our past, we instead grasp tightly to myths that form our identity.[119] Mediated communication forms such as comic books and television programs provide definite description and generic reference that serve to create a sense of the shared world through anonymous consumption.[120] However, the "social circulation of media discourse[s]" reveals the active role readers play in textual interpretation and appropriation of media texts.[121] Between these two functions exist the conflicts not only within a fan community but also within the general American culture.

History is a curious melding of image, sentiment, cultural interpretation, as well as documents and records. Intertextuality factors into the interpretation of textual meaning and community boundaries, which is why it can be so revealing to analyze discussions about shared texts, specifically in regard to questions about the mobility of speech forms from one context to another (between different eras of a comic book or even between different media in which a superhero text is fixed) and about the conditions that encourage the decontextualization and recontextualization of these texts into new meanings. Controversies like the ones cited in this book occur as a result of bringing together timeless cultural attributes and contemporary political situations; the controversies serve as a window through which we can view what we struggle to forget about our history.

This brings us back to the critiques that appeared about the portrayal of Cap in the post-9/11 storyline (such as *The Betrayal of Captain America,* written by Michael Medved and Michael Lackner) and to the accusation that Marvel Comics bowed to liberal influences, allowing the character to change decades of tradition. Tea Party critics made this same charge following the controversy over the use of real-world signs in the comic narrative of *Captain America* volume 5, number 602.

Such reactions appear to be aimed at the superficial image of the text, for any reading of the actual printed text undermines the claims that Marvel was "liberalizing" Captain America in 2002, unless one exclusively reads the earliest stories from the 1940s and 1950s before skipping ahead to consider the fourth volume. Whether these claims are made to outrage other nonreaders or to accomplish some other purpose, numerous rebuttals came from readers, who simply pointed to the text and the character's liberal history.[122] Clearly, one should not make claims about long-standing narratives without at least superficially consulting the body of literature in question, and yet such claims do appear on a regular basis.

This criticism also relates to the threat of boycotting a controversial text (the prevention of which was a likely motive for Marvel's apology concerning the Tea Party signs used in *Captain America* volume 5, number 602). One vocal critic, for example, claimed he had consistently purchased Captain America comic books "since 1972" but indicated that because of the "disgusting" use of the signs in number 602 he would do so "no more."[123] It strains the claim's credibility to think that adopting the views of the New Left in the 1970s and taking an antigovernment stance in 2002 and 2006 were politically acceptable to these readers but that possibly objecting to Tea Party signs (through a Captain America who is not Steve Rogers) is the bridge too far for them.

The breadth and diversity of Captain America narratives, however, allow for a variety of interpretations of the character's value system. As cited in the introduction to this book, Henry Jenkins argues that fans often privilege texts that present attributes they favor over those that do not.[124] This tendency most likely allows different long-standing readers of a comic narrative to arrive at different conclusions regarding what a character should or should value based on which texts form the basis of that memory.

But even scholars engaged in more careful readings run into similar problems. The criticism mounted by Robert Jewett and John Shelton Lawrence, described in chapter 7, is valid, if incomplete. The conflict presented in *Captain America* volume 3, number 16, drew their attention because the extreme conflict originated in New York City and was billed as one in which the "fate of the world" was at stake.[125] They argue that such popular cultural portrayals provided American monomyth framing for the terrorist attacks on September 11, 2001, causing Americans to think of these real events in terms of "good versus evil" and of American forces as the "heroes" of an epic superhero struggle that would determine the "fate of the world." Referencing the advertisements promoting the upcoming *Spirit of America* lithograph by artist Jim Steranko as an example of an attempt to idealize the US war on terror, Jewett and Lawrence "suggest that the time has come for a dignified retirement [of Captain America]."[126]

And yet the lithograph in question was not a new creation. Originally adorning the cover of *The Captain America Marvel Index* by George Olshevesky in 1979, the lithograph was later reproduced as a fund-raiser for the families of those who perished in the World Trade Center attacks. How should one read the lithograph as a text? It depicts Captain America's World War II adventures, but it was created during the 1970s revisionism that sanitized those adventures before being repurposed in 2001 to raise funds for victims of the attacks. Unpacking that particular image requires substantial intertextual and contextual negotiation, and one can see a variety of different meanings potentially embedded within it.

Jewett and Lawrence's explicit criticism of the comic narrative selected also includes some problematic assumptions about the text's claims. As explained in chapter 7, the critique applied to the acts presented in this individual issue is quickly complicated when subsequent issues are consulted and when prior storylines are brought to bear. This example illustrates the problem of analyzing comic books texts, which are themselves positioned in a particular context involving various forms of intertextual continuity and comic book conventions. And just as Jenkins points to fans' tendency to select favored texts as exemplars of a cultural object that deny other unfavored texts, one suspects that a critic of a text would tend to select different exemplars, even ones not exemplary of the text as a whole. Any critique of a long-standing comic book narrative that makes longitudinal claims must strive to account for the positioning of the text within its continuity, the positioning of that continuity within the contemporary state of the medium, and the existing relationship between the fans and the text. Or, such an endeavor must at least locate the reception of the text to argue why a particular reading is troubling to a particular group outside of the fandom of a text.

Captain America in the "Red Glare" story Jewett and Lawrence selected is not acting within the normal conventions of that character at that point in his history. The complaints in the letters column attest to the readers' recognition of that fact.

That is not to say that Jewett and Lawrence's concerns are necessarily ill placed. They provide a list of "fascist notions" that they argue undermine democratic values in stories involving the American monomyth:

* that super power held in the hands of one person can achieve more justice than the workings of democratic institutions;
* that democratic systems of law and order, of constitutional constraint, are fatally flawed when confronted with genuine evil;
* that the community will never suffer from the depredations of such a super leader, whose servanthood is allegedly selfless;
* that the world as a whole requires the services of American superheroism that destroys evildoers through selfless crusades.[127]

These critiques are valid and apply directly to Captain America and to his superpowered colleagues. But the point to consider in selecting texts for analysis is that comic books by their nature and vastness tend to play with conventions and tropes. And certainly Captain America does. The 1940s and 1950s version of the character would clearly fit neatly into the American monomyth formula. But the 1970s version that questioned the established authority broke from that mold on many occasions. The 1990s version of the character, who fought so often to save the lives of his enemies and even to reform them (such as Diamondback), suggests a tension with the typical American monomyth formula, as does the more direct challenges to the military-industrial complex posed in the 2002 series. Had Captain America "retired" at the time of the publication of Jewett and Lawrence's book *Captain America and the Crusade against Evil* in 2003, comic book readers would have been robbed of one of the few overtly critical texts of Bush-era foreign policy at a time when so many other media forms were hesitant to offer much political criticism of any kind.

Jewett and Lawrence's central argument seems strongest when it is attached to films and more episodic media forms, in part because of the limitations of such a narrow text (even films in a series don't generally provide more than one textual offering every few years) and because of the lower level of editorial engagement between film producers and audience than has been witnessed between comic book readers and comic book creators in the past. Films also have the potential to reach an audience much larger than the audience for any comic book title, magnifying their effects. And that is, perhaps, why Jewett and Lawrence's critique is poised to be more salient now than before as Marvel Studios moves into an era in which the movie texts appear to drive a larger portion of the comic creative energies. Whereas comic books prove difficult to critique in this way without a much closer analysis of what readers and fans are doing with the texts, movies lend themselves better to the cultural criticism as offered.

The 2012 Marvel Studios film *The Avengers* served mostly to position Captain America as a natural team leader, though the character does spend some screen time exhibiting suspicion of the government and even questioning the appropriateness of his own patriotic uniform. Though possessing less raw power than some of his contemporaries, Cap's battlefield experience makes him the choice to organize the Avengers' efforts to repel an alien invasion.

The 2014 Marvel Studios film *Captain America: The Winter Soldier* draws heavily on the 2005 Brubaker series, bringing the Bucky Barnes character into the narrative as the brainwashed Soviet assassin Winter Soldier.[128] As in the Brubaker series, the personal connection between Cap and his former partner serves as the foreground for a broader narrative of intrigue. The personal narrative brings Cap and the Winter Soldier into direct and repeated conflict, with Cap struggling to recover his lost friend. The climax of the personal struggle occurs as Cap surrenders himself to Barnes's brutal assault, refusing to lift his hand against his dearest friend. This action begins the process of confusion for Barnes, and the film concludes with the beginning of his journey to rediscover his past and with Cap's determination to pursue and recover his friend.

However, the film's larger narrative interrogates the very notion of state-supported military justice. Captain America and his colleagues become aware of a secret plot within the military-industrial complex to leverage a new class of weapons of mass destruction to wipe out specified threats to a new global order. By launching high-tech hellicarriers with long-range weapons controlled by artificial intelligence, the ominously named Project: Insight adds to post-9/11 national-security concerns the specter of post-Snowden mass-surveillance anxieties and the fears associated with drone strikes.

When Director Nick Fury explains the concept of predicting terror threats and neutralizing them remotely, Cap portrays the system as holding a gun to the heads of everyone on earth and declares, "This isn't freedom, this is fear."

The movie's plot reveals that Cap's World War II nemesis Hydra has infiltrated S.H.I.E.L.D. and has been methodically bending the agency to its agenda. Cap runs afoul of Hydra's plans and becomes a fugitive from the establishment. Fighting members of his own strike team as well as Barnes, Cap and his companions narrowly prevent the assassination of millions of key individuals, expose the top-level Hydra conspiracy, and destroy the superweapons threatening the status quo.

At the core of Cap's initial objection to S.H.I.E.L.D.'s plans to deploy the new superweapons is an indictment of the core neoconservative arguments of projected strength as defense. To drive that critique home, the film links this philosophy to the conspiracies of Hydra, the organization that originally grew (in the first film) from the excesses of Nazi totalitarianism.

By the end of the film, S.H.I.E.L.D. itself lies in ruins, and the military-industrial complex is separated from the superhero community's efforts, apparently Marvel Studios writers' attempt to separate the Marvel superhero narrative from national-security justifications of force.

Whether these concepts can be fully segregated in future film installments remains to be seen. As more such movies are produced, more scholarship and criticism like Jewett and Lawrence's are needed. Disputes over Captain America's patriotism, his use of violence, and his politics appear to stem from the broader concerns about American masculinity. Being a man in the twenty-first century is confusing. The modest gains of feminism, the shift from an industrial to an information-based economy, the commodification of lifestyles—these are but a few of the dramatic changes that have challenged previous eras' patriarchal values. If masculinity is fluid and heavily influenced by media performances, as Kenneth MacKinnon suggests,[129] then it is susceptible to continual crises as those texts evolve. Hypermasculine texts such as Captain America (particularly given the character's patriotic element) fit well within the parameters of those texts in general that are likely to arouse reaction, so watching a character change can be uncomfortable to people who are forced to negotiate their reaction to a perceived decrease in cultural power.

As an extension, the initial entry point to a text may set normative expectations for how future texts should operate. In the various controversies that involved letter-column arguments, there was a tendency to cite specific prior texts, and in those cases the contemporary reading nearly always took a back seat to the prior reading. Perhaps the tyranny of the serial mechanism that Jason Dittmer found, the idea that stories are innately conservative owing to their need to preserve a popular status quo,[130] has a different function over the long term: sowing discord among those who idealize such conceptions of the status quo.

Though fans have a hand in popularizing particular versions of their favorite heroes, creators obviously maintain the greatest influence on how that value system is communicated, and it is striking that such a large number of Marvel creators grew up reading and liking Captain America. Roger Stern, Ed Brubaker, Jim Steranko, Mark Waid, Dan Jurgens, Brian Michael Bendis, and Mark Gruenwald all cite the character as a favorite or influential text in their own fandom.[131] It is clear from the many books chronicling Timely's early years that Jack Kirby modeled at least some of

Captain America's personality on his own life experiences, which included brawling in the alleyways.[132] Roy Thomas's influential work in the 1970s was built on his love of the original Golden Age stories. Mark Gruenwald loved the Stan Lee and Jack Kirby 1960s version. Mark Waid appears to have been a fan primarily of the Thomas era. And Brubaker apparently grew up appreciating the Bronze Age tales by Steve Englehart and Sal Buscema. All of these creators interact with one another, influencing the conception of the character and rewriting the character's historical points of fact. In many ways, comic creation might be considered the ultimate focused act of fandom.

Cap draws the most attention in moments when American cultural values are under scrutiny. Readers from all perspectives appear to identify with the hero, probably because he rarely takes specific stances on particular political issues. He reserves his strongest objections to broad challenges to the philosophic ideas of freedom and equality. Regardless which president sits in the Oval Office, Cap will offer a military salute (over time he has interacted with FDR, Truman, and just about every president since Kennedy). This position also means one must use care when interpreting the significance of the text against the culture of its day. Sometimes popular culture texts reflect mainstream culture, and sometimes they challenge it. Captain America stories clearly do both, and the transition from the late 1960s Kirby stories to the early 1970s Buscema and Englehart stories dramatically demonstrates the difference. In the end, the need to appeal to readers is constant, so wherever Marvel judges its fans to be located vis-à-vis the mainstream culture might be the most significant indicator of how certain texts are intended.

Cap's popularity and relevance paradoxically appear to resonate most with fans when the nation is involved in a direct challenge from other nations or world bodies. Without a doubt, Cap's finest moments, according to fans, occurred during his initial World War II run or in the fourth volume of his comic, issued immediately after 9/11.

In contrast, the more recent Civil War storyline created a paradox of emotion for some readers. Captain America took (in fact led and organized) the side of antiregistration forces, speaking out against the government and those who unquestioningly serve authority. Based on this stance, one might suspect that readers serving in the military would be resistant to the notion of refusing to allow government oversight in combat training. However, according to comic dealers, the vast majority of their military readers sided with Captain America against Iron Man, even though Iron Man's position is pro-military. Said one dealer, "They're kind of against Iron Man because they feel that he's like the corporation going in with the government. He's kind of falling in line."[133]

Though Cap's outlook and values have changed from era to era, his moral code is consistently strong. He believes fiercely in whatever he considers to be right. His devotion to American ideals is absolute: even when he comes into conflict with America's politicians or its laws, his faith in the corrective system of democracy prevents him from complaining.

And yet Captain America is also a cultural commodity, a text produced for economic profit by one of the largest media conglomerates in the world. The profit motive both ensures the survival of the text over long stretches of time and leads to an emphasis on certain frames of focus in the narrative. At this writing, for example, Steve Rogers has endured another depletion of the supersoldier serum in his body.[134] Old and frail, Rogers will undoubtedly explore his loss of masculinity with grace until he returns to health in time to feature prominently in his own comic, coordinated with the release of an *Avengers* or *Captain America* film installment. And as he endures this struggle, others will step in to carry his shield for him. For example, it appears that this time his partner Sam Wilson, the Falcon, will once again take the role of Captain America while Rogers is unable to fulfill it.[135] Once again others will struggle to "live up" to Rogers's career and will acquit themselves admirably with alternative frames of masculinity, even as the Marvel franchise prepares for a resurrection event in which Rogers takes back the Captain America mantle in time for a commercial crossover with film properties and merchandise.

Of course, this cyclical process has been noted on prior occasions. As this book illustrates, Captain America has been "killed" or out of uniform on many previous occasions, only to return triumphantly in a comics and merchandising event. However, given Disney's ownership of Marvel, these absences potentially take on new significance as the character undergoes reformation that both updates and alters previous conventions in order to better embody the contemporary narrative (and marketing) needs.

Disney and its properties have drawn significant criticism from scholars, most notably for their portrayals of race, gender, and political history, given that Disney's cultural offerings "make crucial contributions to [children's] most important discourses of the self."[136] Now that Disney is actively engaged in constructing the narratives of some of the most renowned superhero characters in the world, the implications for how masculinity is modeled for the younger generations should become an area of scholarly interest.

This book has not directly engaged questions of audience aside from fan responses to various storylines, much less engaged the literature about Captain America's potential effect on children (beyond the brief discussion of youth activity in chapter 2 and of the moral panic that emerged during the Wertham claims in the 1950s). The audience for Captain America comic books has proved rather diverse throughout their publication history. However, it should be pointed out that very few Captain America animated cartoons have been available until very recently. The creation of Captain America and Avengers cartoons places a new focus on the younger audiences of those texts and makes some of the previous work on Disney relevant to Marvel's future offerings.

Disney's film and multimedia offerings for children have generated prior critique. The "innocence" that serves as a hallmark of Disney texts "operates on a systematic sanitization of violence, sexuality, and political struggle concomitant with an erasure or repression of difference."[137] In Disney's portrayals of historical events, "the past was cleaned up. . . . Unpleasantries would be dropped from history, and stories of the past would be told in a carefully (and commercially) re-mythologized form to which Americans were becoming accustomed through the movies and television."[138]

Henry Giroux criticizes Disney for its racial portrayals, finding that its films, even when specifically addressing past racial criticisms, largely obscure the legacy of racism in its effort to replace that legacy with "Disney's America . . . a place where people can celebrate America, her people, struggles, victories, courage, setbacks, diversity, heroism, dynamism, pluralism, inventiveness, playfulness, compassion, righteousness, tolerance" and to displace the "historically specific politically constructed 'landscape of power.'"[139]

More broadly, Disney represents "an effort to embody the ideal qualities of a democratic capitalist culture, a fantasy through which contradictions in the social and material relations of a given moment are resolved by the reinscription of those relations in a hiatus between a determining past and an indeterminate future."[140] That tendency to relieve narrative tension by looking forward to a presumed positive future (living happily ever after) appears similar to the destructive updating that comic books undergo, but with different functions. Whereas comic books, positioned as fringe or outlier cultural artifacts, have historically been free to explore controversial subjects and then retroactively erase those explorations from mainstream continuity, the Disney approach has more often focused on a conservative text in the first place. Disney texts taken as a whole have historically and consistently naturalized a "set of values and social markers that privileges certain identities and modes of social organization over others and forecloses solutions to immediate pressing social and economic problems—such as institutionalized racism or gendered economic inequality—by deferring them to the next generation."[141]

If these tendencies now become the manner in which Marvel superhero texts are created, the complexities of American masculinity currently offered by those texts might not translate as well into visual media. The portrayals of some of Marvel's signature African American characters on Disney XD cartoons have already emasculated those heroes' histories and positioning by reducing them in age, in effect eradicating their history, which was forged in 1970s race relations.[142]

Beyond the established race and gender critiques lies the opportunity to specifically explore masculinity as it is presented to young children. Disney's distribution and creation not only elevate the form of superhero narratives (and therefore increase the reach and power of the textual offerings) but also bring the Disney culture to bear on the content-creation process. How Disney communicates masculinity will remain a topic of scholarly interest for some time to come. In some ways, this book, largely concerned with narrative, industry context, and social histories within fandom, comes at a time when Marvel's texts are poised to leave behind those historical structures and evolve into something culturally new. The connection between Disney's culture and Marvel characters' hypermasculinity is but one of several intriguing areas for future study.

For example, juxtaposed against this narrative of personal masculinity sits the symbolism of a nation and the ideological positioning of the country whose flag is represented in Captain America's uniform. As a text, Captain America is "imagined to exist in a world where American force is used only in self-defense or to protect the public" and where America is positioned as a "popular hegemon whose policies produce a safer world."[143] Of course, in the history of his comic book narratives Cap has often found himself at odds with the government and the military-industrial complex even as he embodies both to other people. The 2014 film *Captain America: Winter Soldier* captures some of this tension. The Disney XD *Avengers Assemble* cartoon captures far less. Such observations open the door to intermedia analyses of the Captain America text, in particular how that text positions violence, justice, and the social authority of America's institutions for different audiences. Despite the already large volume of content collected and reported in this book, the rate of future media and consumer offerings featuring Captain America is likely to continue to increase. Walt Disney famously said, "We just make the pictures, and let the professors tell us what they mean,"[144] and one can only see the potential for much more such engagement with Captain America in the future.

Finally, considering Marvel Comics, Marvel Entertainment, and Marvel Studios within the confines of Disney also raises questions about the use of the Marvel characters as cultural symbols outside Disney's corporate offerings. As described in the chapters addressing Marvel's history in the 1970s and 1980s, Marvel has often promoted and celebrated characters by engaging fan activities and reactions. Disney's history looks starkly different in that the company has aggressively opposed unauthorized use of core Disney character images. For example, in 1989 Disney notoriously threatened to sue three daycare facilities in Florida for featuring Disney characters on amateur wall murals, and it tightly regulates how its employees interact with core Disney properties.[145] In response to criticisms of an aggressive antipiracy campaign, Paul Pressler, vice president of Disney licensing, said, "Our characters are the foundation of our business and project the image of our company, so it's imperative that we control them and control how they're used."[146] Such actions (and the successful lobbying efforts to extend the nation's copyright protections for its properties) signal a particular view of the process of gaining and maintaining cultural authority. Beyond merely considering its authority in the framing of the media it produces, Disney often tries to control aspects of reception and even discussion about its characters and products.[147] How Marvel culture will be affected by the Disney culture will be an interesting subject of inquiry in itself.

This book sought to expound on the historical Captain America text, the development and contributions from fans, and the process of popular cultural production as fans and creators struggle with each other over presentation and cultural voice. What Captain America represents changes both with the times and with fans' activity. The influence that readers have over the creative direction of Cap's storyline has been remarkable at times. Though Cap is framed as a leader of public opinion, his values seem to be largely determined by those who read his stories, making him an ongoing artifact of interest to examine.

Notes

Bibliography

Index

Notes

Preface

1. Stephen Johnson, *Everything Bad Is Good for You: How Today's Popular Culture Is Actually Making Us Smarter* (New York: Riverhead Books, 2005).

2. John Storey, *Inventing Popular Culture: From Folklore to Globalization* (Hoboken, NJ: Wiley & Sons, 2009), 2.

3. Herbert Marcuse, *Eros and Civilization*, 2nd ed. (Boston: Beacon, 1966), 26–27.

1. Introduction

1. George Gene Gustines, "Captain America Is Dead; National Hero since 1941," *New York Times*, Mar. 8, 2007, at http://www.nytimes.com/2007/03/08/books/08capt .html, accessed Mar. 7, 2007.

2. "Captain America Is Dead; National Hero since 1941," *New York Times on the Web*, Readers' Comments, Mar. 7, 2007, at http://news.blogs.nytimes.com/2007/03/07 /captain-america-is-dead-national-hero-since-1941/, accessed Mar. 7, 2007, misspellings and capitalization as given in the originals.

3. Quoted in Tom Leonard, "Captain America Killed When US Needs Him," *Telegraph*, Oct. 3, 2007, at http://www.telegraph.co.uk/news/worldnews/1545017/Cap tain-America-killed-when-US-needs-him.html, accessed Feb. 28, 2010.

4. Quoted in ibid.

5. Ricardo Alberich, Joe Miro-Julia, and Francesc Rosselló, "Marvel Universe Looks Almost Like a Real Social Network," *Statistical Mechanic*, Feb. 2002, 9.

6. Jonathan Gray, Cornel Sandvoss, and C. Lee Harrington, "Introduction: Why Study Fans?" in *Fandom: Identities and Communities in a Mediated World*, ed. Jonathan Gray, Cornel Sandvoss, and C. Lee Harrington (New York: New York Univ. Press, 2007), 1–18.

7. Ibid., 9, 10.

8. Michael Denning, *Mechanical Accents: Dime Novels and Working-Class Culture* (London: Verso, 1987), 26.

9. James W. Loewen, *Lies My Teacher Told Me: Everything Your American History Textbook Got Wrong* (New York: Simon & Schuster, 2007).

10. Claude Lévi-Strauss, *Structural Anthropology* (Garden City, NY: Anchor Books, 1963), 57.

11. Jason Dittmer, "The Tyranny of the Serial: Popular Geopolitics, the Nation, and Comic Book Discourse," *Antipode* 39, no. 2 (Mar. 2007): 247–68.

12. Jason Dittmer, "Retconning America: Captain America in the Wake of World War II and the McCarthy Hearings," in *The Amazing Transforming Superhero! Essays on the Revision of Characters in Comic Books, Film, and Television,* ed. Terrence R. Wandtke (Jefferson, NC: McFarland, 2007), 36.

13. Terrence R. Wandtke, "Introduction," in *The Amazing Transforming Superhero!* ed. Wandtke, 14–15.

14. Richard Reynolds, *Super Heroes: A Modern Mythology* (Jackson: Univ. of Mississippi Press, 1992).

15. Matthew Wolf-Meyer, "The World Ozymandias Made: Utopias in the Superhero Comic, Subculture, and the Conservation of Difference," *Journal of Popular Culture* 36, no. 3 (2003): 497–517.

16. For examples of these observations, see Benedict R. Anderson, *Imagined Communities: Reflections on the Origin and Spread of Nationalism* (London: Verso, 1983); Bernard Bailyn, *On the Teaching and Writing of History: Responses to a Series of Questions* (Hanover, NH: Montgomery Endowment, Dartmouth College; distributed by Univ. Press of New England, 1994); T. H. Breen, *The Marketplace of Revolution: How Consumer Politics Shaped American Independence* (New York: Oxford Univ. Press, 2004); Jack P. Greene, *Pursuits of Happiness: The Social Development of Early Modern British Colonies and the Formation of American Culture* (Chapel Hill : Univ. of North Carolina Press, 1988); John Higham, *History: Professional Scholarship in America* (Baltimore: Johns Hopkins Univ. Press, 1983); Richard T. Hughes, *Myths America Lives By* (Champaign: Univ. of Illinois Press, 2004); Gary B. Nash, *The Unknown American Revolution: The Unruly Birth of Democracy and the Struggle to Create America* (New York: Viking, 2005); Peter Novick, *That Noble Dream: The "Objectivity Question" and the American Historical Profession* (Cambridge: Cambridge Univ. Press, 1988); Jeffrey L. Pasley, Andrew W. Robertson, and David Waldstreicher, eds., *Beyond the Founders: New Approaches to the Political History of the Early American Republic* (Chapel Hill: Univ. of North Carolina Press, 2004); Arthur M. Schlesinger Jr., *The Cycles of American History* (Boston: Houghton Mifflin, 1986); and David Waldstreicher, *In the Midst of Perpetual Fetes: The Making of American Nationalism, 1776–1820* (Chapel Hill: Univ. of North Carolina Press, 1997).

17. Umberto Eco, *The Role of the Reader: Explorations in the Semiotics of Texts* (Bloomington: Indiana Univ. Press, 1979), 114.

18. Stan Lee and Jack Kirby, "Captain America Joins the Avengers," *The Avengers* 1, no. 4 (Mar. 1963).

19. Reynolds, *Super Heroes*, 44.

20. John Rhett Thomas, "The Spotlight Interview with Mark Millar," *Marvel Spotlight: Civil War*, June 2007, 22–23, emphasis in original.

21. Gillian Cohen, *Memory in the Real World*, 2nd ed. (Hove, UK: Psychology Press, 1996).

22. Maurice Halbwachs, *The Collective Memory* (New York: Harper & Row, 1980), 69.

23. Henry Jenkins, *Textual Poachers: Television Fans and Participatory Culture* (New York: Routledge, 1992).

24. Michael Medved and Michael Lackner, *The Betrayal of Captain America*, White Paper (Washington, DC: Foundation for the Defense of Democracies, Apr. 2003).

25. Jenkins, *Textual Poachers*, 55.

26. Johnson, *Everything Bad Is Good for You*.

27. Reynolds, *Super Heroes*, 74.

28. Wolf-Meyer, "The World Ozymandias Made."

29. Joe Simon and Jack Kirby, "Meet Captain America," *Captain America Comics* 1, no. 1 (Mar. 1941): 1–8.

30. Gary Engle, "What Makes Superman so Darned American?" in *Superman at Fifty: The Persistence of a Legend!* ed. Dennis Dooley and Gary Engle (New York: Collier, 1987), 79–87.

31. Thomas Andrae, "From Menace to Messiah: The History and Historicity of Superman," in *American Media and Mass Culture*, ed. Donald Lazere (Berkeley: Univ. of California Press, 1987), 124–38.

32. Geoff Klock, *How to Read Superhero Comics and Why* (New York: Continuum, 2002), 13.

33. Andrew MacDonald and Virginia MacDonald, "Sold American: The Metamorphosis of Captain America," *Journal of Popular Culture* 10, no. 1 (1976): 253.

34. Salvatore Mondello, "Spider-Man: Superhero in the Liberal Tradition," *Journal of Popular Culture* 10, no. 1 (1976): 232–38.

35. Matthew Paul McAllister, "Comic Books and AIDS," *Journal of Popular Culture* 26, no. 2 (1992): 1–24.

36. Will Brooker, *Batman Unmasked: Analyzing a Cultural Icon* (New York: Continuum, 2001).

37. Mike. S. DuBose, "Holding Out for a Hero: Reaganism, Comic Book Vigilantes, and Captain America," *Journal of Popular Culture* 40, no. 6 (2007): 915–35.

38. For example, see Janice Hume, "Changing Characteristics of Heroic Women in Midcentury Mainstream Media," *Journal of Popular Culture* 34, no. 1 (2000): 9–29, and Mitra C. Emad, "Reading Wonder Woman's Body: Mythologies of Gender and Nation," *Journal of Popular Culture* 39, no. 6 (2006): 954–84.

39. Valerie Palmer-Mehta and Kellie Hay, "A Superhero for Gays? Gay Masculinity and Green Lantern," *Journal of American Culture* 28, no. 4 (2005): 390–404.

40. Jack G. Shaheen, "Arab Images in American Comic Books," *Journal of Popular Culture* 28, no. 1 (1994): 123–33.

41. Eco, *The Role of the Reader*, 109.

42. Although there are a variety of opinions about the designated ages of comic books, it is generally accepted that the Golden Age of comic books began with the introduction of Superman in *Actions Comics* number 1 (June 1938) and gave way to the Silver Age in October 1956 with the introduction of the modern Flash in *Showcase* number 4. A Bronze Age is thought to have begun in the early 1970s when several of the prominent creators retired and the Comics Code that regulated comic content was relaxed to allow greater freedom of control for authors. Authors have identified several subsequent ages, but the boundaries are heavily disputed. See the discussion about Peter Coogan's demarcations later in this chapter.

43. Tony Bennett and Janet Woollacott, *Bond and Beyond: The Political Career of a Popular Hero* (London: Macmillan, 1987), 19.

44. Max J. Skidmore and Joey Skidmore, "More Than Mere Fantasy: Political Themes in Contemporary Comic Books," *Journal of Popular Culture* 17, no. 1 (1983): 91.

45. Robert Genter, "'With Great Power Comes Great Responsibility': Cold War Culture and the Birth of Marvel Comics," *Journal of Popular Culture* 40, no. 6 (2007): 953–78.

46. Saul Braun, "Shazam! Here Comes Captain Relevant," *New York Times Magazine*, May 2, 1971, 41.

47. Stan Lee and George Mair, *Excelsior! The Amazing Life of Stan Lee* (New York: Fireside, 2002), 114.

48. Peter Coogan, *Superhero: The Secret Origin of a Genre* (Austin, TX: Monkey-Brain, 2006), 193–94.

49. Mark Voger, *The Dark Age: Grim, Great, & Gimmicky Post-modern Comics* (Raleigh, NC: TwoMorrows, 2006).

50. Kenneth Mackinnon, *Representing Men: Maleness and Masculinity in the Media* (London: Arnold, 2003), 3.

51. Ulla Hakala, *Adam in Ads: A Thirty Year Look at Mediated Masculinities in Advertising in Finland and the US* (Tampere, Finland: Esa Print Tampere, 2006), 57.

52. Mackinnon, *Representing Men*, 11.

53. Michael Kimmel, "Masculinity as Homophobia: Fear, Shame, and Silence in the Construction of Gender Identity," in *Feminism and Masculinities*, ed. Peter Murphy (Oxford: Oxford Univ. Press, 2004), 184.

54. Mackinnon, *Representing Men*, 9–10.

55. Julie D'Acci, "Television, Representation, and Gender," in *The Television Studies Reader*, ed. Robert C. Allen and Annette Hill (New York: Routledge, 2004), 379.

56. Mackinnon, *Representing Men*, 9.

57. Garry Whannel, *Media Sports Stars: Masculinities and Moralities* (London: Routledge, 2002), 127.

58. R. W. Connell, *Gender and Power: Society, the Person, and Sexual Politics* (Palo Alto, CA: Stanford Univ. Press, 1987), 215.

59. Mackinnon, *Representing Men*, 5.

60. Michael A. Messner, "When Bodies Are Weapons: Masculinity and Violence in Sport," *International Review for the Sociology of Sport* 25, no. 3 (Sept. 1990): 214.

61. Jonathan Watson, *Male Bodies: Health, Culture, and Identity* (Buckingham, UK: Open Univ. Press, 2005), 43; R. W. Connell, *Masculinities* (Oxford: Polity Press, 1995).

62. Whannel, *Media Sports Stars*, 127.

63. Mackinnon, *Representing Men*, 11.

64. Frank Springer and Roy Thomas, "What If the Invaders Had Stayed Together after World War Two?" *What If?* 1, no. 4 (Aug. 1977).

65. Simcha Weinstein, *Up, Up, and Oy Vey! How Jewish History, Culture, and Values Shaped the Comic Book Superhero* (Baltimore: Leviathan, 2006), 47.

66. Joe Simon, "Beware! Captain America Is Coming!" *The Human Torch* 1, no. 3 (Dec. 1940).

67. "Rushed Hot off the Press," *Marvel Mystery Comics* 1, no. 15 (Jan. 1941).

68. Michael J. Vassallo, "A Golden Age Reunion: Two Timely Talks with Allen Bellman," *Alter Ego* 3, no. 32 (Jan. 2004): 20.

2. The Anti-Hitler Crusader (1940–1949)

1. Simon and Kirby, "Meet Captain America," 1.

2. Ibid., 7.

3. Les Daniels, *Comix: A History of Comic Books in America* (New York: Outerbridge, 1971), 36.

4. Simon and Kirby, "Meet Captain America," 8.

5. "Captain America Wants You!" (advertisement), *Captain America Comics* 1, no. 5 (Aug. 1941).

6. "Captain America Declares a 'State of Unlimited Junior National Emergency'!" (advertisement), *Captain America Comics* 1, no. 7 (Oct. 1941).

7. Joe Simon and Jim Simon, *The Comic Book Makers* (Lebanon, NJ: Vanguard, 2003), 45.

8. Robert Jewett, *The Captain America Complex: The Dilemma of Zealous Nationalism* (Philadelphia: Westminster Press, 1973).

9. Robert Jewett, *The Captain America Complex: The Dilemma of Zealous Nationalism*, 2nd ed. (Santa Fe: Bear, 1984), 205.

10. John Shelton Lawrence and Robert Jewett, *The Myth of the American Superhero* (Grand Rapids, MI: Eerdmans, 2002).

11. Joseph Campbell, *The Hero with a Thousand Faces* (New York: Pantheon, 1949).

12. Robert Jewett and John Shelton Lawrence, *Captain America and the Crusade against Evil: The Dilemma of Zealous Nationalism* (Grand Rapids, MI: Eerdmans, 2003), 29.

13. Robert Jewett, *Mission and Menace: Four Centuries of American Religious Zeal* (Minneapolis: Fortress Press, 2008), 238.

14. Jewett and Lawrence, *Captain America and the Crusade against Evil*, 28.

15. Jewett, *Mission and Menace*.

16. Richard Slotkin, *Regeneration through Violence: The Mythology of the American Frontier, 1600–1860* (Middletown, CT: Wesleyan Univ. Press, 1973), 562.

17. Gerard Jones, *Men of Tomorrow: Geeks, Gangsters, and the Birth of the Comic Book* (New York: Basic Books, 2004), 200.

18. Bradford W. Wright, *Comic Book Nation: The Transformation of Youth Culture in America* (Baltimore: Johns Hopkins Univ. Press, 2001).

19. Harry Shorten and Irving Novick, "The Shield: G-Man-Extraordinary," *Pep Comics* 1, no. 1 (Jan. 1940).

20. Jules Feiffer, *The Great Comic Book Heroes* (Seattle: Fantagraphic Books, 2003), 59.

21. Hughes, *Myths America Lives By*, 6.

22. Ibid., 114–19. See also Jewett, *Mission and Menace*, 237.

23. Hughes, *Myths America Lives By*, 102–4.

24. Ibid., 168–73.

25. Ibid., 155.

26. Chris Hedges, *War Is a Force That Gives Us Meaning* (New York: PublicAffairs, 2002), 147.

27. Hughes, *Myths America Lives By*, 8.

28. Christopher Knowles, *Our Gods Wear Spandex: The Secret History of Comic Book Heroes* (San Francisco: Weiser, 2007), 16.

29. Ibid., 131.

30. Jewett, *Mission and Menace*, 236.

31. Robert Jewett and John Shelton Lawrence, *The American Monomyth* (Garden City, NY: Anchor Press, 1977), 248.

32. Ron Goulart, "Captain America and the Super-Patriots," *Comic Buyer's Guide*, Apr. 22, 1988, 36.

33. Though many have pointed out that Superman is more closely tied to American patriotism today, that character did not become associated with patriotism until World War II, a few years after his creation.

34. Edward L. Feder, *Comic Book Regulation* (Berkeley, CA: Bureau of Public Administration, 1955), 2.

35. Mike Nolan, "The Timely Comics Super-Hero Index (1939–1957)," *Alter Ego* 3, no. 57 (Mar. 2006): 3–64.

36. Jones, *Men of Tomorrow*, 200.

37. Jordan Raphael and Tom Spurgeon, *Stan Lee and the Rise and Fall of the American Comic Book* (Chicago: Chicago Review Press, 2003), 13.

38. Joe Simon and Jack Kirby, "Case #2: Trapped in the Nazi Strong-hold," *Captain America Comics* 1, no. 2 (Apr. 1941): 7.

39. Simon and Simon, *The Comic Book Makers*, 45.

40. Ibid., 43.

41. Ibid., 52.

42. Joe Simon and Jack Kirby, "The Gruesome Secret of the Dragon of Death," *Captain America Comics* 1, no. 5 (Aug. 1941).

43. Feiffer, *The Great Comic Book Heroes*, 59.

44. "Captain America Battles the Horde of the Vulture!" *Captain America Comics* 1, no. 14 (May 1942).

45. "The Vampire Strikes," *All Winners Comics* 1, no. 42 (July 1942).

46. "Captain America and Mikado's Super-Shell," *Captain America Comics* 1, no. 18 (Sept. 1942): 7.

47. "Mystery of the Atomic Boomerang," *Captain America Comics* 1, no. 51 (Dec. 1945): 9.

48. Ibid., 16.

49. Matthew Paul McAllister, "Cultural Argument and Organizational Constraint in the Comic Book Industry," *Journal of Communication* 40, no. 1 (Winter 1990): 58.

50. Roy Thomas, "Marvel's Most Timely Heroes," in *The Golden Age of Marvel Comics*, vol. 1.1, ed. Tom Brevoort (New York: Marvel Comics, 1997), 6.

51. Raphael and Spurgeon, *Stan Lee*, 52.

52. "The Private Life of Captain America," *Captain America Comics* 1, no. 59 (Oct. 1946).

53. "When Friends Turn Foes," *Captain America Comics* 1, no. 65 (Jan. 1948).

54. Betsy Ross (or the Golden Age Betty Ross) should not be confused with the Betty Ross who is the romantic interest to the Silver Age Bruce Banner, a.k.a. the Incredible Hulk. Timely/Marvel has often repurposed character names and concepts when they fall out of common memory.

55. "Golden Girl," *Captain America Comics* 1, no. 66 (Apr. 1948): 12.

56. "Lightning Cult," *Marvel Comics* 1, no. 86 (June 1948).

57. "The Case of Joey Arnold," *Captain America Comics* 1, no. 68 (Sept. 1948).

58. "A Case of Conscience," *Captain America Comics* 1, no. 68 (Sept. 1948).

59. "The Enigma of the Death Doll," *Captain America Comics* 1, no. 68 (Sept. 1948).

60. "Weird Tales of the Wee Males," *Captain America Comics* 1, no. 69 (Nov. 1948).

61. "No Man Is an Island," *Captain America Comics* 1, no. 69 (Nov. 1948).

62. "Worlds at War," *Captain America Comics* 1, no. 70 (Nov. 1948), republished as "The Men Who Conquered the Earth," *Journey into Unknown Worlds* 1, no. 7 (Oct. 1951).

63. "The Red Skull Strikes Again," *Captain America's Weird Tales* 1, no. 74 (Oct. 1949).

64. "The Leopard and His Killer Mob," *Captain America Comics* 1, no. 50 (Oct. 1945): 3–6.

65. "Captain America and the Bloodthirsty Baron," *USA Comics* 1, no. 17 (Oct. 1945): 3.

66. "The Saboteur of Death," *Captain America Comics* 1, no. 30 (Sept. 1943): 4.

67. Joe Simon and Jack Kirby, "The Unholy Legion," *Captain America Comics* 1, no. 4 (June 1941); "The Canal of Lurking Death," *Captain America Comics* 1, no. 31 (Oct. 1943).

68. "Tojo's Terror Masters," *Captain America Comics* 1, no. 42 (Oct. 1944): 17.

69. Joe Simon and Jack Kirby, "The Chess Board of Death," *Captain America Comics* 1, no. 1 (Mar. 1941): 5.

70. "The Mystery of Hangman's Island," *All Select* 1, no. 4 (July 1944): 13.

71. "Captain America and the Tunnel of Terror!" *Captain America Comics* 1, no. 15 (June 1942): 3–4.

72. Ibid., 5–6.

73. "Your Life Depends on It," *Captain America Comics* 1, no. 19 (Oct. 1942): 1–2.

74. Ibid., 4, suspension points in original.

75. "On to Berlin," *Captain America Comics* 1, no. 19 (Oct. 1942): 16.

76. Ibid., 22.

77. "The Walking Dead," *Captain America Comics* 1, no. 50 (Oct. 1945): 3.

78. Ibid., 17.

79. "Mystery of the Atomic Boomerang," 9.

80. Joe Simon and Jack Kirby, "The Riddle of the Red Skull," *Captain America Comics* 1, no. 1 (Mar. 1941): 4.

81. Feiffer, *The Great Comic Book Heroes*, 59.

82. Robert MacDougall, "Red, Brown, and Yellow Perils: Images of the American Enemy in the 1940s and 1950s," *Journal of Popular Culture* 32, no. 4 (Spring 1999): 59–75.

83. Allan Nevins, "How We Felt about the War," in *While You Were Gone: A Report on Wartime Life in the United States*, ed. Jack Goodman (New York: Simon and Schuster, 1946), 13, quoted in MacDougall, "Red, Brown, and Yellow Perils," 61.

84. William W. Savage Jr., *Commies, Cowboys, and Jungle Queens: Comic Books and America, 1945–1954* (Middletown, CT: Wesleyan Univ. Press, 1998), 10.

85. "The Vampire Strikes," 2.

86. Ibid., 12.

87. MacDougall, "Red, Brown, and Yellow Perils," 62.

88. For example, see "The Vultures of Violent Death," *Captain America Comics* 1, no. 28 (July 1943): 10.

89. For example, see "The Seven Sons of Satan," *Captain America Comics* 1, no. 37 (Apr. 1944): 3.

90. For example, see "The Cylinder of Death," *USA Comics* 1, no. 10 (Sept. 1943): 3.

91. "Tojo's Terror Masters," 7.

92. Ibid.

93. "The Case of the Flying Submarine!" *USA Comics* 1, no. 7 (Feb. 1943).

94. "Castle of Doom," *Captain America Comics* 1, no. 38 (May 1944).

95. For example, see "Captain America and the Invasion from Mars," *Captain America Comics* 1, no. 15 (June 1942): 17.

96. "The Case of the Phantom Engineer," *Captain America Comics* 1, no. 29 (Aug. 1943): 6.

97. "The Shadows of Death," *Captain America Comics* 1, no. 43 (Dec. 1944): 9.

98. Wright, *Comic Book Nation*, 54.

99. "The Riddle of the Totem Pole," *USA Comics* 1, no. 16 (July 1945): 9.

100. Ibid., 12.

101. Wright, *Comic Book Nation*, 37.

102. "The Vault of the Doomed," *Captain America Comics* 1, no. 22 (Jan. 1943): 9.

103. "Captain America Fights When the Crocodile Strikes!" *Captain America Comics* 1, no. 19 (Oct. 1942).

104. Simon and Simon, *The Comic Book Makers*, 45.

105. "The Coming of Agent Zero," *Young Allies* 1, no. 1 (July 1941): 6.

106. Ibid., 9.

107. "The Red Skull and the Graveyard of Doom," *Young Allies* 1, no. 1 (July 1941): 9–10.

108. "Voyage to No-Man's-Land," *Young Allies* 1, no. 1 (July 1941): 3.

109. "Outwitting the Bloodthirsty Tyrants," *Young Allies* 1, no. 1 (July 1941): 7.

110. "The Strange Case of the Malay Idol," *All Winners Comics* 1, no. 2 (Oct. 1941): 3.

111. "The Fiend That Was the Fakir," *Captain America Comics* 1, no. 20 (Nov. 1942): 13.

112. "The Idol of Doom!" *Captain America Comics* 1, no. 23 (Feb. 1943): 2.

113. Betsy Ross was sometimes called "Betty Ross." At times, the two seem at times to be separate characters, but both appear to be FBI agents or military operatives, depending on the story. Once the war ended, Betsy Ross, now blond, became a teacher at the Lee Academy, where she is recruited to be Cap's partner.

114. "The Talons of the Vulture," *Captain America Comics* 1, no. 32 (Nov. 1943): 13.

115. "Symphony of Death," *Captain America Comics* 1, no. 49 (Aug. 1945): 3.

116. "The Cylinder of Death," 13.

117. "Golden Girl," 9.

118. Ibid., 12.

119. Jewett, *The Captain America Complex*, 2nd ed., 2, 10.

3. Commie Smasher! (1953–1954)

1. Jones, *Men of Tomorrow*, 234.

2. Roy Thomas, "Introduction," in *Marvel Masterworks: Atlas Era Heroes*, vol. 1.1 (New York: Marvel, 2007), vii.

3. "The Outer World of Doom," *The Human Torch* 1, no. 35 (Nov. 1949): 1–8.

4. James T. Patterson, *Grand Expectations: The United States, 1945–1974* (New York: Oxford Univ. Press, 1996), 59–60.

5. Savage, *Commies, Cowboys, and Jungle Queens*, 15.

6. Thomas, "Marvel's Most Timely Heroes," 7; Raphael and Spurgeon, *Stan Lee*, 56.

7. Thomas, "Marvel's Most Timely Heroes," 8.

8. Savage, *Commies, Cowboys, and Jungle Queens*, 59.

9. Ibid., 113.

10. "The Return of the Human Torch," *Young Men* 1, no. 24 (Dec. 1953): 4.

11. Ibid., 6.

12. Ibid., 9.

13. Stan Lee and John Romita, "Back from the Dead," *Young Men* 1, no. 24 (Dec. 1953).

14. Stan Lee and Mort Lawrence, "The Girl Who Was Afraid," *Men's Adventures* 1, no. 27 (May 1954): 7.

15. Stan Lee and John Romita, "The Betrayers," *Captain America . . . Commie Smasher!* 1, no. 76 (May 1954): 6.

16. Stan Lee and John Romita, "The Man with No Face," *Captain America . . . Commie Smasher!* 1, no. 77 (July 1954): 4, suspension points in original.

17. Stan Lee and John Romita, "Come to the Commies," *Captain America . . . Commie Smasher!* 1, no. 76 (May 1954): 6.

18. Savage, *Commies, Cowboys, and Jungle Queens*, 54.

19. "The League of Hate," *Captain America Comics* 1, no. 49 (Aug. 1945): 15.

20. "Captain America and the Tunnel of Terror!"

21. "Top Secret," *Young Men* 1, no. 25 (Feb. 1954): 6, suspension points in original.

22. Thomas, "Introduction," ix.

23. "Captain America Turns Traitor," *Young Men* 1, no. 26 (Mar. 1954).

24. Ibid., 4.

25. Ibid., 7, suspension points in original.

26. "The Return of the Red Skull," *Young Men* 1, no. 27 (Apr. 1954).

27. Lee and Romita, "The Betrayers," 6, suspension points in original.

28. Stan Lee and John Romita, "Captain America Strikes," *Captain America . . . Commie Smasher!* 1, no. 76 (May 1954).

29. "Come to the Commies," 6, suspension points in original.

30. Lee and Lawrence, "The Girl Who Was Afraid."

31. "The Cargo of Death," *Young Men* 1, no. 28 (June 1954): 3.

32. Stan Lee and John Romita, "You Die at Midnight," *Captain America . . . Commie Smasher!* 1, no. 77 (July 1954).

33. "The Man with No Face."

34. Stan Lee and John Romita, "Captain America," *Captain America . . . Commie Smasher!* 1, no. 77 (July 1954).

35. Ibid., 4.

36. Ibid., 2.

37. Ibid., 6, suspension points in original.

38. "Kill Captain America," *Men's Adventures* 1, no. 28 (July 1954): 7.

39. Stan Lee and John Romita, "His Touch Is Death!" *Captain America . . . Commie Smasher!* 1, no. 78 (Sept. 1954).

40. Stan Lee and John Romita. "The Green Dragon!" *Captain America . . . Commie Smasher!* 1, no. 78 (Sept. 1954).

41. Stan Lee and John Romita, "The Hour of Doom," *Captain America . . . Commie Smasher!* 1, no. 78 (Sept. 1954): 6, suspension points in original.

42. Wright, *Comic Book Nation*, 123.

43. Ibid.

44. Savage, *Commies, Cowboys, and Jungle Queens*, 37–38.

45. Raphael and Spurgeon, *Stan Lee*, 57.

46. Andrae, "From Menace to Messiah."

47. Quoted in Judith Crist, "Horror in the Nursery," *Collier's*, Mar. 1948, 22.

48. Quoted in ibid.

49. Gerson Legman, *Love and Death: A Study in Censorship* (New York: Breaking Point, 1949).

50. Frederic Wertham, *Seduction of the Innocent* (New York: Rinehart, 1954), 190.

51. *Code of the Comics Magazine Association of America* (New York: Comics Magazine Association of America, Oct. 26, 1954), 36.

52. Amy Kiste Nyberg, *Seal of Approval: The History of the Comics Code* (Jackson: Univ. Press of Mississippi, 1998), 125–26.

53. Quoted in Ronin Ro, *Tales to Astonish: Jack Kirby, Stan Lee, and the American Comic Book Revolution* (New York: Bloomsbury, 2004), 51.

54. Ibid., 52.

55. Wright, *Comic Book Nation*, 123.

56. Ibid., 182.

57. Les Daniels, *Superman: The Complete History* (New York: DC Comics, 1998), 99–100.

58. Les Daniels, *Batman: The Complete History* (New York: DC Comics, 1999), 69.

59. Bill Boichel, "Batman: Commodity as Myth," in *The Many Lives of the Batman,* ed. Roberta E. Pearson and William Uricchio (London: Routledge 1991), 13.

4. The Man out of Time (1963–1969)

1. Nyberg, *Seal of Approval*, 125–26.

2. "Mystery of the Human Thunderbolt," *Showcase* 1, no. 4 (Oct. 1956).

3. "S.O.S. Green Lantern," *Showcase* 1, no. 22 (Oct. 1959).

4. "The World of No Return," *The Justice League of America* 1, no. 1 (Oct.–Nov. 1960).

5. Les Daniels, *Marvel: Five Fabulous Decades of the World's Greatest Comics* (New York: Abradale, 1991), 78–81.

6. Lee and Mair, *Excelsior!* 114.

7. Stan Lee, *Origins of Marvel Comics* (New York: Marvel Comics Group, 1974), 5.

8. Genter, "'With Great Power Comes Great Responsibility.'"

9. Stan Lee and Jack Kirby, "The Fantastic Four," *The Fantastic Four* 1, no. 1 (Nov. 1961): 9, suspension points in original.

10. Jewett and Lawrence, *Captain America and the Crusade against Evil*, 29.

11. Raphael and Spurgeon, *Stan Lee*, 91.

12. Ro, *Tales to Astonish*, 74.

13. Steve Clark, letter, *The Avengers* 1, no. 20 (Sept. 1965): 32–33.

14. Stan Lee and Jack Kirby, "The Coming of the Sub-Mariner," *The Fantastic Four* 1, no. 4 (May 1962): 8.

15. Ibid., 13.

16. Stan Lee and Jack Kirby, "The Hulk," *The Incredible Hulk* 1, no. 1 (May 1962).

17. Ibid., 23.

18. Ibid., 24, suspension points in original.

19. Lee, *Origins of Marvel Comics*, 76; Peter Sanderson, *Classic Marvel Superheroes* (New York: Barnes and Nobel, 2005), 75.

20. Stan Lee and Steve Ditko, "Spider-Man!" *Amazing Fantasy* 1, no. 15 (Aug. 1962).

21. Douglas Wolk, *Reading Comics: How Graphic Novels Work and What They Mean* (Cambridge, MA: Da Capo, 2007), 161.

22. Lee and Mair, *Excelsior!* 126.

23. Stan Lee and Bill Everett, "The Origin of Daredevil," *Daredevil* 1, no. 1 (Apr. 1964).

24. Stan Lee and Jack Kirby, "X-Men," *The X-Men* 1, no. 1 (Sept. 1963): 10.

25. Stan Lee and Jack Kirby, "Thor the Mighty! And the Stone Men from Saturn!" *Journey into Mystery* 1, no. 83 (Aug. 1962).

26. Stan Lee, *Son of Origins of Marvel Comics* (New York: Marvel Comics Group, 1975), 82. For Pym, see Stan Lee and Jack Kirby, "The Man in the Ant Hill," *Tales to Astonish* 1, no. 27 (Jan. 1962), and for Ant-Man see Stan Lee and Jack Kirby, "Return of the Ant-Man," *Tales to Astonish* 1, no. 35 (Sept. 1962).

27. Lee, *Son of Origins of Marvel Comics*, 46.

28. Stan Lee and Don Heck, "Iron Man Is Born," *Tales of Suspense* 1, no. 39 (Mar. 1963).

29. Stan Lee and Jack Kirby, "Sgt. Fury and His Howling Commandoes," *Sgt. Fury and His Howling Commandoes* 1, no. 1 (May 1963).

30. Ro, *Tales to Astonish*, 78.

31. Stan Lee and Jack Kirby, "The Coming of the Avengers," *The Avengers* 1, no. 1 (Sept. 1963).

32. Stan Lee and Jack Kirby, "The Avengers Battle the Space Phantom," *The Avengers* 1, no. 2 (Nov. 1963).

33. Stan Lee and Jack Kirby, "The Human Torch Meets Captain America," *Strange Tales* 1, no. 114 (Nov. 1963): 18.

34. Ro, *Tales to Astonish*, 82.

35. Lee and Kirby, "Captain America Joins the Avengers," 4.

36. Ibid., 10.

37. Stan Lee and Jack Kirby, "The Mighty Avengers Meet the Masters of Evil," *The Avengers* 1, no. 6 (July 1964): 20, suspension points in original.

38. Stan Lee and Don Heck, "Now by My Hand Shall Die a Villain," *The Avengers* 1, no. 15 (Apr. 1965): 19.

39. Lee and Kirby, "The Mighty Avengers Meet the Masters of Evil," 12.

40. Lee and Kirby, "Captain America Joins the Avengers," 11.

41. Stan Lee and Don Heck, "Once an Avenger . . . ," *The Avengers* 1, no. 23 (Dec. 1965): 4.

42. Stan Lee and Don Heck, "From the Ashes of Defeat—!" *The Avengers* 1, no. 24 (Jan. 1966): 4.

43. Stan Lee and Dick Ayers, "The Old Order Changeth!" *The Avengers* 1, no. 16 (May 1965).

44. Paul Laiken, Larry Lieber, and Don Heck, "Even Avengers Can Die," *The Avengers* 1, no. 14 (Mar. 1965): 2, suspension points in original.

45. Stan Lee and Don Heck, "When the Commissar Commands," *The Avengers* 1, no. 18 (July 1965): 2.

46. Stan Lee and Don Heck, "Enter—Dr. Doom!" *The Avengers* 1, no. 25 (Feb. 1966): 4, suspension points in original.

47. Stan Lee and Jack Kirby, "In Mortal Combat with Captain America," *Tales of Suspense* 1, no. 58 (Oct. 1964).

48. Stan Lee and Jack Kirby, "Captain America," *Tales of Suspense* 1, no. 59 (Nov. 1964).

49. Stan Lee and Jack Kirby, "The Strength of the Sumo," *Tales of Suspense* 1, no. 61 (Jan. 1965): 2–3.

50. David Mackidd, letter, *The Avengers* 1, no. 22 (Nov. 1965): 33; Richard Kenney, letter, *The Avengers* 1, no. 27 (Apr. 1966): 24.

51. Stan Lee and Jack Kirby, "The Origin of Captain America," *Tales of Suspense* 1, no. 63 (Mar. 1965): 5.

52. Ibid.

53. Stan Lee and Jack Kirby, "The Hero That Was!" *Captain America* 1, no. 109 (Jan. 1969): 6; Stan Lee and Jim Steranko, "Lest We Forget," *Captain America* 1, no. 112 (Apr. 1969): 5.

54. Stan Lee and Jack Kirby, "This Monster Unmasked," *Captain America* 1, no. 100 (Apr. 1968): 13.

55. Lee and Kirby, "The Origin of Captain America," 10.

56. Rick Wrigley, letter, *Tales of Suspense* 1, no. 68 (Aug. 1965): 33; Mark Leader, letter, *Tales of Suspense* 1, no. 68 (Aug. 1965): 33.

57. Stan Lee, Johnny Romita, and Frank Ray, "If a Hostage Should Die!" *Tales of Suspense* 1, no. 77 (May 1966): 4, suspension points in original.

58. Stan Lee and George Tuska, "The Sleeper Shall Awaken," *Tales of Suspense* 1, no. 72 (Dec. 1965): 10.

59. Stan Lee and Jack Kirby, "The Sleeper Strikes!" *Captain America* 1, no. 102 (June 1968): 7.

60. Stan Lee and Dick Ayers, "30 Minutes to Live!" *Tales of Suspense* 1, no. 75 (Mar. 1966): 5.

61. Ibid., 6.

62. Stan Lee and Jack Kirby, "If the Past Be Not Dead," *Captain America* 1, no. 107 (Nov. 1968): 6.

63. Stan Lee and Jack Kirby, "A Time to Die—a Time to Live!" *Tales of Suspense* 1, no. 95 (Nov. 1967).

64. Roy Thomas and John Buscema, "Magneto Walks the Earth," *The Avengers* 1, no. 47 (Dec. 1967).

65. Roy Thomas and John Buscema, "Death Calls for the Arch Heroes," *The Avengers*, 1, no. 52 (May 1968).

66. Stan Lee and Jack Kirby, "When Wakes the Sleeper!" *Captain America* 1, no. 101 (May 1968): 17–18.

67. Stan Lee and Jack Kirby, "The Weakest Link!" *Captain America* 1, no. 103 (July 1968): 19–20.

68. Stan Lee and Jack Kirby, "In the Name of Batroc!" *Captain America* 1, no. 105 (Sept. 1968): 20, suspension points in original.

69. Lee and Kirby, "The Hero That Was!" 18.

70. Stan Lee and Jim Steranko, "No Longer Alone," *Captain America* 1, no. 110 (Feb. 1969).

71. Albert Rodriquez, letter, *Captain America* 1, no. 110 (Feb. 1969): 23.

72. Kenneth Burke, letter, *Captain America* 1, no. 114 (June 1969): 23.

73. Rick Ellrod, letter, *Captain America* 1, no. 114 (June 1969): 23.

74. See J. Richard Stevens, "'Let's Rap with Cap': Redefining 'American Patriotism' through Popular Discourse and Letters," *Journal of Popular Culture* 44, no. 3 (2011): 606–32.

75. Stan Lee and Gene Colan, "The Coming of the Falcon," *Captain America* 1, no. 117 (Sept. 1969).

76. Marvel's first *black* superhero, the Black Panther, debuted in Stan Lee and Jack Kirby, "The Black Panther," *The Fantastic Four* 1, no. 52 (July 1966). Predating the Falcon by three years, the Panther was the king of the fictional African nation Wakanda. In addition, although African American scientist Bill Foster was introduced in *The Avengers* number 32 in 1966, he didn't become a superhero until 1975 in *Luke Cage, Power Man* number 24.

77. Stan Lee and Gene Colan, "Mission: Stamp Out Hell's Angels," *Captain America* 1, no. 128 (Aug. 1970).

78. For an extended discussion of the imagery of the motorcycle in this transition, see J. Richard Stevens, "Easy Riding: The Liberalization of Captain America through Motorcycle Journey," *International Journal of Motorcycle Studies* 8, no. 2 (Fall 2012): 1–27.

79. Stan Lee and Gene Colan, "Up against the Wall," *Captain America* 1, no. 130 (Oct. 1970): 7.

80. Ibid., 15.

81. Stan Lee and Gene Colan, "They Call Him—Stone Face!" *Captain America and the Falcon* 1, no. 134 (Feb. 1971).

82. MacDonald and MacDonald, "Sold American," 253.

5. The Liberal Crusader (1969–1979)

1. Jack Kerouac, *On The Road* (New York: Viking Press, 1957).

2. Frank Robbins and Irv Novick, "One Bullet Too Many," *Batman* 1, no. 217 (Dec. 1969).

3. Mike Gold, "Crisis on Silver Age Earth: The Year (or so) the Future Started," *Alter Ego* 3, no. 32 (Jan. 2004): 11.

4. Herb Trimpe, *The Hulk* (cover art), *Rolling Stone* 1, no. 91 (Sept. 1971).

5. Ted White, "Stan Lee Meets [Castle of] Frankenstein," *Alter Ego* 3, no. 74 (Dec. 2007): 14, suspension points in original.

6. Quoted in Jim Amash, "'I Let People Do Their Jobs!': A Conversation with Vince Fago—Artist, Writer, and Third Editor-in-Chief of Timely/Marvel Comics," *Alter Ego* 3, no. 11 (Nov. 2001): 15.

7. Lee and Colan, "The Coming of the Falcon."

8. Lee and Colan, "They Call Him—Stone Face!"

9. Lee and Kirby, "Sgt. Fury and His Howling Commandos."

10. Stan Lee and Don Heck, "The Sign of the Serpent!" *The Avengers* 1, no. 32 (Sept. 1966).

11. Stan Lee and John Romita, "In the Clutches of . . . the Kingpin!" *The Amazing Spider-Man* 1, no. 51 (Aug. 1967).

12. Stan Lee and John Romita, "The Night of the Prowler," *The Amazing Spider-Man* 1, no. 78 (Sept. 1969).

13. Stan Lee and Gene Colan, "Brother Take My Hand," *Daredevil* 1, no. 47 (Dec. 1969).

14. Lee and Kirby, "The Black Panther."

15. Mike Bourne, "Stan Lee, the Marvel Bard: An Interview Conducted by Mike Bourne, 1970," *Alter Ego* 3, no. 74 (Dec. 2007): 30.

16. Steve Englehart and Sal Buscema, "The Falcon Fights Alone," *Captain America and the Falcon* 1, no. 154 (Oct. 1972): 6.

17. Stan Lee and John Romita, "The Badge and Betrayal!" *Captain America and the Falcon* 1, no. 139 (July 1971).

18. Steve Englehart and Sal Buscema, " . . . If He Loseth His Soul," *Captain America and the Falcon* 1, no. 161 (May 1973): 15.

19. Gerry Conway and Sal Buscema, "All the Colors . . . of Evil!" *Captain America and the Falcon* 1, no. 149 (May 1972): 11, suspension points in original.

20. Dennis O'Neil and Neal Adams, "Earthquake Beware My Power," *Green Lantern/Green Arrow* 1, no. 87 (Dec. 1971–Jan. 1972): 7.

21. Gary Friedrich and John Romita, "Power to the People!" *Captain America and the Falcon* 1, no. 143 (Nov. 1971): 33.

22. Gary Friedrich and John Romita, "Hydra over All," *Captain America and the Falcon* 1, no. 144 (Dec. 1971): 13–14, suspension points in original.

23. Zack Smith, "The Nomad Saga: Englehart and Buscema on Captain America's Identity Crisis," *Back Issue* 1, no. 20 (Feb. 2007): 17.

24. Will Jacobs and Gerard Jones, *The Comic Book Heroes: From the Silver Age to the Present* (New York: Crown, 1985), 129.

25. Steve Englehart and Sal Buscema, "The Incredible Origin of the Other Captain America," *Captain America and the Falcon* 1, no. 155 (Nov. 1972).

26. Englehart and Buscema, "The Falcon Fights Alone," 3.

27. Ibid., 5.

28. Dittmer, "Retconning America," 44–45.

29. Steve Englehart and Sal Buscema, "Two into One Won't Go," *Captain America and the Falcon* 1, no. 156 (Dec. 1972).

30. Dittmer, "Retconning America," 48–49.

31. Roger McKenzie, Michael Fleischer, Sal Buscema, and Don Perlin, "Death Dive," *Captain America* 1, no. 236 (Aug. 1979).

32. Steve Englehart and Sal Buscema, "Beware of Serpents," *Captain America and the Falcon* 1, no. 163 (July 1973).

33. Ibid., 28, suspension points in original.

34. Steve Englehart, letter response, *Captain America and the Falcon* 1, no. 169 (Jan. 1974): 19.

35. Steve Englehart, Steve Gerber, and Sal Buscema, "Veni, Vidi, Vici, Viper!" *Captain America and the Falcon* 1, no. 157 (Jan. 1973): 21, suspension points in original.

36. Englehart and Buscema, "Beware of Serpents," 6, suspension points in original.

37. J. Y. Smith, "H. R. Haldeman Dies," *Washington Post*, Nov. 13, 1993, at http://www.washingtonpost.com/ac2/wp-dyn?pagename=article&contentId=A99231-1993Nov13, accessed May 5, 2008.

38. Steve Englehart, Mike Friedrich, and Sal Buscema, "When a Legend Dies!" *Captain America and the Falcon* 1, no. 169 (Jan. 1974): 11.

39. Steve Englehart and Sal Buscema, " . . . Before the Dawn!" *Captain America and the Falcon* 1, no. 175 (July 1974): 32.

40. Skidmore and Skidmore, "More Than Mere Fantasy," 91.

41. Smith, "The Nomad Saga," 17.

42. Ibid., 18.

43. Steve Englehart and Frank Robbins, "Nomad: No More!" *Captain America and the Falcon* 1, no. 183 (Mar. 1975): 30–32, suspension points in original.

44. Steve Englehart and Herb Trimpe, "Cap's Back!" *Captain America and the Falcon* 1, no. 184 (Apr. 1975): 10–11.

45. Steve Englehart, John Warner, and Frank Robbins, "Mind Cage," *Captain America and the Falcon* 1, no. 186 (June 1975): 14.

46. Steve Englehart and Frank Robbins, "Scream the Scarlet Skull!" *Captain America and the Falcon* 1, no. 185 (May 1975): 6, suspension points in original.

47. Shannon E. Riley, "The Man Who Saved the Justice League of America: Writer Steve Englehart Brings Drama, Discord, and Deceit to DC's Premier Super-Team," *Back Issue* 1, no. 45 (Dec. 2010): 14.

48. Quoted in Jerry Boyd, "Black Marvels: A Look at the House of Ideas' Black Superheroes of the 1970s," *Back Issue* 1, no. 8 (Feb. 2005): 19.

49. Bill Mantlo and Frank Robbins, "The Trial of the Falcon," *Captain America and the Falcon* 1, no. 191 (Nov. 1975): 6.

50. Ibid., 10.

51. Englehart, Warner, and Robbins, "Mind Cage," 2.

52. Adilifu Nama, *Super Black: American Pop Culture and Black Superheroes* (Austin: Univ. of Texas Press, 2011), 77.

53. Jeffrey A. Brown, *Black Superheroes, Milestone Comics, and Their Fans* (Jackson: Univ. of Mississippi Press, 2001), 20.

54. Quoted in Michael Aushenker, "Red, White, Blue, Black, and Proud! Captain America and the Falcon," *Back Issue* 1, no. 22 (June 2007): 28.

55. Quoted in Zack Smith, "Brubaker and Casey's Captain America Influences," *Back Issue* 1, no. 20 (Feb. 2007): 24.

56. Quoted in ibid.

57. Stan Lee, John Romita, and Jim Mooney, "Crisis on Campus," *The Amazing Spider-Man* 1, no. 68 (Jan. 1969).

58. Stan Lee and Gil Kane, "And Now the Goblin," *The Amazing Spider-Man* 1, no. 96 (May 1971); Stan Lee and Gil Kane, "In the Grip of the Goblin," *The Amazing Spider-Man* 1, no. 97 (June 1971); Stan Lee and Gil Kane, "The Goblin's Last Gasp," *The Amazing Spider-Man* 1, no. 98 (July 1971).

59. Hubert H. Crawford, *Crawford's Encyclopedia of Comic Books* (Middle Village, NY: Jonathan David, 1978), 345.

60. Dennis O'Neil and Neal Adams, *Green Lantern/Green Arrow* 1, no. 1 (2004); Dennis O'Neil and Neal Adams, *Green Lantern/Green Arrow* 1, no. 2 (2004).

61. Jack Kirby, "The Madbomb: Screamer in the Brain!" *Captain America and the Falcon* 1, no. 193 (Jan. 1976).

62. Ro, *Tales to Astonish*, 183.

63. Jack Kirby, "Dawn's Early Light," *Captain America and the Falcon* 1, no. 200 (Aug. 1976).

64. Ro, *Tales to Astonish*, 185.

65. Jack Kirby, "The Trojan Horde," *Captain America and the Falcon* 1, no. 194 (Feb. 1976): 10–11, suspension points in original.

66. Kirby, "Dawn's Early Light," 11, suspension points in original.

67. Roy Thomas, Dan Glut, and John Buscema, "The Search for Steve Rogers," *Captain America and the Falcon* 1, no. 217 (Jan. 1978).

68. Stan Lee and Gene Colan, "To Stalk the Spider-Man," *Captain America and the Falcon* 1, no. 137 (May 1971): 3.

69. Ibid., 2.

70. Stan Lee and John Romita, "The Unholy Alliance," *Captain America and the Falcon* 1, no. 141 (Sept. 1971): 7.

71. Ibid.

72. Friedrich and Romita, "Hydra over All," 7, suspension points in original.

73. Gary Friedrich, Gil Kane, and John Romita, "Skyjacked!" *Captain America and the Falcon* 1, no. 145 (Jan. 1972).

74. Roy Thomas, "World War II Forever (but Only in Comic Books)," *Alter Ego* 3, no. 20 (Jan. 2003): 3.

75. Roy Thomas and Sal Buscema, "When Strikes the Squadron Sinister," *The Avengers* 1, no. 70 (Nov. 1969).

76. Roy Thomas and Sal Buscema, "Endgame!" *The Avengers* 1, no. 71 (Dec. 1969).

77. Roy Thomas and Frank Robbins, "The Coming of the Invaders," *Giant-Size Invaders* 1, no. 1 (June 1975): 14.

78. Roy Thomas, George Tuska, and Pablo Marcus, "The Way It REALLY Was," *Captain America and the Falcon* 1, no. 215 (Nov. 1977): 10.

79. Roy Thomas, Frank Robbins, and Frank Springer, "God Save the King," *The Invaders* 1, no. 15 (Apr. 1977): 2.

80. Roy Thomas, Frank Robbins, and Frank Springer, "Enter: The Mighty Destroyer!" *The Invaders* 1, no. 18 (July 1977): 17.

81. Roy Thomas and Frank Robbins, "Blitzkrieg at Bermuda," *The Invaders* 1, no. 3 (Nov. 1975): 14.

82. Steve Gerber, Sal Buscema, John Tartag, and Mike Esposito, "Devastation," *Captain America* 1, no. 225 (Sept. 1978).

83. Fredric C. Bartlett, *Remembering* (Cambridge: Cambridge Univ. Press, 1932), cited in Cohen, *Memory in the Real World*, 77.

84. Robert A. Bjork, "The Updating of Human Memory," in *The Psychology of Learning and Motivation: Advances in Research and Theory*, 12th ed., ed. Gordon H. Bower (New York: Academic Press, 1978), 235–39.

85. Halbwachs, *The Collective Memory*, 69.

86. "Mystery of the Atomic Boomerang."

87. "Tojo's Terror Masters," 17.

88. Simon and Kirby, "Meet Captain America," 7.

89. "The Saboteur of Death," 4.

90. Klock, *How to Read Superhero Comics and Why*, 13.

6. The Hypercommercialized Leader (1979–1990)

1. Michael Thomas, "Jim Shooter Interview: Part 1," *Comic Book Resources*, Oct. 6, 2000, http://www.comicbookresources.com/print.php?type=ar&id=147, accessed June 12, 2012.

2. Quoted in Dwight Jon Zimmerman, "The Marvel Reference Library," *Marvel Age* 1, no. 39 (June 1986): 18–21.

3. Quoted in ibid., 20–21.

4. Peter Sanderson, "Guidebook to the Cosmos: *The Official Handbook of the Marvel Universe*," *Marvel Age* 1, no. 1 (Apr. 1983): 13.

5. Mark Gruenwald, "Just How Strong Is . . . Spider-Man?" *The Amazing Spider-Man Annual* 1, no. 15 (1981): 39–41.

6. Zimmerman, "The Marvel Reference Library," 20.

7. Danny Fingeroth, "The Marvel Saga: The Official History of the Marvel Universe," *Marvel Age* 1, no. 32 (Nov. 1985): 27.

8. Quoted in Zimmerman, "The Marvel Reference Library," 20.

9. "What Is *Marvel Age?*" *Marvel Age* 1, no. 1 (Apr. 1983): 1.

10. "Announcing: Marvel Press!" *Marvel Age* 1, no. 10 (Jan. 1984): 6.

11. Carol Kalish and Mark Lerer, "The Origins of Marvel Press," *Marvel Age* 1, no. 11 (Feb. 1984): 14.

12. Steve Saffel, "Introducing the Marvel Super Heroes Role Playing Game," *Marvel Age* 1, no. 18 (Sept. 1984): 18–20.

13. Dwight Jon Zimmerman, "The Transformers," *Marvel Age* 1, no. 17 (Aug. 1984): 8.

14. Dwight Jon Zimmerman, "The G.I. Joe File," *Marvel Age* 1, no. 15 (June 1984): 8.

15. Quoted in Dwight Jon Zimmerman, "G.I. Joe Update," *Marvel Age* 1, no. 20 (Nov. 1984): 21.

16. Quoted in Zimmerman, "The Transformers," 8.

17. Sholly Fisch, "Star Spotlight: He-Man and the Masters of the Universe," *Marvel Age* 1, no. 38 (Apr. 1986): 18.

18. "Newswatch," *Marvel Age* 1, no. 11 (Feb. 1984): 6.

19. Mark Lerer, "Are You Ready for Marvel Super Heroes Secret Wars?" *Marvel Age* 1, no. 12 (Mar. 1984): 10.

20. "Postscript: A Visit with Jim Shooter," *Marvel Age* 1, no. 20 (Nov. 1984): 14.

21. Dwight Jon Zimmerman, "The MARVEL AGE Interview: Jim Shooter," *Marvel Age* 1, no. 27 (June 1985): 10.

22. Ibid., 12.

23. Quoted in Sholly Fisch, "The Return of Frank Miller," *Marvel Age* 1, no. 37 (Mar. 1986): 19.

24. Sholly Fisch, "The Punisher," *Marvel Age* 1, no. 33 (Dec. 1985): 14.

25. Sholly Fisch, "The Punisher," *Marvel Age* 1, no. 51 (June 1987): 18.

26. Quoted in Daniels, *Marvel*, 210.

27. Voger, *The Dark Age*, 6.

28. Joe Queenan, "Drawing on the Dark Side," *New York Times Magazine*, Apr. 30, 1989, 32.

29. "The Top Ten," *Marvel Age* 1, no. 63 (June 1988): 8.

30. "Marvel Top Twenty," *Marvel Age* 1, no. 85 (Feb. 1990): 8.

31. Steve Bierly, letter, *Captain America* 1, no. 293 (May 1984): 23.

32. Richard E. Homburger, letter, *Captain America* 1, no. 293 (May 1984): 23.

33. Thomas, Tuska, and Marcus, "The Way It REALLY Was," 6.

34. Chris Claremont, Roger McKenzie, Sal Buscema, and Don Perlin, "From the Ashes," *Captain America* 1, no. 237 (Sept. 1979).

35. Matt Kaufman, letter, *Captain America* 1, no. 241 (Jan. 1980): 31; Matt Kaufman, letter, *Captain America* 1, no. 246 (June 1980): 31; Lon Levy, letter, *Captain America* 1, no. 280 (Apr. 1983): 24.

36. Roger McKenzie and Don Perlin, "The Way of All Flesh!" *Captain America* 1, no. 244 (Apr. 1980): 11.

37. J. M. DeMatteis and Paul Neary, "An American Christmas," *Captain America* 1, no. 292 (Apr. 1984): 9.

38. Mark Gruenwald and Paul Neary, "Nomad Madcap Cap . . . ," *Captain America* 1, no. 309 (Sept. 1985): 11.

39. Mark Gruenwald and Paul Neary, "Serpents of the World Unite," *Captain America* 1, no. 310 (Oct. 1985).

40. Mark Gruenwald and Paul Neary, "Working . . . ," *Captain America* 1, no. 311 (Nov. 1985): 6, suspension points in original.

41. Jim Shooter, David Michelini, and Mike Zeck, "Rite of Passage!" *Captain America* 1, no. 259 (July 1981).

42. Mark Gruenwald and Paul Neary, "Justice Is Served?" *Captain America* 1, no. 318 (June 1986).

43. Mark Gruenwald and Paul Neary, "Deface the Nation," *Captain America* 1, no. 312 (Dec. 1985).

44. Nancy Leigh Brown, "The MARVEL AGE Interview: Mike Carlin," *Marvel Age* 1, no. 23 (Feb. 1985): 20.

45. Adam Phillips, "The New Talent Department," *Marvel Age* 1, no. 30 (Sept. 1985): 14, 15.

46. Thomas, Glut, and Buscema, "The Search for Steve Rogers."

47. Steve Gerber, Sal Buscema, John Tartag, and Mike Esposito, "Monumental Menace," *Captain America and the Falcon* 1, no. 222 (June 1978).

48. Bill Kunkel and Al Wenzel, "Deathgarden," *Marvel Team-Up* 1, no. 71 (July 1978).

49. Mark Evanier, Sal Buscema, and Dave Simons, "Sound of the Silencer," *Marvel Premiere* 1, no. 49 (Aug. 1979).

50. Roger McKenzie, Sal Buscema, John Tartag, and Mike Esposito, "A Serpent Lurks Below," *Captain America* 1, no. 228 (Dec. 1978): 10.

51. Charles K. Tagoe, letter, *Captain America* 1, no. 232 (Apr. 1979): 31.

52. David Michelinie, John Byrne, and Gene Day, "On the Matter of Heroes," *The Avengers* 1, no. 181 (Mar. 1979): 15.

53. David Michelinie and John Byrne, "The Redoubtable Return of Crusher Creel!" *The Avengers* 1, no. 183 (May 1979): 14, suspension points in original.

54. David Michelinie and John Byrne, "Death on the Hudson!" *The Avengers* 1, no. 184 (June 1979): 10.

55. David Michelinie and George Perez, "Interlude," *The Avengers* 1, no. 194 (Apr. 1980).

56. Jim Owsley, "Creating a New Limited Series: *The Falcon*," *Marvel Age* 1, no. 7 (Oct. 1983): 13.

57. Jim Owlsey and Paul Smith, "Winners and Losers!" *The Falcon* 1, no. 1 (Nov. 1983).

58. Jim Owlsey and Paul Smith, "Faith!" *The Falcon* 1, no. 3 (Jan. 1984).

59. Jim Owlsey and Paul Smith, "Resurrection!" *The Falcon* 1, no. 4 (Feb. 1984): 7.

60. Ibid., 22.

61. J. M. DeMatteis and Mike Zeck, "Mean Streets," *Captain America* 1, no. 272 (Aug. 1982).

62. J. M. DeMatteis and Mike Zeck, "Yesterday's Shadows!" *Captain America* 1, no. 275 (Nov. 1982).

63. J. M. DeMatteis and Mike Zeck, "Oh, Thus Be It Ever," *Captain America* 1, no. 278 (Feb. 1983).

64. Roger Stern and John Byrne, "Dragon Man," *Captain America* 1, no. 248 (Aug. 1980).

65. J. M. DeMatteis and Mike Zeck, "The Man Who Made a Difference!" *Captain America* 1, no. 267 (Mar. 1982): 7.

66. J. M. DeMatteis and Mike Zeck, "Peace on Earth, Good Will to Man," *Captain America* 1, no. 268 (Apr. 1982): 6.

67. J. M. DeMatteis and Sal Buscema, "Diverging," *Captain America* 1, no. 284 (Aug. 1983).

68. DeMatteis and Zeck, "Yesterday's Shadows!"

69. J. M. DeMatteis and Mike Zeck, "Of Monsters and Men," *Captain America* 1, no. 279 (Mar. 1983): 16.

70. J. M. DeMatteis and Mike Zeck, "On Your Belly You Shall Crawl and Dust You Shall Eat!" *Captain America* 1, no. 282 (June 1983): 11.

71. DeMatteis and Neary, "An American Christmas," 22.

72. J. M. DeMatteis and Mike Zeck, "Someone Who Cares!" *Captain America* 1, no. 270 (June 1982): 20–22.

73. Steve Greydanus, letter, *Captain America* 1, no. 302 (Feb. 1985): 23.

74. Gruenwald and Neary, "Working. . . ."

75. Mark Gruenwald and Paul Neary, "Creatures of Love," *Captain America* 1, no. 316 (Apr. 1986).

76. Mark Gruenwald and Paul Neary, "Death Throws," *Captain America* 1, no. 317 (May 1986): 6.

77. Howard T. Kidd, letter, *Captain America* 1, no. 323 (Nov. 1986): 23.

78. DeMatteis and Zeck, "Someone Who Cares!"

79. J. M. DeMatteis and Mike Zeck, "In Thy Image," *Captain America* 1, no. 277 (Jan. 1983).

80. DeMatteis and Zeck, "Of Monsters and Men," 19–21, suspension points in original.

81. J. M. DeMatteis and Paul Neary, "Things Fall Apart," *Captain America* 1, no. 296 (Aug. 1984): 15–16, suspension points in original.

82. Scott Lobdell and Mark Pacella, "The Walking Wounded," *Alpha Flight* 1, no. 106 (Mar. 1992).

83. J. M. DeMatteis and Mike Zeck, "Before the Fall," *Captain America* 1, no. 281 (May 1983).

84. DeMatteis and Zeck, "On Your Belly You Shall Crawl and Dust You Shall Eat!"

85. DeMatteis and Buscema, "Diverging," 8, suspension points in original.

86. Mark Gruenwald and Paul Neary, "Stop Making Sense," *Captain America* 1, no. 307 (July 1985): 3–4, suspension points in original.

87. Gruenwald and Neary, "Nomad Madcap Cap. . . ."

88. Gruenwald and Neary, "Serpents of the World Unite."

89. Mark Gruenwald and Paul Neary, "Mission: Murder MODOK," *Captain America* 1, no. 313 (Jan. 1986): 21; Mark Gruenwald and Paul Neary, "The Hard Sell," *Captain America* 1, no. 315 (Mar. 1986).

90. Mark Gruenwald and Paul Neary, "Overkill," *Captain America* 1, no. 319 (July 1986): 14–15, suspension points in original.

91. Mark Gruenwald and Kieron Dwyer, "The Snake Pit," *Captain America* 1, no. 342 (June 1988).

92. Denny O'Neil and Luke McDonnell, "Firebrand's Revenge," *Iron Man* 1, no. 172 (July 1983).

93. David Michelinie, Mark Bright, and Bob Layton, "Who Guards the Guardsmen?" *Iron Man* 1, no. 228 (Mar. 1988): 21.

94. Mark Gruenwald and Kieron Dwyer, "Break-In," *Captain America* 1, no. 341 (May 1988): 1–8.

95. Jim Shooter and Don Heck, "The War Begins," *Secret Wars* 1, no. 1 (May 1984): 14.

96. Ibid., 17.

97. Jim Shooter and Don Heck, "Prisoners of War!" *Secret Wars* 1, no. 2 (June 1984): 14.

98. Jim Shooter and Don Heck, "Tempest without, Crisis within!" *Secret Wars* 1, no. 3 (July 1984): 8, suspension points in original.

99. Jim Shooter and Don Heck, "The Battle of the Four Armies!" *Secret Wars* 1, no. 5 (Sept. 1984): 16.

100. Ibid., 18.

101. Jim Shooter and Don Heck, "Invasion!" *Secret Wars* 1, no. 8 (Dec. 1984): 20, suspension points in original.

102. Jim Shooter and Don Heck, "Death to the Beyonder!" *Secret Wars* 1, no. 10 (Feb. 1985): 8–9, suspension points in original.

103. Ibid., 22, suspension points in original.

104. Jim Shooter and Don Heck, " . . . Nothing to Fear," *Secret Wars* 1, no. 12 (Apr. 1985): 28, suspension points in original.

105. Charles David Haskell, letter, *Marvel Age* 1, no. 20 (Nov. 1984): 11; Henry Kujawa, letter, *Marvel Age* 1, no. 20 (Nov. 1984): 12.

106. Mark Gruenwald and Paul Neary, "The Body in Question," *Captain America* 1, no. 308 (Aug. 1985): 20.

107. Kaufman, letter, June 1980, 31.

108. Roger Stern, letter response, *Captain America* 1, no. 246 (June 1980): 31.

109. Roger Stern and John Byrne, "Cap for President!" *Captain America* 1, no. 250 (Oct. 1980): 31, suspension points in original.

110. Thomas, Tuska, and Marcus, "The Way It REALLY Was."

111. J. M. DeMatteis and Ron Wilson, "The Shadows of the Past," *Captain America Annual* 1, no. 6 (1982).

112. DeMatteis and Zeck, "The Man Who Made a Difference!" 4.

113. Ibid., 6.

114. Ibid., 22.

115. Ibid., 31.

116. DeMatteis and Zeck, "Peace on Earth, Good Will to Man," 6, suspension points in original.

117. David Anthony Kraft and Alan Kupperberg, "The Mystery X," *Captain America* 1, no. 271 (July 1982).

118. Peter David and Sal Velluto, "High Heat," *Captain America Goes to War against—Drugs* 1, no. 1 (1990).

119. DeMatteis and Zeck, "Yesterday's Shadows!" 7.

120. Ibid., 20.

121. DeMatteis and Zeck, "In Thy Image."

122. J. M. DeMatteis and Mike Zeck, "Sermon of the Straw," *Captain America* 1, no. 280 (Apr. 1983): 7, suspension points in original.

123. Ibid., 13.

124. Ibid., 20.

125. DeMatteis and Neary, "An American Christmas," 18, suspension points in original.

126. Ibid., 22.

127. Ibid., suspension points in original.

128. "The Riddle of the Totem Pole," 12.

129. J. M. DeMatteis and Paul Neary, "Das Ende," *Captain America* 1, no. 300 (Dec. 1984): 20, suspension points in original.

130. Michael Hartford, letter, *Captain America* 1, no. 304 (Apr. 1985): 23.

131. Mark Gruenwald, "Changing of the Guard," *Captain America* 1, no. 306 (June 1985): 23, emphasis and suspension points in original.

132. Peter Sanderson, "A Tale of Two Captains: An Interview with Mark Gruenwald on Captain America," *Amazing Heroes* 1, no. 146 (Aug. 1, 1988): 21–29.

133. Millard P. Griffin Jr., letter, *Captain America* 1, no. 310 (Oct. 1985): 23.

134. Mark Gruenwald and Paul Neary, "The Little Bang Theory," *Captain America* 1, no. 320 (Aug. 1986): 15.

135. Mark Gruenwald, "Mark's Remarks," *Marvel Age* 1, no. 84 (Jan. 1990): 9.

136. Gruenwald and Neary, "Working . . . ," 21.

137. Gruenwald and Neary, "Deface the Nation," 13.

138. Ibid., 18–19, suspension points in original.

139. Ibid., 22.

140. Paul Weissburg, letter, *Captain America* 1, no. 318 (June 1986): 23.

141. Norman Breyfogle, letter, *Captain America* 1, no. 318 (June 1986): 23, emphasis in original.

142. Mark Gruenwald and Paul Neary, "Ultimatum," *Captain America* 1, no. 321 (Sept. 1986): 17.

143. Ibid.

144. Mark Gruenwald, Paul Neary, and John Beatty, "Clashing Symbols," *Captain America* 1, no. 327 (Mar. 1987).

145. Frank Miller and David Mazucchelli, "God and Country," *Daredevil* 1, no. 232 (July 1986); Frank Miller and David Mazucchelli, "Armageddon," *Daredevil* 1, no. 233 (Aug. 1986).

146. Mark Gruenwald and Paul Neary, "Soldier, Soldier," *Captain America* 1, no. 331 (July 1987).

147. Mark Gruenwald and Paul Neary, "The Choice," *Captain America* 1, no. 332 (Aug. 1987): suspension points in original.

148. Mark Gruenwald and Kieron Dwyer, "Power Struggle," *Captain America* 1, no. 338 (Feb. 1988).

149. Jim Snapp, letter, *Captain America* 1, no. 339 (Mar. 1988): 23.

150. Mark Gruenwald and Tom Morgan, "Natural Calling," *Captain America* 1, no. 336 (Dec. 1987): 7.

151. Sanderson, "A Tale of Two Captains," 23.

152. Ibid., 23–24.

153. Mark Gruenwald and Kieron Dwyer, "Don't Tread on Me," *Captain America* 1, no. 344 (Aug. 1988).

154. Mark Gruenwald and Kieron Dwyer, "Surrender," *Captain America* 1, no. 345 (Sept. 1988).

155. Mark Gruenwald and Kieron Dwyer, "Out of Commission," *Captain America* 1, no. 348 (Dec. 1988): 8–9, suspension points in original.

156. Mark Gruenwald and Kieron Dwyer, "Seeing Red," *Captain America* 1, no. 350 (Feb. 1989): 43.

157. Tom DeFalco and Ron Frenz, "The Hero and the Hammer," *The Mighty Thor* 1, no. 390 (Apr. 1988): 15, 21.

158. Abelardo D. Flores, letter, *Captain America* 1, no. 354 (June 1980): 31.

159. Gerber et al., "Devastation."

160. Mike W. Bar, Frank Springer, and Pablo Marcos, "Fear Grows in Brooklyn!" *Captain America* 1, no. 241 (Jan. 1980): 14, 15, 23.

161. Ibid., 27.

162. Ibid., suspension points in original.

163. Roger Stern and John Byrne, "Blood on the Moors," *Captain America* 1, no. 254 (Feb. 1981): 27.

164. Ibid., italics added to sound effect.

165. Roger Stern and John Byrne, "The Living Legend," *Captain America* 1, no. 255 (Mar. 1981). And see Peter Sanderson, "Book XII: A Legend Reborn!" *Marvel Saga* 1, no. 12 (Nov. 1986): 22–24, for the comparison.

166. J. M. DeMatteis and Paul Neary, "Field of Vision," *Captain America* 1, no. 293 (May 1984): 18.

167. Gruenwald and Neary, "Overkill."

168. Quoted in Daniels, *Batman*, 209.

169. Gruenwald and Neary, "The Little Bang Theory," 21.

170. Gruenwald and Neary, "Ultimatum."

171. Ibid., 4.

172. Mark Gruenwald and Paul Neary, "Super-Patriot Is Here," *Captain America* 1, no. 323 (Nov. 1986): 22.

173. Jesse Guzman, letter, *Captain America* 1, no. 327 (Mar. 1987): 23.

174. Don Daley and Daryl Edelman, letter response, *Captain America* 1, no. 327 (Mar. 1987): 23, emphasis in original.

175. Lorne Teitelbaum, letter, *Captain America* 1, no. 328 (Apr. 1987): 23.

176. Pierre Comtois, letter, *Captain America* 1, no. 328 (Apr. 1987): 23.

177. Don Daley and Daryl Edelman, letter response, *Captain America* 1, no. 328 (Apr. 1987): 23.

178. Quoted in Zimmerman, "The Marvel Reference Library," 20.

179. Peter Sanderson, "Book I: The Saga Begins . . . !" *Marvel Saga* 1, no. 1 (Dec. 1985): 3.

180. Sanderson, "Book XII: A Legend Reborn!" 22.

181. Lamont Ridgell, letter, *Captain America* 1, no. 340 (Apr. 1988): 23, emphasis in original.

182. Ralph Macchio and Marc Siry, letter response, *Captain America* 1, no. 340 (Apr. 1988): 23.

183. Harold C. Holy, letter, *Captain America* 1, no. 341 (May 1988): 23.

184. Mark Gruenwald and Kieron Dwyer, "Freedom of Speech," *Captain America* 1, no. 341 (May 1988): 10.

7. The Superficial Icon (1990–2002)

1. Stan Lee, "Stan's Soapbox," *Marvel Age* 1, no. 51 (June 1987): 15.

2. New World Pictures Ltd., *Annual Report* (Los Angeles: New World Pictures, 1986), 20.

3. Dan Raviv, *Comic Wars: How Two Tycoons Battled over the Marvel Comics Empire—and Both Lost* (New York: Broadway Books, 2002), 36.

4. Ibid.

5. Voger, *The Dark Age*, 7.

6. Wright, *Comic Book Nation*, 279.

7. Voger, *The Dark Age*, 62.

8. Will Allred, "Mark Waid Interview," *Comic Book Resources*, Mar. 5, 2002, http://www.comicbookresources.com/news/newsitem.cgi?id=969, accessed July 5, 2010.

9. Bill Peterson and Emily D. Gerstein, "Fighting and Flying: Archival Analysis of Threat, Authoritarianism, and the North American Comic Book," *Political Psychology* 26, no. 6 (2005): 893.

10. Mark Waid and Ron Garney, "Sanctuary," *Captain America* 1, no. 454 (Aug. 1996).

11. Scott Lobdell, Mark Waid, Andy Kubert, and Joe Bennett, "With Great Power . . . ," *Onslaught: Marvel Universe* 1, no. 1 (Oct. 1996).

12. Jim Valentino and Rob Liefeld, "Awaken the Thunder," *The Avengers* 2, no. 1 (Nov. 1996): 14.

13. Rob Liefeld and Jeph Loeb, "Patriotism," *Captain America* 2, no. 3 (Jan. 1997).

14. Sean Howe, *Marvel Comics: The Untold Story* (New York: HarperCollins, 2012), 388–89.

15. Jewett and Lawrence, *Captain America and the Crusade against Evil*, 6.

16. Ibid., 34–35.

17. Mark Waid and Ron Garney, "Operation: Rebirth Conclusion," *Captain America* 1, no. 448 (Feb. 1996): 39.

18. Mark Waid and Andy Kubert, "Turnabout," *Captain America* 3, no. 14 (Feb. 1999): 31, suspension points in original.

19. Mark Waid and Andy Kubert, "First Gleaming," *Captain America* 3, no. 15 (Mar. 1999): 28–29, suspension points in original.

20. Mark Waid and Andy Kubert, "Red Glare," *Captain America* 3, no. 16 (Apr. 1999): 11.

21. Mark Waid and Andy Kubert, "A Tale of Morality and Failure: Extreme Prejudice," *Captain America* 3, no. 17 (May 1999): 3.

22. Ibid., 18.

23. Harris Mankey, letter, *Captain America* 3, no. 20 (Aug. 1999): 32.

24. Jeanette Langley, letter, *Captain America* 3, no. 20 (Aug. 1999): 32, suspension points around "well" in original.

25. Jeremy Baldwin, letter, *Captain America* 3, no. 22 (Oct. 1999): 32.

26. Mark Waid and Andy Kubert, "Triumph of the Will," *Captain America* 3, no. 19 (July 1999): 4.

27. It should be noted that the terminology here intersects in an interesting manner with the 1935 Nazi propaganda film *Triumph of the Will*. Seen as an exemplar of the "Nazi religion," the film positions political struggle as an intersection of military might and religious fervor. Though it is doubtful the comic book creators themselves intended this intertextual connection, it nonetheless exists and would serve as the starting point for an interesting exploration of the functions of propaganda from two different perspectives.

28. Scot W. Myers, letter, *Captain America* 3, no. 22 (Oct. 1999): 32.

29. Steve Chun, letter, *Captain America* 3, no. 25 (Jan. 2000): 31.

30. Robert Wisham, letter, *Captain America* 3, no. 25 (Jan. 2000): 31.

31. Bob Harras and Steve Epting, "Empire's End," *The Avengers* 1, no. 347 (May 1992): 31.

32. Ibid.

33. Mark Gruenwald and Rik Levins, "After the Storm," *Captain America* 1, no. 401 (June 1992): 2.

34. Ibid., 12, suspension points in original.

35. Len Kaminski and Kevin Hopgood, "Kids These Days," *Iron Man* 1, no. 303 (Apr. 1994): 13, suspension points in original.

36. Mark Gruenwald, Dave Hoover, and Danny Bulanadi, "Twilight's Last Gleaming," *Captain America* 1, no. 443 (Sept. 1995): 20, 27.

37. Ibid., 15.

38. Mark Waid and Ron Garney, "Plan 'B,'" *Captain America* 1, no. 452 (June 1996): 16.

39. Jim Valentino and Rob Liefeld, "In Love & War," *The Avengers* 2, no. 3 (Jan. 1997): 28.

40. Walt Simonson and Michael Ryan, "Shadowbox," *The Avengers* 2, no. 9 (July 1997): 9.

41. Liefeld and Loeb, "Patriotism," 4.

42. Mark Waid and Ron Garney, "Sentinel of Liberty!" *Captain America: Sentinel of Liberty* 1, no. 1 (Sept. 1998): 17, suspension points in original.

43. Jewett and Lawrence, *Captain America and the Crusade against Evil*, 41.

44. Mark Waid and Ron Garney, "Capmania," *Captain America* 3, no. 4 (Apr. 1998): 30, suspension points in original.

45. Dan Jurgens, "A Gulf so Wide," *Captain America* 3, no. 39 (Mar. 2001): 3–6, suspension points in original.

46. Mark Gruenwald and Dave Hoover, "Fighting Chance Part One: Super Patriot Games," *Captain America* 1, no. 425 (Mar. 1994): 23, suspension points in original.

47. Dan Jurgens, "When Strikes Protocide," *Captain America* 3, no. 35 (Nov. 2000): 27, suspension points in original.

48. Dan Jurgens, "Candor," *Captain America* 3, no. 43 (July 2001): 25.

49. Tom Englehart, *The End of Victory Culture: Cold War America and the Disillusioning of a Generation* (New York: Basic Books, 1995).

50. Joanne P. Sharp, "Reel Geographies of the New World Order: Patriotism, Masculinity, and Geopolitics in Post–Cold War American Movies," in *Rethinking Geopolitics*, ed. Gearóid Ó Tuathail and Simon Dalby (New York: Routledge, 1998), 164.

51. Klaus Theweleit, *Male Fantasies, Volume One: Women, Floods, Bodies, History* (Minneapolis: Univ. of Minnesota Press, 1987).

52. Susan Jeffords, *Hard Bodies: Hollywood Masculinity in the Reagan Era* (New Brunswick, NJ: Rutgers Univ. Press, 1994), 24–25.

53. Tania Modleski, *Feminism without Women: Culture and Criticism in a "Postfeminist" Age* (New York: Routledge, 1991).

54. Susan Jeffords, "The Big Switch: Hollywood Masculinity in the Nineties," in *Film Theory Goes to the Movies*, ed. Jim Collins, Hilary Radner, and Ava Preacher Collins (New York: Routledge, 1993), 196–208.

55. Mark Gruenwald and Rik Levins, "No Man's Land," *Captain America* 1, no. 391 (Sept. 1991): 1–2.

56. Ibid., 19.

57. Mark Gruenwald and Rik Levins, "Superia Unbound," *Captain America* 1, no. 392 (Oct. 1991): 24.

58. Gruenwald and Levins, "No Man's Land," 6.

59. Doug Murray and Wayne Vansant, "Back in the Real World," *The 'Nam* 1, no. 41 (Feb. 1990).

60. John Byrne, "Darker Than Scarlet," *Avengers West Coast* 2, no. 56 (Mar. 1990): 29, suspension points in original.

61. Mark Gruenwald and Paul Neary, "The Chasm," *Captain America* 1, no. 322 (Oct. 1986): 4.

62. Englehart and Buscema, "Two into One Won't Go."

63. Mark Gruenwald and Ron Lim, "Cap's Night Out," *Captain America* 1, no. 371 (June 1990).

64. Yann Roblou, "Complex Masculinities: The Superhero in Modern American Movies," *Culture, Society, & Masculinity* 4, no. 1 (2012): 78.

65. Lynn Segal, *Slow Motion: Changing Masculinities, Changing Men* (London: Virago Press, 1990), 123.

66. Mark Gruenwald and Ron Lim, "Sold on Ice," *Captain America* 1, no. 372 (July 1990): 13, suspension points in original.

67. Mark Gruenwald and Dave Hoover, "Policing the Nation," *Captain America* 1, no. 428 (June 1994).

68. Gruenwald, Hoover, and Bulanadi, "Twilight's Last Gleaming."

69. Mark Waid and Ron Garney, "Old Soldiers Never Die," *Captain America* 1, no. 445 (Nov. 1995).

70. Stan Lee and John Buscema, *How to Draw Comics the Marvel Way* (New York: Fireside, 1978), 46.

71. Ben Morse, "The Wizard Retrospective: Captain America," *Wizard Magazine*, May 2007, 44.

72. Watson, *Male Bodies*, 43; Connell, *Masculinities*.

73. Mark Gruenwald and Dave Hoover, "The Next Generation," *Captain America* 1, no. 431 (Sept. 1994): 3, suspension points in original.

74. Mark Gruenwald and Dave Hoover, "Snake Bites," *Captain America* 1, no. 434 (Dec. 1994): 13.

75. Mark Gruenwald and Dave Hoover, "Snake, Battle, and Toll," *Captain America* 1, no. 435 (Jan. 1995): 19, suspension points in original.

76. Mark Waid and Ron Garney, "The Return of Steve Rogers, Captain America," *Captain America* 3, no. 1 (Jan. 1998): 40, suspension points in original.

77. Ibid., 26, suspension points in original.

78. Mark Waid and Ron Garney, "American Graffiti," *Captain America* 3, no. 2 (Feb. 1998): 35.

79. Mark Waid and Dale Eaglesham, "Hoaxed," *Captain America* 3, no. 7 (July 1998): 26–30, suspension points in original.

80. Mark Waid and Andy Kubert, "Plausible Deniability," *Captain America* 3, no. 13 (Jan. 1999): 3.

81. Joe Casey and Pablo Ralmondi, "Full Court Press," *Captain America Annual 1999* 1, no. 1 (Jan. 1999): 28.

82. Dan Jurgens and Andy Kubert, "Twisted Tomorrows, Part 2," *Captain America* 3, no. 26 (Feb. 2000).

83. Dan Jurgens and Andy Kubert, "Twisted Tomorrows," *Captain America* 3, no. 25 (Jan. 2000): 27.

84. Kurt Busiek and George Pérez, "Showdown," *Avengers* 3, no. 23 (Dec. 1999): 10.

85. Michelinie and Byrne, "The Redoubtable Return of Crusher Creel."

86. Kurt Busiek and George Pérez, "Harsh Judgments," *The Avengers* 3, no. 24 (Jan. 2000).

87. Kurt Busiek and George Pérez, "New Order," *The Avengers* 3, no. 27 (Apr. 2000).

88. Mark Gruenwald and Rik Levins, "To Have and to Have Not," *Captain America* 1, no. 418 (Aug. 1993): 30.

89. Mark Waid and Andy Kubert, "American Nightmare, Part 1: The Bite of Madness," *Captain America* 3, no. 9 (Sept. 1998).

90. Mark Gruenwald and Rik Levins, "Gauntlet," *Captain America* 1, no. 421 (Nov. 1993): 23.

91. Mark Waid, letter, *Captain America* 1, no. 454 (Aug. 1996): 32.

8. Captain America's Responses to the War on Terror (2002–2007)

1. Jewett and Lawrence, *Captain America and the Crusade against Evil*.

2. Summarized from ibid., 24–25.

3. Waid and Garney, "Sentinel of Liberty," 17.

4. Ann Coulter, "This Is War: We Should Invade Their Countries," *National Review*, Sept. 13, 2001, at http://old.nationalreview.com/coulter/coulter.shtml, accessed Jan. 4, 2011.

5. J. Michael Stracynski and John Romita Jr., "Stand Tall," *The Amazing Spider-Man* 2, no. 36 (Dec. 2001): 4.

6. Ibid., 14.

7. Julian E. Barnes, "Tough Call, Spider-Man," *New York Times*, Oct. 8, 2001, C9.

8. Jason Cornwell, "Line of Fire Reviews: Amazing Spider-Man #36," *Comics Bulletin*, Nov. 15, 2001, at http://www.comicsbulletin.com/reviews/100586882411959.htm, accessed Jan. 21, 2011.

9. Brian David-Marshall and Igor Kordey, "Relics," *Captain America* 3, no. 50 (Feb. 2002): 65–75.

10. Evan Dorkin and Kevin Maguire, "Stars and Stripes Forever," *Captain America* 3, no. 50 (Feb. 2002): 84–91.

11. Wright, *Comic Book Nation*, 284.

12. Mike Cotton, "We Will Never Forget," *Wizard Magazine* 1, no. 133 (Oct. 2002).

13. John Ney Rieber and John Cassaday, "Dust," *Captain America* 4, no. 1 (June 2002).

14. Jewett and Lawrence, *Captain America and the Crusade against Evil*, xiv.

15. John Ney Rieber and John Cassaday, "Above the Law," *Captain America* 4, no. 5 (Oct. 2002): 27–29, suspension points in original.

16. John Ney Rieber and John Cassaday, "Warlords, Part 3," *Captain America* 4, no. 6 (Dec. 2002): 29–31, suspension points in original.

17. Chuck Austen and Jae Lee, "The Extremists, Part 4," *Captain America* 4, no. 10 (May 2003): 31, suspension points in original.

18. John M. Murphy, "'Our Mission and Our Moment': George W, Bush and September 11th," *Rhetoric & Public Affairs* 6, no. 4 (Winter 2003): 607–32.

19. Quoted in Dan Balz and Bob Woodward, "America's Chaotic Road to War: Bush's Global Strategy Began to Take Shape in First Frantic Hours after Attack," *Washington Post*, Jan. 27, 2002.

20. Howard Zinn, "The Greatest Generation?" *The Progressive*, Oct. 2001, at http://www.progressive.org/0901/zinn1001.html, accessed Jan. 22, 2011.

21. Chuck Austen and Jae Lee, "The Extremists, Part 5," *Captain America* 4, no. 11 (June 2003): 27.

22. Robert Morales and Chris Bachalo, "Homeland, Part Two," *Captain America* 4, no. 22 (Mar. 2004).

23. Chuck Austen and Jae Lee, "Ice, Part 2," *Captain America* 4, no. 13 (July 2003): 31.

24. Chuck Austen and Jae Lee, "Ice, Part 3," *Captain America* 4, no. 14 (Aug. 2003): 24.

25. Geoff Johns and Olivier Coipel, "Infections," *The Avengers* 3, no. 66 (June 2003): 29.

26. Geoff Johns and Olivier Coipel, "The Great Escape," *The Avengers* 3, no. 69 (Sept. 2003): 20.

27. Ibid., 28, suspension points in original.

28. Geoff Johns and Olivier Coipel, "The Great Escape," *The Avengers* 3, no. 70 (Oct. 2003): 30.

29. Sam Raimi, dir., *Spider-Man* (Culver City, CA: Sony Pictures Entertainment, 2002).

30. Brian Michael Bendis, Phil Hester, and Andy Parks, *Ultimate Marvel Team-Up* 1, no. 2 (Oct. 2001): 15.

31. Ernie Estrella, "Mark Millar Interview," *PopCultureShock*, Dec. 7, 2004, at http://www.popcultureshock.com/features.php?id=874, accessed Jan. 7, 2010.

32. Andy Khouri, "MARK MILLAR, ULTIMATELY," *CBR News: The Comic Wire*, July 25, 2007, at http://www.comicbookresources.com/news/newsitem.cgi?id=11294, accessed Jan. 2, 2010.

33. Warren Ellis, Brandon Peterson, and Justin Ponsor, *Ultimate Extinction* 1, no. 2 (Apr. 2006): 7–8, suspension points in original.

34. Mark Millar and Brian Hitch, "Hulk Does Manhattan," *The Ultimates* 1, no. 5 (July 2002): 14, 24.

35. Warren Ellis, Brandon Peterson, and Justin Ponsor, *Ultimate Extinction* 1, no. 4 (June 2006): 17–18.

36. Mark Millar and Chris Bachalo, "Ultimates vs. Ultimate X-Men," *Ultimate War* 1, no. 2 (Feb. 2003): 21.

37. E. J. Dionne, *Why Americans Hate Politics* (New York: Simon & Schuster, 1991), 56.

38. As summarized in Irwin Stelzer, "Neoconservatives and Their Critics: An Introduction," in *The Neocon Reader*, ed. Irwin Stelzer (New York: Grove Press, 2004), 4.

39. Irving Kristol, "The Neoconservative Persuasion," *Weekly Standard*, Aug. 25, 2003, at http://www.weeklystandard.com/Utilities/printer_preview.asp?idArticle=3000&R=785F27881, accessed Mar. 4, 2009.

40. Ira Chernus, *Monsters to Destroy: The Neoconservative War on Terror and Sin* (Boulder, CO: Paradigm, 2006).

41. Charles Krauthammer, "The Real New World Order: The American and the Islamic Challenge," *Weekly Standard*, Nov. 12, 2001, at http://weeklystandard.com/Content/Public/Articles/000/000/000/456zfygd.asp, accessed Sept. 17, 2010.

42. David Brooks, "The Age of Conflict: Politics and Culture after September 11," *Weekly Standard*, Nov. 5, 2001, at http://weeklystandard.com/Content/Public/Articles/000/000/000/424hwkwa.asp?pg=2, accessed July 5, 2006.

43. Stephen Solarz, Richard Perle, Elliot Abrams, Richard V. Allen, Richard Armitage, Jeffrey T. Bergner, John Bolton, Stephen Bryen, Richard Burt, Frank Carlucci, et al., "Open Letter to the President," Feb. 18, 1998, at http://www.iraqwatch.org/perspectives/rumsfeld-openletter.htm, accessed June 10, 2010.

44. William Kristol and Robert Kagan, "Introduction: National Interest and Global Responsibility," in *Present Dangers: Crisis and Opportunity in American Foreign and Defense Policy*, ed. Robert Kagan (San Francisco: Encounter Books, 2000), 14.

45. Khouri, "MARK MILLAR, ULTIMATELY."

46. Mark Millar and Brian Hitch, "Thunder," *The Ultimates* 1, no. 4 (June 2002): 13–15.

47. Sam Evans, "Bryan Hitch: *The Ultimates* Visionary," *SBC Interviews*, Aug. 23, 2002, at http://www.comicsbulletin.com/features/103008397674473.htm, accessed June 17, 2012.

48. Mark Millar and Brian Hitch, "21st Century Boy," *The Ultimates* 1, no. 3 (May 2002): 4.

49. Ibid., 19.

50. Ibid., 20.

51. Mark Millar and Brian Hitch, "Homeland Security," *The Ultimates* 1, no. 7 (Sept. 2002): 10.

52. Millar and Hitch, "21st Century Boy," 20.

53. Mark Millar and Brian Hitch, "Giant Man vs. the Wasp," *The Ultimates* 1, no. 6 (Aug. 2002): 3.

54. Arune Singh, "Ultimate Sequel: Mark Millar Talks '*Ultimates 2*,'" *Comic Book Resources*, Oct. 22, 2004, at http://www.comicbookresources.com/news/printthis.cgi?id=4339, accessed Feb. 12, 2010.

55. Khouri, "MARK MILLAR, ULTIMATELY."

56. Mark Millar and Brian Hitch, "Dead Man Walking," *The Ultimates* 2 1, no. 2 (Mar. 2005): 15.

57. Mark Millar and Brian Hitch, "The Trial of the Hulk," *The Ultimates* 2 1, no. 3 (Apr. 2005): 6.

58. Mark Millar and Brian Hitch, "Wolf in the Fold," *The Ultimates* 2 1, no. 7 (Sept. 2005): 12–13, suspension points in original.

59. Estrella, "Mark Millar Interview."

60. Brian Michael Bendis, Trevor Hairsine, and Danny Miki, *Ultimate Six* 1, no. 5 (Feb. 2004): 19, suspension points in original.

61. Mark Millar and Brian Hitch, "Grand Theft America," *The Ultimates 2* 1, no. 9 (Jan. 2006): 24.

62. Ibid., 26–27.

63. Brian Michael Bendis and Butch Guice, "Ultimate Origins Part 1," *Ultimate Origins* 1, no. 1 (Aug. 2008).

64. Millar and Hitch, "21st Century Boy," 7.

65. Bendis and Guice, "Ultimate Origins Part 1," 12–13.

66. Chuck Austen and Jae Lee, "Ice, Part 5," *Captain America* 4, no. 16 (Oct. 2003): 7.

67. Millar and Hitch, "Giant Man vs. the Wasp," 11.

68. Robert Morales and Kyle Baker, *Captain America: Truth* (New York: Marvel Comics, 2009).

69. Rebecca Wanzo, "Wearing Hero-Face: Black Citizens and Melancholic Patriotism in *Truth: Red, White, and Black*," *Journal of Popular Culture* 42, no. 2 (2009): 341.

70. Ibid.

71. Robert Morales and Kyle Baker, "The Math," *Truth: Red, White, & Black* 1, no. 5 (May 2003): 9–10.

72. Robert Morales and Kyle Baker, "The Whitewash," *Truth: Red, White, & Black* 1, no. 6 (June 2003): 9–10.

73. Robert Morales and Kyle Baker, "The Blackvine," *Truth: Red, White, & Black* 1, no. 7 (July 2003): 5–8.

74. Mark Millar and Steve McNiven, "Civil War: Part One of Seven," *Civil War* 1, no. 1 (July 2006).

75. Ibid., 23.

76. Brian Michael Bendis and Howard Chaykin, "New Avengers: Disassembled, Part One," *The New Avengers* 1, no. 21 (Aug. 2006): 2, suspension points in original.

77. Ed Brubaker and Steve Epting, "Winter Kills," *Winter Soldier: Winter Kills* 1, no. 1 (Feb. 2007): 4–7, suspension points in original.

78. Ed Brubaker and Steve Epting, "The Death of the Dream," *Captain America* 5, no. 25 (Mar. 2007): 13, suspension points in original.

79. Ed Brubaker and Mike Perkins, "The Drums of War," *Captain America* 5, no. 22 (Nov. 2006): 15, suspension points in original.

80. Christos Gage and Jeremy Haun, "Rubicon," *Civil War: Casualties of War* 1, no. 1 (Feb. 2007): 15–16.

81. Mark Millar and Steve McNiven, "Civil War: Part Three of Seven," *Civil War* 1, no. 3 (Sept. 2006): 15.

82. J. Michael Stracynski and Ron Garney, "The War at Home, Part 3 of 6," *The Amazing Spider-Man* 1, no. 534 (Sept. 2006): 22.

83. Gage and Haun, "Rubicon," 26, suspension points and bold in original.

84. Mark Twain, *Glances at History* (suppressed), quoted in J. Michael Stracynski and Ron Garney, "The War at Home, Part 6 of 7," *The Amazing Spider-Man* 1, no. 537 (Dec. 2006): 12–13.

85. Ibid., 14.

86. J. Michael Stracynski and Ron Garney, "The War at Home, Part 7 of 7," *The Amazing Spider-Man* 1, no. 538 (Jan. 2007): 5.

87. Reginald Hudlin and Manuel Garcia, "Inside Man," *Black Panther* 4, no. 23 (Feb. 2007): 22.

88. For an in-depth look at the portrayal of news media in this narrative, see J. Richard Stevens, "On the Front Line: Portrayals of War Correspondents in Marvel Comics' *Civil War: Front Line*," *Image of the Journalist in Popular Culture Journal* 1, no. 1 (Fall 2009): 37–69.

89. Mark Millar and Steve McNiven, "Civil War: Part Seven of Seven," *Civil War* 1, no. 7 (Jan. 2007).

90. Paul Jenkins and Ramon Bachs, "Embedded, Part Eleven," *Civil War: Front Line* 1, no. 11 (Apr. 2007): 12, suspension points in original.

91. Ibid., 14.

92. Ibid., 16, suspension points and bold in original.

93. Brian Michael Bendis and Alex Malley, "The Confession," *Civil War: The Confession* 1, no. 1 (May 2007): 21, suspension points and bold in original.

94. Barry Glassner, *The Culture of Fear: Why Americans Are Afraid of the Wrong Things* (New York: Basic Books, 1999); Frank Füredi, *Culture of Fear: Risk-Taking and the Morality of Low Expectation* (New York: Continuum, 2002); David L. Altheide, *Creating Fear: News and the Construction of Crisis* (New York: Aldine de Gruyter, 2002).

95. Chernus, *Monsters to Destroy*.

96. Ellen Goodman, "Post–September 11 Dilemmas for Journalists," *Boston Globe*, Dec. 7, 2001.

97. Celestine Bohlen, "Think Tank; in New War on Terrorism, Words Are Weapons, Too," *New York Times*, Sept. 29, 2001, at http://query.nytimes.com/gst/fullpage.html?res=9B04EFDA163DF93AA1575AC0A9679C8B63, accessed Jan. 2, 2008.

98. Bendis and Malley, "The Confession," 6, suspension points and bold in original.

9. The Death and Rebirths of Captain America (2007–2014)

1. Damian Fowler, "Why Captain America Had to Die," *Guardian*, Mar. 12, 2007, at http://www.theguardian.com/books/booksblog/2007/mar/12/whycaptainamericahadtodie, accessed Apr. 4, 2007.

2. Ari Emanuel, "Did Bush and Cheney Kill Captain America?" *Huffington Post*, Mar. 8, 2007, at http://www.huffingtonpost.com/ari-emanuel/did-bush-and-cheney-kill-_b_42967.html, accessed Apr. 4, 2007.

3. Cited in Bryant Jordan, "Captain America, 89; Defender of Freedom," *Navy Times*, Mar. 14, 2007, at http://www.navytimes.com/entertainment/books/life_captain america_obit070314/, accessed May 12, 2007.

4. Molly Rebuttal, "Captain America's Death a Bush Indictment?" *blonde sagacity*, Mar. 12, 2007, at http://mobyrebuttal.blogspot.com/2007/03/captain-americas-death -bush-indictment.html, accessed Apr. 4, 2007.

5. Quoted in Ethan Sacks, "Captain America Killed! Marvel Comic Book Hero Shot Dead by Sniper," *New York Daily News*, Mar. 9, 2007, at http://www.nydailynews .com/entertainment/music-arts/captain-america-killed-article-1.217626, accessed Mar. 10, 2007.

6. Quoted in Gustines, "Captain America Is Dead."

7. For the view from the left, see aghrivaine, "Captain America: Death of Liberty—a Eulogy," *Quotidian Loveliness*, Mar. 9, 2007, at http://aghrivaine.livejournal.com/538118 .html, accessed Apr. 4, 2007. For the view from the right, see Wordsmith from Nantucket, "Breaking News: Captain America Assassinated! (as in: 'Character Assassination')," *Sparks from the Anvil*, Mar. 8, 2007, at http://hammeringsparksfromtheanvil.blogspot.com/2007 /03/breaking-news-captain-america-dead.html, accessed Apr. 4, 2007.

8. Edward Douglas, "Marvel Studios Sets Four More Release Dates!" *SuperHeroHype*, May 5, 2008, at http://www.superherohype.com/features/articles/96489-mar vel-studios-sets-four-more-release-dates, accessed Dec. 8, 2012; Jon Favreau, dir., *Iron Man* (Burbank, CA: Marvel Studios, 2008); Jon Favreau, dir., *Iron Man 2* (Burbank, CA: Marvel Studios, 2010); Kenneth Branagh, dir., *Thor* (Burbank, CA: Marvel Studios, 2011); Joe Johnston, dir., *Captain America: The First Avenger* (Burbank, CA: Marvel Studios, 2011); and Joss Whedon, dir., *The Avengers* (Burbank, CA: Marvel Studios, 2012).

9. Quoted in Benjamin Svetkey, "Barack Obama: Celebrity in Chief," *Entertainment Weekly*, Nov. 21, 2008, at http://www.ew.com/ew/article/0,,20241874,00.html, accessed Dec. 8, 2012.

10. Brooks Barnes and Michael Cieply, "Disney Swoops into Action, Buying Marvel for $4 Billion," *New York Times*, Aug. 31, 2009, at http://www.nytimes.com/2009/09/01 /business/media/01disney.html, accessed Sept. 1, 2009; David Goldman, "Disney to Buy Marvel for $4 Billion," *CNN Money*, Aug. 31, 2009, at http://money.cnn.com/2009/08/31 /news/companies/disney_marvel/, accessed Sept. 1, 2009.

11. Jack Mathis, *Valley of the Cliffhangers Supplement* (Chicago: Jack Mathis Advertising, 1995), 3.

12. Jim Harmon and Donald F. Glut, "The Long-Underwear Boys: 'You've Met Me, Now Meet My Fist!'" in *The Great Movie Serials: Their Sound and Fury* (New York: Routledge, 1972), 264–65.

13. Ibid., 263.

14. Richard Hurst, *Republic Studios: Beyond Poverty Row and the Majors* (New York: Scarecrow Press, 2007), 124.

15. Chuck McCleary, "How the Serials Rate," *Serial World* 1, no. 3 (1975): 6–7.

16. Howe, *Marvel Comics*, 195.

17. However, not all Marvel characters' film rights are controlled by Marvel and Disney, owing to previous licensing contract. Sony maintains the film rights to Spider-Man and Ghost Rider, and Fox holds the rights to the X-Men, Daredevil, and the Fantastic Four.

18. Cullen Bunn, Matt Fraction, Christopher Yost, and Scot Eaton, *Battle Scars* 1, no. 4 (Apr. 2012): 20.

19. Cullen Bunn, Matt Fraction, Christopher Yost, and Scot Eaton, *Battle Scars* 1, no. 5 (May 2012): 15.

20. Cullen Bunn, Matt Fraction, Christopher Yost, and Scot Eaton, *Battle Scars* 1, no. 6 (June 2012): 19.

21. Quoted in Brian Truitt, "Agent Coulson Charges into Comics with 'Battle Scars,'" *USA Today*, Apr. 24, 2012, at http://usatoday30.usatoday.com/life/comics/story/2012-04 -25/Agent-Coulson-Avengers-movie-comic-books/54508162/1, accessed May 5, 2012.

22. Brian Michael Bendis and Mark Bagley, "The Assembling," *Avengers Assemble* 1, no. 1 (May 2012).

23. Brian Michael Bendis and Mark Bagley, *Avengers Assemble* 1, no. 5 (Sept. 2012).

24. Anthony R. Mills, *American Theology, Superhero Comics, and Cinema* (New York: Routledge, 2013), 184.

25. Jonathan Hickman and Jerome Opeña, "Avengers World," *The Avengers* 5, no. 1 (Feb. 2013): 19–20.

26. Ed Brubaker and Mark Morales, "American Dreamers, Part I," *Captain America* 6, no. 1 (Sept. 2011): 11.

27. Hydra originally appeared in *Strange Tales* number 135 (Aug. 1965). Originally portrayed as a terrorist organization, it was later retconned as an outgrowth of the defeated Nazi movement under Baron Von Strucker and then was retconned to be an ancient organization that evolved over many moments of world history.

28. For example, see Brian Michael Bendis and Renato Guedes, *The Avengers* 4, no. 21 (Mar. 2012): 16; Brubaker and Morales, "American Dreamers, Part I," 2.

29. Bob Chipman, "Stars and Stripes," *Escapist Magazine*, Apr. 1, 2011, at http:// www.escapistmagazine.com/articles/view/columns/moviebob/8745-Stars-and-Stripes.3, accessed May 4, 2012.

30. Ben Morse, "The Big Questions: Ed Brubaker Addresses the Hot Topics Facing Marvel in the Wake of the Star-Spangled Avenger's Death," *Wizard Magazine*, May 2007, 27.

31. J. Michael Stracynski and Oliver Coipel, *Thor* 3, no. 11 (Nov. 2008): 9.

32. Bendis and Malley, "The Confession," 12–13.

33. Jeph Loeb and Leinil Yu, "Denial," *Fallen Son: The Death of Captain America* 1, no. 1 (June 2007); Jeph Loeb and Ed McGuinness, "Anger," *Fallen Son: The Death*

of Captain America 1, no. 2 (June 2007); Jeph Loeb and John Romita Jr., "Bargaining," *Fallen Son: The Death of Captain America* 1, no. 3 (July 2007); Jeph Loeb and David Finch, "Depression," *Fallen Son: The Death of Captain America* 1, no. 4 (July 2007); Jeph Loeb and John Cassaday, "Acceptance," *Fallen Son: The Death of Captain America* 1, no. 5 (Aug. 2007).

34. Stracynski and Coipel, *Thor* 3, no. 11.

35. Jim Krueger, Alex Ross, and Steve Sadowski, "Old Soldiers, New Wars," *Avengers/Invaders* 1, no. 1 (July 2008).

36. Brian Michael Bendis and Bill Tan, *The New Avengers* 1, no. 41 (July 2008).

37. Ed Brubaker and Steve Epting, "The Man Who Bought America: Part Three," *Captain America* 5, no. 39 (Aug. 2008); Ed Brubaker and Steve Epting, "The Man Who Bought America: Part Four," *Captain America* 5, no. 40 (Sept. 2008).

38. Paul Jenkins and Paolo Rivera, "Captain America," *Mythos: Captain America* 1, no. 1 (Aug. 2008); Jeph Loeb and Tim Sale, "It Happened One Night," *Captain America: White* 1, no. 1 (Sept. 2008).

39. Charles Knauf and Mitch Breitweiser, "Operation: Zero Point," *Captain America: Theater of War; Operation: Zero Point* 1, no. 1 (Dec. 2008); Kyle Higgins, Alec Siegel, and Agustin Padilla, "Prisoners of Duty," *Captain America: Theater of War; Prisoners of Duty* 1, no. 1 (Feb. 2010): 29.

40. Paul Jenkins and Elia Bonetti, "Ghosts of My Country," *Captain America: Theater of War; Ghosts of My Country* 1, no. 1 (Dec. 2009).

41. Paul Jenkins and Fernando Blanco, "To Soldier On," *Captain America: Theater of War; to Soldier On* 1, no. 1 (Oct. 2009).

42. David Morrell and Mitch Breitweiser, "Now You See Me, Now You Don't," *Captain America: The Chosen* 1, no. 1 (Nov. 2007).

43. David Morrell and Mitch Breitweiser, "Fear in a Handful of Dust," *Captain America: The Chosen* 1, no. 4 (Dec. 2007): 17.

44. Ibid., 21.

45. David Morrell and Mitch Breitweiser, "Multitude," *Captain America: The Chosen* 1, no. 6 (Feb. 2008): 20, 25.

46. Loeb and Romita, "Bargaining."

47. Ed Brubaker and Paco Medina, "Patriot," *Young Avengers Presents Patriot* 1, no. 1 (Mar. 2008).

48. Matt Fraction and Ariel Olivetti, "Goin' out West," *Punisher War Journal* 2, no. 6 (June 2007): 7–8.

49. Matt Fraction and Ariel Olivetti, "Blood and Sand," *Punisher War Journal* 2, no. 7 (July 2007).

50. Matt Fraction and Ariel Olivetti, "Heroes and Villains," *Punisher War Journal* 2, no. 11 (Nov. 2007).

51. Ed Brubaker, Michael Lark, and Steve Epting, "Out of Time, Part 5," *Captain America* 5, no. 5 (May 2005): 11.

52. Ed Brubaker and Steve Epting, "The Winter Soldier, Part 1 of 6," *Captain America* 5, no. 8 (Aug. 2005); Ed Brubaker and Steve Epting, "The Winter Soldier, Part 3 of 6," *Captain America* 5, no. 11 (Nov. 2005).

53. Ed Brubaker and Steve Epting, "The Winter Soldier Conclusion," *Captain America* 5, no. 14 (Feb. 2006): 16.

54. Ed Brubaker and Steve Epting, "The Death of the Dream, Part Three: White Lies," *Captain America* 5, no. 27 (Aug. 2007): 4.

55. Ed Brubaker and Steve Epting, "The Burden of Dreams, Part Three," *Captain America* 5, no. 33 (Feb. 2008).

56. Tom Leonard, "Gun-Toting Captain America Comes Back to Life," *Telegraph*, Jan. 29, 2008, at http://www.telegraph.co.uk/news/main.jhtml?xml=/news/2008/01/28/wcomic128.xml, accessed Feb. 3, 2008.

57. Ed Brubaker and Steve Epting, "The Burden of Dreams, Part Four," *Captain America* 5, no. 34 (Mar. 2008).

58. Though "William Burnside" is now known to be the name of the 1950s Captain America character, the alternative Captain America faced in the 1970s, and the Grand Director faced in the 1980s, the name "William Burnside" was not introduced until 2010 in Brubaker and Ross, "Two Americas, Part I," in issue 602 of *Captain America*.

59. Mark Gruenwald and Tom Morgan, "Baptism by Fire," *Captain America* 1, no. 335 (Nov. 1987).

60. Englehart and Buscema, "Two into One Won't Go."

61. Ed Brubaker and Luke Ross, "Two Americas, Part One," *Captain America* 5, no. 602 (Mar. 2010): 15–16.

62. Warner Todd Huston, "Marvel Comics: Captain America Says Tea Parties Are Dangerous and Racist," *Publius Forum* 8 (Feb. 2010), at http://www.publiusforum.com/2010/02/08/marvel-comics-captain-america-says-tea-parties-are-dangerous-and-racist/, accessed Mar. 12, 2010.

63. mailloux, "Tea Party Activists Beware . . . Captain America Is onto You!" *RedState*, Feb. 3, 2010, at http://www.redstate.com/mailloux/2010/02/03/tea-party-activists-beware-captain-america-is-onto-you/, accessed Mar. 14, 2008.

64. tgusa, comment, *Dr. Bulldog and Ronin*, Feb. 9, 2010, at http://doctorbulldog.wordpress.com/2010/02/09/marvel-comics-turn-tea-party-patriots-into-racist-villains/, accessed Mar. 14, 2010.

65. avideditor, comment on Joshua Rhett Miller, "Tea Party Jab to Be Zapped from Captain America Comic, Writer Says," *Avid Editor's Insights*, Feb. 9, 2010, at http://avideditor.wordpress.com/2010/02/09/captan-america-is-used-to-portray-the-tea-party-movement-as-dangerous-and-racist/, accessed Apr. 10, 2010.

66. Gsoteapartygirl, "For All You Comics Fans . . . ," *Greensboro Tax Day Tea Party*, Feb. 10, 2010, at http://gsoteaparty.wordpress.com/2010/02/10/for-all-you-comics-fans/, accessed Mar. 14, 2010.

67. Glenn Beck, "Glenn Beck: Where Are the Weathermen Now?" *GlenBeck.com*, July 28, 2010, at http://www.glennbeck.com/content/articles/article/198/43522/, accessed Aug. 4, 2010.

68. nicedeb, "Captain America Takes On the Tea-Partiers," *Nice Deb*, Feb. 8, 2010, at http://nicedeb.wordpress.com/2010/02/08/captain-america-takes-on-the-tea-partiers/, accessed Mar. 14, 2010.

69. David Weigel, "Scenes from the New American Tea Party," *Washington Independent*, Feb. 27, 2009, at http://washingtonindependent.com/31868/scenes-from-the-new-american-tea-party, accessed Mar. 14, 2010.

70. Joshua Rhett Miller, "Tea Party Jab to Be Zapped from Captain America Comic, Writer Says," *FoxNews.com*, Feb. 10, 2010, at http://www.foxnews.com/politics/2010/02/09/tea-party-reference-captain-america-removed/, accessed Apr. 14, 2010.

71. Quoted in Kiel Phegley, "Political Controversy and the Heroic Age," *Comic Book Resources*, Feb. 10, 2010, at http://www.comicbookresources.com/?page=article&id=24784, accessed Apr. 14, 2010.

72. Brendan McGuirk, "Why Marvel Owes No Apology to Captain America's 'Tea Party,'" *Comics Alliance*, Feb. 11, 2010, at http://comicsalliance.com/captain-america-tea-party-controversy/, accessed Mar. 14, 2010; Alex Boney, "Captain America's Uncomfortable Tea Party," *GutterGeek*, Feb. 2010, at http://guttergeek.com/2010/Feb.2010/capteaparty/capteaparty.html, accessed Mar. 14, 2010.

73. Ed Brubaker and Ed Guice, "Two Americas Conclusion," *Captain America* 5, no. 605 (June 2010).

74. Ed Brubaker and Ed Guice, "No Escape, Part 3," *Captain America* 5, no. 608 (Sept. 2010).

75. Ed Brubaker and Ed Guice, "The Trial of Captain America, Part 5," *Captain America* 5, no. 615 (Apr. 2011).

76. Matt Fraction and Stuart Immonen, "Fear Itself 3: The Hammer That Fell on Yancy Street," *Fear Itself* 1, no. 3 (Sept. 2011).

77. Ed Brubaker and Butch Guice, *Fear Itself Chapter 7.1: Captain America*, Jan. 2012.

78. Brian Michael Bendis and Leinil Yu, *Secret Invasion* 1, no. 8 (Jan. 2009).

79. Ed Brubaker and Bryan Hitch, "Captain America: Reborn, Part 1," *Captain America: Reborn* 1, no. 1 (Sept. 2009).

80. Ed Brubaker and Bryan Hitch, "Captain America: Reborn, Part 2," *Captain America: Reborn* 1, no. 2 (Oct. 2009): 23.

81. Ed Brubaker and Bryan Hitch, "Captain America: Reborn, Part 4," *Captain America: Reborn* 1, no. 4 (Jan. 2010): 27.

82. Ed Brubaker and Bryan Hitch, "Captain America: Reborn, Part 5," *Captain America: Reborn* 1, no. 5 (Feb. 2010).

83. Ed Brubaker and Bryan Hitch, "Captain America: Reborn, Part 6," *Captain America: Reborn* 1, no. 6 (Mar. 2010).

84. Ed Brubaker and Butch Guice, "Who Will Wield the Shield?" *Captain America: Who Will Wield the Shield?* 1, no. 1 (Feb. 2010): 25.

85. Brian Michael Bendis and Oliver Coipel, *Siege* 1, no. 1 (Mar. 2010): 22.

86. Brian Michael Bendis and Oliver Coipel, *Siege* 1, no. 3 (May 2010): 12.

87. Brian Michael Bendis and Oliver Coipel, *Siege* 1, no. 4 (June 2010).

88. Brian Michael Bendis and Alan Davis, "Brothers in Arms," *Avengers: Prime* 1, no. 5 (Feb. 2011): 25.

89. Ed Brubaker and Mike Deodato Jr., "Secret Histories, Part 1," *Secret Avengers* 1, no. 1 (July 2010): 19, suspension points in original.

90. James Asmus and Ibraim Roberson, "Escape from the Negative Zone," *Steve Rogers: Super-Soldier Annual* 1, no. 1 (June 2011): 21.

91. Nick Spencer and Scot Eaton, *Secret Avengers* 1, no. 12.1 (June 2011): 18–19, suspension points in original.

92. Ibid., 20.

93. Ibid., 22, suspension points in original.

94. Brian Michael Bendis and Bryan Hitch, "It Came from Outer Space (Knight)!" *The Avengers* 4, no. 12.1 (June 2011).

95. Rick Remender and Carlos Pacheco, *Captain America* 7, no. 14 (Feb. 2014): 11–12, suspension points in original.

96. Ed Brubaker and Mike Deodato Jr., "Eyes of the Dragon, Part 4," *Secret Avengers* 1, no. 9 (Mar. 2011).

97. Bendis and Hitch, "It Came from Outer Space (Knight)!" 13, 17.

98. Brian Michael Bendis and Walt Simonson, *The Avengers* 4, no. 25 (June 2012): 6–7, suspension points in original.

99. Jonathan Hickman and Steve Epting, "Infinity," *New Avengers* 3, no. 3 (Apr. 2013).

100. Rick Remender and Daniel Acuña, *Uncanny Avengers* 1, no. 9 (Aug. 2013): 18.

101. Brian Michael Bendis and Daniel Acuña, *The Avengers* 4, no. 24 (May 2012).

102. Rick Remender and John Romita Jr., *Captain America* 7, no. 6 (June 2013): 1, suspension points in original.

103. Hickman and Epting, "Infinity."

104. Ben McCool and Craig Rousseau, "The Star Lord," *Captain America and the Korvac Saga* 1, no. 4 (May 2011): 19.

105. Rick Remender and Patrick Zircher, "Red Light Nation," *Secret Avengers* 1, no. 21.1 (Mar. 2011): 13.

106. Rick Remender and John Cassaday, *Uncanny Avengers* 1, no. 2 (Jan. 2013): 7.

107. Rick Remender and John Cassaday, *Uncanny Avengers* 1, no. 3 (Feb. 2013): 13, suspension points in original.

108. Dan Abnett and Andy Lanning, "Like a Streak of Light," *I Am an Avenger* 1, no. 3 (Jan. 2011): 9, suspension points in original.

109. Rick Remender and John Romita Jr., *Captain America* 7, no. 10 (Oct. 2013): 7.

110. Brian Michael Bendis and John Romita Jr., "Next Avengers, Part 1," *The Avengers* 4, no. 1 (July 2009): 5–6, suspension points in original.

111. Rick Remender and John Romita Jr., *Captain America* 7, no. 8 (Aug. 2013): 13.

112. Remender and Romita, *Captain America* 7, no. 14: 3.

113. Rick Remender and Carlos Pacheco, "A Fire in the Rain," *Captain America* 7, no. 11 (Nov. 2013): 3, suspension points in original.

114. Ibid., 20.

115. Quoted in Jordan, "Captain America, 89."

116. Stern and Byrne, "Blood on the Moors," 27.

117. Ed Brubaker, Butch Guice, Howard Chaykin, Rafael Albuquerque, and Mitch Breitweiser, "Red, White, and Blue-Blood," *Captain America* 5, no. 601 (Sept. 2008).

118. Roger Scruton, *An Intelligent Person's Guide to Philosophy* (New York: Penguin Books, 1996), 8.

119. Hughes, *Myths America Lives By.*

120. Anderson, *Imagined Communities*, 33–36.

121. Deborah Spitulnik, "The Social Circulation of Media Discourse and the Mediation of Communities," *Journal of Linguistic Anthropology* 6, no. 2 (1997): 161–87.

122. For example, see Jacob Heilbrunn, "Captain America Was Us," *Los Angeles Times*, Mar. 9, 2007, at http://articles.latimes.com/2007/mar/09/opinion/oe-heilbrunn9, accessed May 10, 2010; Barb Lien-Cooper, "Captain America: A Patriot for Our Time?" *Sequential Tart* 6, no. 12 (Dec. 2003), at http://www.sequentialtart.com/archive/dec03/art_1203_7.shtml, accessed Feb. 2, 2015; Jet-Poop, "Captain America, Traitor?" *Everything2*, May 20, 2003, at http://everything2.com/title/Captain+America%252C+Traitor%253F, accessed Aug. 13, 2005.

123. Roger Cotton, comment, *Hunting Muses*, Jan. 29, 2010, at http://natewinchester.wordpress.com/2010/01/29/so-what-are-you-a-captain-of/, accessed Mar. 14, 2010.

124. Jenkins, *Textual Poachers.*

125. Jewett and Lawrence, *Captain America and the Crusade against Evil*, 6.

126. Ibid., 329–30, 9. See also "Vanguard Productions Presents THE SPIRIT OF AMERICA Print by JIM Steranko," n.d., at http://www.vanguardproductions.net/steranko/soa/, accessed June 17, 2006.

127. Jewett and Lawrence, *Captain America and the Crusade against Evil*, 42–43.

128. Anthony Russo and Joe Russo, dirs., *Captain America: Winter Soldier* (Los Angeles: Marvel Studios, 2014).

129. MacKinnon, *Representing Men.*

130. Dittmer, "The Tyranny of the Serial."

131. Morse, "The Big Questions," 30–48.

132. Howe, *Marvel Comics*, 16; Wright, *Comic Book Nation*, 35; Thomas Andrae, *Creators of the Superheroes* (Neshannock, PA: Hermes Press, 2011), 115; Ro, *Tales to Astonish*, 1–2.

133. Quoted in Bryant Jordan, "Hero vs. Hero: Civil War Breaks Out in the Marvel Universe!" *Army Times*, June 26, 2006, at http://www.armytimes.com/legacy/new/0-ARMYPAPER-1873086.php, accessed Feb. 2, 2011.

134. Rick Remender and Nic Klein, "Super-Soldier No More," *Captain America* 7, no. 21 (Aug. 2014).

135. Sam Wilson briefly wore the Captain America uniform in Mark Waid's series *Captain America: Sentinel of Liberty*, numbers 8 and 9. The story, which appeared in 1999, was retroactively set in the 1970s adventures featuring Cap and the Falcon. See Mark Waid and Cully Hamner, "Flashpoint," *Captain America: Sentinel of Liberty* 1, no. 8 (Apr. 1999); Mark Waid and Dale Braithwaite, "Back in Black," *Captain America: Sentinel of Liberty* 1, no. 9 (May 1999).

136. Susan Miller and Greg Rode, "The Movie You See, the Movie You Don't: How Disney Do's that Old Time Derision," in *From Mouse to Mermaid: The Politics of Film, Gender, and Culture*, ed. Elizabeth Bell, Lynda Haas, and Laura Sells (Bloomington: Indiana Univ. Press, 1995), 86.

137. Elizabeth Bell, Lynda Haas, and Laura Sells, "Introduction: Walt's in the Movies," in *From Mouse to Mermaid*, ed. Bell, Haas, and Sells, 7.

138. Stephen M. Fjellmann, *Vinyl Leaves: Walt Disney World and America* (Boulder, CO: Westview, 1992), 59.

139. Henry Giroux, *The Mouse That Roared: Disney and the End of Innocence* (New York: Rowman & Littlefield, 1999), 41, 109.

140. Nicholas Sammond, *Babes in Tomorrowland: Walt Disney and the Making of the American Child, 1930–1960* (Durham, NC: Duke Univ. Press, 2005), 381.

141. Ibid., 23.

142. J. Richard Stevens, "Ultimate Race Presentations: Racial Adaptations of Marvel's Falcon and Luke Cage in 2013 Disney Superhero Cartoons," paper presented at the Annual National Meeting of the Popular Culture Association/American Culture Association, Chicago, Apr. 17, 2014.

143. Jason Dittmer, *Captain America and the Nationalist Superhero* (Philadelphia: Temple Univ. Press, 2013), 134.

144. Quoted in Bell, Haas, and Sells, "Introduction," 1.

145. Janet Wasko, *Understanding Disney: The Manufacture of Fantasy* (Cambridge, UK: Polity Press, 2001).

146. Quoted in Max Knudson, "Piracy Battle Not Child's Play for Disney; Company Zealously Guards Rights to Mickey, Goofy, Donald, and the Gang," *Deseret News*,

Apr. 28, 1989, at http://www.deseretnews.com/article/44429/PIRACY-BATTLE-NOT
-CHILDS-PLAY-FOR-DISNEY.html?pg=all, accessed July 5, 2013.

147. It is well known among media scholars who study popular culture that Disney
tightly regulates and sometimes outright opposes scholarship perceived to be critical of
its corporate culture, its processes of labor, or even its characters. I feel I would be remiss
if I did not recount my own struggles to involve Marvel in the production of this book.
Though I had gained the rights to use Captain America images from comic books in my
previously published works, when it came time to clear the images for this book, I met
significant and unexpected resistance from Marvel.

In the past, Marvel's primary concerns were the use of characters in cover illustrations, derogatory portrayals of the characters, and the promotional use of characters. During the permissions process, I quickly agreed not to feature an official image of Captain
America or any Marvel characters on the cover of the book when objections were raised.
Then came a request to reduce the number of illustrations from forty-four to ten and to
resubmit my proposal. Then arrived an objection to the terms of the rights requested.
After adjustments and a resubmission, Marvel then responded with an objection to my
book's "scope" and a claim that Marvel doesn't provide rights for such works. My referrals
to many previous examples of more substantial requests for use of images in similar academic works (including my own) and two further requests drew no further response. I did
manage to get a member of the Marvel staff on the phone who had working knowledge
of the permissions process and was bluntly told that I needed to understand that "Disney
is charge now" and that "the rules have changed."

This book contains no images of Marvel or Disney properties.

Bibliography

Abnett, Dan, and Andy Lanning. "Like a Streak of Light." *I Am an Avenger* 1, no. 3 (Jan. 2011).

aghrivaine. "Captain America: Death of Liberty—a Eulogy." *Quotidian Loveliness*, Mar. 9, 2007. At http://aghrivaine.livejournal.com/538118.html. Accessed Apr. 4, 2007.

Alberich, Ricardo, Joe Miro-Julia, and Francesc Rselló. "Marvel Universe Looks Almost Like a Real Social Network." *Statistical Mechanic*, Feb. 2002, 1–14.

Allred, Will. "Mark Waid Interview." *Comic Book Resources*, Mar. 5, 2002. At http://www.comicbookresources.com/news/newsitem.cgi?id=969. Accessed June 17, 2005.

Altheide, David L. *Creating Fear: News and the Construction of Crisis.* New York: Aldine de Gruyter, 2002.

Amash, Jim. "'I Let People Do Their Jobs!': A Conversation with Vince Fago—Artist, Writer, and Third Editor-in-Chief of Timely/Marvel Comics." *Alter Ego* 3, no. 11 (Nov. 2001): 8–27.

Anderson, Benedict R. *Imagined Communities: Reflections on the Origin and Spread of Nationalism.* London: Verso, 1983.

Andrae, Thomas. "From Menace to Messiah: The History and Historicity of Superman." In *American Media and Mass Culture*, edited by Donald Lazere, 124–38. Berkeley: Univ. of California Press, 1987.

"Announcing: Marvel Press!" *Marvel Age* 1, no. 10 (Jan. 1984): 6.

Asmus, James, and Ibraim Roberson. "Escape from the Negative Zone." *Steve Rogers: Super-Soldier Annual* 1, no. 1 (June 2011).

Aushenker, Michael. "Red, White, Blue, Black, and Proud! Captain America and the Falcon." *Back Issue* 1, no. 22 (June 2007): 25–30.

Austen, Chuck, and Jae Lee. "The Extremists, Part 4." *Captain America* 4, no. 10 (May 2003).

————. "The Extremists, Part 5." *Captain America* 4, no. 11 (June 2003).

————. "Ice, Part 2." *Captain America* 4, no. 13 (July 2003).

————. "Ice, Part 3." *Captain America* 4, no. 14 (Aug. 2003).

————. "Ice, Part 5." *Captain America* 4, no. 16 (Oct. 2003).

avideditor. Comment on Joshua Rhett Miller, "Tea Party Jab to Be Zapped from Captain America Comic, Writer Says." *Avid Editor's Insights*, Feb. 9, 2010. At http://avideditor.wordpress.com/2010/02/09/captan-america-is-used-to-portray-the-tea-party-movement-as-dangerous-and-racist/. Accessed Apr. 10, 2010.

Bailyn, Bernard. *On the Teaching and Writing of History: Responses to a Series of Questions*. Hanover, NH: Montgomery Endowment, Dartmouth College; distributed by Univ. Press of New England, 1994.

Baldwin, Jeremy. Letter. *Captain America* 3, no. 122 (Oct. 1999).

Balz, Dan, and Bob Woodward. "America's Chaotic Road to War: Bush's Global Strategy Began to Take Shape in First Frantic Hours after Attack." *Washington Post*, Jan. 27, 2002.

Bar, Mike W., Frank Springer, and Pablo Marcos. "Fear Grows in Brooklyn!" *Captain America* 1, no. 241 (Jan. 1980).

Barnes, Brooks, and Michael Cieply. "Disney Swoops into Action, Buying Marvel for $4 Billion." *New York Times*, Aug. 31, 2009. At http://www.nytimes.com/2009/09/01/business/media/01disney.html. Accessed Sept. 1, 2009.

Barnes, Julian E. "Tough Call, Spider-Man." *New York Times*, Oct. 8, 2001.

Bartlett, Fredric C. *Remembering*. Cambridge: Cambridge Univ. Press, 1932.

Beck, Glenn. "Glenn Beck: Where Are the Weathermen Now?" *GlenBeck.com*, July 28, 2010. At http://www.glennbeck.com/content/articles/article/198/43522/. Accessed Aug. 4, 2010.

Bell, Elizabeth, Lynda Haas, and Laura Sells. "Introduction: Walt's in the Movies." In *From Mouse to Mermaid: The Politics of Film, Gender, and Culture*, edited by Elizabeth Bell, Lynda Haas, and Laura Sells, 1–17. Bloomington: Indiana Univ. Press, 1995.

Bendis, Brian Michael, and Daniel Acuña. *The Avengers* 4, no. 24 (May 2012).

Bendis, Brian Michael, and Mark Bagley. "The Assembling." *Avengers Assemble* 1, no. 1 (May 2012).

————. *Avengers Assemble* 1, no. 5 (Sept. 2012).

Bendis, Brian Michael, and Howard Chaykin. "New Avengers: Disassembled, Part One." *The New Avengers* 1, no. 21 (Aug. 2006).

Bendis, Brian Michael, and Oliver Coipel. *Siege* 1, no. 1 (Mar. 2010).

————. *Siege* 1, no. 3 (May 2010).

————. *Siege* 1, no. 4 (June 2010).

Bendis, Brian Michael, and Alan Davis. "Brothers in Arms." *Avengers: Prime* 1, no. 5 (Feb. 2011).

Bendis, Brian Michael, and Renato Guedes. *The Avengers* 4, no. 21 (Mar. 2012).

Bendis Brian Michael, and Butch Guice. "Ultimate Origins Part 1." *Ultimate Origins* 1, no. 1 (Aug. 2008).

Bendis, Brian Michael, Trevor Hairsine, and Danny Miki. *Ultimate Six* 1, no. 5 (Feb. 2004).

Bendis, Brian Michael, Phil Hester, and Andy Parks. *Ultimate Marvel Team-Up* 1, no. 2 (Oct. 2001).

Bendis, Brian Michael, and Bryan Hitch. "It Came from Outer Space (Knight)!" *The Avengers* 4, no. 12.1 (June 2011).

Bendis, Brian Michael, and Alex Malley. "The Confession." *Civil War: The Confession* 1, no. 1 (May 2007).

Bendis, Brian Michael, and John Romita Jr. "Next Avengers, Part 1." *The Avengers* 4, no. 1 (July 2009).

Bendis, Brian Michael, and Walt Simonson. *The Avengers* 4, no. 25 (June 2012).

Bendis, Brian Michael, and Bill Tan. *The New Avengers* 1, no. 41 (July 2008).

Bendis, Brian Michael, and Leinil Yu. *Secret Invasion* 1, no. 8 (Jan. 2009).

Bennett, Tony, and Janet Woollacott. *Bond and Beyond: The Political Career of a Popular Hero*. London: Macmillan, 1987.

Bierly, Steve. Letter. *Captain America* 1, no. 293 (May 1984).

Bjork, Robert A. "The Updating of Human Memory." In *The Psychology of Learning and Motivation: Advances in Research and Theory*, 12th ed., edited by Gordon H. Bower, 235–39. New York: Academic Press, 1978.

Bohlen, Celestine. "Think Tank; in New War on Terrorism, Words Are Weapons, Too." *New York Times*, Sept. 29, 2001. At http://query.nytimes.com/gst/fullpage.html?res=9B04EFDA163DF93AA1575AC0A9679C8B63. Accessed Jan. 2, 2008.

Boichel, Bill. "Batman: Commodity as Myth." In *The Many Lives of the Batman*, edited by Roberta E. Pearson and William Uricchio, 4–17. London: Routledge, 1991.

Boney, Alex. "Captain America's Uncomfortable Tea Party." *GutterGeek*, Feb. 2010. At http://guttergeek.com/2010/February2010/capteaparty/capteaparty.html. Accessed Mar. 14, 2010.

Bourne, Mike. "Stan Lee, the Marvel Bard: An Interview Conducted by Mike Bourne, 1970." *Alter Ego* 3, no. 74 (Dec. 2007): 26–34.

Boyd, Jerry. "Black Marvels: A Look at the House of Ideas' Black Superheroes of the 1970s." *Back Issue* 1, no. 8 (Feb. 2005): 17–21.

Branagh, Kenneth, dir. *Thor*. Burbank, CA: Marvel Studios, 2011.

Braun, Saul. "Shazam! Here Comes Captain Relevant." *New York Times Magazine*, May 2, 1971.

Breen, T. H. *The Marketplace of Revolution: How Consumer Politics Shaped American Independence*. New York: Oxford Univ. Press, 2004.

Breyfogle, Norman. Letter. *Captain America* 1, no. 318 (June 1986).

Brooker, Will. *Batman Unmasked: Analyzing a Cultural Icon*. New York: Continuum, 2001.

Brooks, David. "The Age of Conflict: Politics and Culture after September 11." *Weekly Standard*, Nov. 5, 2001. At http://weeklystandard.com/Content/Public /Articles/000/000/000/424hwkwa.asp?pg=2. Accessed July 5, 2006.

Brown, Jeffrey A. *Black Superheroes, Milestone Comics, and Their Fans*. Jackson: Univ. of Mississippi Press, 2001.

Brown, Nancy Leigh. "The MARVEL AGE Interview: Mike Carlin." *Marvel Age* 1, no. 23 (Feb. 1985): 18–21.

Brubaker, Ed, and Mike Deodato Jr. "Eyes of the Dragon, Part 4." *Secret Avengers* 1, no. 9 (Mar. 2011).

———. "Secret Histories, Part 1." *Secret Avengers* 1, no. 1 (July 2010).

Brubaker, Ed, and Steve Epting. "The Burden of Dreams, Part Three." *Captain America* 5, no. 33 (Feb. 2008).

———. "The Burden of Dreams, Part Four." *Captain America* 5, no. 34 (Mar. 2008).

———. "The Death of the Dream." *Captain America* 5, no. 25 (Mar. 2007).

———. "The Death of the Dream, Part Three: White Lies." *Captain America* 5, no. 27 (Aug. 2007).

———. "The Man Who Bought America: Part Three." *Captain America* 5, no. 39 (Aug. 2008).

———. "The Man Who Bought America: Part Four." *Captain America* 5, no. 40 (Sept. 2008).

———. "Winter Kills." *Winter Soldier: Winter Kills* 1, no. 1 (Feb. 2007).

———. "The Winter Soldier Conclusion." *Captain America* 5, no. 14 (Feb. 2006).

———. "The Winter Soldier, Part 1 of 6." *Captain America* 5, no. 8 (Aug. 2005).

———. "The Winter Soldier, Part 3 of 6." *Captain America* 5, no. 11 (Nov. 2005).

Brubaker, Ed, and Butch Guice. *Fear Itself Chapter 7.1: Captain America*, Jan. 2012.

———. "No Escape, Part 3." *Captain America* 5, no. 608 (Sept. 2010).

———. "The Trial of Captain America, Part 5." *Captain America* 5, no. 615 (Apr. 2011).

———. "Two Americas Conclusion." *Captain America* 5, no. 605 (June 2010).

———. "Who Will Wield the Shield?" *Captain America: Who Will Wield the Shield?* 1, no. 1 (Feb. 2010).

Brubaker, Ed, Butch Guice, Howard Chaykin, Rafael Albuquerque, and Mitch Breitweiser. "Red, White, and Blue-Blood." *Captain America* 5, no. 601 (Sept. 2008).

Brubaker, Ed, and Bryan Hitch. "Captain America: Reborn, Part 1." *Captain America: Reborn* 1, no. 1 (Sept. 2009).

———. "Captain America: Reborn, Part 2." *Captain America: Reborn* 1, no. 2 (Oct. 2009).

——— "Captain America: Reborn, Part 4." *Captain America: Reborn* 1, no. 4 (Jan. 2010).

———. "Captain America: Reborn, Part 5." *Captain America: Reborn* 1, no. 5 (Feb. 2010).

———. "Captain America: Reborn, Part 6." *Captain America: Reborn* 1, no. 6 (Mar. 2010).

Brubaker, Ed, Michael Lark, and Steve Epting. "Out of Time, Part 5." *Captain America* 5, no. 5 (May 2005).

Brubaker, Ed, and Paco Medina. "Patriot." *Young Avengers Presents Patriot* 1, no. 1 (Mar. 2008).

Brubaker, Ed, and Mark Morales. "American Dreamers, Part I." *Captain America* 6, no. 1 (Sept. 2011).

Brubaker, Ed, and Mike Perkins. "The Drums of War." *Captain America* 5, no. 22 (Nov. 2006).

Brubaker, Ed, and Luke Ross. "Two Americas, Part One." *Captain America* 5, no. 602 (Mar. 2010).

Bunn, Cullen, Matt Fraction, Christopher Yost, and Scot Eaton. *Battle Scars* 1, no. 4 (Apr. 2012).

———. *Battle Scars* 1, no. 5 (May 2012).

———. *Battle Scars* 1, no. 6 (June 2012).

Burke, Kenneth. Letter. *Captain America* 1, no. 114 (June 1969).

Busiek, Kurt, and George Pérez. "Harsh Judgments." *The Avengers* 3, no. 24 (Jan. 2000).

———. "New Order." *The Avengers* 3, no. 27 (Apr. 2000).

———. "Showdown." *The Avengers* 3, no. 23 (Dec. 1999).

Byrne, John. "Darker Than Scarlet." *Avengers West Coast* 2, no. 56 (Mar. 1990).

Campbell, Joseph. *The Hero with a Thousand Faces.* New York: Pantheon, 1949.

"The Canal of Lurking Death." *Captain America Comics* 1, no. 31 (Oct. 1943).

"Captain America and the Bloodthirsty Baron." *USA Comics* 1, no. 17 (Oct. 1945).

"Captain America and the Invasion from Mars." *Captain America Comics* 1, no. 15 (June 1942).

"Captain America and Mikado's Super-Shell." *Captain America Comics* 1, no. 18 (Sept. 1942).

"Captain America and the Tunnel of Terror!" *Captain America Comics* 1, no. 15 (June 1942).

"Captain America Battles the Horde of the Vulture!" *Captain America Comics* 1, no. 14 (May 1942).

Captain America Comics 1, no. 13 (Apr. 1942).

"Captain America Declares a 'State of Unlimited Junior National Emergency'!" (advertisement). *Captain America Comics* 1, no. 7 (Oct. 1941).

"Captain America Fights When the Crocodile Strikes!" *Captain America Comics* 1, no. 19 (Oct. 1942).

"Captain America Is Dead; National Hero since 1941." *New York Times on the Web,* Readers' Comments, Mar. 7, 2007. At http://news.blogs.nytimes.com/2007/03/07/captain-america-is-dead-national-hero-since-1941/. Accessed Mar. 7, 2007.

"Captain America Turns Traitor." *Young Men* 1, no. 26 (Mar. 1954).

"Captain America Wants You!" (advertisement). *Captain America Comics* 1, no. 5 (Aug. 1941).

"The Cargo of Death." *Young Men* 1, no. 28 (June 1954).

"A Case of Conscience." *Captain America Comics* 1, no. 68 (Sept. 1948).

"The Case of the Flying Submarine!" *USA Comics* 1, no. 7 (Feb. 1943).

"The Case of Joey Arnold." *Captain America Comics* 1, no. 68 (Sept. 1948).

"The Case of the Phantom Engineer." *Captain America Comics* 1, no. 29 (Aug. 1943).

Casey, Joe, and Pablo Ralmondi. "Full Court Press." *Captain America Annual 1999* 1, no. 1 (Jan. 1999).

"Castle of Doom." *Captain America Comics* 1, no. 38 (May 1944).

Chernus, Ira. *Monsters to Destroy: The Neoconservative War on Terror and Sin.* Boulder, CO: Paradigm, 2006.

Chipman, Bob. "Stars and Stripes." *Escapist Magazine*, Apr. 1, 2011. At http://www.escapistmagazine.com/articles/view/columns/moviebob/8745-Stars-and -Stripes.3. Accessed May 4, 2012.

Chun, Steve. Letter. *Captain America* 3, no. 25 (Jan. 2000).

Claremont, Chris, Roger McKenzie, Sal Buscema, and Don Perlin. "From the Ashes." *Captain America* 1, no. 237 (Sept. 1979).

Clark, Steve. Letter. *The Avengers* 1, no. 20 (Sept. 1965).

Code of the Comics Magazine Association of America. New York: Comics Magazine Association of America, Oct. 26, 1954.

Cohen, Gillian. *Memory in the Real World.* 2nd ed. Hove, UK: Psychology Press, 1996.

"The Coming of Agent Zero." *Young Allies* 1, no. 1 (July 1941).

Comtois, Pierre. Letter. *Captain America* 1, no. 328 (Apr. 1987).

Connell, R. W. *Gender and Power: Society, the Person, and Sexual Politics.* Palo Alto, CA: Stanford Univ. Press, 1987.

———. *Masculinities.* Oxford: Polity Press, 1995.

Conway, Gerry, and Sal Buscema. "All the Colors . . . of Evil!" *Captain America and the Falcon* 1, no. 149 (May 1972).

Coogan, Peter. *Superhero: The Secret Origin of a Genre.* Austin, TX: Monkey-Brain, 2006.

Cornwell, Jason. "Line of Fire Reviews: Amazing Spider-Man #36." *Comics Bulletin*, Nov. 15, 2001. At http://www.comicsbulletin.com/reviews/100586882 411959.htm. Accessed Jan. 21, 2011.

Cotton, Mike. "We Will Never Forget." *Wizard Magazine* 1, no. 133 (Oct. 2002).

Cotton, Roger. Comment. *Hunting Muses*, Jan. 29, 2010. At http://natewinchester .wordpress.com/2010/01/29/so-what-are-you-a-captain-of/. Accessed Mar. 14, 2010.

Coulter, Ann. "This Is War: We Should Invade Their Countries." *National Review*, Sept. 13, 2001. At http://old.nationalreview.com/coulter/coulter.shtml. Accessed Jan. 4, 2011.

Crawford, Hubert H. *Crawford's Encyclopedia of Comic Books.* Middle Village, NY: Jonathan David, 1978.

Crist, Judith. "Horror in the Nursery." *Collier's*, Mar. 1948.

"The Cylinder of Death." *USA Comics* 1, no. 10 (Sept. 1943).

D'Acci, Julie. "Television, Representation, and Gender." In *The Television Studies Reader,* edited by Robert C. Allen and Annette Hill, 373–88. New York: Routledge, 2004.

Daley, Don, and Daryl Edelman. Letter response. *Captain America* 1, no. 327 (Mar. 1987).

———. Letter response. *Captain America* 1, no. 328 (Apr. 1987).

Daniels, Les. *Batman: The Complete History.* New York: DC Comics, 1999.

———. *Comix: A History of Comic Books in America.* New York: Outerbridge, 1971.

———. *Marvel: Five Fabulous Decades of the World's Greatest Comics.* New York: Abradale, 1991.

———. *Superman: The Complete History.* New York: DC Comics, 1998.

David, Peter, and Sal Velluto. "High Heat." *Captain America Goes to War against—Drugs* 1, no. 1 (1990).

David-Marshall, Brian, and Igor Kordey. "Relics." *Captain America* 3, no. 50 (Feb. 2002).

DeFalco, Tom, and Ron Frenz. "The Hero and the Hammer." *The Mighty Thor* 1, no. 390 (Apr. 1988).

DeMatteis, J. M., and Sal Buscema. "Diverging." *Captain America* 1, no. 284 (Aug. 1983).

DeMatteis, J. M., and Paul Neary. "An American Christmas." *Captain America* 1, no. 292 (Apr. 1984).

———. "Das Ende." *Captain America* 1, no. 300 (Dec. 1984).

———. "Field of Vision." *Captain America* 1, no. 293 (May 1984).

———. "Things Fall Apart." *Captain America* 1, no. 296 (Aug. 1984): 15–16.

DeMatteis, J. M., and Ron Wilson. "The Shadows of the Past." *Captain America Annual* 1, no. 6 (1982).

DeMatteis, J. M., and Mike Zeck. "Before the Fall." *Captain America* 1, no. 281 (May 1983).

———. "In Thy Image." *Captain America* 1, no. 277 (Jan. 1983).

———. "The Man Who Made a Difference!" *Captain America* 1, no. 267 (Mar. 1982).

———. "Mean Streets." *Captain America* 1, no. 272 (Aug. 1982).

———. "Of Monsters and Men." *Captain America* 1, no. 279 (Mar. 1983).

———. "Oh, Thus Be It Ever." *Captain America* 1, no. 278 (Feb. 1983).

———. "On Your Belly You Shall Crawl and Dust You Shall Eat!" *Captain America* 1, no. 282 (June 1983).

———. "Peace on Earth, Good Will to Man." *Captain America* 1, no. 268 (Apr. 1982).

———. "Sermon of the Straw." *Captain America* 1, no. 280 (Apr. 1983).

———. "Someone Who Cares!" *Captain America* 1, no. 270 (June 1982).

———. "Yesterday's Shadows!" *Captain America* 1, no. 275 (Nov. 1982).

Denning, Michael. *Mechanical Accents: Dime Novels and Working-Class Culture.* London: Verso, 1987.

Dionne, E. J. *Why Americans Hate Politics.* New York: Simon & Schuster, 1991.

Dittmer, Jason. *Captain America and the Nationalist Superhero.* Philadelphia: Temple Univ. Press, 2013.

———. "Retconning America: Captain America in the Wake of World War II and the McCarthy Hearings." In *The Amazing Transforming Superhero! Essays on the Revision of Characters in Comic Books, Film, and Television,* edited by Terrence R. Wandtke, 33–51. Jefferson, NC: McFarland, 2007.

———. "The Tyranny of the Serial: Popular Geopolitics, the Nation, and Comic Book Discourse." *Antipode* 39, no. 2 (Mar. 2007): 247–68.

Dorkin, Evan, and Kevin Maguire. "Stars and Stripes Forever." *Captain America* 3, no. 50 (Feb. 2002).

Douglas, Edward. "Marvel Studios Sets Four More Release Dates!" *SuperHeroHype,* May 5, 2008. At http://www.superherohype.com/features/articles/96489 -marvel-studios-sets-four-more-release-dates. Accessed Dec. 8, 2012.

DuBose, Mike S. "Holding Out for a Hero: Reaganism, Comic Book Vigilantes, and Captain America." *Journal of Popular Culture* 40, no. 6 (2007): 915–35.

Eco, Umberto. *The Role of the Reader: Explorations in the Semiotics of Texts.* Bloomington: Indiana Univ. Press, 1979.

Ellis, Warren, Brandon Peterson, and Justin Ponsor. *Ultimate Extinction* 1, no. 2 (Apr. 2006).

———. *Ultimate Extinction* 1, no. 4 (June 2006).

Ellrod, Rick. Letter. *Captain America* 1, no. 114 (June 1969).

Emad, Mitra C. "Reading Wonder Woman's Body: Mythologies of Gender and Nation." *Journal of Popular Culture* 39, no. 6 (2006): 954–84.

Emanuel, Ari. "Did Bush and Cheney Kill Captain America?" *Huffington Post,* Mar. 8, 2007. At http://www.huffingtonpost.com/ari-emanuel/did-bush-and -cheney-kill-_b_42967.html. Accessed Apr. 4, 2007.

Engle, Gary. "What Makes Superman so Darned American?" In *Superman at Fifty: The Persistence of a Legend!* edited by Dennis Dooley and Gary Engle, 79–87. New York: Collier, 1987.

Englehart, Steve. Letter response. *Captain America and the Falcon* 1, no. 169 (Jan. 1974).

Englehart, Steve, and Sal Buscema. " . . . Before the Dawn!" *Captain America and the Falcon* 1, no. 175 (July 1974).

———. "Beware of Serpents." *Captain America and the Falcon* 1, no. 163 (July 1973).

———. "The Falcon Fights Alone." *Captain America and the Falcon* 1, no. 154 (Oct. 1972).

———. " . . . If He Loseth His Soul." *Captain America and the Falcon* 1, no. 161 (May 1973).

———. "The Incredible Origin of the Other Captain America." *Captain America and the Falcon* 1, no. 155 (Nov. 1972).

———. "Two into One Won't Go." *Captain America and the Falcon* 1, no. 156 (Dec. 1972).

Englehart, Steve, Mike Friedrich, and Sal Buscema. "When a Legend Dies!" *Captain America and the Falcon* 1, no. 169 (Jan. 1974).

Englehart, Steve, Steve Gerber, and Sal Buscema. "Veni, Vidi, Vici, Viper!" *Captain America and the Falcon* 1, no. 157 (Jan. 1973).

Englehart, Steve, and Frank Robbins. "Nomad: No More!" *Captain America and the Falcon* 1, no. 183 (Mar. 1975).

———. "Scream the Scarlet Skull!" *Captain America and the Falcon* 1, no. 185 (May 1975).

Englehart, Steve, and Herb Trimpe. "Cap's Back!" *Captain America and the Falcon* 1, no. 184 (Apr. 1975).

Englehart, Steve, John Warner, and Frank Robbins. "Mind Cage." *Captain America and the Falcon* 1, no. 186 (June 1975).

Englehart, Tom. *The End of Victory Culture: Cold War America and the Disillusioning of a Generation.* New York: Basic Books, 1995.

"The Enigma of the Death Doll." *Captain America Comics* 1, no. 68 (Sept. 1948).

Estrella, Ernie. "Mark Millar Interview." *PopCultureShock*, Dec. 7, 2004. At http://www.popcultureshock.com/features.php?id=874. Accessed Jan. 7, 2010.

Evanier, Mark, Sal Buscema, and Dave Simons. "Sound of the Silencer." *Marvel Premiere* 1, no. 49 (Aug. 1979).

Evans, Sam. "Bryan Hitch: *The Ultimates* Visionary." *SBC Interviews*, Aug. 23, 2002. At http://www.comicsbulletin.com/features/103008397674473.htm. Accessed June 17, 2012.

Favreau, Jon, dir. *Iron Man.* Burbank, CA: Marvel Studios, 2008.

———, dir. *Iron Man 2*. Burbank, CA: Marvel Studios, 2010.

Feder, Edward L. *Comic Book Regulation*. Berkeley, CA: Bureau of Public Administration, 1955.

Feiffer, Jules. *The Great Comic Book Heroes*. Seattle: Fantagraphic Books, 2003.

"The Fiend That Was the Fakir." *Captain America Comics* 1, no. 20 (Nov. 1942).

Fingeroth, Danny. "The Marvel Saga: The Official History of the Marvel Universe." *Marvel Age* 1, no. 32 (Nov. 1985): 27.

Fisch, Sholly. "The Punisher." *Marvel Age* 1, no. 33 (Dec. 1985): 14–15.

———. "The Punisher." *Marvel Age* 1, no. 51 (June 1987): 18–21.

———. "The Return of Frank Miller." *Marvel Age* 1, no. 37 (Mar. 1986): 18–23.

———. "Star Spotlight: He-Man and the Masters of the Universe." *Marvel Age* 1, no. 38 (Apr. 1986): 18–20.

Fjellmann, Stephen M. *Vinyl Leaves: Walt Disney World and America*. Boulder, CO: Westview, 1992.

Flores, Abelardo D. Letter. *Captain America* 1, no. 354 (June 1980).

Fowler, Damian. "Why Captain America Had to Die." *Guardian*, Mar. 12, 2007. At http://www.theguardian.com/books/booksblog/2007/mar/12/whycaptain americahadtodie. Accessed Apr. 4, 2007.

Fraction, Matt, and Stuart Immonen. "Fear Itself 3: The Hammer That Fell on Yancy Street." *Fear Itself* 1, no. 3 (Sept. 2011).

Fraction, Matt, and Ariel Olivetti. "Blood and Sand." *Punisher War Journal* 2, no. 7 (July 2007).

———. "Goin' Out West." *Punisher War Journal* 2, no. 6 (June 2007).

———. "Heroes and Villains." *Punisher War Journal* 2, no. 11 (Nov. 2007).

Friedrich, Gary, Gil Kane, and John Romita. "Skyjacked!" *Captain America and the Falcon* 1, no. 145 (Jan. 1972).

Friedrich, Gary, and John Romita. "Hydra over All." *Captain America and the Falcon* 1, no. 144 (Dec. 1971).

———. "Power to the People!" *Captain America and the Falcon* 1, no. 143 (Nov. 1971).

Füredi, Frank. *Culture of Fear: Risk-Taking and the Morality of Low Expectation*. New York: Continuum, 2002.

Gage, Christos, and Jeremy Haun. "Rubicon." *Civil War: Casualties of War* 1, no. 1 (Feb. 2007).

Genter, Robert. "'With Great Power Comes Great Responsibility': Cold War Culture and the Birth of Marvel Comics." *Journal of Popular Culture* 40, no. 6 (2007): 953–78.

Gerber, Steve, Sal Buscema, John Tartag, and Mike Esposito. "Devastation." *Captain America* 1, no. 225 (Sept. 1978).

———. "Monumental Menace." *Captain America and the Falcon* 1, no. 222 (June 1978).

Giroux, Henry. *The Mouse That Roared: Disney and the End of Innocence.* New York: Rowman & Littlefield, 1999.

Glassner, Barry. *The Culture of Fear: Why Americans Are Afraid of the Wrong Things.* New York: Basic Books, 1999.

Gold, Mike. "Crisis on Silver Age Earth: The Year (or so) the Future Started." *Alter Ego* 3, no. 32 (Jan. 2004): 3–12.

"Golden Girl." *Captain America Comics* 1, no. 66 (Apr. 1948).

Goldman, David. "Disney to Buy Marvel for $4 billion." *CNN Money*, Aug. 31, 2009. At http://money.cnn.com/2009/08/31/news/companies/disney_marvel/. Accessed Sept. 1, 2009.

Goodman, Ellen. "Post–September 11 Dilemmas for Journalists." *Boston Globe*, Dec. 7, 2001.

Goulart, Ron. "Captain America and the Super-Patriots." *Comic Buyer's Guide*, Apr. 22, 1988.

Gray, Jonathan, Cornel Sandvoss, and C. Lee Harrington. "Introduction: Why Study Fans?" In *Fandom: Identities and Communities in a Mediated World*, edited by Jonathan Gray, Cornel Sandvoss, and C. Lee Harrington, 1–18. New York: New York Univ. Press, 2007.

Greene, Jack P. *Pursuits of Happiness: The Social Development of Early Modern British Colonies and the Formation of American Culture.* Chapel Hill: Univ. of North Carolina Press, 1988.

Greydanus, Steve. Letter. *Captain America* 1, no. 302 (Feb. 1985).

Griffin, Millard P., Jr. Letter. *Captain America* 1, no. 310 (Oct. 1985).

Gruenwald, Mark. "Changing of the Guard." *Captain America* 1, no. 306 (June 1985).

———. "Just How Strong Is . . . Spider-Man?" *The Amazing Spider-Man Annual* 1, no. 15 (1981): 39–41.

———. "Mark's Remarks." *Marvel Age* 1, no. 84 (Jan. 1990): 9.

Gruenwald, Mark, and Kieron Dwyer. "Break-In." *Captain America* 1, no. 341 (May 1988).

———. "Don't Tread on Me." *Captain America* 1, no. 344 (Aug. 1988).

———. "Freedom of Speech." *Captain America* 1, no. 341 (May 1988).

———. "Out of Commission." *Captain America* 1, no. 348 (Dec. 1988).

———. "Power Struggle." *Captain America* 1, no. 338 (Feb. 1988).

———. "Seeing Red." *Captain America* 1, no. 350 (Feb. 1989).

———. "The Snake Pit." *Captain America* 1, no. 342 (June 1988).

———. "Surrender." *Captain America* 1, no. 345 (Sept. 1988).

Gruenwald, Mark, and Dave Hoover. "Fighting Chance Part One: Super Patriot Games." *Captain America* 1, no. 425 (Mar. 1994).

———. "The Next Generation." *Captain America* 1, no. 431 (Sept. 1994).

———. "Policing the Nation." *Captain America* 1, no. 428 (June 1994).

———. "Snake, Battle, and Toll." *Captain America* 1, no. 435 (Jan. 1995).

———. "Snake Bites." *Captain America* 1, no. 434 (Dec. 1994).

Gruenwald, Mark, Dave Hoover, and Danny Bulanadi. "Twilight's Last Gleaming." *Captain America* 1, no. 443 (Sept. 1995).

Gruenwald, Mark, and Rik Levins. "After the Storm." *Captain America* 1, no. 401 (June 1992).

———. "Gauntlet." *Captain America* 1, no. 421 (Nov. 1993).

———. "No Man's Land." *Captain America* 1, no. 391 (Sept. 1991).

———. "Superia Unbound." *Captain America* 1, no. 392 (Oct. 1991).

———. "To Have and to Have Not." *Captain America* 1, no. 418 (Aug. 1993).

Gruenwald, Mark, and Ron Lim. "Cap's Night Out." *Captain America* 1, no. 371 (June 1990).

———. "Sold on Ice." *Captain America* 1, no. 372 (July 1990).

Gruenwald, Mark, and Tom Morgan. "Baptism by Fire." *Captain America* 1, no. 335 (Nov. 1987).

———. "Natural Calling." *Captain America* 1, no. 336 (Dec. 1987).

Gruenwald, Mark, and Paul Neary. "The Body in Question." *Captain America* 1, no. 308 (Aug. 1985).

———. "The Chasm." *Captain America* 1, no. 322 (Oct. 1986).

———. "The Choice." *Captain America* 1, no. 332 (Aug. 1987).

———. "Creatures of Love." *Captain America* 1, no. 316 (Apr. 1986).

———. "Death Throws." *Captain America* 1, no. 317 (May 1986).

———. "Deface the Nation." *Captain America* 1, no. 312 (Dec. 1985).

———. "The Hard Sell." *Captain America* 1, no. 315 (Mar. 1986).

———. "Justice Is Served?" *Captain America* 1, no. 318 (June 1986).

———. "The Little Bang Theory." *Captain America* 1, no. 320 (Aug. 1986).

———. "Mission: Murder MODOK." *Captain America* 1, no. 313 (Jan. 1986).

———. "Nomad Madcap Cap. . . ." *Captain America* 1, no. 309 (Sept. 1985).

———. "Overkill." *Captain America* 1, no. 319 (July 1986).

———. "Serpents of the World Unite." *Captain America* 1, no. 310 (Oct. 1985).

———. "Soldier, Soldier." *Captain America* 1, no. 331 (July 1987).

———. "Stop Making Sense." *Captain America* 1, no. 307 (July 1985).

———. "Super-Patriot Is Here." *Captain America* 1, no. 323 (Nov. 1986).

———. "Ultimatum." *Captain America* 1, no. 321 (Sept. 1986).

———. "Working. . . ." *Captain America* 1, no. 311 (Nov. 1985).

Gruenwald, Mark, Paul Neary, and John Beatty. "Clashing Symbols." *Captain America* 1, no. 327 (Mar. 1987).

Gsoteapartygirl. "For All You Comics Fans . . ." *Greensboro Tax Day Tea Party*, Feb. 10, 2010. At http://gsoteaparty.wordpress.com/2010/02/10/for-all-you -comics-fans/. Accessed Mar. 14, 2010.

Gustines, George Gene. "Captain America Is Dead; National Hero since 1941." *New York Times*, Mar. 8, 2007. At http://www.nytimes.com/2007/03/08 /books/08capt.html. Accessed Mar. 7, 2007.

Guzman, Jesse. Letter. *Captain America* 1, no. 327 (Mar. 1987).

Hakala, Ulla. *Adam in Ads: A Thirty Year Look at Mediated Masculinities in Advertising in Finland and the US*. Tampere, Finland: Esa Print Tampere, 2006.

Halbwachs, Maurice. *The Collective Memory*. New York: Harper & Row, 1980.

Harmon, Jim, and Donald F. Glut. "The Long-Underwear Boys: 'You've Met Me, Now Meet My Fist!'" In *The Great Movie Serials: Their Sound and Fury*, 235–74. New York: Routledge, 1972.

Harras, Bob, and Steve Epting. "Empire's End." *The Avengers* 1, no. 347 (May 1992).

Hartford, Michael. Letter. *Captain America* 1, no. 304 (Apr. 1985).

Haskell, Charles David. Letter. *Marvel Age* 1, no. 20 (Nov. 1984): 11.

Hedges, Chris. *War Is a Force That Gives Us Meaning*. New York: PublicAffairs, 2002.

Heilbrunn, Jacob. "Captain America Was Us." *Los Angeles Times*, Mar. 9, 2007. At http://articles.latimes.com/2007/mar/09/opinion/oe-heilbrunn9. Accessed May 10, 2010.

Hickman, Jonathan, and Steve Epting. "Infinity." *New Avengers* 3, no. 3 (Apr. 2013).

Hickman, Jonathan, and Jerome Opeña. "Avengers World." *The Avengers* 5, no. 1 (Feb. 2013).

Higgins, Kyle, Alec Siegel, and Agustin Padilla. "Prisoners of Duty." *Captain America: Theater of War; Prisoners of Duty* 1, no. 1 (Feb. 2010).

Higham, John. *History: Professional Scholarship in America*. Baltimore: Johns Hopkins Univ. Press, 1983.

Holy, Harold C. Letter. *Captain America* 1, no. 341 (May 1988).

Homburger, Richard E. Letter. *Captain America* 1, no. 293 (May 1984).

Howe, Sean. *Marvel Comics: The Untold Story*. New York: HarperCollins, 2012.

Hudlin, Reginald, and Manuel Garcia. "Inside Man." *Black Panther* 4, no. 23 (Feb. 2007).

Hughes, Richard T. *Myths America Lives By*. Champaign: Univ. of Illinois Press, 2004.

Hume, Janice "Changing Characteristics of Heroic Women in Midcentury Mainstream Media." *Journal of Popular Culture* 34, no. 1 (2000): 9–29.

Hurst, Richard, *Republic Studios: Beyond Poverty Row and the Majors*. New York: Scarecrow Press, 2007.

Huston, Warner Todd. "Marvel Comics: Captain America Says Tea Parties Are Dangerous and Racist." *Publius Forum* 8 (Feb. 2010). At http://www.publius forum.com/2010/02/08/marvel-comics-captain-america-says-tea-parties-are -dangerous-and-racist/. Accessed Mar. 12, 2010.

"The Idol of Doom!" *Captain America Comics* 1, no. 23 (Feb. 1943).

Jacobs, Will, and Gerard Jones. *The Comic Book Heroes: From the Silver Age to the Present*. New York: Crown, 1985.

Jeffords, Susan. "The Big Switch: Hollywood Masculinity in the Nineties." In *Film Theory Goes to the Movies*, edited by Jim Collins, Hilary Radner, and Ava Preacher Collins, 196–208. New York: Routlege, 1993.

———. *Hard Bodies: Hollywood Masculinity in the Reagan Era*. New Brunswick, NJ: Rutgers Univ. Press, 1994.

Jenkins, Henry. *Textual Poachers: Television Fans and Participatory Culture*. New York: Routledge, 1992.

Jenkins, Paul, and Ramon Bachs. "Embedded, Part Eleven." *Civil War: Front Line* 1, no. 11 (Apr. 2007).

Jenkins, Paul, and Fernando Blanco. "To Soldier On." *Captain America: Theater of War; to Soldier On* 1, no. 1 (Oct. 2009).

Jenkins, Paul, and Elia Bonetti. "Ghosts of My Country." *Captain America: Theater of War; Ghosts of My Country* 1, no. 1 (Dec. 2009).

Jenkins, Paul, and Paolo Rivera. "Captain America." *Mythos: Captain America* 1, no. 1 (Aug. 2008).

Jet-Poop. "Captain America, Traitor?" *Everything2*, May 20, 2003. At http://every
thing2.com/title/Captain+America%252C+Traitor%253F. Accessed Aug. 13,
2005.

Jewett, Robert. *The Captain America Complex: The Dilemma of Zealous Nationalism*. Philadelphia: Westminster Press, 1973.

———. *The Captain America Complex: The Dilemma of Zealous Nationalism*.
2nd ed. Sante Fe: Bear, 1984.

———. *Mission and Menace: Four Centuries of American Religious Zeal*. Minneapolis: Fortress Press, 2008.

Jewett, Robert, and John Shelton Lawrence. *The American Monomyth*. Garden
City, NY: Anchor Press, 1977.

———. *Captain America and the Crusade against Evil: The Dilemma of Zealous
Nationalism*. Grand Rapids, MI: Eerdmans, 2003.

Johns, Geoff, and Olivier Coipel. "The Great Escape." *The Avengers* 3, no. 69
(Sept. 2003).

———. "The Great Escape." *The Avengers* 3, no. 70 (Oct. 2003).

———. "Infections." *The Avengers* 3, no. 66 (June 2003).

Johnson, Stephen. *Everything Bad Is Good for You: How Today's Popular Culture
Is Actually Making Us Smarter*. New York: Riverhead Books, 2005.

Johnston, Joe, dir. *Captain America: The First Avenger*. Burbank, CA: Marvel
Studios, 2011.

Jones, Gerard. *Men of Tomorrow: Geeks, Gangsters, and the Birth of the Comic
Book*. New York: Basic Books, 2004.

Jordan, Bryant. "Captain America, 89; Defender of Freedom." *Navy Times*, Mar.
14, 2007. At http://www.navytimes.com/entertainment/books/life_captain
america_obit070314/. Accessed May 12, 2007.

———. "Hero vs. Hero: Civil War Breaks Out in the Marvel Universe!" *Army
Times*, June 26, 2006. At http://www.armytimes.com/legacy/new/0-ARMY
PAPER-1873086.php. Accessed Feb. 2, 2011.

Jurgens, Dan. "Candor." *Captain America* 3, no. 43 (July 2001).

———. "A Gulf so Wide." *Captain America* 3, no. 39 (Mar. 2001).

———. "When Strikes Protocide." *Captain America* 3, no. 35 (Nov. 2000).

Jurgens, Dan, and Andy Kubert. "Twisted Tomorrows." *Captain America* 3, no.
25 (Jan. 2000).

———. "Twisted Tomorrows, Part 2." *Captain America* 3, no. 26 (Feb. 2000).

Kalish, Carol, and Mark Lerer. "The Origins of Marvel Press." *Marvel Age* 1, no.
11 (Feb. 1984): 14–15.

Kaminski, Len, and Kevin Hopgood. "Kids These Days." *Iron Man* 1, no. 303 (Apr. 1994).

Kaufman, Matt. Letter. *Captain America* 1, no. 241 (Jan. 1980).

———. Letter. *Captain America* 1, no. 246 (June 1980).

Kenney, Richard. Letter. *The Avengers* 1, no. 27 (Apr. 1966).

Kerouac, Jack. *On the Road*. New York: Viking Press, 1957.

Khouri, Andy. "MARK MILLAR, ULTIMATELY." *CBR News: The Comic Wire*, July 25, 2007. At http://www.comicbookresources.com/news/newsitem .cgi?id=11294. Accessed Jan. 2, 2010.

Kidd, Howard T. Letter. *Captain America* 1, no. 323 (Nov. 1986).

"Kill Captain America." *Men's Adventures* 1, no. 28 (July 1954).

Kimmel, Michael. "Masculinity as Homophobia: Fear, Shame, and Silence in the Construction of Gender Identity." In *Feminism and Masculinities*, edited by Peter Murphy, 182–99. Oxford: Oxford Univ. Press, 2004.

Kirby, Jack. "Dawn's Early Light." *Captain America and the Falcon* 1, no. 200 (Aug. 1976).

———. "The Madbomb: Screamer in the Brain!" *Captain America and the Falcon* 1, no. 193 (Jan. 1976).

———. "The Trojan Horde." *Captain America and the Falcon* 1, no. 194 (Feb. 1976).

Klock, Geoff. *How to Read Superhero Comics and Why*. New York: Continuum, 2002.

Knauf, Charles, and Mitch Breitweiser. "Operation: Zero Point." *Captain America: Theater of War; Operation: Zero Point* 1, no. 1 (Dec. 2008).

Knowles, Christopher. *Our Gods Wear Spandex: The Secret History of Comic Book Heroes*. San Francisco: Weiser, 2007.

Knudson, Max. "Piracy Battle Not Child's Play for Disney; Company Zealously Guards Rights to Mickey, Goofy, Donald, and the Gang." *Deseret News*, Apr. 28, 1989. At http://www.deseretnews.com/article/44429/PIRA CY-BATTLE-NOT-CHILDS-PLAY-FOR-DISNEY.html?pg=all. Accessed July 5, 2013.

Kraft, David Anthony, and Alan Kupperberg. "The Mystery X." *Captain America* 1, no. 271 (July 1982).

Krauthammer, Charles. "The Real New World Order: The American and the Islamic Challenge." *Weekly Standard*, Nov. 12, 2001. At http://weeklystandard .com/Content/Public/Articles/000/000/000/456zfygd.asp. Accessed Sept. 17, 2010.

Kristol, Irving. "The Neoconservative Persuasion." *Weekly Standard*, Aug. 25, 2003. At http://www.weeklystandard.com/Utilities/printer_preview.asp?id Article=3000&R=785F27881. Accessed Mar. 4, 2009.

Kristol, William, and Robert Kagan. "Introduction: National Interest and Global Responsibility." In *Present Dangers: Crisis and Opportunity in American Foreign and Defense Policy*, edited by Robert Kagan, 3–24. San Francisco: Encounter Books, 2000.

Krueger, Jim, Alex Ross, and Steve Sadowski. "Old Soldiers, New Wars." *Avengers/Invaders* 1, no. 1 (July 2008).

Kujawa, Henry. Letter. *Marvel Age* 1, no. 20 (Nov. 1984): 12.

Kunkel, Bill, and Al Wenzel. "Deathgarden." *Marvel Team-Up* 1, no. 71 (July 1978).

Laiken, Paul, Larry Lieber, and Don Heck. "Even Avengers Can Die." *The Avengers* 1, no. 14 (Mar. 1965).

Langley, Jeanette. Letter. *Captain America* 3, no. 120 (Aug. 1999).

Lawrence, John Shelton, and Robert Jewett. *The Myth of the American Superhero*. Grand Rapids, MI: Eerdmans, 2002.

Leader, Mark. Letter. *Tales of Suspense* 1, no. 68 (Aug. 1965).

"The League of Hate." *Captain America Comics* 1, no. 49 (Aug. 1945).

Lee, Stan. *Origins of Marvel Comics*. New York: Marvel Comics Group, 1974.

———. *Son of Origins of Marvel Comics*. New York: Marvel Comics Group, 1975.

———. "Stan's Soapbox." *Marvel Age* 1, no. 51 (June 1987): 15.

Lee, Stan, and Dick Ayers. "30 Minutes to Live!" *Tales of Suspense* 1, no. 75 (Mar. 1966).

———. "The Old Order Changeth!" *The Avengers* 1, no. 16 (May 1965).

Lee, Stan, and John Buscema. *How to Draw Comics the Marvel Way*. New York: Fireside, 1978.

Lee, Stan, and Gene Colan. "Brother Take My Hand." *Daredevil* 1, no. 47 (Dec. 1969).

———. "The Coming of the Falcon." *Captain America* 1, no. 117 (Sept. 1969).

———. "Mission: Stamp Out Hell's Angels." *Captain America* 1, no. 128 (Aug. 1970).

———. "They Call Him—Stone Face!" *Captain America and the Falcon* 1, no. 134 (Feb. 1971).

———. "To Stalk the Spider-Man." *Captain America and the Falcon* 1, no. 137 (May 1971).

———. "Up against the Wall." *Captain America* 1, no. 130 (Oct. 1970).

Lee, Stan, and Steve Ditko. "Spider-Man!" *Amazing Fantasy* 1, no. 15 (Aug. 1962).

Lee, Stan, and Bill Everett. "The Origin of Daredevil." *Daredevil* 1, no. 1 (Apr. 1964).

Lee, Stan, and Don Heck. "Enter—Dr. Doom!" *The Avengers* 1, no. 25 (Feb. 1966).

———. "From the Ashes of Defeat—!" *The Avengers* 1, no. 24 (Jan. 1966).

———. "Iron Man Is Born." *Tales of Suspense* 1, no. 39 (Mar. 1963).

———. "Now by My Hand Shall Die a Villain." *The Avengers* 1, no. 15 (Apr. 1965).

———. "Once an Avenger. . . ." *The Avengers* 1, no. 23 (Dec. 1965).

———. "The Sign of the Serpent!" *The Avengers* 1, no. 32 (Sept. 1966).

———. "When the Commissar Commands." *The Avengers* 1, no. 18 (July 1965).

Lee, Stan, and Gil Kane. "And Now the Goblin." *The Amazing Spider-Man* 1, no. 96 (May 1971).

———. "The Goblin's Last Gasp." *The Amazing Spider-Man* 1, no. 98 (July 1971).

———. "In the Grip of the Goblin." *The Amazing Spider-Man* 1, no. 97 (June 1971).

Lee, Stan, and Jack Kirby. "The Avengers Battle the Space Phantom." *The Avengers* 1, no. 2 (Nov. 1963).

———. "The Black Panther." *The Fantastic Four* 1, no. 52 (July 1966).

———. "Captain America." *Tales of Suspense* 1, no. 59 (Nov. 1964).

———. "Captain America Joins the Avengers." *The Avengers* 1, no. 4 (Mar. 1963).

———. "The Coming of the Avengers." *The Avengers* 1, no. 1 (Sept. 1963).

———. "The Coming of the Sub-Mariner." *The Fantastic Four* 1, no. 4 (May 1962).

———. "The Fantastic Four." *The Fantastic Four* 1, no. 1 (Nov. 1961).

———. "The Hero That Was!" *Captain America* 1, no. 109 (Jan. 1969).

———. "The Hulk." *The Incredible Hulk* 1, no. 1 (May 1962).

———. "The Human Torch Meets Captain America." *Strange Tales* 1, no. 114 (Nov. 1963).

———. "If the Past Be Not Dead." *Captain America* 1, no. 107 (Nov. 1968).

———. "In Mortal Combat with Captain America." *Tales of Suspense* 1, no. 58 (Oct. 1964).

———. "In the Name of Batroc!" *Captain America* 1, no. 105 (Sept. 1968).

———. "The Man in the Ant Hill." *Tales to Astonish* 1, no. 27 (Jan. 1962).

———. "The Mighty Avengers Meet the Masters of Evil." *The Avengers* 1, no. 6 (July 1964).

———. "The Origin of Captain America." *Tales of Suspense* 1, no. 63 (Mar. 1965).

———. "Return of the Ant-Man." *Tales to Astonish* 1, no. 35 (Sept. 1962).

———. "Sgt. Fury and His Howling Commandoes." *Sgt. Fury and His Howling Commandoes* 1, no. 1 (May 1963).

———. "The Sleeper Strikes." *Captain America* 1, no. 102 (June 1968).

———. "The Strength of the Sumo." *Tales of Suspense* 1, no. 61 (Jan. 1965).

———. "This Monster Unmasked." *Captain America* 1, no. 100 (Apr. 1968).

———. "Thor the Mighty! And the Stone Men from Saturn!" *Journey into Mystery* 1, no. 83 (Aug. 1962).

———. "A Time to Die—A Time to Live!" *Tales of Suspense* 1, no. 95 (Nov. 1967).

———. "The Weakest Link!" *Captain America* 1, no. 103 (July 1968).

———. "When Wakes the Sleeper!" *Captain America* 1, no. 101 (May 1968).

———. "X-Men." *The X-Men* 1, no. 1 (Sept. 1963).

Lee, Stan, and Mort Lawrence. "The Girl Who Was Afraid." *Men's Adventures* 1, no. 27 (May 1954).

Lee, Stan, and George Mair. *Excelsior! The Amazing Life of Stan Lee.* New York: Fireside, 2002.

Lee, Stan, and John Romita. "Back from the Dead." *Young Men* 1, no. 24 (Dec. 1953).

———. "The Badge and Betrayal!" *Captain America and the Falcon* 1, no. 139 (July 1971).

———. "The Betrayers." *Captain America . . . Commie Smasher!* 1, no. 76 (May 1954).

———. "Captain America." *Captain America . . . Commie Smasher!* 1, no. 77 (July 1954).

———. "Captain America Strikes." *Captain America . . . Commie Smasher!* 1, no. 76 (May 1954).

———. "Come to the Commies." *Captain America . . . Commie Smasher!* 1, no. 76 (May 1954).

———. "The Green Dragon!" *Captain America . . . Commie Smasher!* 1, no. 78 (Sept. 1954).

———. "His Touch Is Death!" *Captain America . . . Commie Smasher!* 1, no. 78 (Sept. 1954).

———. "The Hour of Doom." *Captain America . . . Commie Smasher!* 1, no. 78 (Sept. 1954).

———. "In the Clutches of . . . the Kingpin!" *The Amazing Spider-Man* 1, no. 51 (Aug. 1967).

———. "The Man with No Face." *Captain America . . . Commie Smasher!* 1, no. 77 (July 1954).

———. "The Night of the Prowler." *The Amazing Spider-Man* 1, no. 78 (Sept. 1969).

———. "The Unholy Alliance." *Captain America and the Falcon* 1, no. 141 (Sept. 1971).

———. "You Die at Midnight." *Captain America . . . Commie Smasher!* 1, no. 77 (July 1954).

Lee, Stan, John Romita, and Jim Mooney. "Crisis on Campus." *The Amazing Spider-Man* 1, no. 68 (Jan. 1969).

Lee, Stan, Johnny Romita, and Frank Ray. "If a Hostage Should Die!" *Tales of Suspense* 1, no. 77 (May 1966).

Lee, Stan, and Jim Steranko. "Lest We Forget." *Captain America* 1, no. 112 (Apr. 1969).

———. "No Longer Alone." *Captain America* 1, no. 110 (Feb. 1969).

Lee, Stan, and George Tuska. "The Sleeper Shall Awaken." *Tales of Suspense* 1, no. 72 (Dec. 1965).

Legman, Gerson. *Love and Death: A Study in Censorship.* New York: Breaking Point, 1949.

Leonard, Tom. "Captain America Killed When US Needs Him." *Telegraph,* Oct. 3, 2007. At http://www.telegraph.co.uk/news/worldnews/1545017/Captain-America-killed-when-US-needs-him.html. Accessed Feb. 28, 2010.

———. "Gun-Toting Captain America Comes Back to Life." *Telegraph,* Jan. 29, 2008. At http://www.telegraph.co.uk/news/main.jhtml?xml=/news/2008/01/28/wcomic128.xml. Accessed Feb. 3, 2008.

"The Leopard and His Killer Mob." *Captain America Comics* 1, no. 50 (Oct. 1945).

Lerer, Mark. "Are You Ready for Marvel Super Heroes Secret Wars?" *Marvel Age* 1, no. 12 (Mar. 1984): 9–11.

Lévi-Strauss, Claude. *Structural Anthropology.* Garden City, NY: Anchor Books, 1963.

Levy, Lon. Letter. *Captain America* 1, no. 280 (Apr. 1983).

Liefeld, Rob, and Jeph Loeb. "Patriotism. " *Captain America* 2, no. 3 (Jan. 1997).

Lien-Cooper, Barb. "Captain America: A Patriot for Our Time?" *Sequential Tart* 6, no. 12 (Dec. 2003). At http://www.sequentialtart.com/archive/dec03 /art_1203_7.shtml. Accessed Feb. 2, 2015.

"Lightning Cult." *Marvel Comics* 1, no. 86 (June 1948).

Lobdell, Scott, and Mark Pacella. "The Walking Wounded." *Alpha Flight* 1, no. 106 (Mar. 1992).

Lobdell, Scott, Mark Waid, Andy Kubert, and Joe Bennett. "With Great Power. . . ." *Onslaught: Marvel Universe* 1, no. 1 (Oct. 1996).

Loeb, Jeph, and John Cassaday. "Acceptance." *Fallen Son: The Death of Captain America* 1, no. 5 (Aug. 2007).

Loeb, Jeph, and David Finch. "Depression." *Fallen Son: The Death of Captain America* 1, no. 4 (July 2007).

Loeb, Jeph, and Ed McGuinness. "Anger." *Fallen Son: The Death of Captain America* 1, no. 2 (June 2007).

Loeb, Jeph, and John Romita Jr. "Bargaining." *Fallen Son: The Death of Captain America* 1, no. 3 (July 2007).

Loeb, Jeph, and Tim Sale. "It Happened One Night." *Captain America: White* 1, no. 1 (Sept. 2008).

Loeb, Jeph, and Leinil Yu. "Denial." *Fallen Son: The Death of Captain America* 1, no. 1 (June 2007).

Loewen, James W. *Lies My Teacher Told Me: Everything Your American History Textbook Got Wrong.* New York: Simon & Schuster, 2007.

Macchio, Ralph, and Marc Siry. Letter response. *Captain America* 1, no. 340 (Apr. 1988).

MacDonald, Andrew, and Virginia MacDonald. "Sold American: The Metamorphosis of Captain America." *Journal of Popular Culture* 10, no. 1 (1976): 239–58.

MacDougall, Robert. "Red, Brown, and Yellow Perils: Images of the American Enemy in the 1940s and 1950s." *Journal of Popular Culture* 32, no. 4 (Spring 1999): 59–75.

Mackidd, David. Letter. *The Avengers* 1, no. 22 (Nov. 1965).

Mackinnon, Kenneth. *Representing Men: Maleness and Masculinity in the Media.* London: Arnold, 2003.

mailloux. "Tea Party Activists Beware . . . Captain America Is onto You!" *Red-State*, Feb. 3, 2010. At http://www.redstate.com/mailloux/2010/02/03/tea-par ty-activists-beware-captain-america-is-onto-you/. Accessed Mar. 14, 2008.

Mankey, Harris. Letter. *Captain America* 3, no. 120 (Aug. 1999).

Mantlo, Bill, and Frank Robbins. "The Trial of the Falcon." *Captain America and the Falcon* 1, no. 191 (Nov. 1975).

Marcuse, Herbert. *Eros and Civilization*. 2nd ed. Boston: Beacon, 1966.

"Marvel Top Twenty." *Marvel Age* 1, no. 85 (Feb. 1990): 8.

Mathis, Jack. *Valley of the Cliffhangers Supplement*. Chicago: Jack Mathis Advertising, 1995.

McAllister, Matthew Paul. "Comic Books and AIDS." *Journal of Popular Culture* 26, no. 2 (1992): 1–24.

———. "Cultural Argument and Organizational Constraint in the Comic Book Industry." *Journal of Communication* 40, no. 1 (Winter 1990): 55–71.

McCleary, Chuck. "How the Serials Rate." *Serial World* 1, no. 3 (1975): 6–7.

McCool, Ben, and Craig Rousseau. "The Star Lord." *Captain America and the Korvac Saga* 1, no. 4 (May 2011).

McGuirk, Brendan. "Why Marvel Owes No Apology to Captain America's 'Tea Party.'" *Comics Alliance*, Feb. 11, 2010. At http://comicsalliance.com/captain-america-tea-party-controversy/. Accessed Mar. 14, 2010.

McKenzie, Roger, Sal Buscema, John Tartag, and Mike Esposito. "A Serpent Lurks Below." *Captain America* 1, no. 228 (Dec. 1978).

McKenzie, Roger, Michael Fleischer, Sal Buscema, and Don Perlin. "Death Dive." *Captain America* 1, no. 236 (Aug. 1979).

McKenzie, Roger, and Don Perlin. "The Way of All Flesh!" *Captain America* 1, no. 244 (Apr. 1980).

Medved, Michael, and Michael Lackner. *The Betrayal of Captain America*. White Paper. Washington, DC: Foundation for the Defense of Democracies, Apr. 2003. At http://www.defenddemocracy.org/index.php?option=com_content&task=view&id=11782096&Itemid=102. Accessed Dec. 5, 2009.

"The Men Who Conquered the Earth." *Journey into Unknown Worlds* 1, no. 7 (Oct. 1951).

Messner, Michael A. "When Bodies Are Weapons: Masculinity and Violence in Sport." *International Review for the Sociology of Sport* 25, no. 3 (Sept. 1990): 203–20.

Michelinie, David, Mark Bright, and Bob Layton. "Who Guards the Guardsmen?" *Iron Man* 1, no. 228 (Mar. 1988).

Michelinie, David, and John Byrne. "Death on the Hudson!" *The Avengers* 1, no. 184 (June 1979).

———. "The Redoubtable Return of Crusher Creel!" *The Avengers* 1, no. 183 (May 1979).

Michelinie, David, John Byrne, and Gene Day. "On the Matter of Heroes." *The Avengers* 1, no. 181 (Mar. 1979).

Michelinie, David, and George Perez. "Interlude." *The Avengers* 1, no. 194 (Apr. 1980).

Millar, Mark, and Chris Bachalo. "Ultimates vs. Ultimate X-Men." *Ultimate War* 1, no. 2 (Feb. 2003).

Millar, Mark, and Brian Hitch. "21st Century Boy." *The Ultimates* 1, no. 3 (May 2002).

———. "Dead Man Walking." *The Ultimates* 2 1, no. 2 (Mar. 2005).

———. "Giant Man vs. the Wasp." *The Ultimates* 1, no. 6 (Aug. 2002).

———. "Grand Theft America." *The Ultimates* 2 1, no. 9 (Jan. 2006).

———. "Homeland Security." *The Ultimates* 1, no. 7 (Sept. 2002).

———. "Hulk Does Manhattan." *The Ultimates* 1, no. 5 (July 2002).

———. "Thunder." *The Ultimates* 1, no. 4 (June 2002).

———. "The Trial of the Hulk." *The Ultimates* 2 1, no. 3 (Apr. 2005).

———. "Wolf in the Fold." *The Ultimates* 2 1, no. 7 (Sept. 2005).

Miller, Frank, and David Mazucchelli. "Armageddon." *Daredevil* 1, no. 233 (Aug. 1986).

———. "God and Country." *Daredevil* 1, no. 232 (July 1986).

Millar, Mark, and Steve McNiven. "Civil War: Part One of Seven." *Civil War* 1, no. 1 (July 2006).

———. "Civil War: Part Three of Seven." *Civil War* 1, no. 3 (Sept. 2006).

———. "Civil War: Part Seven of Seven." *Civil War* 1, no. 7 (Jan. 2007).

Miller, Joshua Rhett. "Tea Party Jab to Be Zapped from Captain America Comic, Writer Says." *FoxNews.com*, Feb. 10, 2010. At http://www.foxnews.com/politics /2010/02/09/tea-party-reference-captain-america-removed/. Accessed Apr. 14, 2010.

Miller, Susan, and Greg Rode. "The Movie You See, the Movie You Don't: How Disney Do's That Old Time Derision." In *From Mouse to Mermaid: The Politics of Film, Gender, and Culture*, edited by Elizabeth Bell, Lynda Haas, and Laura Sells, 86–106. Bloomington: Indiana Univ. Press, 1995.

Mills, Anthony R. *American Theology, Superhero Comics, and Cinema*. New York: Routledge, 2013.

Modleski, Tania. *Feminism without Women: Culture and Criticism in a "Postfeminist" Age*. New York: Routledge, 1991.

Molly Rebuttal. "Captain America's Death a Bush Indictment?" *blonde sagacity*, Mar. 12, 2007. At http://mobyrebuttal.blogspot.com/2007/03/captain-ameri cas-death-bush-indictment.html. Accessed Apr. 4, 2007.

Mondello, Salvatore. "Spider-Man: Superhero in the Liberal Tradition." *Journal of Popular Culture* 10, no. 1 (1976): 232–38.

Morales, Robert, and Chris Bachalo. "Homeland, Part Two." *Captain America* 4, no. 22 (Mar. 2004).

Morales, Robert, and Kyle Baker. "The Blackvine." *Truth: Red, White & Black* 1, no. 7 (July 2003).

———. *Captain America: Truth.* New York: Marvel Comics, 2009.

———. "The Math." *Truth: Red, White, & Black* 1, no. 5 (May 2003).

———. "The Whitewash." *Truth: Red, White, & Black* 1, no. 6 (June 2003).

Morrell, David, and Mitch Breitweiser. "Fear in a Handful of Dust." *Captain America: The Chosen* 1, no. 4 (Dec. 2007).

———. "Multitude." *Captain America: The Chosen* 1, no. 6 (Feb. 2008).

———. "Now You See Me, Now You Don't." *Captain America: The Chosen* 1, no. 1 (Nov. 2007).

Morse, Ben. "The Big Questions: Ed Brubaker Addresses the Hot Topics Facing Marvel in the Wake of the Star-Spangled Avenger's Death." *Wizard Magazine*, May 2007.

———. "The Wizard Retrospective: Captain America." *Wizard Magazine*, May 2007.

Murphy, John M. "'Our Mission and Our Moment': George W. Bush and September 11th." *Rhetoric & Public Affairs* 6, no. 4 (Winter 2003): 607–32.

Murray, Doug, and Wayne Vansant. "Back in the Real World." *The 'Nam* 1, no. 41 (Feb. 1990).

Myers, Scot W. Letter. *Captain America* 3, no. 22 (Oct. 1999).

"Mystery of the Atomic Boomerang." *Captain America Comics* 1, no. 51 (Dec. 1945).

"The Mystery of Hangman's Island." *All Select* 1, no. 4 (July 1944).

"Mystery of the Human Thunderbolt." *Showcase* 1, no. 4 (Oct. 1956).

Nama, Adilifu. *Super Black: American Pop Culture and Black Superheroes.* Austin: Univ. of Texas Press, 2011.

Nash, Gary B. *The Unknown American Revolution: The Unruly Birth of Democracy and the Struggle to Create America.* New York: Viking, 2005.

Nevins, Allan. "How We Felt about the War." In *While You Were Gone: A Report on Wartime Life in the United States*, edited by Jack Goodman, 3–27. New York: Simon and Schuster, 1946.

New World Pictures Ltd. *Annual Report.* Los Angeles: New World Pictures, 1986.

"Newswatch." *Marvel Age* 1, no. 11 (Feb. 1984): 6.

nicedeb. "Captain America Takes On the Tea-Partiers." *Nice Deb*, Feb. 8, 2010. At http://nicedeb.wordpress.com/2010/02/08/captain-america-takes-on-the-tea-partiers/. Accessed Mar. 14, 2010.

Nolan, Mike. "The Timely Comics Super-Hero Index (1939–1957)." *Alter Ego* 3, no. 57 (Mar. 2006): 3–64.

"No Man Is an Island." *Captain America Comics* 1, no. 69 (Nov. 1948).

Novick, Peter. *That Noble Dream: The "Objectivity Question" and the American Historical Profession.* Cambridge: Cambridge Univ. Press, 1988.

Nyberg, Amy Kiste. *Seal of Approval: The History of the Comics Code.* Jackson: Univ. Press of Mississippi, 1998.

O'Neil, Dennis, and Neal Adams. "Earthquake Beware My Power." *Green Lantern/Green Arrow* 1, no. 87 (Dec. 1971–Jan. 1972).

———. *Green Lantern/Green Arrow* 1, no. 1 (2004).

———. *Green Lantern/Green Arrow* 1, no. 2 (2004).

O'Neil, Denny, and Luke McDonnell. "Firebrand's Revenge." *Iron Man* 1, no. 172 (July 1983).

"On to Berlin." *Captain America Comics* 1, no. 19 (Oct. 1942).

"The Outer World of Doom." *The Human Torch* 1, no. 35 (Nov. 1949).

"Outwitting the Bloodthirsty Tyrants." *Young Allies* 1, no. 1 (July 1941).

Owsley, Jim. "Creating a New Limited Series: *The Falcon.*" *Marvel Age* 1, no. 7 (Oct. 1983): 13–14.

Owlsey, Jim, and Paul Smith. "Faith!" *The Falcon* 1, no. 3 (Jan. 1984).

———. "Resurrection!" *The Falcon* 1, no. 4 (Feb. 1984).

———. "Winners and Losers!" *The Falcon* 1, no. 1 (Nov. 1983).

Palmer-Mehta, Valerie, and Kellie Hay. "A Superhero for Gays? Gay Masculinity and Green Lantern." *Journal of American Culture* 28, no. 4 (2005): 390–404.

Pasley, Jeffrey L., Andrew W. Robertson, and David Waldstreicher, eds. *Beyond the Founders: New Approaches to the Political History of the Early American Republic.* Chapel Hill: Univ. of North Carolina Press, 2004.

Patterson, James T. *Grand Expectations: The United States, 1945–1974.* New York: Oxford Univ. Press, 1996.

Peterson, Bill, and Emily D. Gerstein. "Fighting and Flying: Archival Analysis of Threat, Authoritarianism, and the North American Comic Book." *Political Psychology* 26, no. 6 (2005): 887–904.

Phegley, Kiel. "Political Controversy and the Heroic Age." *Comic Book Resources,* Feb. 10, 2010. At http://www.comicbookresources.com/?page=article&id=24784. Accessed Apr. 14, 2010.

Phillips, Adam. "The New Talent Department." *Marvel Age* 1, no. 30 (Sept. 1985): 13–15.

"Postscript: A Visit with Jim Shooter." *Marvel Age* 1, no. 20 (Nov. 1984): 13–15.

"The Private Life of Captain America." *Captain America Comics* 1, no. 59 (Oct. 1946).

Queenan, Joe. "Drawing on the Dark Side." *New York Times Magazine,* Apr. 30, 1989.

Raimi, Sam, dir. *Spider-Man.* Culver City, CA: Sony Pictures Entertainment, 2002.

Raphael, Jordan, and Tom Spurgeon. *Stan Lee and the Rise and Fall of the American Comic Book.* Chicago: Chicago Review Press, 2003.

Raviv, Dan. *Comic Wars: How Two Tycoons Battled over the Marvel Comics Empire—and Both Lost.* New York: Broadway Books, 2002.

"The Red Skull and the Graveyard of Doom." *Young Allies* 1, no. 1 (July 1941).

"The Red Skull Strikes Again." *Captain America's Weird Tales* 1, no. 74 (Oct. 1949).

Remender, Rick, and Daniel Acuña. *Uncanny Avengers* 1, no. 9 (Aug. 2013).

Remender, Rick, and John Cassaday. *Uncanny Avengers* 1, no. 2 (Jan. 2013).

———. *Uncanny Avengers* 1, no. 3 (Feb. 2013).

Remender, Rick, and Nic Klein. "Super-Soldier No More." *Captain America* 7, no. 21 (Aug. 2014).

Remender, Rick, and Carlos Pacheco. *Captain America* 7, no. 14 (Feb. 2014).

———. "A Fire in the Rain." *Captain America* 7, no. 11 (Nov. 2013).

Remender, Rick, and John Romita Jr. *Captain America* 7, no. 6 (June 2013).

———. *Captain America* 7, no. 8 (Aug. 2013).

———. *Captain America* 7, no. 10 (Oct. 2013).

Remender, Rick, and Patrick Zircher. "Red Light Nation." *Secret Avengers* 1, no. 21.1 (Mar. 2011).

"The Return of the Human Torch." *Young Men* 1, no. 24 (Dec. 1953).

"The Return of the Red Skull." *Young Men* 1, no. 27 (Apr. 1954).

Reynolds, Richard, *Super Heroes: A Modern Mythology.* Jackson: Univ. of Mississippi Press, 1992.

"The Riddle of the Totem Pole." *USA Comics* 1, no. 16 (July 1945).

Ridgell, Lamont. Letter. *Captain America* 1, no. 340 (Apr. 1988).

Rieber, John Ney, and John Cassaday. "Above the Law." *Captain America* 4, no. 5 (Oct. 2002).

———. "Dust." *Captain America* 4, no. 1 (June 2002).

———. "Warlords, Part 3." *Captain America* 4, no. 6 (Dec. 2002).

Riley, Shannon E. "The Man Who Saved the Justice League of America: Writer Steve Englehart Brings Drama, Discord, and Deceit to DC's Premier Super-Team." *Back Issue* 1, no. 45 (Dec. 2010): 13–25.

Ro, Ronin. *Tales to Astonish: Jack Kirby, Stan Lee, and the American Comic Book Revolution*. New York: Bloomsbury, 2004.

Robbins, Frank, and Irv Novick. "One Bullet Too Many." *Batman* 1, no. 217 (Dec. 1969).

Roblou, Yann. "Complex Masculinities: The Superhero in Modern American Movies." *Culture, Society, & Masculinity* 4, no. 1 (2012): 76–91.

Rodriquez, Albert. Letter. *Captain America* 1, no. 110 (Feb. 1969).

"Rushed Hot off the Press." *Marvel Mystery Comics* 1, no. 15 (Jan. 1941).

Russo, Anthony, and Joe Russo, dirs. *Captain America: Winter Soldier*. Los Angeles: Marvel Studios, 2014.

"The Saboteur of Death." *Captain America Comics* 1, no. 30 (Sept. 1943).

Sacks, Ethan. "Captain America Killed! Marvel Comic Book Hero Shot Dead by Sniper." *New York Daily News*, Mar. 9, 2007. At http://www.nydailynews.com/entertainment/music-arts/captain-america-killed-article-1.217626. Accessed Mar. 10, 2007.

Saffel, Steve. "Introducing the Marvel Super Heroes Role Playing Game." *Marvel Age* 1, no. 18 (Sept. 1984): 18–20.

Sammond, Nicholas. *Babes in Tomorrowland: Walt Disney and the Making of the American Child, 1930–1960*. Durham, NC: Duke Univ. Press, 2005.

Sanderson, Peter. "Book I: The Saga Begins . . . !" *Marvel Saga* 1, no. 1 (Dec. 1985).

———. "Book XII: A Legend Reborn!" *Marvel Saga* 1, no. 12 (Nov. 1986).

———. *Classic Marvel Super Heroes*. New York: Barnes and Noble, 2005.

———. "Guidebook to the Cosmos: *The Official Handbook of the Marvel Universe*." *Marvel Age* 1, no. 1 (Apr. 1983): 13–16.

———. "A Tale of Two Captains: An Interview with Mark Gruenwald on Captain America." *Amazing Heroes* 1, no. 146 (Aug. 1988): 21–29.

Savage, William W., Jr. *Commies, Cowboys, and Jungle Queens: Comic Books and America, 1945–1954*. Middletown, CT: Wesleyan Univ. Press, 1998.

Schlesinger, Arthur M., Jr. *The Cycles of American History.* Boston: Houghton Mifflin, 1986.

Scruton, Roger. *An Intelligent Person's Guide to Philosophy.* New York: Penguin Books, 1996.

Segal, Lynn. *Slow Motion: Changing Masculinities, Changing Men.* London: Virago Press, 1990.

"The Seven Sons of Satan." *Captain America Comics* 1, no. 37 (Apr. 1944).

"The Shadows of Death." *Captain America* 1, no. 43 (Dec. 1944).

Shaheen, Jack G. "Arab Images in American Comic Books." *Journal of Popular Culture* 28, no. 1 (1994): 123–33.

Sharp, Joanne P. "Reel Geographies of the New World Order: Patriotism, Masculinity, and Geopolitics in Post–Cold War American Movies." In *Rethinking Geopolitics*, edited by Gearóid Ó Tuathail and Simon Dalby, 152–69. New York: Routlege, 1998.

Shooter, Jim, and Don Heck. "The Battle of the Four Armies!" *Secret Wars* 1, no. 5 (Sept. 1984).

———. "Death to the Beyonder!" *Secret Wars* 1, no. 10 (Feb. 1985).

———. "Invasion!" *Secret Wars* 1, no. 8 (Dec. 1984).

———. " . . . Nothing to Fear." *Secret Wars* 1, no. 12 (Apr. 1985).

———. "Prisoners of War!" *Secret Wars* 1, no. 2 (June 1984).

———. "Tempest without, Crisis within!" *Secret Wars* 1, no. 3 (July 1984).

———. "The War Begins." *Secret Wars* 1, no. 1 (May 1984).

Shooter, Jim, David Michelini, and Mike Zeck. "Rite of Passage!" *Captain America* 1, no. 259 (July 1981).

Shorten, Harry, and Irving Novick. "The Shield: G-Man-Extraordinary." *Pep Comics* 1, no. 1 (Jan. 1940).

Simon, Joe. "Beware! Captain America Is Coming!" *The Human Torch* 1, no. 3 (Dec. 1940).

Simon, Joe, and Jack Kirby. "Case #2: Trapped in the Nazi Strong-hold." *Captain America Comics* 1, no. 2 (Apr. 1941).

———. "The Chess Board of Death." *Captain America Comics* 1, no. 1 (Mar. 1941).

———. "The Gruesome Secret of the Dragon of Death." *Captain America Comics* 1, no. 5 (Aug. 1941).

———. "Meet Captain America." *Captain America Comics* 1, no. 1 (Mar. 1941).

———. "The Riddle of the Red Skull." *Captain America Comics* 1, no. 1 (Mar. 1941).

———. "The Unholy Legion." *Captain America Comics* 1, no. 4 (June 1941).

Simon, Joe, and Jim Simon. *The Comic Book Makers.* Lebanon, NJ: Vanguard, 2003.

Simonson, Walt, and Michael Ryan. "Shadowbox." *The Avengers* 2, no. 9 (July 1997).

Singh, Arune. "Ultimate Sequel: Mark Millar Talks 'Ultimates 2.'" *Comic Book Resources,* Oct. 22, 2004. At http://www.comicbookresources.com/news/print this.cgi?id=4339. Accessed Feb. 12, 2010.

Skidmore, Max J., and Joey Skidmore. "More Than Mere Fantasy: Political Themes in Contemporary Comic Books." *Journal of Popular Culture* 17, no. 1 (1983): 83–92.

Slotkin, Richard. *Regeneration through Violence: The Mythology of the American Frontier, 1600–1860.* Middletown, CT: Wesleyan Univ. Press, 1973.

Smith, J. Y. "H. R. Haldeman Dies." *Washington Post,* Nov. 13, 1993. At http://www .washingtonpost.com/ac2/wp-dyn?pagename=article&contentId=A99231-19 93Nov13. Accessed May 5, 2008.

Smith, Zack. "Brubaker and Casey's Captain America Influences." *Back Issue* 1, no. 20 (Feb. 2007): 24.

———. "The Nomad Saga: Englehart and Buscema on Captain America's Identity Crisis." *Back Issue* 1, no. 20 (Feb. 2007): 16–23.

Snapp, Jim. Letter. *Captain America* 1, no. 339 (Mar. 1988).

Solarz, Stephen, Richard Perle, Elliot Abrams, Richard V. Allen, Richard Armitage, Jeffrey T. Bergner, John Bolton, Stephen Bryen, Richard Burt, Frank Carlucci, et al. "Open Letter to the President." Feb. 18, 1998. At http://www .iraqwatch.org/perspectives/rumsfeld-openletter.htm. Accessed June 10, 2010.

"S.O.S. Green Lantern." *Showcase* 1, no. 22 (Oct. 1959).

Spencer, Nick, and Scot Eaton. *Secret Avengers* 1, no. 12.1 (June 2011).

Spitulnik, Deborah. "The Social Circulation of Media Discourse and the Mediation of Communities." *Journal of Linguistic Anthropology* 6, no. 2 (1997): 161–87.

Springer, Frank, and Roy Thomas. "What If the Invaders Had Stayed Together after World War Two?" *What If?* 1, no. 4 (Aug. 1977).

Stelzer, Irwin. "Neoconservatives and Their Critics: An Introduction." In *The Neocon Reader,* edited by Irwin Stelzer, 3–28. New York: Grove Press, 2004.

Stern, Roger. Letter response. *Captain America* 1, no. 246 (June 1980).

Stern, Roger, and John Byrne. "Blood on the Moors." *Captain America* 1, no. 254 (Feb. 1981).

————. "Cap for President!" *Captain America* 1, no. 250 (Oct. 1980).

————. "Dragon Man." *Captain America* 1, no. 248 (Aug. 1980).

————. "The Living Legend." *Captain America* 1, no. 255 (Mar. 1981).

Stevens, J. Richard. "Easy Riding: The Liberalization of Captain America through Motorcycle Journey." *International Journal of Motorcycle Studies* 8, no. 2 (Fall 2012): 1–27.

————. "'Let's Rap with Cap': Redefining 'American Patriotism' through Popular Discourse and Letters." *Journal of Popular Culture* 44, no. 3 (2011): 606–32.

————. "On the Front Line: Portrayals of War Correspondents in Marvel Comics' *Civil War: Front Line*." *Image of the Journalist in Popular Culture Journal* 1, no. 1 (Fall 2009): 37–69.

————. "Ultimate Race Presentations: Racial Adaptations of Marvel's Falcon and Luke Cage in 2013 Disney Superhero Cartoons." Paper presented at the Annual National Meeting of the Popular Culture Association/American Culture Association, Chicago, Apr. 17, 2014.

Storey, John. *Inventing Popular Culture: From Folklore to Globalization*. Hoboken, NJ: Wiley & Sons, 2009.

Stracynski, J. Michael, and Oliver Coipel. *Thor* 3, no. 11 (Nov. 2008).

Stracynski, J. Michael, and Ron Garney. "The War at Home, Part 3 of 6." *The Amazing Spider-Man* 1, no. 534 (Sept. 2006).

————. "The War at Home, Part 6 of 7." *The Amazing Spider-Man* 1, no. 537 (Dec. 206).

————. "The War at Home, Part 7 of 7." *The Amazing Spider-Man* 1, no. 538 (Jan. 2007).

Stracynski, J. Michael, and John Romita Jr. "Stand Tall." *The Amazing Spider-Man* 2, no. 36 (Dec. 2001).

"The Strange Case of the Malay Idol." *All Winners Comics* 1, no. 2 (Oct. 1941).

Svetkey, Benjamin. "Barack Obama: Celebrity in Chief." *Entertainment Weekly*, Nov. 21, 2008. At http://www.ew.com/ew/article/0,,20241874,00.html. Accessed Dec. 8, 2012.

"Symphony of Death." *Captain America* 1, no. 49 (Aug. 1945).

Tagoe, Charles K. Letter. *Captain America* 1, no. 232 (Apr. 1979).

"The Talons of the Vulture." *Captain America Comics* 1, no. 32 (Nov. 1943).

Teitelbaum, Lorne. Letter. *Captain America* 1, no. 328 (Apr. 1987).

tgusa. Comment. *Dr. Bulldog and Ronin*, Feb. 9, 2010. At http://doctorbulldog .wordpress.com/2010/02/09/marvel-comics-turn-tea-party-patriots-into-racist -villains/. Accessed Mar. 14, 2010.

Theweleit, Klaus. *Male Fantasies, Volume One: Women, Floods, Bodies, History.* Minneapolis: Univ. of Minnesota Press, 1987.

Thomas, John Rhett. "The Spotlight Interview with Mark Millar." *Marvel Spotlight: Civil War,* June 2007, 16–24.

Thomas, Michael. "Jim Shooter Interview: Part 1." *Comic Book Resources,* Oct. 6, 2000. At http://www.comicbookresources.com/print.php?type=ar&id=147. Accessed June 17, 2011.

Thomas, Roy. "Introduction." In *Marvel Masterworks: Atlas Era Heroes,* vol. 1, vi–ix. New York: Marvel Publishing, 2007.

———. "Marvel's Most Timely Heroes." In *The Golden Age of Marvel Comics,* vol. 1, no. 1, edited by Tom Brevoort, 4–8. New York: Marvel Comics, 1997.

———. "World War II Forever (but Only in Comic Books)." *Alter Ego* 3, no. 20 (Jan. 2003): 3–14.

Thomas, Roy, and John Buscema. "Death Calls for the Arch Heroes." *The Avengers* 1, no. 52 (May 1968).

———. "Magneto Walks the Earth." *The Avengers* 1, no. 47 (Dec. 1967).

Thomas, Roy, and Sal Buscema. "Endgame!" *The Avengers* 1, no. 71 (Dec. 1969).

———. "When Strikes the Squadron Sinister." *The Avengers* 1, no. 70 (Nov. 1969).

Thomas, Roy, Dan Glut, and John Buscema. "The Search for Steve Rogers." *Captain America and the Falcon* 1, no. 217 (Jan. 1978).

Thomas, Roy, and Frank Robbins. "Blitzkrieg at Bermuda." *The Invaders* 1, no. 3 (Nov. 1975).

———. "The Coming of the Invaders." *Giant-Size Invaders* 1, no. 1 (June 1975).

Thomas, Roy, Frank Robbins, and Frank Springer. "Enter: The Mighty Destroyer!" *The Invaders* 1, no. 18 (July 1977).

———. "God Save the King." *The Invaders* 1, no. 15 (Apr. 1977).

Thomas, Roy, George Tuska, and Pablo Marcus. "The Way It REALLY Was." *Captain America and the Falcon* 1, no. 215 (Nov. 1977).

"Tojo's Terror Masters." *Captain America Comics* 1, no. 42 (Oct. 1944).

"Top Secret." *Young Men* 1, no. 25 (Feb. 1954).

"The Top Ten." *Marvel Age* 1, no. 63 (June 1988): 8.

Trimpe, Herb. *The Hulk* (cover art). *Rolling Stone* 1, no. 91 (Sept. 1971).

Truitt, Brian. "Agent Coulson Charges into Comics with 'Battle Scars.'" *USA Today,* Apr. 24, 2012. At http://usatoday30.usatoday.com/life/comics/story/2012-04-25/Agent-Coulson-Avengers-movie-comic-books/54508162/1. Accessed May 5, 2012,

Valentino, Jim, and Rob Liefeld. "Awaken the Thunder." *The Avengers* 2, no. 1 (Nov. 1996).

———. "In Love & War." *The Avengers* 2, no. 3 (Jan. 1997).

"The Vampire Strikes." *All Winners Comics* 1, no. 42 (July 1942).

"Vanguard Productions Presents THE SPIRIT OF AMERICA Print by JIM Steranko." 2002. http://www.vanguardproductions.net/steranko/soa/. Accessed June 17, 2006.

Vassallo, Michael J. "A Golden Age Reunion: Two Timely Talks with Allen Bellman." *Alter Ego* 3, no. 32 (Jan. 2004): 3–44.

"The Vault of the Doomed." *Captain America Comics* 1, no. 22 (Jan. 1943).

Voger, Mark. *The Dark Age: Grim, Great, & Gimmicky Post-modern Comics*. Raleigh, NC: TwoMorrows, 2006.

"Voyage to No-Man's-Land." *Young Allies* 1, no. 1 (July 1941).

"The Vultures of Violent Death." *Captain America Comics* 1, no. 28 (July 1943).

Waid, Mark. Letter. *Captain America* 1, no. 454 (Aug. 1996).

Waid, Mark, and Dale Braithwaite. "Back in Black." *Captain America: Sentinel of Liberty* 1, no. 9 (May 1999).

Waid, Mark, and Dale Eaglesham. "Hoaxed." *Captain America* 3, no. 7 (July 1998).

Waid, Mark, and Ron Garney. "American Graffiti." *Captain America* 3, no. 2 (Feb. 1998).

———. "Capmania." *Captain America* 3, no. 4 (Apr. 1998).

———. "Old Soldiers Never Die." *Captain America* 1, no. 445 (Nov. 1995).

———. "Operation: Rebirth Conclusion." *Captain America* 1, no. 448 (Feb. 1996).

———. "Plan 'B.'" *Captain America* 1, no. 452 (June 1996).

———. "The Return of Steve Rogers, Captain America." *Captain America* 3, no. 1 (Jan. 1998).

———. "Sanctuary." *Captain America* 1, no. 454 (Aug. 1996).

———. "Sentinel of Liberty!" *Captain America: Sentinel of Liberty* 1, no. 1 (Sept. 1998).

Waid, Mark, and Cully Hamner. "Flashpoint." *Captain America: Sentinel of Liberty* 1, no. 8 (Apr. 1999).

Waid, Mark, and Andy Kubert. "American Nightmare, Part 1: The Bite of Madness." *Captain America* 3, no. 9 (Sept. 1998).

———. "First Gleaming." *Captain America* 3, no. 15 (Mar. 1999).

———. "Plausible Deniability." *Captain America* 3, no. 13 (Jan. 1999).

————. "Red Glare." *Captain America* 3, no. 16 (Apr. 1999).

————. "A Tale of Morality and Failure: Extreme Prejudice." *Captain America* 3, no. 17 (May 1999).

————. "Triumph of the Will." *Captain America* 3, no. 19 (July 1999).

————. "Turnabout." *Captain America* 3, no. 14 (Feb. 1999).

Waldstreicher, David. *In the Midst of Perpetual Fetes: The Making of American Nationalism, 1776–1820.* Chapel Hill: Univ. of North Carolina Press, 1997.

"The Walking Dead." *Captain America Comics* 1, no. 50 (Oct. 1945).

Wandtke, Terrence R. "Introduction." In *The Amazing Transforming Superhero! Essays on the Revision of Characters in Comic Books, Film, and Television,* edited by Terrence R. Wandtke, 1–32. Jefferson, NC: McFarland, 2007.

Wanzo, Rebecca. "Wearing Hero-Face: Black Citizens and Melancholic Patriotism in *Truth: Red, White, and Black.*" *Journal of Popular Culture* 42, no. 2 (2009): 339–62.

Wasko, Janet. *Understanding Disney: The Manufacture of Fantasy.* Cambridge, UK: Polity Press, 2001.

Watson, Jonathan. *Male Bodies: Health, Culture, and Identity.* Buckingham, UK: Open Univ. Press, 2005.

Weigel, David. "Scenes from the New American Tea Party." *Washington Independent,* Feb. 27, 2009. At http://washingtonindependent.com/31868/scenes-from-the-new-american-tea-party. Accessed Mar. 14, 2010.

Weinstein, Simcha. *Up, Up, and Oy Vey! How Jewish History, Culture, and Values Shaped the Comic Book Superhero.* Baltimore: Leviathan, 2006.

"Weird Tales of the Wee Males." *Captain America Comics* 1, no. 69 (Nov. 1948).

Weissburg, Paul. Letter. *Captain America* 1, no. 318 (June 1986).

Wertham, Frederic. *Seduction of the Innocent.* New York: Rinehart, 1954.

Whannel, Garry. *Media Sports Stars: Masculinities and Moralities.* London: Routledge, 2002.

"What Is *Marvel Age?*" *Marvel Age* 1, no. 1 (Apr. 1983): 1.

Whedon, Joss, dir. *The Avengers.* Burbank, CA: Marvel Studios, 2012.

"When Friends Turn Foes." *Captain America Comics* 1, no. 65 (Jan. 1948).

White, Ted. "Stan Lee Meets [Castle of] Frankenstein." *Alter Ego* 3, no. 74 (Dec. 2007): 5–15.

Wisham, Robert. Letter. *Captain America* 3, no. 25 (Jan. 2000).

Wolf-Meyer, Matthew. "The World Ozymandias Made: Utopias in the Superhero Comic, Subculture, and the Conservation of Difference." *Journal of Popular Culture* 36, no. 3 (2003): 497–517.

Wolk, Douglas. *Reading Comics: How Graphic Novels Work and What They Mean.* Cambridge, MA: Da Capo, 2007.

Wordsmith from Nantucket. "Breaking News: Captain America Assassinated! (as in: 'Character Assassination')." *Sparks from the Anvil,* Mar. 8, 2007. At http://hammeringsparksfromtheanvil.blogspot.com/2007/03/breaking-news-captain-america-dead.html. Accessed Apr. 4, 2007.

"The World of No Return." *The Justice League of America* 1, no. 1 (Nov. 1960).

"Worlds at War." *Captain America Comics* 1, no. 70 (Nov. 1948).

Wrigley, Rick. Letter. *Tales of Suspense* 1, no. 68 (Aug. 1965).

Wright, Bradford W. *Comic Book Nation: The Transformation of Youth Culture in America.* Baltimore: Johns Hopkins Univ. Press, 2001.

"Your Life Depends on It." *Captain America Comics* 1, no. 19 (Oct. 1942).

Zimmerman, Dwight Jon. "The G.I. Joe File." *Marvel Age* 1, no. 15 (June 1984): 8–12.

———. "G.I. Joe Update." *Marvel Age* 1, no. 20 (Nov. 1984): 21–24.

———. "The MARVEL AGE Interview: Jim Shooter." *Marvel Age* 1, no. 27 (June 1985): 10–13.

———. "The Marvel Reference Library." *Marvel Age* 1, no. 39 (June 1986): 18–21.

———. "The Transformers." *Marvel Age* 1, no. 17 (Aug. 1984): 8–10.

Zinn, Howard. "The Greatest Generation?" *The Progressive,* Oct. 2001. At http://www.progressive.org/0901/zinn1001.html. Accessed Jan. 22, 2011.

Index

Acrobat (as Captain America), 82
Adams, Neal, 105, 115
Adventures of Superman, The (television program), 59, 69, 73
Agent Axis, 120
AIM (Advanced Idea Mechanics), 205
Alberich, Ricardo, 3
All Select Comics, 38, 44, 154
All Winners Comics, 37, 38, 48, 53
Amazing Fantasy, 80
Amazing Spider-Man, The, 115, 126, 212, 213
American Dream, 47, 111, 143, 150, 153, 155, 159, 160, 166, 170, 186, 205, 221, 222, 277, 278, 280
American monomyth, xi, xv, 11, 18–19, 28–29, 34, 47, 69, 72, 78, 121, 161, 176, 179, 189, 198, 211, 212, 216, 220, 271, 278, 280, 284–86; Captain America breaks free of, 261; defined, 29
Andrae, Thomas, 11
Atlas Comics. *See* Marvel Comics
atomic weapons, 37, 46, 58, 61, 63, 79, 155, 186, 194, 218, 231; Captain America's criticism of, 37, 46, 186, 194; Captain America's endorsement of, 63
Avengers, 8, 82–89, 95; "Avengers: Disassembled," 240; Cap become leader, 85, 95–96, 146; and Galactic Storm,

191–92; origin, 82; racial quota for membership, 136–37, 206–7; "Red Zone" critique, 222–23; Secret Avengers, 272–75
Avengers, The (Marvel Studios film), 260–61
Avengers Assemble, 260
Avison, Al, 38

"Ballad of the Incredible Hulk, The" (song), 99
Baron Blood, 171–72, 282
Baron Zemo, 84–85, 141, 270
Batman (film), 259
Batman (television program), 74
Batman, 30, 48, 55, 58, 71, 73, 75, 130; analyzed, 12; in films, 259; on television, 74
Batroc, 91, 196
Battlestar, 180–82
Battlestar Galactica, 125
Bellman, Allen, 23
Bendis, Brian Michael, 277, 307
Bennett, Tony, 13
Beyonder, 129, 147, 152
Black Crow, 158–60, 179
Black Panther, 90, 101, 114, 134, 137, 249, 311n76
Black Widow, 202, 203, 260, 276

Blade, 101

Bradley, Isaiah, 16, 20, 214, 241

Brooker, Will, 12

Brooks, David, 228

Brubaker, Ed, 2, 115, 242, 256, 262, 264, 265, 269, 277, 288; comments on Cap's assassination, 262

Bucky, 16, 25, 27, 36–39, 43–54, 61–67, 83–84, 88, 106, 119, 120, 141–42, 146, 155, 159, 176, 177, 180–82, 197, 200, 213, 230, 242–44, 253, 265, 280, 282, 286; as Captain America, 265, 266–70, 271, 272; death, 83–84; of the 1950s (Jack Monroe), 142–44; of the 1980s (Lamar Hoskins), 180–82; as Winter Soldier (comics), 242, 243–44, 265–66; as Winter Soldier (films). *See also* Battlestar; Nomad

Buscema, Sal, 20, 289

Bush, George W., 218, 223, 230–32, 256–57

Byrne, John, 172, 178

Campbell, Joseph, 28, 216, 230

Captain America, 16; anti-drug stances of, 155–56, 201; assassination of, 1, 3, 254, 256–57; Bucky Barnes as (*see* Bucky); Clint Barton as (*see* Hawkeye); Isaiah Bradley as (*see* Bradley, Isaiah); William Burnside as, 10, 57–74, 105–7, 140, 266–67, 269, 335n58; as the Captain, 168–71; Frank Castle as, 265; comic appearances while "dead," 262; conflicts with Iron Man, 145–46, 192, 245–51, 254, 256; and drugs, 155–56; in films, 257–65; fired by government, 169–70, 193; has never killed, 120,

174, 195, 281; "Hazy continuity" of, 7–8; against killing, 120, 122, 150, 173–75, 189, 193, 194, 195, 210–12, 218, 221, 277; kills opponents, 25, 37, 43, 48, 49, 51, 55, 61, 65, 66, 68, 88, 92, 122, 119, 172, 175, 187, 216; "Moral center of the Marvel universe," 281; 1960s re-emergence, 8, 82–83; as Nomad, 110–12; origin of, 24–25, 45, 87–88, 92, 119–20, 127, 154, 171, 172, 178, 186, 241, 261, 264, 270, 276–77; other people as, 16, 20; prominence in Marvel Universe, 3, 151; quits, 90, 110–12, 168; Roscoe as, 111; as superspy, 272–76; on television, 259; threatens or uses torture, 43–44; against torture, 120; Ultimate Captain America, 224–27, 229, 232, 235–39; John Walker as (*see* Walker, John); Sam Wilson as (*see* Falcon)

Captain America, 21, 22, 90, 91, 92, 93, 94

Captain America (New World Pictures film), 259

Captain America (Republic Film serial films), 258–59

Captain America Comics, 2, 21, 22, 24, 26, 30, 35, 36, 37, 38, 39, 40, 41, 42, 43, 57, 58; cancelled, 57, 58; date of issue one, 21; first issue, 24

"Captain America Complex," 28, 32, 41, 47, 187, 211, 215, 220, 247

Captain America Goes to War against—Drugs, 156

Captain America: Sentinel of Liberty, 194

Captain America's Weird Tales, 40, 58, 64

Captain America: The First Avenger
      (Marvel Studios film), 257, 261–64
Captain America: The Winter Soldier
      (Marvel Studios film), 286–87, 293
Captain Marvel, 258
Carlin, Michael, 133, 134
Carter, Peggy, 88, 112; as Agent 13, 118
Carter, Sharon, 117–18, 135, 189,
      193–95, 205, 212, 213, 240, 243–45,
      278, 280
China, 48, 62, 65–66
Civil War (Marvel event), 9, 210, 242–57,
      289
Clinton, Bill, 195
Colan, Gene, 101
Comics Code, 69–74, 75, 95, 115, 122,
      171, 300n42
Communists, 59, 61–62, 64–68, 81
Conway, Gerry, 113
Coogan, Peter, 14–15
Coulter, Ann, 212
counterculture, 197, 227
Cox, Dave, 107–8
Cooper, Valerie, 169
Crossbones, 193
Cyclops, 277

Daredevil, 80–81, 130, 166
Daredevil, 101, 130, 166
Dark Knight Returns, The, 9, 12, 130
DC Comics (Detective Comics), 7, 38,
      51, 58, 73, 74, 75–76, 99, 101, 115,
      119; as National Comics, 58, 75
DeFalco, Tom, 130–31
DeMatteis, J. M., 140, 155, 159
Destroyer, 120
Diamondback, 144, 201–02, 286
Disney. *See* Walt Disney Company

Disney, Walt, 293
Ditko, Steve, 76, 80
Dittmer, Jason, 5, 106–7, 288
D-man, 207
Downey Jr., Robert, 259
DuBose, Mike, 12

Easy Rider (film), 94, 99
Eco, Umberto, 7, 12–13
Electro, 66
Elektra, 130
Engle, Gary, 11
Englehart, Steve, 20, 21, 105–16, 289
Erskine, Abraham. *See* Reinstein, Joseph
Everyman, 155

Falcon (Sam Wilson), 3, 93–94,
      100–108, 113–17, 135–39, 179–80,
      186–87, 206, 240, 266–69, 275, 290;
      as Avenger, 136–37; fan reaction to,
      113–14; as Captain America, 290,
      339n135; declining popularity of, 117;
      1983 limited series, 240; as "Snap,"
      113, 138
fan culture, 4–6, 10, 33, 125, 127; fan
      resources used by Marvel, 125–26;
      fans become creators, 119, 124; fans
      object to text, 11, 92–94, 113–14, 116,
      175–77, 184, 267–68, 269; "Sentinels
      of Liberty," 26–27, 52
Fantastic Four, 76–79, 82, 84, 147, 149
Fantastic Four, 78, 79, 101
Feiffer, Jules, 30
Femme Force, 118–19
Fighting American, 73
Fingeroth, Danny, 126–27, 177–78
Flag-Smasher, 163–65

Flash, 14, 75
Foster, Bill, 101, 311n76
Free Spirit, 203
Friedrich, Gary, 104–5, 116
Fury, Nick, 81–82, 88, 118, 139, 176,
    186, 218, 225, 227, 260, 266, 276,
    287, 309, 311, 332, 354, 360; agent
    of S.H.I.E.L.D., 118, 139, 186,
    218; in films, 260, 287; race-
    changed for comics, 260, 276;
    Ultimate Nick Fury, 225, 227–30,
    231, 235, 239–40

Galactus, 188, 277–78
Gargoyle, 79–80
Garney, Ron, 194, 203, 208
German American Bund, 36, 44, 63;
    objection to Captain America Comics
    #1, 36; portrayed in comics, 44
Germans, 48–50, 55
G. I. Joe: A Real American Hero, 128,
    183
G. I. Max, 166
Golden Girl (Betsy Ross/Betty Ross),
    39–40, 54–44, 65, 155
Goodman, Martin, 25–27, 36, 38, 41,
    57–58, 59, 76, 81, 99, 124
Gray, Jonathan, 4
Green Lantern, 75, 101, 103, 117
Green Lantern/Green Arrow, 115
Gruenwald, Mark, 126, 140, 160–61,
    163, 166, 167–68, 173, 177, 180–81,
    200, 204, 288–89; editorials of, 161,
    162, 229, 230, 231, 232, 235, 239–40,
    260

Halbwachs, Maurice, 9, 122
Haldeman, H. R., 108

Hama, Larry, 128
Harrington, C. Lee, 4
Hawkeye (Clint Barton), 85, 95–96,
    136–37, 260, 265; As Captain
    America, 264–65
He-Man and the Masters of the Universe,
    129
Hill, Maria, 242–43
Hitch, Bryan, 226, 230, 232–34, 238,
    260
Hitler, Adolf, 21, 36, 40, 45, 50, 60, 120,
    241, 261
homosexuality, 12, 71, 141–42
Hughes, Richard T., 31–33, 47
Hulk, Incredible, 79–80, 81, 82, 84, 99,
    126, 147, 149, 224, 226, 230, 232,
    235, 237, 238, 259, 260, 277; origin,
    79–84, 147, 149, 224, 226, 230, 232,
    235, 38, 260; on television, 259
Human Torch (Jim Hammond), 21, 26,
    35, 36, 38, 39, 52, 57–60, 244
Human Torch (Johnny Storm), 77, 78,
    79, 82, 148, 149
Human Torch Comics, 21, 57; cancelled,
    57
Hydra, 261–62, 287, 333n27

Image Comics, 131, 185, 194
Incredible Hulk, 81, 99, 303
Incredible Hulk, The (television pro-
    gram), 224
Invaders, 119–23, 146, 175, 154, 175,
    176–78, 263
Invaders, The, 22, 119, 120, 121, 122,
    146, 176, 178
Invisible Girl/Invisible Woman (Sue
    Storm), 77–78
Iran-Contra scandal, 167, 196
Iron Man (film), 257, 259

Iron Man, 81–83, 86, 90, 145–46, 192,
 245–54, 256, 263, 271, 290; alcoholism, 145; in films, 257, 259, 260
Iron Man 2 (film), 257
Isabella, Tony, 113

Jack Kirby Collector, 114
Jackson, Samuel L., 227, 229–30, 260;
 drawn as Ultimate Nick Fury, 227,
 229–30; as Nick Fury in Marvel
 films, 260
Japanese, 21, 37–38, 43, 45–50, 53, 64,
 69, 122
Jarvis, Edwin, 204
Jenkins, Henry, 10–11, 283, 285, 299
Jet Black, 277, 278
Jewett, Robert, xv, 28–32, 34, 41, 47, 56,
 187, 189, 196, 210–11, 216, 220, 247,
 284–86, 288
Jones, Gabriel, 81, 100–101, 112–13
Jones, Rick, 79–80, 84
Jones, Whitewash, 52, 53
Jurgens, Dan, 288
Justice League of America (JLA), 15,
 75–76, 82, 119

Kang the Conqueror, 188
Kennedy, John F., xii, 83, 289; assassinated, 83
Kirby, Jack, 25, 31, 32, 38, 45, 73, 76–78,
 81–88, 90, 92, 93, 95, 96–97, 99, 100,
 115–16, 171, 172, 178, 288–89; bases
 Captain America on life experiences, 288–89; co-creates Captain
 America, 45; co-creates Fighting
 American, 73; devastated by Kennedy Assassination, 83; fans object
 to 1960s stories of, 88; hired back to

Marvel, 76; leaves Marvel, 92, 99;
 leaves Timely, 38; returns to Marvel,
 93, 115
Klock, Geoff, 11, 122
Korean War, 59–69
Korvac, Michael, 188, 190
Krauthammer, Charles, 228
Kristol, Irving, 227
Kristol, William, 228

Lackner, Michael, 10, 220, 283–84
Lavender, 39, 55
Lawrence, John Shelton, xv, 28–29, 34,
 61, 187, 189, 196, 210–11, 216, 220,
 247, 284–86, 288
Lawrence, Mort, 61
Lee, Jim, 185, 186
Lee, Stan, 36, 38, 39, 68, 76–77, 78–90,
 95, 99, 100, 101, 106, 119, 120, 124, 154,
 289; first Captain America story, 36
Leila. *See* Taylor, Leila
Lennon, John, 116
Liefeld, Rob, 185, 186, 201–2
Loki, 82, 236

MacDonald, Andrew, 12, 97
MacDonald, Virginia, 12, 97
MacDougal, Robert, 48, 49
Mackinnon, Kenneth, 17
Magneto, 150, 277
Mantlo, Bill, 113
Man with No Face, 62, 120
Marvel Age, 127–28
Marvel Comics: Atlas era, 9, 57–58;
 Disney purchase of, 257; financial
 difficulty of, 184, 185–87; Silver Age,
 75–82; Timely era, 22, 23, 25–27,
 28–56

Marvel Comics, 39
"Marvel Method," 22, 78
Marvel Mystery Comics, 21, 26, 57; cancelled, 57
Marvel Saga, 126–27, 177–78
Marvel Studios, 11, 257, 259; created, 184
Marvel Superheroes Secret Wars, 129, 146–52
Marvel Tales, 57
Marvel Team-Up, 135, 224
masculinity, 11, 17–19, 103–4, 107–8, 134, 143, 161, 171, 173, 199, 200–202, 208, 237, 239, 274, 277, 288, 290, 291, 292; defined, 18
Master Man, 120
Masters of Evil, 84, 85
McAllister, Matthew, 12
McCarthyism, 93, 106–7, 121
McFarlane, Todd, 185
McKenzie, Roger, 152–53
Medved, Michael, 10, 220, 283–84
Millar, Mark, 9, 224–38, 260
Miller, Frank, 130
Mills, Anthony, 261
Miro-Julia, Joe, 3
Miss America, 39, 120
Mondello, Salvatore, 12
Moon Knight, 276
Morales, Robert, 241
Mr. Fantastic (Reed Richards), 76, 77, 147, 149, 230

'Nam, The, 200
Namor, the Sub-Mariner, 26, 35, 38, 39, 57, 59, 79, 82, 83–84, 119–20, 244; cancelled, 57; helps revive Cap, 83; as Invader, 120; 1960s revival, 79; television project, 59

National Publications. *See* DC Comics (Detective Comics)
Native Americans, 30–32, 37, 50–51, 158–60, 179, 217
Nazis, 31, 36, 42–44, 50, 52–53, 55, 62, 64, 67, 105, 150, 207, 261
neoconservatism, 227–37
New York Times, 1, 213
New York Times Magazine, 1, 131, 213
9/11. *See* September 11, 2001, attacks
Nixon, Richard, 8, 21, 106, 109–10, 111–12
Nomad, 110–12, 142–44, 172–73, 207; Jack Munroe as, 142–44, 172–73, 207; Steve Rogers becomes, 110
Norris, Chuck, 130, 196
Northstar, 142
Nova, 278
nuclear weapons. *See* atomic weapons
Nuke, 166, 275, 279–80

Obama, Barack, 257, 267, 271–72
Official Handbook of the Marvel Universe, The, 126–27, 177
Olshevesky, George, 125–26, 284
O'Neil, Dennis, 115, 119, 128
Osborn, Norman, 270–72, 279
Owsley, Jim. *See* Priest, Christopher

Paladin, 199
Perleman, Ronald, 184
Priest, Christopher (Jim Owsley), 137–38, 240
Professor X (Charles Xavier), 147, 150
Protocide, 187, 198
Prowler, 101
Punisher, 130–31, 171, 173–74, 192, 197; as Captain America, 265

Pym, Henry, 81, 82, 83, 85, 86, 235, 308n26; as Ant-Man, 81, 82,308n26; as Giant-man, 82, 83, 85, 86, 235

Quasar, 192
Quesada, Joe, 213, 269
Quicksilver, 85

race relations in comics, 48–54, 100–106, 115, 137–39, 179–82, 186, 206–7, 239–41, 291, 292–93; in Bronze Age, 100–106; in Golden Age, 48–54; in 1980s, 137–39, 179–82; in 1990s, 206–7; relevant comics dealing with, 115; in 2000s, 239–41
Rambo, 170, 196
Reagan, Ronald, 28, 124, 138, 152, 156, 167–69, 195, 199
Redpath, Inali, 217–19
Red Skull, 36, 40, 47, 53, 84, 89, 90–91, 96, 2014, 111–13, 141, 152, 159, 166, 169, 186, 187–91, 222, 261, 267, 271, 278; 1950s Red Skull, 61, 64; Sinthea Schmidt, 270
Reinstein, Joseph (Abraham Erskine), 87, 92, 119, 176, 178, 292
Remender, Rick, 276–77
retroactive continuity (retcon), 7, 73, 84, 105, 106, 107, 113, 120, 140, 142, 176, 194, 221, 241, 242, 262, 265, 266, 281, 298, 333n27; defined, 7
Reynolds, Richard, 6, 8, 11
Richards, Gail, 230
Rieber, John Ney, xiv, 215–17, 257
Roberston, Robbie, 101
Rogers, Ian, 279
Rolling Stone, 99
Romita, John, 61, 68, 73

Roosevelt, Franklin D., 24, 41, 172
Rosenthal, Bernie, 139–46, 155–56, 167, 179
Rosselló, Francesc, 3
Roth, Arnie, 141–42
Russians, 54, 62–64

Sandvoss, Cornel, 4
Savage, William, 48, 58–60, 62, 68
Scarlet Witch (Wanda Maximoff), 85, 240
Schwartz, Julius, 75
Scourge, 173–74
Secret Empire, 109–10, 111
Secret Wars. *See Marvel Superheroes Secret Wars*
Seduction of the Innocent. See Wertham, Frederic
Senate hearings. *See* US Senate, Subcommittee to Investigate Juvenile Delinquency
Sentinels of Liberty, 26–27, 52
September 11, 2001, attacks, 1–2, 5, 11, 14, 19, 22, 196, 210–17, 222, 246, 252–53, 284
Serpent Society, 144–45
Serpent Squad, 108
Sgt. Fury and His Howling Commandos, 81–82, 176
Shark, 120
S.H.I.E.L.D. (Supreme Headquarters, International Espionage, Law-Enforcement Division/ Strategic Hazard Intervention Espionage Logistics Directorate), 113, 117–19, 135, 189, 194–95, 198, 212, 242–44, 260, 275, 267
Shield, 30, 34–35
Shooter, Jim, 124–30, 177

Shores, Syd, 38

Siege (Marvel event), 271–72

Simon, Joe, 2, 27, 21–32, 36, 38, 45, 52, 73, 171

Skidmore, Joey, 13, 109

Skidmore, Max, 13, 109

Skrulls, 231, 263, 270, 272, 279

Sleepers (Nazi robots), 89–90

Slotkin, Richard, 20

Sons of the Serpent, 100

Spider-Man, 12, 80, 115, 125–26, 129, 131, 135, 146, 184–85, 212–13, 223–24, 235, 246–49, 278; anti-drug stories in, 151; and Captain America, 278; as national metaphor, 246–49; origin, 80; and September 11, 212–13; *Ultimate Spider-Man*, 223–24, 235

Spider-Man, 184

Spider-Man and His Amazing Friends (television program), 129

Spitfire, 120

Spysmasher, 258

Squadron Sinister/Squadron Supreme, 119

Star Trek, 125

Star Wars, 124–25, 129

Steele, John, 276

Steranko, Jim, 92, 172, 178, 284, 288

Stern, Roger, 152–54, 172, 178–79, 288

Storey, John, xi

Strange Tales, 82

Sub-Mariner. *See* Namor, the Sub-Mariner

Superia, 199, 200

Superman, 7, 12–14, 30, 33, 25, 55, 58–60, 69, 73–75, 268

Tales of Suspense, 81, 86, 87, 90, 95, 96; Captain America joins, becomes *Captain America*, 90; first appearance of Iron Man, 81

Tales to Astonish, 81, 82

al-Tariq, Faysal, 216, 220

Taylor, Leila, 102–3

Thing (Benjamin Grimm), 76, 78

Thomas, Roy, 64, 99–100, 119–22, 124, 146, 154–55, 176, 289

Thor, 81–83, 147–49, 170, 194, 232–34, 237, 260, 262, 271, 276; in films, 257; Ultimate Thor, 232–34, 237

Thor (film), 257

Timely Comics. *See* Marvel Comics

Togo, 48–49

Toro, 36, 39, 47, 52, 60, 61, 64, 119, 200

Toy Biz, 186

Transformers, The, 128

"transhistorical presence," 6

Triathlon, 207

Trimpe, Herb, 99

Truman, Harry, 154, 186, 194, 289

Truth: Red, White, and Black, 20, 240

Twain, Mark, quoted by Captain America, 248

tyranny of the serial, 5

Ultimate Marvel Team-Up, 224

Ultimates, The, 214, 224–40, 260, 262

Ultimate Spider-Man, 223–24, 235

Union Jack, 120, 172

USA Comics, 42, 50, 159

US Senate, Subcommittee to Investigate Juvenile Delinquency, 71–72, 75

Vietnam War, 28, 81, 86, 93, 105, 130, 132, 265

Viper (Jordan Stryke), 108

Viper (Madame Hydra), 145
Voger, Mark, 15, 131

Waid, Mark, 185, 190, 194, 203, 208–9, 288, 289; editorials, 203–4, 205
Walker, John, 16, 165–66, 167, 168–71, 180, 187; as Captain America, 167–71, 180, 187; as Super-Patriot, 165–66, 167, 180
Walt Disney Company, 257, 259, 290, 291, 292, 293–94, 340–41; copyright attitudes of, 293–94, 340n147; historic critiques, 291–94; purchase of Marvel, 257, 259
Wandtke, Terrence R., 6
Warrior Woman, 120
Wasp, 82, 83, 85, 147, 149, 240
Watcher, 188, 190
Watchmen, 9, 12, 130
Watergate scandal, 93, 110, 133, 187

Wertham, Frederic, 70–72, 291
What If?, 19–20
Whizzer, 39, 120
Wolverine, 130–31, 147–51, 192, 197, 277
Wonder Man, 278–79
Wonder Woman, 35, 74, 75; on television, 74
Woollacott, Janet, 13
Wright, Bradford W., 30, 50–52, 67–68, 214

X-Men, 7, 81, 130–31, 147–50, 226–27, 277

Young Allies, 38, 52–53
Young Men, 59, 60, 61, 64, 65, 87

Zeck, Mike, 129–30